D1329587

PLACE IN RETURN BOX to remove this checkout from your record.
TO AVOID FINES return on or before date due.
MAY BE RECALLED with earlier due date if requested.

DATE DUE	DATE DUE	DATE DUE

We Are Not What We Seem

We Are Not What We Seem

Black Nationalism and Class Struggle in the American Century

Rod Bush

NEW YORK UNIVERSITY PRESS

New York and London

NEW YORK UNIVERSITY PRESS
New York and London

Library of Congress Cataloging-in-Publication Data
Bush, Roderick D., 1945–
We are not what we seem : Black nationalism and class struggle in
the American century / Roderick D. Bush
p. cm.
Includes bibliographical references and index.
ISBN 0-8147-1317-3 (cloth : alk. paper)
1. Afro-Americans—Civil rights—History—20th century. 2. Black
nationalism—United States—History—20th century. 3. Afro-Americans—
Politics and government. 4. Social classes—United States—History—
20th century. 5. United States—Race relations.   I. Title.

E185.61.B98 1998
305.896'073—ddc21   98-25483
                              CIP

New York University Press books are printed on acid-free paper,
and their binding materials are chosen for strength and durability.

Manufactured in the United States of America

10 9 8 7 6 5 4 3 2 1

For Melanie and Sarafina Bush
Malik Bush
Thembi Bush Tillman
Sojourner Bush
Margaret J. Bush
Terence K. Hopkins

Contents

Acknowledgments

I often felt lonely and isolated while working on this project over the last ten years, but the very attempt to communicate reinforces the profoundly social aspect of this experience. This act of communication draws upon a dizzying array of mentors, enablers, and supporters without which this effort would not have been possible. This number is much larger than I can mention here, but I would like to express my love and gratitude to some of the key people.

This work is dedicated to my family and to a beloved mentor who passed away last January. Terence K. Hopkins was a friend, mentor, and role model as a scholar, a writer, a teacher, and a human being. He always gave more than seemed humanly possible to any task. He worked diligently, tirelessly, and unremittingly with me to state my ideas clearly and fully, forcefully and carefully. We talked for hours and hours about the movements, the world-economy, and the need to understand the processes of the capitalist world-economy. We made plans to do joint work once this project was done. He made a profound mark upon those whom he advised, but the world does not know the intellectual impact of this man because he worked mostly through advising and teaching others, even his peers.

The first circle of support comes from my wife, my children, and my parents. First and foremost is my wife, my soulmate, and comrade, Melanie Bush. As a mentor and critic, as an intellectual companion without compare, she has been a singular inspiration. From our first meeting and eventual collaboration as militants, she has always been my role model. Her tireless energy and devotion to unselfish service and mentorship is a constant reminder of how humane we can all strive to be. Her personal and intellectual integrity and depth daily enriches my life and my scholarship. Over the course of this project she gave birth to our love child, Sarafina Fidelia, completed her own M.P.H. and completed the course work for a Ph.D. in anthropology. While doing all of this she helped me to keep my eyes on the prize, reaffirmed our common values (humility, the mass line), and gave unselfishly of her own insights on many issues germane to this project.

All of my children in their own way provided invaluable support. Although my youngest, Sarafina, was born during this process, she has grown up and has increasingly provided moral and emotional support, and clearly reflects the values that we espouse. Malik, my oldest, is a constant intellectual companion willing to talk for hours about "the movement," its objectives, and how a new generation could make its own mark upon the world. Thembi, my oldest daughter, is loving and responsible and capable. She keeps up with everyone, makes sure they are all right. She makes sure that I am doing what I am supposed to be doing. Sojourner, my middle daughter, has much of the adventurous spirit, the daring, and the rebelliousness that kept me in trouble. They are all a source of joy, inspiration, and support.

I would also like to express my deepest appreciation to my mother, Margaret J. Bush, a source of emotional and spiritual support for all of these fifty-two years, and who always encouraged me to follow my dream. I am also indebted to her for my strong commitment to being my brother's keeper, and for my strong opposition to all forms of injustice. In this category there are, of course, many others, but most notably my grandmother, Arbesto Johnson (Barkoo), and my Aunt Honey (Margie Whipper) both of whom taught me more than I can ever remember. I should also say a word of thanks to my father, David Bush Jr., who encouraged me and was always willing to listen to me, no matter how wild my ideas seemed, especially in the 1960s and 1970s. He died in 1981, his body wracked with pain from overwork at the local automobile factory.

Now I turn to my intellectual debt.

I am very grateful to Immanuel Wallerstein who encouraged me to return to school, and indeed whose work inspired me to go back to school at such a late stage in my life. Immanuel is not only one of the greatest scholars of our time, but also a kind and decent human being who truly believes in the democratic and egalitarian ideas that he writes about. He always took time out of his very busy schedule to consult with me about whatever. I am also indebted to Andrew "Chip" Maxwell, Dale Tomich, and Darryl Thomas my professors at the State University of New York at Binghamton who were always there when I needed them.

I would like to express my appreciation to a few of the people to whom I owe a special intellectual debt and who served as role models for me. Again these are too many to mention, but certain ones demand special recognition: Abdul Alkalimat and Bill Sales for their contributions to Black Studies *and* the Black Liberation Movement; Robin D. G. Kelley for his exemplary scholarship steeped in the egalitarian traditions of our foremothers and forefathers, for broadening the scope of our vision, and for being an extraordinary human being who gives unselfishly of time, advice, and support; James and Grace Boggs for the political education that they have provided for my generation and for others as well; Frances Fox Piven, whose *Poor People's Movements* (with Richard Cloward) served as a model for this project and who helped me clarify my views at an early stage in the project; Cedric Robinson, whose *Black Marxism* is the most exemplary chronicle of the Black radical tradition; W. E. B. Du Bois, whose insights for nearly a century have made an inestimable contribution to our understanding of the capitalist world-system and the place of people of color in it; Samir Amin, whose work first introduced me to the world-systems perspective; Giovanni Arrighi, whose work on capitalism and the working class has very much informed my work; Stephen Steinberg, whose work on racial inequality is without peer; Amiri Baraka, who always says what he means, yet tirelessly counsels that we unite and not split, a model of intellectual integrity and revolutionary commitment; Arcee James, who taught me very early in life the importance of independent and critical thought; Stanley Levine, who in endless discussions has taught me much about the traps of ideological rigidity; Omali Yeshitela, whose writings and leadership have been very important in maintaining the continuity of one section of the Black Liberation Movement; Mickey Dean, whose friendship and mentorship have been very important in my development; James Ogunusi, whose generous spirit has been a constant inspiration to me over the past few years and who fed me endless articles to help me with this project; and Yusuf Nuruddin, who has made me aware of a number of documents which deepened my comprehension of this area of scholarship.

There are many others who have gave me considerable encouragement and support in the course of this undertaking. My mother- and father-in-law, Roz and Stan Levine, my brothers-in-law, Ethan Levine and Larry Levine; my former colleagues at the Educational Opportunity Center in Brooklyn (especially Dorothy Braithwaite, Louise Lloyd, Peggy Richardson, Vernon Charms, Lois Rosado, DeSana Stone, Danny Locario, Yvonne Ward, Tony Belcher, Helen Jennings, Frank Riley, Dick Riseling,

Dwayne Sampson, and Bill Yates), Beth Harding and Chris Butters, Julie and Richard Culley, Dave Walters at Brooklyn College, Alean Rush at Memorial AME Zion church, and too many others to name. They always insisted on being kept apprised of my progress and problems, and had helpful comments and advice at every turn. My good friend of some forty years, Renzie D. Taylor, has kept up with the status of this project since its inception.

At the State University of New York at Binghamton I owe a debt to many for discussions, encouragement, and various types of assistance. Among that group I must recognize Nettie Rathje, Nancy Hall, Gloria Hopkins, Pat Washington, Farouk Tabak, Aiguo Lu, Bob Ostertag, Jean Claude Gerlus, Owen Brown, Donna DeVoist, James Geschwender, Mark Selden, and Martin Murray.

A number of colleagues at Seton Hall have provided important support for this project. Foremost has been Dr. William Sales, my chair, mentor, and friend. Dr. Robert Hallissey, Jo Renee Formicola, Bernhard Scholtz, and Roslyn Jenkins provided valuable assistance at different points during this project. Tayari Sekou Onaje of the Uhuru Organization and the Campaign to Free Black and New Afrikan Political Prisoners spent many hours discussing the movement and the political situation at Seton Hall with me.

Apart from these institutional locations, a number of scholars have gone out of their way to be of help to me. They have given unselfishly of their time, their advice, and resources. Among this group are Gerald Horne of the University of North Carolina, Joseph Wilson of Brooklyn College, Michael Schwartz of the State University of New York at Stony Brook, Komozi Woodard of Sarah Lawrence College, Alphonso Pinkney of Hunter College, Paul Takagi of the University of California at Berkeley, John Horton of the University of California at Los Angeles, and Melvin Oliver of the University of California at Los Angeles, Steven Rosenthal of Hampton University, Walda Katz Fishman of Howard University, and Alan Spector of Purdue University. I am also grateful to Jack Newfield of the *New York Post*, Milton Coleman of the *Washington Post*, and Karl Evanzz of the *Washington Post* for their generosity in sharing resources.

I owe a special debt to the Ford Foundation for providing a postdoctoral fellowship that allowed me a year to work on this project with a reduced teaching load. Christine O'Brien and her staff at the Fellowship Office were exemplary in their work of raising up young scholars. In that same category the University Research Council at Seton Hall University provided me with two summer fellowships to work on this project.

There is another category of assistance that has been very valuable for me over the years, my relationship with and the nurturance provided by sisters and brothers in the struggle for social change. This is a cast of thousands, but I can name only a few here: Elizabeth Sutherland Martinez, Tony and Cecilia Platt, Greg Shank, Mabel Stewart, Mary Denny, Laura Benne, Vanda Sendzimir, Bill Felice, Leonard Harrison, Lance Hill and Eileen San Juan, Duane and Brenda Vann, Ron Washington, Harry Armstrong, Gerald Armstrong, Tom Bodenheimer, Barbara Bishop, Janja Lalich, Carol Cannon and Mike Carter, Sobukwe Bambatta, Elombe Brath, Modibo, Frank Chapman, Phil Thorne, Sam Jenkins, Kim Maddox, Susanne Jonas, Erika Huggins, Keith Carson, John George, Ronald V. Dellums, Arthur Paris, Ed McCaughan, Olga Talamante, Richard Schauffler, James and Connie Smith, Mrs. Everlener Wright, Charles Scott Jr., Finas Hall, Mary Cobbins, Janis Lewin, Patti McSherry, Esther Madriz and Steve Richardson, Nancy Stein, Nancy Strohl and Peter Siegel, Joseph Starr, and many, many others.

A second category of family and friends far removed from this project but who have given me love, nurturance, and reassurance throughout my life should be mentioned here. First my uncles, Thomas Bush, Billy Bush, and James Craddock, and my aunt, Harriet Bush. My cousins, Gloria Springer, Alfreda Adams, and Lillian Williams. Then my brothers, Michael, Leonard, and David Bush III. I owe an additional debt to a number of dear friends not yet mentioned: Juanita Reed and Elizabeth Ellis, Dennis Talbert, and Michael Bonner.

Finally I would like to thank Niko Pfund and Despina Papazoglou Gimbel of New York University Press for their energetic support and visionary work on behalf of making this book a reality.

We Are Not What We Seem

Introduction
Reassessing Black Power

Each day when you see us black folk upon the dusty land of the farms or upon the hard pavement of the city streets, you usually take us for granted and think you know us, but our history is far stranger than you suspect, and we are not what we seem.
—Richard Wright, *Twelve Million Black Voices*

Imagine European history from the days of Christ to the present telescoped into three hundred years and you can comprehend the drama which our consciousness has experienced! Brutal, bloody, crowded with suffering and abrupt transitions, the lives of us black folk represent the most magical and meaningful picture of human experience in the Western world. Hurled from our native African homes into the center of the most complex and highly industrialized civilization the world has ever known, we stand today with a consciousness and memory such as few people possess. . . .

We black folk, our history and our present being, are a mirror of all the manifold experiences of America. What we want, what we represent, what we endure is what America *is*. If we black folk perish, America will perish. If America has forgotten her past, then let her look into the mirror of our consciousness and she will see the *living* past living in the present, for our memories go back, through our black folk of today, through the recollections of our black parents, and through the tales of slavery told by our black grandparents, to the time when none of us black or white, lived in this fertile land.   —Richard Wright, *Twelve Million Black Voices*

The nation was shocked by the appearance of more than a million Black men in Washington, DC in response to the call put forth by the African American Leadership Summit, led by Minister Louis Farrakhan and the Reverend Benjamin Chavis. Before the October 16,

1995, march, pundits were openly contemptuous of the organizers, and wrote smugly of the inconsequential nature of this march compared to the 1963 March on Washington led by Dr. Martin Luther King, Jr.

The differences between the two marches could hardly be overstated, but did this mean that the latter was inconsequential? More than one million Black men did not think so. However, unlike the 1963 march for inclusion and civil rights, this march did not emphasize demands on the government. Instead it called for Black men to atone for their sins against the Black community, Black women, Black children, and one another. This march included Black men from all walks of life, but the ambience of the march was decidedly nationalist and not integrationist.

Black nationalism is routinely vilified in the media, is seldom taken seriously by white scholars, and is the butt of sarcasm in the popular discourse. The corporate media's coverage of leaders and activists who are sympathetic to Black nationalism is reflexively skeptical, if not oppositional, and generously indulges those political forces antagonistic to Black nationalism. Among the opponents of Black nationalism, the Anti-Defamation League of B'nai B'rith (ADL) has been perhaps the most effective. The Anti-Defamation League is a major Jewish organization whose primary concern historically has been exposing and combating anti-Semitism. But as the socioeconomic and geopolitical clout of the Jewish population has increased in the post–World War II period, the ADL has increasingly made common cause with the WASP establishment, often broadening its surveillance to include "subversives" of all sorts. Thus Black radicals and Black nationalists are both abhorrent to the ADL, not because they are anti-Semitic per se (although some clearly are), but because of their relationship to or sympathy for larger geopolitical forces to which the ADL and the WASP establishment are opposed.

The ADL's critique of Black leaders carries a great deal more moral authority than any made by the WASP establishment, but these critiques play differently to different audiences. When the ADL issues a report highlighting the anti-Semitic utterances of major Black nationalist leaders, it compromises the moral credibility of these leaders (and their followers) among substantial sections of the population not already sympathetic to Black nationalism. However, attacks by organizations like the ADL may increase the stature of these Black nationalist spokespersons among those who interpret them as standing up to the white man (Jewish or otherwise). Black radicals, most of whom manifest some degree of nationalist consciousness, often find themselves in a conundrum of sorts in these situations, because they understand that anti-Black racism among Jewish people is simply a subset of (and not at all different from) white racism in general, but have not themselves fully examined the third worldist assumptions behind the simplistic "Zionism is racism" formulation.

We might all benefit from a sober intellectual and political discussion of the impact of geopolitical alliances on intergroup relations and what Michael Lerner terms left-wing anti-Semitism.[1] But the ADL's focus on the more outrageous statements of the Nation of Islam's Minister Farrakhan and the notoriously provocative statements of Farrakhan's former lieutenant, Khallid Abdul Muhammad, has not been conducive to principled discussion.

This complex issue deserves serious analysis, not the facile or opportunistic commentary it is too often accorded. I will return to this issue later in the book; I simply want to emphasize here that African Americans largely supported the 1995 march because its positive thrust on behalf of Black people outweighed their concern about the sensibilities of Jews and other whites, most of whom are felt to demonstrate precious little sensitivity to Black people's pain. In light of this perceived insensitivity to Black pain and suffering, and an unambiguous hostility among many whites, the very presumption that Blacks could want no more than inclusion in the white-dominated social system is an egregious form of racial arrogance that served to blind the white public to the mounting nationalist sentiment in the Black community. And the disparagement of Black nationalism by some left-leaning Black intellectuals made absolutely no difference. The white and Black critics of the nationalist sentiments of the marchers could not comprehend how in this time of profound social crisis so many Black people could turn away from the possibility of help from the state and articulate a need to "do for self." Do we have here simply a "dialogue of the deaf"?

In reality the situation is much more complex than the public drama indicates. The intensification of nationalist consciousness among the Black population almost always appears to most whites as a great ideological transformation, and a quite unfathomable transformation at that. But it should be no mystery. Black nationalism has been a significant component of African American social thought for more than two hundred years, varying in intensity according to time, place, and circumstance. Throughout this work we will be at pains to explicate and understand the ebb and flow of nationalist thought and practice among African Americans. But the public drama of which we are now in the midst has more recent causes.

Black Power and the Underclass

The 1960s were a turbulent period in African American history and U.S. history more generally. A proud and militant Black movement had marched to center stage. The civil rights movement had defeated Jim Crow and set the stage for the incorporation of large sections of the Black middle class into the social system. The number of Black elected officials increased exponentially. But for some (Martin Luther King, Jr., the civil rights radicals in the Student Nonviolent Coordinating Committee [SNCC], and large numbers of ordinary Black people outside the South) the lesson of that victory was that something more fundamental was needed. The radical wing of the civil rights movement began to call for a new approach to freedom and equality for Black people, which it summed up in the slogan Black Power. King agreed with the substantive need to go beyond the victories of 1964–65, but disagreed with the tactics of the Black Power militants.

The Black Power slogan, however, had broad appeal throughout the various strata of the African American population, and each gave its own interpretation to the slogan. Some advocates of Black Power used it as a means of pluralist integration into the existing system. This segment of Black Power advocates assumed that fair access to the levers of power for talented and educated Blacks and other people of color was the solution to America's race problems. It was this conception that President Richard M. Nixon had in mind when he announced himself in favor of Black Power or Black capitalism. The radical wing of the Black Power movement, which demanded more substantive transformations of U.S. society, was subject to repression by the police, the FBI, and other elements of the local, state, and national security apparatus. Daniel Patrick Moynihan called on President Nixon to initiate a period of benign neglect with regard to race relations, because the major work had been done, and what was needed now more than anything was a cooling off of the rhetoric.

In the late 1970s the Black sociologist William Julius Wilson perhaps unwittingly codified this approach in his notion of the "declining significance of race." Wilson argued that social, political, and economic changes during the course of the twentieth century had greatly altered American institutions, such that race was no longer the primary determinant of the life chances of the African American population. The success of the civil rights revolution, among other things, meant that educated and talented Blacks had virtually equal access to employment opportunities with whites. Thus the life chances of the Black population were now much more impacted by social class position. Wilson was not an apologist for the racial status quo; he thought an attack on its flanks via class-based mobilization would be more effective than a frontal attack, which he considered to be divisive. But Wilson's relatively conservative use of class analysis backfired, and major elements of his argument were co-opted by the Right to argue for a color-blind approach to discrimination. This meant that white racism could not be addressed, since any color-conscious perspective was inherently racist. In this argument racial discrimination was not anchored in a historically evolved system of white privilege, but was a discriminatory action in the present, regardless of race.

The 1970s saw a great deal of rhetoric about the success of the civil rights revolution. Supposedly racial discrimination and prejudice had been ended. Blacks of ability had quickly taken advantage of new opportunities to climb to positions of status in our society. Of those who were not capable, not very much was said. But they increasingly appeared as scapegoats in the intensifying law-and-order rhetoric that had come to replace racial rhetoric as a means of making invidious distinctions between the deserving and the undeserving.

The Black freedom struggle had all but faded from public view, replaced by the machinations of newly elected officials who had come to power in the post–civil rights era. But the Black freedom struggle gained new visibility with the decision of the Reverend Jesse Jackson to run for president of the United States under the banner of the Rainbow Coalition, a multiracial coalition rooted among those sectors of the population who were locked out of the political process. This concept drew on the lessons of the radical struggles of the 1960s and 1970s, and drew its most enduring strength from the reinvigoration of the cadres of those struggles. But the impetus for Jackson's run came largely from the deliberations of the Black elite.

Jackson himself was a marginal figure among the liberal Black establishment and was unpopular among some Jewish members of the liberal coalition, who thought of him as an ally to the PLO and felt that he harbored anti-Semitic sentiments. In this context, the Jewish Defense League

(JDL), a paramilitary right-wing sect that had been instrumental (with FBI support) in fanning the flames of Black-Jewish antagonism in 1968, immediately sprang into action and threatened Jackson's life. Jackson called on Farrakhan and the Nation of Islam to provide security for him during the initial stage of his candidacy.

The die was cast. This series of events set the stage for Jackson's "Hymietown" remarks and effectively killed the promise of a rainbow coalition for the foreseeable future. The JDL had played the FBI's game in the past and was a fellow traveler in the world of agents provocateurs. The more liberal ADL had also cooperated with U.S. intelligence organizations in its battle against "subversives." This was classic COINTELPRO. Twenty years ago the conservative leadership of the Nation of Islam had played the FBI's (and CIA's) game in the assassination of Malcolm X. We do not know to what extent the state's counterinsurgency apparatus reaches into the Nation of Islam today, but this is by no means a closed question.

In December 1986, when young Michael Griffith was chased to his death by a white racist mob in Howard Beach, Queens, the issue of justice and equality for Black people in the United States regained the high profile it had been denied since the 1970s. The Howard Beach murder not only provided the focus for a revitalized movement against racism in New York City, it sparked a national debate about the circumstances that led to the murder, and the systemic processes that were its basis.

One group of organizers called for a boycott of white businesses, among others things. But Jesse Jackson argued that such tactics did not attack the real source of the problems. He asserted that we needed to move away from the racial battleground to the economic common ground, and that the boardrooms of the *New York Times*, ABC, CBS, NBC, and so forth were more segregated than Howard Beach.[2]

Local activists accused Jackson of doing a "perfect Cuomo,"[3] that is, providing a political light show rather than taking a real stand. There ensued in the pages of the *City Sun* (a black-owned, grassroots-oriented New York City weekly) a debate about race and class that illuminated some—but not all—of the positions that surfaced in this debate.[4]

The local activists who received the highest profile in the Howard Beach situation, the Reverend Al Sharpton and attorneys Alton Maddox and C. Vernon Mason, called for a new civil rights movement. Although they tended toward greater militance and a stronger nationalist position, they were more a part of the civil rights mainstream; but they were distinct from Jackson, whose emphasis on the Rainbow Coalition led him to avoid nationalist rhetoric altogether. (We will see later, however, that there were consistently strong nationalist elements in Jackson's approach.)

The split within the civil rights mainstream was mirrored by a split among the radicals. But here there was more variation. Those allied with the Rainbow Coalition tended to either agree with Jackson or argue for a variation on his notion of class analysis.[5] Andy Pollack, a white trade unionist, argued for a more nuanced analysis of class and race that did not unduly or mechanically privilege class. But no nationalist position was presented.

I was surprised by the tone of the *City Sun* debate. What a difference twenty years made. During the heyday of the Black Power movement, its activists and analysts argued assertively that the major problem facing Black people is not racism (something in the minds of white people), but colonialism, a material relation between the Black population and the North American state. This analysis most often included a conception of class analysis and a critique of capitalism, but it also held fast to the necessity of conceptualizing the nature of the African American national question. This is of course the more radical wing of the Black Power movement. There were other positions. But my point is that the lessons of the Black Power movement should have been recapitulated in these debates in the *City Sun*. They were not.

Only a few relatively small revolutionary nationalist organizations continued the tradition established in the Black Power movement. These included the Patrice Lumumba Coalition, the Community Self-Defense Program, the New African Peoples Organization, and the African People's Socialist Party (the largest of the above named organizations, but one with no cadres in New York City). Later the Black Men's Committee Against Crack, the Patrice Lumumba Coalition, and the New York Eight would form the December 12th Coalition around the attempt to obtain justice for Tawana Brawley. This organization would bring a more cohesive revolutionary nationalist analysis to the Black activist movement in New York City.

The call for Black Power was based precisely on Black people's awareness that the civil rights movement did not address the key issues that would result in genuine empowerment. What was needed was not more "civil rights," but human rights. The problem facing the African American people was not a "Negro" problem or an American problem, but a human problem that could not be solved merely by the attainment of civil rights; it required a long-range strategy for independence and self-determination.

The "domestic (or internal) colonialism" analysis made by relatively small organizations, such as the Community Self-Defense Program (in Brooklyn) and the African People's Socialist Party, may seem antiquated in this day of high technology, globalization, and the theory of a hopelessly impoverished Black "underclass." Yet this was not the case a short twenty years ago.

In the wake of the Black Power movement and the spontaneous rebellions by the Black working class in the 1960s, the "internal colonialism" thesis on the nature of Black existence in the United States was very popular. But as many of the cadre of the movement moved to more or less orthodox Marxist and liberal positions, this thesis lost much of its currency. From the orthodox Marxists' perspective the internal colony analysis did not seem realistic; they believed that the most logical strategy for revolutionary change in the United States was a mass insurrection and seizure of power in the name of the working class.

The retreat from the "internal colonialism" thesis took place largely during the 1970s when the forces seeking equality and justice felt they were in a position to actually challenge those who held state power in the United States. While such optimism may have seemed absurd during the heyday of Ronald Reagan's conservative triumphalism, we should not forget that the multiple movements for racial equality, gender equality, a new international order, peace, third world liberation, and workers' and students' rights collectively exerted an enormous pressure on the system between 1965 and 1980, so that within the liberal center itself voices were raised about a crisis of "governability." Samuel Huntington's call for "a greater degree of moderation in democracy" in the liberal Trilateral Commission can be seen as preparing the ground for the rise to prominence of a xenophobic, racist, and jingoistic right wing within the ruling establishment.

During the 1960s the interracial movement for equality, the Black Power movement, and the uprising of the Black population in hundreds of cities across the country had wrested concessions from the federal government in the form of the Civil Rights Act of 1964, the Voting Rights Act of 1965, the Equal Opportunity Act of 1965, the Demonstration Cities (Model Cities) Act of 1966, and so forth. These concessions occurred at a time when the long postwar boom was coming to an end, and the ability of the system to provide Keynesian demand stimulation solutions was similarly coming to an end.

Consequently the worsening plight of the Black poor in the face of these concessions was used as a weapon to turn back the clock on liberal reforms and win a newly insecure white working and middle class away from any support or sympathy for the welfare of the Black population. The intensification of the Black movement and the simultaneous decline of U.S. world hegemony, symbolized by the defeat of the U.S. armed forces and its allies in Vietnam, set the stage for a conservative counter-attack against the "new class" of liberal welfare state bureaucrats and their Black allies, who, conservatives argued, were undermining America's world position, moral fabric, and national character.

In my mind the 1960s and 1970s' struggles for racial equality had been at the center of a great social and intellectual drama. Thus in the 1980s I was troubled by what seemed to me to be a feeble intellectual response to the revival of the issue of racial oppression. The grandeur of the 1960s was nowhere evident. I was sympathetic to the internal colonialism thesis and to class analysis, and believed there must be some synthesis of the insights provided by the two approaches. I puzzled over why the movement of the late 1980s seemed such a pale comparison to the movement of the 1960s. I thought this might be a misperception on my part. It seemed we needed a more thorough analysis. I hope to contribute in some small way to meeting that need.

The Black Power movement of the 1960s was part of a tumultuous period in both U.S. and world history. We desperately need to understand the history of that movement as a whole. Beyond the events of that period, we need to situate the movement(s) within the larger social world of which it was a part. We need to ascertain to what extent the Black Power movement was an expression of a universal social situation. To what extent was the movement a particularized response to the unique social situation of African Americans? Is Black Power simply one more version of ethnic politics or something with wider import? How does the existing social structure set the context for the movement, its constraints, and its possibilities?

I hold that the demand for Black Power constitutes a logical, rational, and sensible response to the social structure of the capitalist world-economy, and particularly the configuration of social groups in the United States. The Left's traditional invocation of false consciousness as a means of explaining the Black Power movement and its antagonist, white racism, is fundamentally mistaken. From the late 1970s this fundamentally flawed strategy has been re-elaborated into a new orthodoxy in liberal and left-liberal intellectual and political circles, which call for a universal approach to the problems of the "disadvantaged" rather than a race-specific approach. This new orthodoxy received its most crucial imprimatur in two works by the Black social democratic scholar William Julius Wilson, *The Declining Significance of Race* and *The Truly Disadvantaged: The Inner City, the Underclass, and Public Policy*.

In reality this new orthodoxy is simply a re-elaboration of theses that were earlier articulated by Daniel Patrick Moynihan, and even earlier by the Swedish social scientist Gunnar Myrdal. The Chicago school of sociology, which produced important Black sociologists such as E. Franklin Frazier and Charles Johnson, was primarily concerned with the assimilation of immigrants into the mainstream of American society. Any adjustments these groups sought to make on their own terms were viewed as pathological. By the time of the formation of the Chicago school at the turn of the century, this approach was well established.

In opposition to liberal universalism and the top-down coalition that is its political counterpart, I will argue that a true universalism can be constructed only from the bottom up. Liberal universalism is only a formula for a return to the status quo ante, circa 1965, the very status quo against which the Black Power revolt of the 1960s was directed.

Let us recall briefly the general line of the Black Power movement of the 1960s. Whereas the civil rights movement had been based on appeals to morality and conscience, all other groups understood that their position was based on power. Carmichael and Hamilton argued that Black Power was a call for Black people to unite, to recognize our heritage, and to build a sense of community:

> The concept of Black Power rests on a fundamental premise: *Before a group can enter the open society, it must first close ranks.* By this we mean group solidarity is necessary before a group can operate effectively from a bargaining position of strength in a pluralistic society. Traditionally, each new ethnic group in this society has found the route to social and political viability through the organization of its own institutions with which to represent its needs within the larger society . . . the American melting pot has not melted. Italians vote for Rubino over O'Brien; Irish for Murphy over Goldberg, etc.[6]

This rather unremarkable observation was met by a barrage of criticisms from a broad range of political and ideological perspectives. The arguments of the declared defenders of the status quo are not the main object of our critique here. That the people who opposed the civil rights movements would also oppose the notion of Black Power even more strenuously is not surprising. What *appears* to be more of an anomaly is the resistance of liberal and left intellectuals and organizations to the rise of a militant quasi-nationalist ideology among Black activists and in Black communities around the country.

Bayard Rustin's late 1960s comments were the prototype of left-wing criticism of the Black Power movement.[7] Rustin argued that the Black Power movement was "nothing but the economic and political philosophy of Booker T. Washington given a 1960's militant shot in the arm and brought up to date."[8] While we may now shrink from this rhetorical overkill, there was (and is) a considerable consensus in left and liberal intellectual and political circles that Black Power was not a serious critique of the status quo. Such critics viewed Black Power as simply a means for the Black middle class to gain a piece of the pie.[9] These self-righteous criticisms of the Black (barely) bourgeoisie, however, can just as easily be viewed as a defense of privilege for those who saw this emergent Black bourgeoisie as encroaching on *their* privileges. Thus they argued for class analysis as a more effective means of understanding social inequality in the United States. Social policy in turn should be oriented toward class rather than racial interests, because class unites while race divides.

Class analysis *is* an important tool in allowing us to understand the dynamics of a capitalist world. But it has been used much too carelessly and sometimes opportunistically by scholars, journalists, and political activists. The liberal/left/social democratic attack on the Black Power movement and the elaboration of the notion of a behaviorally defined "underclass" reveal a peculiar pattern in class analysis that cripples rather than strengthens the attack on the structural inequality deeply embedded in the capitalist system.

While there has been a great deal of emphasis on how the Black Power movement alienated white workers, little attention is given to the response of the upper and ruling strata. The Black Power movement generated intense opposition to the extent that it raised claims that could not easily be met in the context of the existing framework of social relations.

However, some of the middle-class elements in the movement were more interested in gaining access to middle-class lifestyles and privilege than in promoting equality for all Black people. Thus the liberal section of the establishment (both Black and white) was able to court, seduce, and co-opt individuals and whole sections of the movement. Both the civil rights movement and the Black Power movement were united front movements, and thus contained both prosystemic and antisystemic thrusts. The liberal center attempted to promote the prosystemic thrusts (Black capitalism, some forms of cultural nationalism, liberal integrationism), and fiercely repressed the antisystemic thrusts (most notably the Black Panther Party, but many others as well).

If we turn briefly to the structural context in which the various expressions of Black Power came to contend with the racial status quo, we can better understand the thrust of this argument. In the latter half of the 1960s the postwar expansion of the capitalist world-economy was still perceived to be in process (some even thought that the prosperity of the postwar period would never end, that the business cycle had been conquered by Keynesian economic strategies) and U.S. world hegemony was still intact. The radical wing of the Black Power movement thus was a disruptive influence and an impediment to the smooth incorporation of the Black middle class into the system. This led the most progressive section of the liberal center and aspiring members, including the moderate civil rights leadership and social democrats, who viewed the Black Power movement as needlessly disruptive, to initiate a ferocious and unprincipled attack on the Black Power movement. To the extent that the Left (especially the top leadership of the CPUSA) felt itself to be building a united front (antimonopoly coalition), it too attacked this movement.

Perhaps the best way to understand the concerted attack on Black Power is to view it as a desperate maneuver by the liberal center to undermine a movement that attempted to articulate the grievances of the most openly rebellious section of the population. The radical section of the Black Power movement potentially constituted the most effective challenge to the hegemony of the ruling coalition in the post–World War II period (which by the 1960s very definitely included some leaders of the labor movement and sought to incorporate members of the moderate civil rights establishment as well). The structure and membership of this ruling coalition were being expanded because it now quite self-consciously presided over the hegemonic power in the capitalist world-economy.

Once the radical wing of the Black Power movement had been militarily defeated,[10] and the moderate and conservative sections safely co-opted, the question remained of what to do about the massive lower stratum of the Black population, which had not benefited from the civil rights revolution and whose militancy the radicals attempted to articulate. In a shameless display of disingenuousness, increasingly conservative social scientists and journalists blamed the Black Power movement and the New Left (not the war in Vietnam) for the collapse of the societal consensus for the War on Poverty. They attributed the poverty of the lower stratum of the Black population and other communities of color to the cultural deficits of the poor, disingenuously co-opting the work of Oscar Lewis in emphasizing the class dimension of racial and ethnic subordination. They deftly shifted the definition of class to hinge on the "culture" of a particular group rather than its relationship to other groups in a social structure.

Paradoxically, the myth of the underclass obscures bona fide class analysis while posing as such. It confuses rather than clarifies. It seems designed to justify the increasing polarization of wealth and poverty by affixing the blame for this state of affairs on the victims. By the late 1970s the long postwar expansion of the economy had evidently come to an end, and U.S. world hegemony was under challenge from many quarters (Southeast Asia, Southern Africa, Central America). The catastrophic decline in the living standards of significant sectors of the population within U.S. borders further delegitimated the social system. The myth of the underclass deflected blame from the system to the behavior of individuals.

The attack on the Black Power movement and the myth of the underclass highlight a momentous shift in public sensibilities and sympathy regarding people of color (particularly Blacks as arch-symbol of the dangerous classes) and the poor. In the 1970s the Left began a massive ideological shift away from the "excesses" and romanticism of the 1960s toward more pragmatic (and "universal") approaches to fostering social change. For most this shift is believed to have come about as a consequence of our clearer understanding of the social system based on a scientific analysis of capitalism. By the 1980s, when many of the militants of the national and social movements began to sense that these movements were collectively in a fundamental crisis, I began to reevaluate the 1970s ideological shift in the Black liberation movement and in the Left more broadly.

Far from the hardheaded, nonromantic revolutionary viewpoint that we envisioned, the appropriation of the Third International tradition (antirevisionist Marxism-Leninism)[11] by segments of the Black Left and the wider New Left was a confused step, in which genuine a desire for a new approach was combined with a retreat from the real world. Revolutionary Marxism lent a new coherence to our arguments and our ability to understand the world, but we were too formulaic in our analysis and thus moved as often as not away from the revolutionary end that we desired. The new pragmatism of the revolutionaries meant that the retreat was less obvious than it otherwise would have been.

While the revolutionaries viewed themselves as reconnecting with a revolutionary history that they had arrogantly brushed aside in their youthful exuberance and historical ignorance, their actual separation from that history in the real world (the antagonism against the Old Left communists and socialists) meant that they had no real comprehension of it. Thus while the failure of the Third International forces could be considered a tragedy, even considering its mean-spirited component, can we say that the reversion to Third International strategy by a section of the 1960s New Left and Black Left was little more than farce?[12]

Such an unqualified dismissal tells us little about the real dynamics of the social movements involved, even though the criticism of the organizations' methodology may have some validity. As a judgment, however, it can become as much a parody as the attempt by the Black Left and radical New Left to mimic the successes of the Third International by mimicking its language and political lines.[13] In the following section I will attempt to summarize in more detail the criticism of the Black Power movement as elaborated by William Julius Wilson. Then I will introduce my own assessment of the import of class analysis as a tool to help oppressed strata understand and resist the forces that are devastating their lives. I will attempt to show how racism operates in the capitalist world-economy, and especially in the United States. I will show that the "declining significance of race" thesis is patently false and simpleminded, and that it does not work even as practical tactic, since it falsifies that which is so obviously true and impacts the lives of all people in the United States. Its perpetrators are also its victims; the bystanders are also key actors. At the same time I will attempt to show how class analysis, as a component of the analysis of a historical social system, capitalism, can be used to enable us to understand the depth and breadth of racism.

Black Power Movement: Wrong Turn for the Civil Rights Movement?

Although I am reluctant to begin this book with such an extensive discussion of a body of scholarship that has come before it, I find it virtually impossible to engage in any analysis of the ways Black economic life has been debated in this country in recent years without spending some time on the work of William Julius Wilson. Wilson's sophisticated and highly intelligent discussion of Black poverty is enormously important but also deeply problematic. Any discussion of how strategies of social transformation interface with America's racial dilemma cannot avoid coming to terms with the deliberations of this towering figure in the nation's intellectual life.

Starting with an analysis first proposed by Bayard Rustin in "From Protest to Politics," Wilson argues that from 1955 to 1965 the chief objective of the civil rights movement was to integrate public accommodations and remedy Black disenfranchisement. These, he says, are matters of constitutional rights and basic human dignity, and thus could be addressed as issues of civil rights. Despite victories in the area of civil rights, a more complex and fundamental set of problems remained to be addressed for which the "rights" acquired provided no vehicle: jobs, education, and housing.[14]

The gains of the civil rights movement, according to Wilson, mainly profited the Black middle class. To confront the more fundamental issues of social and economic conditions would require a different strategy, one that moved beyond the limited vision of race relations. While a few thinkers, such as Kenneth Clark, Lee Rainwater, and Elliot Liebow, discussed the importance of economic relations in determining the structure of inequality, this progressive development was undermined by "a competing mode of analysis stressing racial solidarity which rose at that time to compete with interracialism."[15]

In Wilson's view, struggles for interracialism emerge when the struggle against racial inequality appears hopeful, while struggles emphasizing racial solidarity emerge when minority members view the struggle against racial inequality as hopeless, or when they experience intense disillusionment and frustration after a period of optimism or heightened expectation. Yet Wilson paradoxically blames the Black Power movement for having aggressively polarized Blacks and whites who had been allies in the civil rights movement.

Wilson emphasizes the role of well-meaning and knowledgeable elites (such as Michael Harrington *and* Daniel Patrick Moynihan) who know how to operate within the policy-making establishment, instead of the role of the oppressed strata themselves, who, if not burdened by a culture of poverty, are socially isolated and in any case politically inept. Like "peasants," they need the intellectuals' thought and leadership.

Since the emphasis of the civil rights movement was on race, Wilson contends, little attention was paid to socioeconomic differences in the Black community and their implications for public policy options. Thus "the promising move in the early and mid-1960's to pursue programs of economic reform by defining the problems of *American economic organization* and outlining their effect on the minority community were offset by calls for 'reparations,' or 'Black control of institutions serving the Black community'" (emphasis added).[16] Wilson objects that the movement of these social forces to the fore produced an overly conflictual situation into which a relatively privileged group of Blacks moved to buttress their own competitive positions vis-à-vis the white middle class. In pursuing its own *class* interests in this way, this group undermined white support for measures to achieve racial equality, especially since the economy was now in decline. Support for racial equality, Wilson notes, was strong as long as the economy was expanding and such measures were not perceived as undermining the privileges of the dominant groups. In Wilson's view the political strategy and analysis of the Black Power movement led to a situation in which Black ethnicity became a form of mystification, which made it difficult for Blacks to perceive the inextricable link between their own fate and the structure of the American economy.

For Wilson the trajectory of the civil rights movement and its allied intellectuals up to the mid-1960s was setting the stage for the emergence of an authentic social democratic agenda in the United States. Here Wilson echoes an argument Harrington made nearly twenty years earlier. The emergence of the Black Power movement essentially undermined the process by which a social democratic movement was coming into being.

Harrington had argued that the demand for civil rights could be accommodated within the general expansion of the economy during the 1960s. The war in Vietnam, however, created a general economic squeeze. For Harrington the pursuit of the war meant that the advances of "the Other America" were no longer part of the general increase in economic prosperity, but a source of competition with the white working class and the lower middle class. Prior to this change in the economic conjuncture (from expansion to stagnation), Harrington argues, conditions for a common struggle existed, *"even if they [whites] did not lose their prejudices"* (emphasis added).[17] With the onset of the economic downturn, however, Harrington contends, the new activism of the poor would turn into despair, most of it passive, some of it "dangerously angry."

Harrington's use of the imagery of "hope frustrated" seems a clear attempt to appeal to the elites to stay the course, since he thought that it would require significant involvement on the part of the nonpoor to pursue an effective war against poverty. But what about the involvement of the poor themselves? Unfortunately Harrington's analysis accepts the dependent position of the poor in the United States as a given. So Harrington's analysis (like Wilson's), while addressing what he viewed to be the available policy options, is not adequate as an overall analysis of the political and social dynamics of this period.

In an effort to coalesce with white professional-managerial and blue-collar strata, Wilson and Harrington adopt a conciliatory tone toward some of the beneficiaries of the system of white racial privilege, while deploring the increasing militance of the victims. In their view advocates of "race-specific" policies are detrimental to the interests of the "truly disadvantaged" because they prevent disadvantaged groups in American society from seeing their common interests. Furthermore, Wilson argues that advocates of race-specific policies do so from a self-interested viewpoint, and in a zero-sum society, this means that the needs of the "truly disadvantaged" are pushed to the side.

A more fruitful approach to the pressing problem of the Black underclass, according to Wilson, would be the development of a "universal" program of economic reform that would benefit both advantaged and disadvantaged minority members and women as well. Although the initial thrust of the civil rights movement was to win equal opportunity under the law, the inadequacy of this approach led policy analysts sympathetic to the plight of the disadvantaged to advocate a policy of "equality of results," identified with the War on Poverty. Wilson believes that this approach is "reverse discrimination." He believes that the question of reform is inherently political, and must be couched in terms promoting economic security for all Americans in order to generate a broad-based coalition that would support such reforms.

While I have no doubt that such a political coalition must be constructed, I do not think that the goals of the Harrington-Wilson coalition are likely to reflect the felt needs of the "truly disadvantaged" themselves, given that their input is minimal in this conception. Wilson's manner of presenting the Black Power movement is highly partisan, and follows substantially the antinationalist positions of A. Philip Randolph and Bayard Rustin, who ended up as apologists for the procapitalist, pro-imperialist labor establishments.

This work will not only be a defense of the Black Power movement, it will place the movement in the context of the African American nationalist tradition. It will reply at length to the liberal and social democratic critique of Black Power. I will argue not that social democracy overemphasizes class, but that its mechanical separation of class from race oversimplifies the concept of social class, which is a historically evolved relational category.

Class Analysis and the Racial Divide

With all due respect to Michael Harrington and William Julius Wilson for their herculean efforts in bringing the issue of poverty and social inequality to the forefront of public consciousness and placing it on the social policy agenda of the United States, their tactical efforts largely undermine the contribution that class analysis can make to our understanding of the significance of the racial divide, and the power that the racially subjugated have to bring about fundamental change in our society. I would therefore like to contribute to a reformulation of our understanding of race and class in a world-systems perspective. To do this I want to attempt to relate briefly some intellectual history, with some personal biographical details to help the reader understand where I stand in the debate and why.

Somewhere in the course of the post–World War II expansion of the capitalist world-economy, liberal (and many Marxist) intellectuals in the United States reached a consensus that capitalist development had undermined the structural logic of the Marxian thesis about increasing class polarization and thus fatally diminished the prospects of the rise of an internationalist, revolutionary, and universalistic working-class movement as the agency for the transformation of the capitalist system into a just and egalitarian (socialist) system. These intellectuals often consciously rejected Lenin's injunction to look to the "lower and deeper" section of the working class, since the poor (in the United States at least) were being gradually eliminated.

This consensus was based on their observation that the working class has not over time been reduced to a common mass of labor, more and more impoverished and thus potentially united in its opposition to capitalism. Instead the living standards of the working class in the countries of advanced capitalism had steadily increased with its labor productivity. This change in the life circumstances of the working class resulted in its endorsement of the reform program of social democracy.

In most countries there existed an upper stratum of the working class whose households depended totally on wage labor and a lower stratum whose households only partly depended on wage labor, and for whom capital did not have to bear the total cost of their reproduction (the cost of obtaining the necessities of life for the laborer). This reality amounted to both an objective and a subjective split in the working class and is key to the stability of the capitalist system, economically and politically. Paradoxically, it is also key to the transformation of the system. Furthermore, the split in the working class is reflective of fundamental processes of capitalism, which affects all strata in the world-economy. In the process of class formation (bourgeoisification-proletarianization), we get not two classes, but three: the bourgeoisie, the petty bourgeoisie, and the working class. This configuration of social classes tends to give rise to a set of political dynamics that are fundamentally different from the more polarizing process Marx and Engels envisioned. This is an important factor in analyzing the politics of the capitalist world-economy.

In the core zone (the so-called developed countries of North America, Western Europe, and Japan), which by definition has captured a disproportionate share of the benefits of the system, the upper stratum of the working class has often united with the petty bourgeoisie seeking upward mobility, while taking a defensive position toward the lower working class (as well as other low-ranking groups throughout the world-system). This lower stratum of the working class is often identified as an "ethnic underclass" whose conditions of life stem from the fact that its members belong to a different culture, a "culture of poverty" ("underclass" is the more current terminology, but it too implies that a group is impoverished because of the cultural characteristics of that group).

Class is an objective category. But people also invariably consider themselves to be a part of a number of other types of groups, such as peoples, states, nations, and ethnic groups, all of which are integral (not incidental) to the stratifying processes of the capitalist world-economy. One's beliefs about who are the haves and who are the have-nots tend to be related to the various communities to which one belongs. Furthermore, since communities by definition possess a definite consciousness of themselves (which is seldom the case with classes), these groupings are often more easily mobilized.

The history of African people in the United States is a case in point. African Americans are overwhelmingly a lower-working-class group, and their social movements have largely reflected that fact by elaborating ideas that call for a just and egalitarian world order, rather than simply joining in the competition for benefits *within* the status quo.

An analysis of African American social movements in the twentieth century should show that over time African American social movements shifted from a concern primarily with their own survival and prosperity to a more antisystemic position, which essentially demands a fundamental reordering of the capitalist world-system. This means that the Black movement, because of the class position of its constituency and the consciousness that African Americans have developed in their struggle for justice and equality in the United States, should be the central component of an antisystemic movement in the United States, one that will demand justice not only internally, but externally as well (i.e., internationally).

The details of the above sketch will be spelled out in what follows. The more general objective of this work is to clarify the role of social movements of the urban poor in effecting social transformation. The poor of course are the objects of endless study. Too often these studies have focused on how the poor are different from "you and me." This premise, pervasive in the literature about the impoverished, has tended to blind us, so that we view people as totally overpowered by the extremely difficult circumstances of their lives. The urban poor are thus viewed as objects of overwhelming and debilitating social forces, rather than as subjects who have attempted in their own way to come to grips with their circumstances and change their lives.

My formative intellectual experience took place during a time when a series of militant Black organizations captured the imaginations of Black people throughout the United States. These organizations included the Nation of Islam, the Student Nonviolent Coordinating Committee (SNCC), the Congress of African People, the Black Panther Party, the League of Revolutionary Black Workers, the Youth Organization for Black Unity, Malcolm X Liberation University, and Peoples College. These organizations not only promulgated audacious social theories to explain current conditions, they related these theories to the transformation of the existing social order. In varying degrees these organizations inspired people within and outside the Black communities to support their struggle. But equally, if not more importantly, these organizations (and similar ones) inspired people to struggle for peace, justice, and equality in their own right, *and on behalf of all disadvantaged groups* within the social system. Although the social theories espoused by these organizations might be found wanting by academic standards, the ideas were assimilated widely throughout large sections of the African American, Puerto Rican, and Chicano/Mexicano working classes and intelligentsia, and among women and students of various ethnic groups and social strata. When I later encountered people who seemed to support the goals of justice and equality for the poor and the excluded, but who dismissed the ability of the lower strata to organize and fight for their own interests, I wondered whether we could have possibly experienced the same reality.

That ordinary people and poor people were capable of dreaming of a better life, that they were capable of articulating their dreams and calculating realistically their chances of success or gain, that their horizons were not circumscribed by the narrow horizons of the dominant (especially the ruling) group were among the things that the movement had taught me. It also seemed to me that the dominant group's need to conceal the reality and nature of its privileged positions would lead to a certain moral debasement.

The consequence of this line of intellectual development is that my approach to the process of social transformation is doubly removed from those arguments that focus *only* or *primarily* on the role of the elites in the making of history. I will argue that increasingly the burden of social transformation has weighed on those at the bottom of the social scale. This of course is not to say that social movements of the urban poor do not have among their leaders and memberships people from all strata of the social system.

Furthermore, despite the rules by which groups form their self-identities, in the final analysis all social groups formed under historical capitalism inevitably bear the marks of what Terence Hopkins calls the stratifying processes of the capitalist world-economy. While these stratifying processes cannot be reduced to class formation, I take class formation to be central to these processes. But the process of class formation is not self-evident. This is an empirical question, not a given. We must then specify the manner in which classes are formed rather than relying on ideal-typical descriptions or fantasies.

So the question becomes whether and to what extent analysts need to reconcile the imagery of a united proletariat who have "nothing to lose but their chains" with the reality of a bifurcated working class—a relatively well-to-do section and an increasingly larger low-wage section (at least putatively working class) constantly reproduced on an expanding scale by the processes of the capitalist world-economy. From the point of view of social movements this raises the question of whether this "split" in the working class may give rise to (or has given rise to) a split in the working-class movement. The basic fear is that such a "split" will frustrate the possibility of transforming the capitalist world-economy into a just and egalitarian social system.

Those less interested in (or opposed to) actively promoting social change may argue that the Marxist proposition about class polarization is simply wrong. The real social dynamic in modern societies such as the United States, Western Europe, and Japan is one of increasing complexity. As industrialization proceeds, in this view, we see not class polarization but a more pluralist social organization.

In such a view the major social process is that of industrialization or modernization. Human development, in this conception, consists of adapting to this process of modernization and learning the increasingly complicated skills needed for success in the system. In modern society success is increasingly based on merit. The ideal of a classless society is not socialism or communism, but modern democracies such as the United States. Classlessness is here defined in terms of equality of opportunity and the progressive elimination of differences in inherited status or wealth. Inequality is a positive feature of this system because it reflects differences in innate and/or trained abilities and talents.

Class struggle is not relevant in this conception; the proper subject is the social mobility of the individual. Ultimately those who hold such views declare that social transformation is not possible (or if possible is not desirable), and that the process of modernization is universal. It thus follows that there is no possibility of a social system that follows another logic than that of industrialization/modernization. We have come to the end, not only of ideology, but of fundamental social change as well!

In my view the theory of modernization is the false consciousness of the residents of the most advantaged zones of the capitalist world-economy, and it has spread from there to ruling groups and cadres in selected locales elsewhere. This view is inherently partisan since its adherents capture most of the benefits of the system (including some sections of the working class, although their hold on the benefits is always precarious—as is increasingly evident these days).

This study is based on the threefold assumption that class analysis is a key to the understanding of social transformation in the capitalist world-economy; that social groups are formed by a variety of stratifying processes that cannot be reduced to class formation; and that all of these are processes integral to the allocation of resources and power in the capitalist world-economy (itself a process).

The demand for Black Power stems from intellectuals, organizations, and ordinary people in Black communities in recognition of the fundamental reliance on race and racism as a stratifying principle in the social system in which they are embedded. This social system is a capitalist world-economy, and racism is the means by which classes are allocated across the breadth of the world-system. The demand for Black Power cannot be captured by the Black elite, who are essentially locked into a comprador relationship with the white-dominated but multiracial elite of the U.S. national and world-system.

1

The Contemporary Crisis

The time is past when the white world can exercise unilateral authority and control over the dark world. The independence and power of the dark world is on the increase; the dark world is rising in wealth, power, prestige, and influence. It is the rise of the dark world that is causing the fall of the white world.

As the white man loses his power to oppress and exploit the dark world, the white man's own wealth (power or "world") decreases. . . .

You and I were born at this turning point in history; we are witnessing the fulfillment of prophecy. Our present generation is witnessing the end of colonialism, Europeanism, Westernism, or "White-ism" . . . the end of white supremacy, the end of the evil white man's unjust rule.

—Malcolm X, *The End of White World Supremacy*

They say there is no hope for the youth, but what they mean is there is no hope for the future.

—Tupac Shakur, "Keep Ya Head Up"

There is nothing more painful for me at this stage in my life than to walk down the street and hear footsteps and start to think about robbery and then look around and see it's somebody white and feel relieved. How humiliating.   —Jesse Jackson

Malcolm's words above reflect the utter optimism of the spirit of Bandung, symbolizing the revolt of the third world against white, Western, colonial domination. Yet a mere thirty years later Tupac Shakur's statement seems to summarize the desperation of our own times. Tupac's lament seems to be a stark reversal of Malcolm's hope. Yet appearances are not always what they seem. In this case the apparent reversal of hope for Black people and other subjugated peoples is the most misleading signpost of the current era. We are in the midst of a fundamental transformation of our world, but we must beware of hasty generalizations overwhelmed by the pessimism of the moment. The reality is more complex. Malcolm, Tupac, and Jesse all capture a certain reality. We need to look beneath the surface appearance to understand the true relationship between Malcolm's hope and Tupac's lament.

We should note that the medium through which Tupac's sentiments are expressed is almost as significant as the sentiment itself. Tupac Shakur, son of a former member of the Black Panther Party, speaks through rap music, a cultural form that Frank Owen deemed a "brutal form of musical reportage about life in the inner city free-fire zone, a chilling reflection of the boiling rage and loss of hope felt by young, disenfranchised blacks."[1] Indeed there is much discussion about the loss of hope among Black youth. The popular Black public intellectual Cornel West decries a new nihilism among Black youth.[2] While Jesse Jackson's 1988 presidential campaign urged that our most important task is to "keep hope alive," even he now joins in this chorus, seemingly bringing us full circle.[3] Representatives of the civil rights mainstream increasingly argue that a new civil rights movement in the 1990s must have at its heart the issue of "Black-on-Black" crime and violence, as if it can be understood apart from the cruel economic redundancy of many Black youth, the hateful images of Black youth in the minds, hearts, and eyes of white America, and the outright discriminatory behavior to which they are subjected. Intimidated rather than emboldened by the rightward lurch in U.S. political culture since the 1970s, the civil rights mainstream is also seeking the middle ground by increasingly expressing views that are perilously close to President Clinton's claim that Black-on-Black crime is the nation's number one problem, and that if Martin Luther King were alive today his focus would be on Black crime, not on the struggle for equality.

It all seems so clear *now*. The struggle for civil rights was clearly won in the 1960s. The next phase of the civil rights movement should have been for Black people to prepare themselves to enter the mainstream. Many have done just that. Those who still linger at the bottom of the socioeconomic ladder do so because it is their own fault. Then comes the revisionist punch line: *"we must have the courage to face these unpleasant truths."* Courage indeed.

In view of the "triumph of capitalism" circa 1989, revisionist history now argues, with seemingly perfect hindsight, that Malcolm's (and others') optimism about the spirit of Bandung was clearly misguided. Not only have the national liberation movements that aroused our optimism succumbed to the necessity of a subordinate and dependent position vis à vis Western capitalism, but the socialist states that claimed to be an alternative to capitalism have succumbed to the "magic of the market." The triumphalism of the 1960s and 1970s has turned to dust. The vision of a just and egalitarian world order was a false hope.

According to this revisionist conception, realism demands that we admit that inequality is a natural component of a world in which people are not the same. The failure of the socialist experiments indicates that egalitarianism does not work. Economic prosperity can take place only when the most talented are rewarded for their efforts; the less talented should not be encouraged to aspire to be their equals. The moral philosophy of this new world order is the law of the jungle. Insofar as society elects to include humane considerations in its social policy deliberations, it should be understood that such considerations will inevitably promote a feeling of entitlement among the lower strata and thus should be kept to a minimum and be clearly promoted as a gift of the strong, which the weak should receive gratefully.

Notwithstanding an increasingly conservative consensus that calls for repressive and regressive measures against the poor, the disadvantaged populations are not only *not* grateful, they are positively incensed about continuing injustice and are collectively much stronger than they have been at any time in the past. This combination makes for political dynamite; the conservative backlash has its match in the multifaceted resistance of the oppressed. That this resistance does not take familiar forms means that we tend not to understand its depth until it materializes as it did in South Central Los Angeles.

The protagonists of 1989 in Eastern Europe were fond of pointing out that '89 was '68 turned upside down. The essence of this imagery is that the revolutionary events of 1968 are being reversed by the counterrevolutionary events of 1989. While 1968 might be viewed as a worldwide revolt against U.S. and Western hegemony in the world, 1989 is seen as an affirmation of the values and practices of the capitalist West. I will argue here that this imagery is a misperception of reality, but we should note that the same imagery can be applied to domestic affairs in the United States. I hold that 1989 in the United States is a continuation of 1968, as indeed it was on a world scale. The revolutionary rhetoric of the 1960s is the reality of the 1990s.[4]

The systems of power that were relatively entrenched and secure in the 1960s, and that proved their security with the largess with which they responded to some of the demands of the insurgents, are much less strong in the 1990s. The mature global liberalism of a hegemonic world power has given way to a mean-spirited conservatism on one hand and a Janus-faced neoliberalism on the other. Neoliberalism as a political philosophy is indeed a sign of our times. It is a confusing brew in which politicians seek to act liberal while looking conservative or act conservative while looking liberal, playing to different audiences, as most politicians are wont to do in our political culture. Yet neither approach represents anything more than a holding pattern, incapable of solving the fundamental problems of racism, social polarization, and economic decline on the one hand, and an impending collapse of civil society on the other. We are now entering a time of difficulties that will be as frightening for some as it will be potentially liberating for others. Some of the oppressed possess a fighting spirit and an open disregard for the civilization and system that have demonized them—an attitude that the activists of the 1960s only hoped would come to exist among the masses. As Arrighi, Hopkins, and Wallerstein argue, 1968 was just a rehearsal.[5]

What then is the time of troubles to which I refer? There is widespread concern about violent crime, racial violence, religious violence, and what some feel to be a veritable culture of violence that is wracking the cities of the United States. At the same time the polarization of wealth and income proceeds apace. The crimes of the powerful who are deeply implicated in this state of affairs are often dutifully reported but seem to incite very little media fanfare, except as spectacle (witness the lack of an effective outcry regarding the savings and loan debacle as compared to the public furor about violent imagery in rap music). Moreover, homelessness, joblessness, underemployment, and a veritable war against the poor are the economic essence of our time. It seems clear that the long-festering contradictions of our historical system (of race, class, and poverty; of imperialism and war; of social polarization and economic underdevelopment) are undoing the moorings of our civil society.

This should not surprise us. The concept of contradiction as used here implies that certain practices simultaneously represent the ongoing evolution of a given entity *and* the transformation of that entity. The extent to which any entity evolves in a systemic manner is definitive of that entity. This consistency over time reaffirms the entity's essential nature. But everything also changes over time, and therefore is in a process of transformation. Thus our historical system is stronger than ever by its own light, but this very strength is undermining the foundations of the system. A simple example is the extent to which the increasing mechanization of production is creating massive joblessness.

This is not unique to the particular time during which I sit down to write these words (winter 1997–98). I am not speaking here in terms of what Fernand Braudel calls the time frame of the event.[6] Indeed, the events that could be presented as evidence of a societal (and global) crisis are regularly and dizzyingly evident. The events multiply as we speak—in fact much faster than we can speak: the uprising in South Central Los Angeles following the Rodney King verdict; the conflagration between Blacks and Jews in Crown Heights, Brooklyn (involving the accidental killing of seven-year-old Gavin Cato and the [suspected] revenge murder of Yankel Rosenbaum); the murder of Michael Griffith in Howard Beach, Queens; the murder of Yusuf Hawkins in Bensonhurst, Brooklyn; Colin Ferguson's attempt to gain retribution against white society by gunning down suburbanite commuters on the Long Island Railroad; the assassinations of rap artists Tupac Shakur and the Notorious B.I.G; widespread concern about the popularity of Louis Farrakhan and his controversial (former) lieutenant Khallid Abdul Muhammad (who came to widespread public awareness as a consequence of remarks made at Kean College);[7] the bombing of the World Trade Center in New York City; Baruch Goldstein's rampage against Palestinians as they prayed, the revenge shooting of Hasidic youth on the Brooklyn Bridge, allegedly by a Lebanon national; the appearance of one million Black men in the streets of the nation's capital at Farrakhan's call; and the appearance of more that one million Black women in the streets of Philadelphia. The list is endless.

I do not deny the significance of any of these events, but our most pressing imperative is to look at their meaning and understand to what extent they are signposts of an impending sea change in the political culture of the United States and the modern world.

I intend to argue that the trajectory of African American social movements throughout U.S. history certainly has had some bearing on our current state of affairs, but not in isolation from other factors. That is why it is crucial to situate any review of African American social movements in the context of the larger social world. We need to know the story of the African American freedom struggle, but we will also benefit from understanding it against the backdrop of the ongoing centralization of capital and polarization of wealth, and the crisis of legitimacy of the states in the capitalist world-economy. In this context the practice of the social movements will largely determine how we negotiate this societal or civilizational crisis.

Thus the history of African American social movements is consequential not so much because of the victory of the civil rights movement, but because of its impact on the overall balance of power between the dominant and subordinate groups both in the United States and on a world scale. Some movements that have been failures organizationally and institutionally have been of enormous import for world rapports de force. The revolution of 1848 spread throughout large parts of Europe but was decisively defeated in country after country for the most part within the year. But the Manifesto of the Communist Party was a product of this revolutionary period, and most subsequent revolutions have carried forward the tradition and lessons of 1848. I will argue that the world revolution of 1968 had much the same impact. As George Lipsitz argues, failures in the war of maneuver (the holding of state and other institutional power, control over resources, etc.) do not necessarily mean a failure in the war of position (the struggle for hegemony). Bourgeois hegemony is inherently unstable. The struggles of the oppressed result inevitably in the accumulation of sensibilities that we call a culture of opposition, which survives any individual episode of struggle.[8] At the same time as this culture of opposition builds and deepens among the oppressed, there occurs an evolution or devolution of the capitalist world-economy, ultimately presaging a denouement that substantially strengthens the ability of subordinate strata to contest their domination by the ruling elite. It is therefore important that we do not consider our contemporary crisis merely or primarily a cyclical downturn in the economy. Although the cyclical downturn has been a crucial aspect of the world-economy since the early 1970s, we cannot understand what is happening if we do not also consider the consequent restructuring of production processes and thus of labor markets and labor forces the world over, and the ongoing broadening and deepening of the capitalist process in our society and in the world. It is precisely the broadening and deepening of the capitalist process and not its weakening that sharpens the contradictions of the system and will create the social conditions that will make fundamental social transformation possible.

Although an understanding of the social, economic, and political processes is essential for the telling of our story, this will not be the focus of the story I will seek to tell. It is, however, the crucial framework, the only means by which we can truly grasp the dynamics of the struggle of the African American people for peace, justice, and equality.

There is and has been great consensus regarding the radical democratic nature of the American experiment. It was in the United States that classical liberalism was to achieve its full unfolding. Classical liberalism held that the good of all would best be served if each individual were left as free as possible to pursue their own ends.[9] Classical liberalism came to be so widely identified with the United States that few contested the notion that the United States was indeed the land of opportunity. Yet the claim that the United States is the land of the free and the home of the brave did not apply to all of America's population. For all of the partially justified pride in the greatness and the glories of the United States and the achievements of its civilization, there are few who would dispute that the sorry history of racial injustice, particularly toward Black people, has been the Achilles heel of U.S. democracy.

Nevertheless, there was a period in the late 1970s when there seemed to be an emerging consensus in the middle part of the political spectrum, encompassing most of the Right and the moderate Left as well, which argued that for the most part the civil rights movement had abolished racial discrimination. Henceforth the residue of social inequality as it affected Blacks and other racially subordinate groups was due to other more impersonal "economic" or "cultural" factors. Thus the system worked; equality for all was now guaranteed, except for those who were not prepared to take advantage of it. This was canonized in the late 1970s not by the conservatives, but by a bona fide social democrat, William Julius Wilson, in his award-winning book *The Declining Significance of Race*.[10]

From the mid-1980s with the rise of racist violence—especially in New York City, the bastion of liberalism—the wide consensus about the "declining significance of race" notion collapsed. On the contrary, there was now abundant and clear evidence that racism is stronger than ever. At the very moment of the presumed triumph of capitalism over any competing mode of organization of society (communism, socialism, and national liberation), race remains the most divisive issue in the United States. One might argue that the specter of an intractable, hostile underclass composed mostly of people of color has become the new threat to American society.

Following George Bush and Dan Quayle, President Clinton (in his November 13, 1993, speech at the convention of the all-Black Church of God in Christ in Memphis) has declared that the most significant problem of our time is the lack of morals and values among the African American poor. The liberal *Washington Post and* the neoconservative *Commentary* declared this to be the most important speech of Clinton's presidency. The consensus across the political spectrum of the defenders of the status quo can be matched only by the lack of consensus about what is to be done among that significant portion of the U.S. population who truly believe in freedom and justice for all.

This is due in no small part to the character of the age in which we are living. War and counterrevolution appear to be wiping out the progressive gains of our era, while the struggles of the impoverished majority whose dignity and courage both inspired and brought out the best instincts in the rest of us seem to have subsided, and the oppressed have sunken deeper into a seemingly hopeless poverty.

We inhabit a world that increasingly seems to have come unhinged.

Across town, in white America, the same angst expresses itself in somewhat different terms. Most whites share a strong sense of alarm and dismay about the rise of nationalist consciousness among large sections of the African American population, and about the popularity of leaders such as Minister Louis Farrakhan and Professor Leonard Jeffries. For many if not most white people, this nationalistic attitude among Black youth is part and parcel of the crime and disorder that seem so pervasive. These same people often cannot be bothered with talk about the racist humiliation to which white society has subjected Black people, particularly young Black males and females.

White America's fear of "slave revolts" is widespread. This fear has underwritten a fortress mentality, which closes many whites off from a more objective assessment of the status and nature of race relations in the United States. Rather than an open and nondefensive assessment of race relations and racism, too many whites have reconstructed themselves as victims and have often lost sight of the cruel and brutal victimization of Blacks and other people of color, who are increasingly viewed as "animals" or as people so deficient in character and cultural values that they are beyond the pale of society.

Racial and ethnic discrimination has long been the basis of nationalist mobilizations among those who have been its victims. This is especially the case when these groups feel that the dominant group is absolutely opposed to granting them real equality of opportunity. This indicates to me that white myopia about and absolute intolerance of Black nationalism (despite approval of other peoples' ethnic nationalism, such as that of

Jews, Irish, Poles, etc.) is exceptional, and thus in need of much deeper analysis than it has heretofore received.

The rising antagonism between Black political leaders and organizations and Jewish political leaders and organizations seems to exemplify the contradictory treatment accorded to the ethnic nationalisms of white and Black groups.

Both African Americans and Jewish Americans include in their number people whose political and ideological beliefs reflect variants of nationalist *and* assimilationist views. The range of views in each group is probably similar (although concentrations of people in certain ideological categories probably vary). However, the United States is a capitalist society, characterized by vast discrepancies in wealth and power among peoples, groups, and classes (regardless of how a particular social group identifies itself). Jews are concentrated largely in the intermediate strata of society, and constitute a substantial portion of the wealthy. Blacks are concentrated in the working class, and have only a handful of moderately wealthy people (mostly entertainers and athletes), despite the fact that the Black middle class increased substantially from 1965 to 1980.

In nationalist terms the Black community has reached a level of consciousness and has developed sufficient resources to be able to establish Black control of their own communities. Yet those non-Black people who hold positions of power in the economic and institutional spheres on which African American communities depend, as with almost all privileged groups, are not ready to give up their power and wealth. Thus as the distinguished Afrocentric historian John Henrik Clarke argues, we have a power struggle, pure and simple.[11]

The people most likely to press for Black economic and political control of Black communities are those who are most able to take the positions now held by other racial and ethnic groups. Thus the Black petty bourgeoisie, which seeks to gain influence in sectors of the economy and labor force where Jews are most prominent will likely be at the forefront. The fact that this power struggle is led by the Black middle class, however, does not negate the legitimacy of the grievances that are put forward. That they represent the class interest of a small proportion of the Black community is not relevant to a struggle waged on the terms that normally prevail in bourgeois society: individual and group competition.

The terms of this struggle are rather straightforward, and confirm the principles of nationalist and ethnic group assertion everywhere. It is extremely disingenuous for white public figures and writers to act as if the nationalism of African Americans is totally outside the bounds of reasonable discourse. This is especially and ironically true when we consider that Jewish nationalism at least partially animates those who have unfortunately become some of the primary antagonists of African American nationalism.

In a bourgeois capitalist society (the ideological framework of which is shared by most nationalist and liberal thinkers and activists) there can be no right answer or resolution to this problem; it is inherent in the very nature of a system whose bottom line is competition between individuals and groups, no matter what their social location.

Nationalist movements that have emerged in opposition to the structural inequalities of peoples in the capitalist world-economy have sometimes been able to increase the power of some people in the states that they have formed, but have not been able to affect the continued structural inequality of the world-system. As national liberation movements have come to power in more and more countries in the third world, they have not been able to alter the fundamental inequality of core and periphery and have not been able to lift their countries out of the poverty to which peripheral status in the world-economy consigned them.

Like their socialist and communist cousins, these movements have to be considered failures, and all the formerly egalitarian movements have become resigned to the necessity to submit to the austerity conditions of structural adjustment demanded by the International Monetary Fund. While the reasons for the widespread failure of these strategies for modernizing and catching up with the West are profoundly structural, populations who had hoped to be elevated through these strategies have attempted to understand what *they* did wrong.

Since socialist, communist, and nationalist ideologies were the means of articulating their grievances and fighting to change their conditions, attention has initially focused on the weakness of these ideologies. Religious fundamentalism and ultranationalism have emerged in some cases as guiding ideologies; identity-based politics is a means of attempting to guarantee group cohesion in a world where state authority is increasingly disintegrating.

In the devastated landscape of U.S. inner cities, where the impact of conservative and neoliberal policy has led to the increasing withdrawal of state services, the emergence of nationalist movements such as the Nation of Islam makes unequivocal sense. If the community cannot depend on state services for maintaining social order and cohesion, then it will be necessary to "do for self." This should be an unremarkable conclusion.

But white America's historical memory tends to lead whites more often than not to see only their own fears. Unprecedented levels of public frustration about violent crime are generating very different responses by groups at different ends of the economic ladder. For many African Americans the "do for self" philosophy of the Nation of Islam seems a way out. While this view overlaps with the calls of the conservative and neoliberal public officials for the Black poor to stop "whining" and take responsibility, the implications could not be more different.

Many at the annual meeting of the liberal United Jewish Appeal were said to have booed Martin Peretz, editor in chief of the *New Republic*, when he argued that "so many people in the black population are afflicted by deficiencies, which Jews, for example, didn't (have),"[12] but one wonders whether his thoughts were not more representative of the *white* mainstream. The conception of a Black community brimming with deviants seems to have suffused white America, including the academic community, which should know better. Rather than ask, why do we have the poor, they asked, how are the poor different from you and me. This manner of posing the questions leads in short order to a rather self-evident answer. They are poor *because* they are different from you and me.[13] They operate within a different cultural framework, one that is inferior to the culture of white middle-class America. They are poor and they are culturally deficient. Oscar Lewis's concept of the culture of poverty fit the bill perfectly, although he did not intend the concept to be used (abused) in this manner.[14]

The sociological concept of the culture of poverty enabled social scientists to blame poverty on the poor, and to designate a culture for them that encapsulated their essence, and from which they were able to escape only very slowly, individually, and in exceptional cases. The concept of deviance within which social scientists operated deprived the poor of the dignity of willful disobedience. The poor are deviants, but the deviance itself is structured by their lack of the cultural traits of their white middle-class superiors. Social scientists seem to have no comprehension that we are often dealing with the willful disobedience of human beings who deliberately break the rules to compensate for having been dealt a bad hand.

If we are to move beyond our current stalemate we need to break through to a fresh understanding of the situation. We need a much more profound grasp of our time than the simplicities about a culture of violence, a culture of poverty, the hopeless and hapless underclass, the disincentives of liberal social policy, and indeed the belief that elites on their own can alleviate the crisis that we face. One need not be apocalyptic to understand that the crisis is indeed a profound one, something other than a simple B-phase of economic stagnation worldwide. The economic stagnation will be medium-term (twenty-five to thirty years), but it is temporary; the cycle will swing upward again in time. Economic stagnation is a systemic feature of the capitalist world-economy. The cyclical alternation between stagnation and expansion might be called the breathing of the system. But our contemporary crisis is not simply a response to economic stagnation; it involves changes that correspond more to the deepening of the capitalist process, and thus the slow undoing of the system. This crisis will not go away, as I will argue in greater detail in my concluding chapter.

Only a social revolution of profound proportions can address the momentous difficulties we face, the marginalization of the majority of the earth's population (including larger and larger segments of the populations of the core states, who have often been designated a third world within). Here I do not use "revolution" in the traditional or Leninist sense of the seizure of power by a revolutionary party, which then presumably operates the state on behalf of the working class and popular classes. By revolution I mean a profound *social transformation* that not only redistributes power but democratizes it; empowers ordinary people to participate in and help determine the affairs of state, economy, and society; challenges the law of value that impels all production to center ultimately on the profit motive; establishes a cooperative commonwealth in which production for human needs takes priority over production for exchange.

I believe that the struggle of the African American people, particularly the lower strata (or what Malcolm X called the "field Negroes") is central to this revolutionary transformation of the United States, and by extension of the capitalist world-economy as a whole.

From Black Rage to a Vision of the Future

The epigraphs at the beginning of this chapter, from Malcolm X in 1963 and Tupac Shakur in 1993, appear to be polar opposite projections, but in fact represent different versions (or angles of vision) of the same social reality.

Malcolm X is the central figure in the political imaginations of African American youth in the 1980s and 1990s. Many critics of African American youth deplore what they feel to be the superficiality of Black youth's attachment to Malcolm X. They argue that today's Black youth do not really know what Malcolm is all about; for them he is simply an icon of Black rage. But why is the 1960s and 1970s generation so disdainful and dismissive toward Black youth's embrace of the revolutionary tradition that Malcolm represented? There are probably more than a few reasons. Some of these critics are people who always feared or were ambivalent about what William Sales calls the tradition of field Negro revolt that Malcolm X represented.[15] Others no doubt honestly feel that Black youth have not really done their homework. But if this is the case, we need to get on with the political education instead of haughtily dismissing youth and claiming that our generation truly grappled with the full complexity of the issues while their generation is not fulfilling its historic mission. Challenge is needed, but dismissal sinks all our boats. There is no doubt a considerable amount of plain old generation gap mentality at work here. The attitude of many African Americans over thirty-five toward hip hop music (i.e., it isn't really music, it all sounds the same, just a bunch of kids cursing) confirms my suspicion on this issue. Dismissive sniping by the elders, lamenting youth's failure to follow the trail that *we* blazed, has always generated more heat than light.

Black rage is not trivial. Icons are not unimportant. But where do we go from there? Clearly we are still groping for a direction. The revolutionary movements of the last 150 years are today in crisis. This is not an issue unique to the Black movement. However, the need for dialogue among us is more urgent than ever. While we urgently need a direction, we more urgently need to be able to talk to one another so that we can establish a collective agenda. We do not need more ideological struggle; we have had far too much already. People with different ideologies but similar goals need to be able to sit down and talk about how we achieve these goals.

In the late 1960s and through the mid-1970s ideological struggle between revolutionary nationalists and cultural nationalists occupied much of the movement's energy, and with the frequent provocation of local and federal police agents, sometimes broke out into gunfire. This debate is still simmering below the surface. Today many of the revolutionary nationalists have moved toward some variation of Marxian analysis. Yet there are still signs of the old sectarianism, which we should try to nip in the bud.

After all, the debate itself has been overtaken by events. Most of the young revolutionary-minded people of today are dramatically impacted by cultural practices. In fact what is most significant about this generation of young Black people is precisely the extent to which their cultural practices and preferences are *overtly* oppositional, and pose a direct challenge to the system of racial and social subordination that Black people have suffered in the United States.

There is a special intensity to the cultural productions and practices of Black youth. Given the intensity and ferocity of white America's antagonism to these youth, it is not at all unfathomable that there would emerge a strong countermovement, the substance of which is a proud assertion of Blackness and Afrocentricity. Those who so lightly dismiss these concerns cannot be mindful of the powerful inducements for this attitude in the depth and intensity of societal racism, a system of oppressive humiliation that is unmatched in the history of the world in terms of the psychic scars it leaves on its victims. Sylvia Wynter has called our attention to a radio news report shortly after the acquittal of the police officers involved in the Rodney King beating. According to Wynter, this report stated that "public officials of the judicial system of Los Angeles routinely use the acronym N.H.I. to refer to any case involving a breach of the rights of young, jobless, black males living in the inner city ghetto. N.H.I. means 'no humans involved.'"[16]

The characterization of Black people as subhuman in the popular ideology of white America (see Raymond Franklin's excellent treatment of this issue) has called forth a strong countermovement based on Black pride, Afrocentrism, and ghettocentrism.[17] This has been accompanied by a strong emphasis on authenticity. In the emerging debate about cultural nationalism, then, there is considerable focus on the problematic aspects of the concept of authenticity.

Although the quest for authenticity is often representative of a righteous stand for full justice for the oppressed, critics point out that with regard to culture the concept is problematic because it is so often steeped in essentialist logic. The bedrock of this essentialist logic is the notion of cultural purity, an essence unique to a particular group that is not shared by other groups or that has not included the input of any other group. This is of course just the opposite of what has happened historically.

Most cultures are hybrids in the sense that they are *constructed* from disparate elements; they do not simply reside in a people. As Stuart Hall argues, Black popular culture stems in part from our common African inheritance *and* from our experience under the diasporic conditions in which we have lived. "Selective appropriation, incorporation, and rearticulation of European ideologies, cultures, and institutions, alongside an African heritage . . . led to linguistic innovation in rhetorical stylization of the body, forms of occupying an alien space, heightened expressions, hairstyles, ways of walking, standing, and talking, and a means of constituting and sustaining camaraderie and community."[18]

In Hall's view the weakness of essentialism is that it dehistoricizes difference, and thus mistakes what is historical and cultural for what is natural, biological, and genetic. A cultural politics is not automatically authentic just because the signifier "Black" is applied to it. Note the Clarence Thomas phenomenon.

Notwithstanding the deeply problematic aspects of essentialism and thus to some extent of the new Black nationalism, the essence of Afrocentrism is a response to cultural imperialism. This we can never lose sight of, for it is precisely here where the traditional national liberation movements have been weak.

Thus even if it is important to point out the problematic aspects of essentialism, the purveyors of the new cultural criticism in the United States (of which Henry Louis Gates is the leading example) are on weak grounds because they have no corresponding criticism of liberalism. Indeed, they are often all too eager to tie their own pronouncements to a liberal framework. They do not seem to understand that liberalism as a political philosophy is moribund.

It is precisely on this count that Afrocentrism is correct in its basic impulses. It is a response precisely to the failure of the national liberation movements on a world scale in the nineteenth and twentieth centuries to liberate their peoples from exploitation and oppression, and the failure of the civil rights movement in the United States to meaningfully change the lives of the masses of African Americans outside the South. Intrinsic to the failure of these two movements is their faith in liberal universalism as a tool of *deliverance* (I use this term advisedly and deliberately), despite the otherwise much more radical tenor of the national liberation movements in the peripheral zones of the capitalist world-economy in the twentieth century.

The essence of the Farrakhan debacle can be captured here. Farrakhan is upset about what he believes to be inordinate control over Black professionals, intellectuals, and public figures in athletics and entertainment by Jews. He wants to break that hold and reconstruct the relationship along lines of reciprocity, fairness, and equity.[19] But while the specter of Jewish control over the Black intelligentsia and professional-managerial strata has some basis in fact, as Adolph Reed argues, it is more complicated than is usually indicated by critics like Farrakhan.[20] The control alluded to is not always direct; some examples are Jewish participation and sometimes leadership of such organizations as the NAACP and the National Urban League, and Jewish contributions to philanthropic organizations that fund Black advocacy organizations. On the larger societal level this illusion results primarily from Jewish concentration in the intermediate strata. Jews are the most visible representatives of the white power structure, although Koreans and Arabs are widely felt to be replacing Jews as merchants in Black communities. Thus the particular location of the intermediary means they are often the target of the wrath of both the lower strata and that stratum of the community that will benefit most if they leave the community.

Moreover, Black professionals and intellectuals, as well as public figures in sports and entertainment, are overwhelmingly liberal in persuasion. American liberalism is tied inextricably to and stems largely from Jewish liberalism. For much of the twentieth century liberalism has played what most Black people see as a positive role in the United States vis à vis Black people. With the victory over Jim Crow and the delegitimation of overt discrimination, however, the most pressing issue in Black communities has become the struggle against structural (or institutional) racism. Unlike bigotry or simple discrimination by individual actors, institutional racism refers to arrangements and practices in our basic social institutions that perpetuate favorable treatment toward one group and unfavorable treatment toward another or other groups. It is possible, and it often happens, that institutional racism operates without the conscious intent to discriminate against specific groups (although in such cases there is often a conscious intent to gain advantage for some group). Institutional racism also operates, according to Stephen Steinberg, through the cumulative effects of past discrimination, which places Blacks in a disadvantageous position to compete with others.[21] It is clear that this type of racism is much more deeply entrenched and much more difficult to eradicate than simple discrimination. State intervention is required here on a much larger scale against a phenomenon that is all too systemic.

Here liberalism was of little help. Many of the liberal Jews who fought sincerely against discrimination oppose steps taken to ameliorate structural racism; they see affirmative action as a quota system that would potentially restrict Jewish participation in certain desirable labor markets.[22] Institutional racism affects all Black people but has a much more profound effect on the Black working class, especially its lowest strata.

The old relationship between Blacks and liberalism is thus profoundly changed, although liberalism retains a powerful hold on most Black professionals, intellectuals, and public figures. This is of course understandable in some sense, since liberalism has played such a key role in the advancement of this stratum.

But the crisis of liberalism and the challenge from the Black liberation movement did not begin with Farrakhan and Khallid Abdul Muhammad. In 1964 Malcolm X captured the mood of African American communities in a manner that is most striking and that I think is most illuminating to this issue. In a speech at Harvard University he told the audience that "Black people in this country have become frustrated, disenchanted, disillusioned and probably more set for action now than ever before—not the kind of action that has been set out for them in the past by some of their supposedly liberal white friends, but the kind of action that will get some immediate results." One who is oppressed is not

> looking to the oppressor to give him some system or form of logic or reason. What is logical to the oppressor is not logical to the oppressed. And what is reason to the oppressor is not reason to the oppressed. The black people in this country are beginning to realize that what sounds reasonable to those who exploit us doesn't sound reasonable to us. There just has to be a new system of reason and logic devised by those of us who are at the bottom, if we are to get some results in this struggle.[23]

In light of what we are calling the crisis or collapse of liberalism, we might want to recast the arguments that several authors have made regarding the crisis of Black leadership. One might point out that what they are really addressing is the age-old disjunction between the political program of the Black middle class as a class-for-itself and the needs of the lower strata of the Black population, whose demands the system cannot meet. In contrast to those who lament the iconic uses to which Malcolm X has been put, I think it is all too clear that youth are reaching out for what Malcolm contributed as a leader over and above what seems possible from the thoroughly compromised leadership of the civil rights establishment and their faith in liberal integrationism.

The Continuing Legacy of Malcolm X

The emergence of Malcolm X as a leader of the Black freedom struggle rearticulated and deepened the *revolutionary* tradition of the African American people. William Sales, Jr., contends that while the civil rights movement had been largely a regional movement focused in the South and based in the church, once Jim Crow had been defeated, the movement was not able to relocate and confront the more trenchant conditions of the largely impoverished urban masses.[24] With the victory of the civil rights law and the voting rights law, the conservative fractions (the NAACP and the Urban League) declared victory and the moderate militants (the SCLC and Martin Luther King, Jr.) argued for the continuation of the struggle in the streets through nonviolent direct action. The radical militants who ultimately became the advocates of Black Power (SNCC and CORE), partially from the influence of Malcolm X, began to argue that nonviolence does not seem to work.

The new mood among the radical militants of the civil rights movement was part of an overall restive mood emerging among Black people as a whole. Lerone Bennett argues that this new mood was a buildup of pent-up frustration and rage against oppression, detonated by the violent repression of peaceful, nonviolent demonstrators in Bull Connor's Birmingham in 1963.[25] The route of the moderate civil rights leadership (the SCLC and King) in Chicago and the shooting of James Meredith in Mississippi during his march against fear contributed to this new, more radical mood. During the impasse in the movement brothers and sisters in the street started to set torch to one city after another, beginning in 1963 with Birmingham.

Malcolm had both articulated and personified this new mood. Indeed Sales argues that nationalism is the political orientation of ordinary Black folk.[26] Malcolm gave that mood a coherent ideological expression.

As the civil rights movement floundered about in search of a new direction, those people, sectors of the African American population who had not been a part of the civil rights movement, were moving out on their own using tactics much different from those of the old civil rights coalition. In fact Robin D. G. Kelley has pointed out that the rebellion in Birmingham in 1963 was an expression of working-class revolt in support of the civil rights movement. However, the Black working class responded to the repression of the Bull Connor regime in its own terms.[27]

The traditional civil rights leadership no longer had the initiative. The Black working classes of the urban areas were running ahead of it. Malcolm X had developed the most comprehensive critique of the civil rights movement. He spoke much more to the needs of the urban Black masses than the established civil rights movement, yet he argued for a coalition with the militant wing of the civil rights movement in SNCC and CORE. Unlike the civil rights leadership, Malcolm placed himself squarely in the tradition of field Negro revolt, a tradition that was anti-assimilationist and based on ordinary Black folk. He vigorously fought against the subaltern tradition of the Black middle class and attempted to win Black intellectuals to a revolutionary position. Malcolm X, like perhaps no Black leader before or after him, possessed the unique ability to accomplish these goals.[28]

His story clarifies the centrality of the tradition of field Negro revolt and the significance of the lower stratum of the Black population in the transformation of the structures of oppression and exploitation for all people in the United States, and those victims of U.S. imperial and Western imperial domination throughout the world.[29]

Malcolm X was cut down by assassins' bullets before he could lead this movement into its fuller unfolding. However, there were many who heard Malcolm's message and attempted to implement it. The Black Panther Party, the League of Revolutionary Black Workers, the Black Workers Congress, the Congress of African People, the Youth Organization for Black Unity, Malcolm X Liberation University, Peoples College, the African Liberation Support Committee, the Black New York Action Committee, the Young Lords Party, the Brown Berets, and the African People's Socialist Party were among the many who responded to Malcolm's message.

This self-consciously revolutionary tradition, which coexisted for a while with intense grassroots unrest and activism, was a combustible mixture that provoked strong anxieties among the defenders of the status quo and for a while some sympathy among ordinary white folk. The defenders of the status quo initiated a massive campaign of law and order, which with some variations has continued up to this time.

Crime, Civil Disorder, and Rebellion

Due in no small part to the prevalence of law-and-order rhetoric among public officials, politicians, and the media, the most palpable fear among the public at large seems to be of crime. For the most part conceptions about crime and disorder are steeped in the imagery of inner-city, Black, underclass "tangles of pathology." Ray Franklin's *Shadows of Race and Class* is a sensitive and insightful treatment of this issue. Most treatments of this issue, however, totally ignore the political economy of crime. Moreover, sociological treatments tend to greatly minimize the extent to which so-called deviants are actually willful actors who are involved in their own personal rebellion. This should not be underestimated because there is the appearance of individualism. This rebellion reflects the values and actions of an entire social stratum.[30]

Frances Fox Piven has argued quite persuasively that the defiance of rules is not necessarily simply an instance of the failure of the socializing mechanisms of a society, as presented in classical sociological work of the societal reaction school. Defiance of the rules can also be a challenge to the system of domination on which a social order rests. "Domination and challenge, and thus conformity and deviance are at the center of the history." They are the expressions of a dialectical movement through which societies change or fail to change.[31] In opposition to the Hobbesian notion of a drive to power, classical sociology posited a theory of pure domination in the form of the societal reaction school. This theory denied that conflict was at the center of group life, focusing instead on the consensus achieved via a shared normative orientation through socializing agents. Society thus took the form of a reified consensus from which rules simply emanated. The consensus, such as it is, normally comes from a process of contention whereby the dominant strata seek to rein in rule breakers who broke rules not blindly but with forethought and purpose. Defiant people are thus part of the dynamic through which societies change. Domination is not total.

The critique Piven developed in "Deviant Behavior and the Remaking of the World" is elaborated in a later article entitled "Normalizing Collective Protest."[32] Here Piven and Cloward take resource mobilization theorists to task for overreacting to the malintegration theorists of social movements by blurring the distinction between normative and nonnormative collective behavior. While resource mobilization theorists are attempting to show the rationality of collective action by subordinate strata, what they end up doing is ignoring the powerful role that norms play in the regulation of social life, including relations of domination and subordination. Rule making is a strategy for power.

However, on a daily basis people seek to address in the best way they can what seem to be the main problems of their communities. The issue of drugs is key to Black communities' conception of crime; there has been a great deal of effort to get drugs out of the community. The current influence of the Nation of Islam among mainstream Black leadership is due in no small part to the traditional Black leadership's view (reinforced by African American popular perceptions) that the Nation of Islam has developed by far the most effective strategy in combating drugs.

The African People's Socialist Party, however, has argued that the war on drugs is a subterfuge for criminalizing and repressing low-income Black communities. It argues that Black organizations that become involved in these activities risk becoming an arm of the police forces and thus undermine their ability to pursue a revolutionary solution to the crisis of Black communities in the United States.

It might help if we attempt to put the issue of drugs in perspective as an economic force and as a social psychological force. Juliet Ucelli and Dennis O'Neil point out that cocaine was the definitive drug of the 1980s, reflecting the prevailing social psychology of large segments of the "artistic and technical intelligentsia—advertising and entertainment executives and writers, lawyers, computer programmers."[33] In this era of a culture of aggressive individualism and luxury consumption there occurred a rising and escalating demand for cocaine among this stratum of the population. While the 1980s could be said to have been a party for the upper strata, the lowest strata of the population suffered the opposite fate. Yet the manufacture of crack cocaine by drug dealers in New York City was a stroke of marketing genius in that it made the "master of the universe feeling" universally accessible in the much cheaper variant of cocaine. For those who feel their lack of power most sharply, this drug had wide appeal.

But beyond the problems presented by the users of crack and heroin is of course the business end of the drug problem, the drug economy. Escalating rates of unemployment and underemployment make the drug business an attractive option for many. Because penalties for children under sixteen are far less harsh than for adults, dealers rely to an unprecedented extent on youth as lookouts and runners. Traditional power relations are reversed when youth become the main source of income. The community loses its ability to transmit its values when adults cannot serve as role models and are in fact dependent on youth for cash, often to buy drugs.

For the political elite the drug crisis exacerbates and deepens the legitimation crisis that has wracked all levels of government in the United States and elsewhere. The essence of the legitimation crisis is that not only do things not work, the populace perceives that things are not working. People believe that state institutions and employees, from elected officials and national security officers to cops on the beat and immigration officials, are either complicit in the drug trade or simply incapable of stopping it. What else must people think of a system that cannot do anything about hundreds of thousands of citizens who are homeless and sleeping in the streets?

The drug economy of $150 billion annually is important to banking sectors in Florida and California, and is important in maintaining sales of consumer durables during a time when fewer and fewer people can depend on the formal economy, that is, on formal employment.[34] In part the key to understanding the social situation in our inner cities lies in understanding the impact of these powerful economic forces (which are the underside of the larger formal economy, not a separate and independent entity) and their corresponding impact on community, not the pathologies of the Black and Latino poor.[35]

Nihilism or Opposition?

The conditions of life in the inner cities have led to the widespread adoption of a culture of opposition among Black youth as a means of dealing with the white supremacist beliefs that daily attack Black intelligence, Black ability, Black beauty, and Black character in subtle and not so subtle ways;[36] and as a means of dealing with the harshness of street life (in part a by-product of the drug economy and in part a by-product of the pervasive powerlessness of the inner-city poor).[37] Yet the culture of opposition itself is a statement that the inner-city poor are not simply helpless victims of racism and poverty. I would thus oppose Cornel West's notion that there is a rampant nihilism in Black America, which suffers from a collective clinical depression.[38] In West's presentation one hears echoes of Michael Harrington's suspicion of Black anger. (see Introduction)

West properly notes the central role of the structural dynamics of corporate market institutions and the "ontological wounds and emotional scars inflicted by white supremacist beliefs and images permeating U.S. society and culture." He argues, however, that these wounds and scars have produced "a deep-seated anger, a boiling sense of rage, and a passionate pessimism regarding America's will to justice."[39]

We have here not the peaceful, well-dressed, disciplined, middle-class–oriented civil rights activists of the 1950s and 1960s, but the children of the working class, increasingly marginalized and mired in desperate conditions, who can only begin to evoke the kind of transcendental meaning that West implies in his politics of conversion in the process of struggling to transform the social system that so brutally subjugates them. The Black Panther Party and the Nation of Islam articulated their own versions of a transcendent vision, and the resulting sense of revolutionary mission attracted tens of thousands of the most marginalized members of the Black community into their ranks. One need not agree with every particular of their vision to understand the implications of this phenomenon.

Instead he engages in the age-old myopia of Black socialists and social democrats, whose antinationalist rhetoric has consistently moved them to the right, toward an essentially prosystemic stand.[40] He argues that the crisis in Black leadership has created a vacuum into which have stepped bold and defiant Black nationalist figures "with even narrower visions."[41] West does not consider for a moment his own presumption in using the term "vacuum," as though Black nationalists are somehow interlopers or usurpers.

I fear that West's concern about nihilism in Black America can more accurately be conceived as a fear of the spontaneous, unguided rebellious impulses of African American youth. Here we see again the ambiguity about the tradition of field Negro revolt. The rebellion in South Central Los Angeles proved that the impulse and spirit of rebellion still exist. Those who brand such acts as mere riots miss the essence of such rebellion and the strategic and tactical consensus that they represent. The radicals of the 1960s were antisystemic in their ideology, but the capitalist economy was at the height of the most vigorous expansion in its history. During this time the ruling class promoted a program of liberal reform that promised to expand the benefits to all in due time. Thus, in part, the rebellions of the 1960s reflected impatience at the pace of change. By the 1990s not only had the capitalist economy entered a long phase of stagnation, but also the ruling class had shifted to a decidedly conservative stance, openly calling for limited expectations and proclaiming the existence of an underclass (often Black) that could not be integrated into the economic mainstream.

The economic polarization of the 1960s seemed to be a thing of the past. The liberal reform program of the time seemed to pose a credible threat to poverty. The economic polarization of the 1990s, however, was a consequence of present economic difficulties with little or no hope of alleviation in the foreseeable future. It seemed to portend a deepening of racialized poverty that would become increasingly intractable in tandem with the deepening of the capitalist process. Moreover, the social struggles of the last fifty to sixty years had produced a cumulative political psychology throughout large sectors of the population, which, despite differences, expected more, not less real democracy.

In the 1960s thus some observers began to detect a level of instability at the very height of capitalist civilization such that the mighty United States of America had itself entered into the first stages of a revolutionary situation. This situation was not seen as cataclysmic, but likely to be of long duration. The following indicates a popular statement of this sentiment:

> The rhetoric of the sixties has become the reality of the nineties. The revolution is here—it's just less ideological and more fragmented than predicted. It isn't really against the system but against the white men who mostly run it. Now everyone is sick of white men: the white man who destroyed Native American culture, the white man who practiced slavery and fought to preserve it, the white men with clubs in Birmingham, the white men who beat up gays and raided their bars, the white men with briefcases who launch and carry out every war, the white men on campus who cling to self-serving curricula and control tenure, the white men who dismissed Anita Hill's complaints, the white men who talk about family values while overseeing policies that ravage the lives of millions of American family members, the white men who beat Rodney King."[42]

Wallerstein argues that the decline in the efficiency of the State structures in the core zones and the increasing mass of the "third world within" in the core zones, leading to unprecedented demographic shifts, will be the occasion of increasing social disorder. The situation that has evolved is not merely conjunctural; it is structural. In the late twentieth century, he argues, social disorder will become the norm in the core zones once again, especially in the United States with its very large and increasing complement of the "third world within." This has already started but has been widely misunderstood as simply an increase in crime. In reality what we are seeing is civil warfare.

As we proceed deeper and deeper into our "time of troubles," people will become ever more dismayed because the forms of opposition will not be the forms to which we have become accustomed. Thus there will be an increasing scramble for protection that cannot be provided by the state, which lacks the financial resources and also the necessary legitimation. In New York City supporters of Mayor Rudolph Giuliani, a recently elected law-and-order centrist with strong connections to the police, will no doubt begin to see that the tough policing they desire is beyond the capability of the city.

Arrighi, Hopkins, and Wallerstein have best elaborated on this argument. They detect a declining significance of states as sovereign entities that are key organizing centers of historical capitalism's patterns of development.[43] State networks, they argue, are abridged by trans-state networks, state authority is defied by sectional and secessionist (and drug lord) interests, business and consumerist interests serve as intermediaries in the election of lawmakers and the construction of the law. The state as a site for the betterment of all is increasingly losing legitimacy in this context. These phenomena are intertwined with the ongoing centralization of capital and polarization of wealth in historical capitalism.

The individual states have increasingly been unable to protect their citizens from the ravages of the world-economy and have not been able to guarantee their citizens an increasingly higher standard of living. On the other hand social movements have increased people's expectations of the state in terms of democracy, human rights, equality, and quality of life. It is this crunch that serves as such a severe threat to the legitimation of the state. The Old Left movements, they argue, were not simply organizations with leaders and cadres but were moral communities. The legitimacy these movements claimed carried over when they participated in state power, but it tended to erode over time as national communities themselves tended to disintegrate. New national communities are being formed out of the disintegration of the communist bloc, but they are not an alternative to stateness. Fundamentalist religious movements for whom secular legitimation is a contradiction in terms provide the only alternative to stateness.

According to Arrighi, Hopkins, and Wallerstein,

in between a nationalist movement's replication of stateness and a fundamentalist movement's negation of stateness come various intermediate alternatives, which would appear to pose no long-run alternative to stateness but which promise to remain and to grow as definite locales within the formal jurisdiction of the states and well within the evolving terrain(s) of the movements. These are locales where an "informal economy"—i.e., not state-measured, let alone state-regulated—integrates people in a place, and forms the relational substratum of their moral community.[44]

Such communities grow as state power recedes. The power of the state over them decreases further as they become more and more self-provisioning, and especially as they become better able to protect themselves. Such communities are outside the law and therefore outside civil society itself. They are centers for all types of illegal activities whose spheres of circulation reach throughout the larger society, "but they occupy a territory and that makes them a substitute for state power, not just another source of its corruption. As outsiders we know them by such names as 'inner cities,' 'drug-lord domains,' 'shanty-towns,' and 'warlord fiefs.'"[45]

The Resurrection of Black Nationalism

It is in the context of the contemporary crisis that we must examine the resurrection of Black nationalism as a widespread ideology in Black communities, especially among youth. Khallid Abdul Muhammad's venomous, insensitive remarks have served to divert us from a proper appreciation of the power and depth of nationalist consciousness in the Black community by associating it with anti-Semitism.

Yet when all is said and done, we are called on to examine the content of *any* nationalist program, and ask what is so unique about Black nationalism that it inspires such opprobrium. The strategy of nationalist movements in a multinational state is nation against nation. If indeed Jews, Koreans, and Arabs occupy the positions in the Black community that should by the logic of national development or even simply ethnic pluralism be occupied by Blacks, one would expect antagonism toward these middle-ranking groups. To emphasize that the United States is a "pluralist society" does not satisfactorily deal with this issue, for pluralism in practice has been hierarchical.

The anti-assimilationist groups that have emerged in the third world in the wake of the failure of national liberation movements are of course the analog to the return of the Nation of Islam to popularity and the increasing popularity of Afrocentric ideas. The traditional national liberation movements had some faith in the progressive ideologies of the core zones of the world-system, socialism and liberalism. The extent to which socialism became increasingly liberal socialism, even in the hands of the most radical socialists, Lenin and the Bolsheviks in the Soviet Union, can be seen as a harbinger of the fate of the national liberation movements, which, like the movements of other oppressed strata, succumbed to the lure of Western liberalism.

But liberalism has today collapsed, as have the liberal socialisms of the East, South, and West. All reformist illusions have thus been dashed. It is not the socialist project that has come to an end, but a socialist reformist project that was tied to the coattails of liberalism, which in essence believed in the capacity of the system to reform itself to meet the needs of (some) oppressed strata. Historically liberalism has been about the process of orderly reform as a normal part of the operation of our social, political, and economic institutions. This process of orderly reform is reinforced by the ideology of universalism, a worldview that allows members of all racial and ethnic groups to aspire to high positions in the system if they have the proper educational and social class experience.

The end of the liberal hope gives rise to an assortment of nationalist movements seeking to make their own way into a world that is forever destroyed. Yet there is something very old about nationalist movements among African Americans, and the logic of it is rather straightforward. African Americans are a racially oppressed group, originally brought to the Western Hemisphere as slaves, as cheap labor for the needs of the expanding capitalist world-economy. As long as African Americans remain a racially oppressed group, they will form a community, and thus nationalist consciousness is to be expected. Liberal integrationists may be dismayed, but all the hand wringing about nationalism is counterproductive; it only exposes the bankruptcy of the historical position of liberalism.

On the other hand African Americans are citizens of the United States, and thus are affected by government policies, the legal system, and social institutions. It makes sense for them to make claims on the state. A self-help strategy in and of itself is not adequate, although the building of internal strength is necessary and sensible. Both strategies flow from the conditions of life of African Americans in the United States. There is more of a need for unity between the two currents than ideological debate, which can never end satisfactorily, since the two approaches are in fact responses to different aspects of a singular historical social system.

Thus there is no simple resolution to the two trajectories of the Black movement. There are in reality more than two, but I respond here to the prototypes presented in much of the literature. The movement for equality also takes the form of a movement for integration. While there are qualitative differences between a movement for integration and one for equality, there are also qualitative differences between a struggle for equality and a struggle for justice. In much the same way, there are different strands within nationalism (the distinction between revolutionary nationalism and cultural nationalism has occupied a good deal of our attention over time).

Yet on the whole, all these strategies flow inexorably from the social structures of the capitalist world-economy. Our task is to cease calling for ideological unity; that is simply a recipe for even more and more endless infighting. Ideological diversity is problematic only insofar as we are driven to seek ideological unity. What is much more important than ideological unity is a common program to which we can all aspire without regard to ideology.

Thus what is needed is just the opposite of democratic centralism, which made the old communist movement so feared by the bourgeois governments of the world. While democratic centralism is a powerful tool in obtaining unity of will and unity of action, the democratic part is most often jettisoned, so that the process, while made that much simpler, strays from the democratic goals that were at the heart of the original objectives of the movements.

We need to be able to explicate the different pressures to which certain types of groups are prone. Where do these pressures lead these different groups? Nationalist organizations are pressed to respond to the need for internal strength; there is thus a logic of narrowing the focus in order to strengthen the group in the face of overwhelming external pressures and dangers. Integrationist organizations and socialist organizations tend toward coalition building, and thus attempt to be somewhat inclusive (at least racially and ethnically, if more exclusive class-wise, that is, exclusive of the lower strata of the working class).

These are not mutually exclusive objectives, but it is difficult for one type of organization to do both, given the logic of their long-term objectives. Yet both strategies are needed if a strong movement is to be built. That is why there is a need for unity, and that is why the unity we need is not ideological, but has to be built around a program (as Phil Thompson recently argued in *New York Newsday)*.

The Radicalization of the NAACP?

Black nationalism has been a recurrent feature of African American political, cultural, and social life. In times when racist practices have become most intense, Black people have routinely looked to Africa or to form their own government separate from and independent of the United States government. The particular form that nationalist movements have assumed in the 1990s may not have been anticipated, although they do follow trends in the "third world without" (in Asia, Africa, South and Central America, the Caribbean, the Pacific Islands, etc.).

What was not anticipated very clearly, and what clearly seems to exercise the U.S. power elite as articulated by the neoconservative mandarins of *Commentary* and the *New Republic*, is that those who have traditionally been thought to be supporters of the liberal integrationist program of the ruling class seem to be deserting ship.

The NAACP, which has a long and proud history of fighting for civil rights, under the leadership of Roy Wilkins had more and more entrenched itself in the moderate—even conservative—wing of the civil rights establishment. Increasingly the NAACP lost the support of young Black people, who saw it as a relic of the past. When he was chosen as chair of the NAACP, the Reverend Benjamin Chavis pledged that the NAACP would redefine the sum and substance of the civil rights movement and provide the leadership to transform the quality of life of Black America. Chavis traveled to Los Angeles before the verdict was announced in the second Rodney King trial to listen to and learn from the residents of South Central Los Angeles. In April 1993 he organized a national gang summit to call for a truce in gang warfare across the nation. Chavis has called for outreach to other people of color, Chicanos, Puerto Ricans, Asian Americans, and American Indians.[46]

Arch Puddington of *Commentary* thought it particularly and sadly ironic that at the very moment when there seemed to be a developing consensus about the centrality of Black crime to the problems of the nation (as reflected in Clinton's November 13, 1993, speech before a convention of Black clergy), the NAACP named Benjamin Chavis its new executive director, a person whose career as an activist and writer personifies precisely the kind of mindset that needs to be overcome.[47] Puddington was concerned about Chavis's leftist views and his critique of American society as racist and not a truly democratic society for Black and other third world people. Puddington enumerated a number of issues that show that Chavis should not have been selected to head the NAACP. These include the gang leader summit and of course Chavis's move to open the NAACP and the established Black leadership to Louis Farrakhan and the Nation of Islam.

In a presentation at the House of the Lord Pentecostal Church in Brooklyn, New York, Don Rojas, a former editor of the *New York Amsterdam News* who Chavis appointed national director of communications for the NAACP, argued that the NAACP should have been a big tent organization all along. The sectarianism of the NAACP during especially the reign of Roy Wilkins was a serious error. Rojas was hopeful that there would now be a dramatic change in the NAACP in this regard, as befits the nation's oldest and largest civil rights organization. He fully and enthusiastically supported Chavis's intent to have the NAACP meet with all members of the Black organized community. Revealingly, Rojas pointed out that the NAACP would return to the Pan African tradition of W. E. B. Du Bois.

With regard to Farrakhan, Rojas pointed out that the much-heralded relationship between Blacks and Jews has been an unequal one. Leaders who are now calling for a relationship between equals are being denounced. The NAACP meets with the Anti-Defamation League of B'nai B'rith and the American Jewish Committee; they can certainly meet with the Nation of Islam.

Farrakhan is popular among Black people, Rojas asserted, not because of the Nation of Islam's designation of Jews as the "blood suckers" of the Black nation, but because he is perceived as the only national Black leader who stands up to the white power establishment. This is no doubt a commentary on the legitimacy of the established Black leadership in the eyes of ordinary Black folk, Rojas offered, but he (understandably) declined to elaborate in that direction.

Did Chavis's appointment indicate that at that time there was an emerging sentiment in the NAACP about Jews that is moving in the direction of that of Farrakhan and the Nation of Islam? This seems highly unlikely. Benjamin Chavis condemned Khallid Abdul Muhammad's "demagogic diatribe" in the strongest terms. Rojas argued that although some Jews are members of the ruling class, it is not Jewish power that is responsible for the position of Black people.

In the final analysis the turn of the NAACP to the left proved to be much less sound than Puddington and New York Civil Rights Coalition's Michael Meyers feared.[48] The brief tenure of Benjamin Chavis at the head of the NAACP indicates the powerful potential for social transformation in African American social movements, which, if they are to speak meaningfully to their constituencies, must articulate a vision that will have some potential to address their grievances. Such a vision must of necessity transcend the boundaries of the existing historical system, as I shall attempt to show in what follows.

Powerful currents of resistance and opposition are at work in African American communities and other communities of color. This is manifest in such phenomena as the much maligned hip hop music; the truce between two important African American gangs, the Crips and the Bloods; and the rise of new organizations among subordinate groups and peoples, such as MOTHERS ROC (Mothers Reclaiming Our Children), the Coalition Against Police Abuse,[49] the National Welfare Rights Union, the League for a Revolutionary America, the Campaign for a New Tomorrow, Black Men Against Crack in Brooklyn, and the Community Self-Defense Program, also in Brooklyn.

Our current situation has a history. This history is not simply of interest to the curious, it is part and parcel of our current reality. It is to that history that we will now turn in an effort to deepen our understanding of what has transpired and what we might anticipate for the future of Black liberation and social transformation in the United States.

2

Nothing but a Black Thing?
The Black Freedom Struggle in Context

Histories of the Black freedom struggle have largely focused on individuals and organizations. We have thus witnessed an explosion of empirical histories of specific individuals, such as Malcolm X, W. E. B. Du Bois, Marcus Garvey, and Martin Luther King, and organizations like the Black Panther Party, the Student Nonviolent Coordinating Committee (SNCC), the Southern Christian Leadership Conference (SCLC), and the Congress of Racial Equality (CORE). With some exceptions the more comprehensive studies focus on the civil rights movement.[1]

We seek here to both chronicle and analyze the efforts of those who confronted the North American social system with a vision of fundamental social change on behalf of working-class Blacks, and who sought either self-determination or the transformation of America into a truly egalitarian society.

Too often scholars have viewed Black radicalism as simply a variant of its putative ideological counterparts among the white population. There is indeed much common ground, but there is also a specificity that we ignore at the cost of serious misunderstanding of the significance of social struggle emanating from the African American working class and those intellectuals who seek to speak and act on its behalf. Most significantly, these views seriously misunderstand the significance of nationalist consciousness among the African American working class and its organic intellectuals. Richard Wright argued passionately that the white public should take heed, but also that those whites who were deeply sympathetic to the struggle against racial inequality should not underestimate the significance of this struggle for "we are not what we seem."

Cedric Robinson has also warned against the danger of such a reductionist approach to the Black radical tradition.[2] Robinson argues that a distinctive cultural tradition emerged among the lower stratum of the Black population, a culture of resistance based on resistance to slavery.

This culture of resistance was fundamentally different from the efforts at social equality mounted by the Black middle class. William Sales has also analyzed the distinction between what he conceptualized as the tradition of field Negro revolt articulated by Malcolm X and the progressive but talented tenth egalitarianism of King and the early Du Bois.[3]

Taken as a whole, the initial thrust of the Black movement was for freedom. The enslaved and the small communities of free Blacks constructed a number of strategies to that end, which included seeking to return to Africa, to run away and form autonomous communities or Maroons, and where conditions seemed promising to form independent states (e.g., Haiti). The African slave trade and the system of chattel slavery gave rise over time to a systematic racism that structured people of African descent into particular locations at the bottom of the social structure. The ideological substructure of this system was a set of ideas that disparaged the humanity of African people, asserted that they had made no contribution to civilization, and used religious concepts (the Hamitic myth) to justify treating them as beasts of burden.

This system of oppressive humiliation and superexploitation consolidated people of African descent at the bottom of the socioeconomic ladder in the United States. Because African Americans have been the most sharply defined and historically continuous section of the lower class, the labor movement, an overwhelmingly white institution, has often appealed to racist assumptions. Moreover, the pejorative stereotypes of Blacks are similar to the stereotypes about the entire class of manual workers in more racially homogeneous societies. Thus among the white working class (but certainly not in the organized Left) Blacks are viewed as the American proletariat. Racial prejudice is then inexorably bound up with class status. As Kazin argues, for most workers of European ancestry, the reliable material and psychological benefits of whiteness have far outweighed the faint glimmerings of class unity.[4]

The framework within which social movements will be viewed in this study derives from the concept of "antisystemic movements" developed in the work of Arrighi, Hopkins, and Wallerstein.[5] The importance of the approach used by these authors is that they unfailingly make the link between social movements and social structure. According to Wallerstein,

> As the classes come to be defined vis-à-vis the developing division of labor in the world-economy and the peoples come to be defined vis-à-vis the increasingly rationalized interstate system, the locational concentration of

various oppressed groups gives rise over time to antisystemic movements. These movements have organized in two main forms around two main themes: the social movement around "class" and the national movement around "nation" or people.

The seriously antisystemic (or revolutionary) forms of such movements first emerged in organized form in the nineteenth century. Their general objective—human equality—was by definition incompatible with the functioning of the capitalist world-economy, a hierarchical system based on uneven development, unequal exchange, and the appropriation of surplus value. However, the political structure of the capitalist world-economy—the fact that it was not a single unit but a series of sovereign states—pressed the movements to seek the transformation of the world-system via the achievement of political power within separate states. The organization of these antisystemic movements at the state level had contradictory effects.[6]

While nationalism facilitated the immediate need to achieve political power in a particular state structure, it often hindered the development of principled alliances at the international level.

But there are other contradictions of building power, which we should note as we undertake this study. Frances Fox Piven and Richard A. Cloward emphasize the need for discipline and commitment, but caution against the tendency to project doctrinaire schemes onto movements, and against the tendency to allow the conservative pressures of organizational priorities to undermine the radical aims and objectives of the social movement.[7]

They argue that the achievements of mass movements are due primarily *not* to the requirements of formal organizations but to the reality of mass defiance, which wrests concessions from ruling elites. Thus formally organized movements are much less a threat to the existing order than we sometimes think because they are so highly vulnerable to internal oligarchy and to external integration through their leaderships with (other, organizational) elites. The tendency of formal organization is to blunt the militancy of the movement in the interest of "building the organization."

Piven and Cloward follow Michels, who argued that democracy is not conceivable without organization. The reason for this is very simple: organization is the only means for the creation and implementation of a collective will. Thus organization is particularly important as a weapon for the weak against the strong, that is, for the working class against capital. On the other hand, organization entails its own dangers.

The tendency toward oligarchy stems in part from the simple fact that a fighting organization requires discipline and centralism to ensure the rapid transmission and precise execution of orders. Thus true democracy cannot be established till the fight is over, "and liberty itself must yield to the need for prompt action."[8] While Michels's analysis of oligarchical tendencies in organizations is largely devoid of a notion of subjective betrayal by leadership, he does point out how the revolutionary zeal of the party is undermined by the exigencies of the struggle itself. Although oligarchy in the organization begins simply as a means used to overcome an adversary that is formidable in its power in comparison to the unorganized people, as the strength of the party organization grows, its combativeness vis à vis the state declines. In Michels's words,

> For half a century the socialists have been working in the sweat of their brow to create a model organization. Now, when three million workers have been organized—a greater number than was supposed necessary to secure complete victory over the enemy—the party is endowed with a bureaucracy which in respect of its consciousness of its duties, its zeal, and its submission to the hierarchy, rivals that of the state itself; the treasuries are full, a complex ramification of financial and moral interests extends all over the country. A bold and enterprising tactic would endanger all of this: the work of many decades, the social existence of thousands of leaders and subleaders, the entire party, would be compromised.[9]

It is for this reason that eventually the revolutionary party changes its goals from demolishing the existing state to permeating the state with the personnel and aims of the party.

If the stability of institutional structures implies an acceptance of the rules of the game by the oppressed, and discontent becomes possible when this institutional structure is disrupted, it follows, according to the logic used by Piven and Cloward, that forms of political protest are invariably devised in relation to—and in effect out of—the institutional context in which people live and work. This does not mean that the behavior of movement participants is predetermined in some way, it only means that the most efficacious actions they can take will be upon some institution, some organizational arrangement that is within their reach, and that the tools they use will be fashioned out of the materials they have at hand and have some knowledge of. This of course does not rule out inventiveness—on the contrary, there is invariably much inventiveness. Tactics are not invented out of thin air, however, but come rather from the past and ongoing experiences of the acting collectivity.

The form such action takes is a function not of some abstract attraction to a particular strategy but of certain features of institutional life that frame the weapons the groups have at hand. Thus some people go on strike because their everyday life places them in situations where withholding their labor imposes a cost on employers, who then must seek to restore the peace, either by coming to terms with the strikers or by removing them by some means from the enterprise. Others riot because the most effective action they can take is to disrupt the public space and thereby require authorities to remove them from the public space or address their grievances and needs.

Strategically, classical Marxism assumed an increasing polarization between capitalists and workers in an increasingly homogeneous world. Liberals, social democrats, and some Marxists have argued—wrongly, in my view—that this polarization has *not* taken place, but that the working class has seen a constantly increasing standard of living, while the bottom stratum has been occupied by nonproletarians who cannot properly be the agents of social transformation.

Such views do not invalidate the extent of social polarization within capitalism, they merely rationalize it. Poverty today is not a *paradox* in the midst of affluence, but a condition and a fundamental result produced and continually reproduced by the capital accumulation process. Yet the leaders of the organized workers' movement in the core zones and large sections of the upper and middle strata of the working class in the core zones have been incorporated into the political systems of the core states in alliance with the imperialist domination of the third world *and* of their internal reserves.[10] The working populations of the third world and the internal reserves in the core zones constitute a "subproletarian" stratum that provides the fundamental thrust for social change in the capitalist world-economy. Since the late nineteenth century this "subproletarian" stratum has been geographically concentrated in the periphery and semiperiphery of the world-economy. However, since the 1960s increasingly larger segments of the populations of the core zones are of this stratum, which includes oppressed ethnic groups.

While these groups tend to be politicized along the lines of their "status identities," their fundamental political thrusts tend to be toward an egalitarian social order because their needs can be addressed only in a social order that is fundamentally egalitarian and just.

Moynihan prefaced his (in)famous report on the "Negro" family with the observation that the completion of the Negro revolution should be viewed as the completion of the unfinished American Revolution. Moynihan explicitly viewed the Black revolution of that period as an analogy to India's struggle against British colonialism, the decolonization in Africa, and the increasing tensions between the white world and people of color the world over. If the nation failed to incorporate the Negro into the mainstream, Moynihan noted, we must consider the alternatives: the specter of the Black Muslim doctrine, based on total alienation from the white world; and the attraction of Chinese communism. He argued that the course of world events will be profoundly affected by the success or failure of the Negro revolution in seeking peaceful assimilation of the races in the United States.[11]

By the 1960s the struggle over the *class* distribution of resources in the advanced capitalist countries had resulted in the development of the welfare state, a compromise that subsequently muted the ferocity of class struggle. The working class, however, was defined as male workers of the dominant ethnic groups; thus the marginalization of subordinate ethnic groups was institutionalized. The ethnicization of the working class came to justify the growing inequality within these states. It resulted in weakened working-class solidarity (divide and conquer) and a spreading acceptance of "cultural" explanations of class-structured inequalities.

Despite the apparent lack of class consciousness and appreciation of "proletarian" ideology among the core zone workforce, the ongoing process of centralization and concentration of capital has increased the social power of some sectors of the workforce because of their structural position in the production process.[12] This increasing social power of some sections of the core zone working class had forced capital to distribute more and more of the wealth to them. At the same time, precisely in response to this growing strength of the core zone workforce, capital has increasingly incorporated more and more cheap labor from the peripheral zone of the capitalist world-economy, both in that zone, by the relocation of some production, and in the core zone, by immigration and the technological displacement of skilled workers.[13]

The increasing peripheralization of Africa, Asia, and Latin America led to the rise of nationalist and national liberation movements fighting for independence and sometimes also socialism. In the language of the world socialist movement this meant that the main contradiction had shifted from the conflict between the bourgeoisie and the proletariat in each industrialized nation to the conflict between the masses of the third world and the ruling classes of the core zones and their subaltern allies in the third world. That these movements have often been led by Marxists reflects the convergence (or confusion) that has taken place in the twentieth century between the nationalist and socialist antisystemic movements.

However, nationalist and class-based movements of a particular type continued to emerge in the core and often viewed themselves as revolutionary and socialist. Often these movements were opposed by the traditional workers' movements in the core zones because they were deemed divisive or representative of the class interest of the petty bourgeoisie.

Multiracial equality in the United States will come through, *and only through*, systemic transformation from a capitalist world-economy toward an egalitarian world order. Systemic transformation will be the result of many different forces, working in a coordinated fashion (including ecological/ environmental movements, and the peace and the various rights movements—minority, gay and lesbian, disabled), but systemic transformation will not be possible if the struggle for multiracial equality is not put at the forefront.

Why? Because although class polarization is an essential feature of capitalism, people formation is an integral part of class formation. One's place within the world division of labor is fundamentally determined by ethnicity. Therefore, it is not possible to create an egalitarian society or social system if it is based on the continued exclusion of any group. The egalitarian route is the only possible way; any other route leads back to inequality, exploitation, and oppression.

My assumption is that these social movements have given rise to organizations that have been increasingly working-class in composition and antisystemic in character, especially since World War I, and increasingly over the course of the twentieth century. I hasten to add that this is not a linear development. The successes of the civil rights movement also provided the basis for the rise of increasingly aggressive middle-class nationalist movements, such as those represented by leaders like C. Vernon Mason and Alton Maddox in New York, and Minister Louis Farrakhan on the national (U.S.) level.

During the first part of the twentieth century Black migration to the great U.S. urban centers had only begun. The major organizations of this period represented the interest of the middle classes. Proletarian organizations were largely centered around the workplace. But even during this period some organizations emerged outside the workplace that incorporated increasingly significant numbers of the working class. These organizations were against imperialism and for self-determination. With the increasing integration of African Americans into the active and reserve labor force, the thrust of the nationalist organizations continued to be anti-imperialist, but also became more and more explicitly anticapitalist.

Despite the integration of the Black migrants into the active and reserve labor force, overall the Black experience of enslavement, racial oppression, and exclusion had set them apart from the process of national development in the United States. Black people were often considered a nation within a nation. The urbanization of the rural Black masses in the early twentieth century reinforced rather than lessened Black people's sense of peoplehood. The concentration of Black people led to the proliferation of institutional sites, which generated an increasing complement of organic intellectuals who were crucial actors in deepening and elaborating on this peoplehood.

On the other hand, as the white male section of the working class came increasingly to occupy the upper rungs of the working class, or to move to middle class positions, the "working-class organizations" came increasingly to represent the new interests of these sections of the population. Henceforth their politics reflected the strain of articulating the interests of their cross-class membership.

Socialists have traditionally assumed that the special needs of oppressed "minorities" would be subsumed under the class struggle. Since the 1920s communists have given a special place in both theory and practice to the situation of oppressed "minorities," even though the theoretical justification for these coalitions has always been dubious in the sense that the theory simply served to justify the party's practice rather than truly guiding it (e.g., the Communist Party USA's theory of the Black Belt nation in the South).

In my view both positions are fundamentally mistaken. All efforts to form top-down coalitions miss the fundamental social fact that an effective social movement fully in the interests of the lowest strata must include their significant participation, not as subaltern participants but as leaders. Thus the study of social movements must include a serious analysis of independent movements such as the various Black Power and Black nationalist movements that have often captured center stage. Attempts have been made to marginalize these movements intellectually; there will be a large gap in our knowledge and our praxis if this continues.

The African Blood Brotherhood was the first North American–based Black organization that sought to develop a firm connection between the Black freedom struggle in North America and the revolutionary struggle in Africa. The ABB mass base was among servicemen who were a part of the American Expeditionary Forces in Europe. These men had seen both the grandeur and the shame of Europe. They knew also that they had been used to fight a fight that ultimately was not theirs. More than forty-five years before young Blacks rebelled against being sent to fight in Vietnam, these men said that America is the Black man's battleground.

In May 1919 W. E. B. Du Bois was moved to say that a "new radical Negro spirit had been born in France, which leaves us older radicals far behind."[14] This group was more experienced and more fiercely determined than the generations that had preceded it. They came to call themselves the "New Negro," but the term was a misnomer. Militant opposition to oppression and racism in North America by Black people was not "new." The term makes sense only in contradistinction to the accommodationist approach of the period (1890–1914) that preceded the rise of the "New Negro," particularly as characterized by Booker T. Washington's Tuskegee machine. But the movements of this period reflected both the opportunities of that period and the constraints Black people faced.

The U.S. socialist movement at that time had attracted very few Black people. The socialists of this period were often racists who thought of Black people as natural strikebreakers and enemies of the working class. Many socialists opposed the abolition of slavery because it would create competition for free (white) labor and thus depress the wages of the (white) working people.

It is important to examine social movements in the context of large-scale structural changes in the capitalist world-economy. Thus my discussion of Black social movements will encompass five periods. The first is from 1890 to 1914, which some refer to as the age of imperialism. The second period (1915–30) is the first part of the interwar period, which is marked by a long period of readjustment from the impact of the war on state structures, economic processes, and mentalities. The third period is the second part of the interwar period, which includes the Great Depression and the dislocations it wrought in the U.S. social structure, and World War II, which brought its own crises and opportunities. The fourth period is the postwar period of unprecedented economic expansion; dreams of endless prosperity, promised to be extended this time fully to African Americans; and the consolidation of U.S. hegemony. The fifth period is the crisis of U.S. hegemony.

During the first period, at the beginning of the twentieth century, the socialist movements and Black nationalist movements were separate and distinct groups, often bitterly opposed, and with quite divergent programs. This is the period of the rise of the United States as an imperialist power on the world stage. The period was preceded by radical Reconstruction, the Hayes-Tilden compromise of 1877, and the reversal of the populist collaboration in Texas and elsewhere in the U.S. South, which set the stage for Black nationalist hegemony in the Black social movements, both militant and accommodationist.

During this period the most racially egalitarian white groups were those like the Knights of Labor, the Western Federation of Miners, and the Industrial Workers of the World. These organizations won the support of the most radical Black leaders of that time. When a revolutionary socialist movement matured and seized power in a semicolonial area of the capitalist world, a segment of the Black population, like subject people everywhere, saw this as a lesson with some applicability to their own situation.

Moreover, the process of proletarianization and geographical concentration had begun to take effect during this same period, when a group identity was further molded by attacks against Blacks in these new urban dwellings (as well as in the old ones). The harsh repression, which seemed to allow for only an accommodationist approach like that of Booker T. Washington's Tuskegee machine, had also nurtured an opposition, which in the following period burst into vibrant expressions of militant resistance (the Garvey movement, the African Blood Brotherhood, the New Negro). But we would be mistaken in overdrawing the demarcation between the two approaches, opposition and accomodation. All groups emphasized the need to do for self, to build strong institutions, and to develop our own resources.

In the second period there was some coming together of the socialist and Black nationalist movements. As noted above, the communists (and to a lesser extent the socialists) increasingly recognized the strategic importance of Blacks as an oppressed, largely working-class group in the United States. This recognition, it seems to me, stemmed from their observation of the Garvey movement, the impact of the African Blood Brotherhood, and the influence of the CPSU.

During the 1930s the militance of the working class increased significantly. It was during this period that the CPUSA made its greatest contributions to the struggle of Black people for equality and justice. In the meantime expressions of Black nationalism continued, but on a much smaller scale. With the co-optation of the labor leadership into the ruling coalition and the repression of the Left in the postwar period, the Black movement became the principal antisystemic social movement in the United States.

In addition to the alternating phases of African American social movements there has been an increasing shift in location from rural to urban, and an increasing reflection of proletarian demands and concerns in the movement. The class character of the movement has shifted from primarily Black and white upper-class and upper-middle-class to Black-led and predominantly working- class. The shifts in strategy that we will be reviewing are basically reflections of the changing demography of the African American population.[15]

Race pride, economic nationalism, self-help, and racial solidarity have been advocated as means of gaining acceptance and achieving full equality in "American society" rather than as an ideology of permanent separatism. Thus both Booker T. Washington, the advocate of accommodation, and W. E. B. Du Bois, the advocate of "radical protest," advocated race pride, self-help, racial solidarity, and Black support of Black businesses.

On the other hand, both Marcus Garvey and the Nation of Islam embraced these same objectives, not as means of acceptance into "American society" but as means of building their own "nation."[16] This should not be surprising. As in the wider world, African American nationalist movements in attempting to increase their effectiveness have broadened their base from the bourgeoisie and the intelligentsia and have sought to express the needs of the direct producers (whether referred to as workers or peasants). Wallerstein points out that such movements in India, China, the Arab world, Mexico, and South Africa during this period started out as predominantly "constitutionalist" movements, but over time, as they sought to capture state power, they appealed to the anti-imperialist sentiments of the broad masses and thus became more and more revolutionary.[17]

While appeal to racial solidarity is commonly used by all African American social movements, one can discern three principal themes in African American social movements of the twentieth century: the demand for full rights as citizens, economic radicalism, and African American nationalism. As we will see, these themes were expressed in varying ways in the five periods under discussion here.

3

The Washington–Du Bois Conflict
African American Social Movements in the "Age of Imperialism," 1890–World War I

Some scholars and leaders of radical social movements have followed the Hobson-Lenin thesis in referring to the period at the end of the nineteenth century and beginning of the twentieth century as the age of imperialism. I use the phrase "age of imperialism" to indicate a period during which the core powers scrambled to obtain direct colonial rule in many parts of the third world. That is an indisputable fact. I do not, however, agree with the Hobson-Lenin paradigm, which sees imperialism as a stage of capitalism. Rather, I hold that imperialism is a cyclical constant in which there is a constant alternation between formal empire (as during the period under discussion here) and informal empire (or neocolonialism).[1]

But even if imperialism was not a new stage of capitalism, it was very consequential politically in a number of ways. The advent of the new imperialist era marked the beginning of the United States' ascendancy to hegemony in the world-system. The rise and decline of hegemonies is one of the basic structures of the capitalist world-economy. The story of U.S. hegemony can best be begun in 1873, the beginning of the so-called Great Depression of the nineteenth century.[2] A third important trend during the period 1870–1914 was the prodigious growth and expansion of the European workers' movement.[3]

In addition this moment is also said to mark the end of British world hegemony, in virtue of the increasingly successful competition of the United States and Germany. The new "balance-of-power" situation and the acute great power rivalry that ensued were manifested primarily in these years in the periphery and semiperiphery of the world-system. These manifestations, according to Wallerstein, included the "scramble" for colonies in Africa, Southeastern Asia, and the Pacific; the dismantlement of the Ottoman and Chinese empires; and U.S. military intervention in Mexico, Central America, and the Caribbean. While it was an incident in a peripheral section of Europe, Sarajevo, that triggered the start of World War I, it was not until 1917, with the entry of the United States into the war, that it was acknowledged that the fundamental issue of the war was the struggle between the United States and Germany for control over the world-system.[4]

What then, was the relation of the U.S. North and the U.S. South to the geopolitical issues of this period? In Wallerstein's view the U.S. North was a semiperipheral power seeking to become a core power by snapping the umbilical cord that tied the U.S. South to Britain. According to Du Bois, the English upper classes were strongly in favor of the South, and were certain that the North fought only for a high tariff and "hurt vanity." "Carlyle sneered at people 'cutting each other's throats because one-half of them prefer hiring their servants for life, and the other by the hour.'"[5]

Wallerstein points out that most southern cotton was consumed not in the United States but in Britain. The primary benefactors of slavery in the U.S. South were the primary consumers of its products, the British textile manufacturers. Britain therefore encouraged abolition of the slave trade because it wanted to utilize West Africa as a crop-producing area and deny its competitors slave production. On the other hand, in areas outside its own supply zones (the U.S. South and Brazil), the British upper class encouraged slavery.[6]

The social movements of this period were thus shaped by the rise of U.S. imperialism and the particularities of the class struggle preceding it. In the period from the Civil War to the turn of the century a unified white and Black populist movement and radical Reconstruction were abruptly and brutally reversed. The imperial ambitions of the United States exerted an exceptionally strong conservatizing force among the upper and intermediate strata within U.S. borders.

During this period white Americans in general, not just the labor and popular movements, tended to attribute the spectacular rise of the United States as an economic, military, and imperial power to its Anglo-Saxon superiority.[7] This set the pattern for the global expansion of U.S. imperialism, a pattern that involved an alliance between the white ruling classes and their subaltern cadres, located mainly in the core, but also throughout the colonial world. This pattern was modeled loosely on the relations between Blacks and whites in the United States.

This period was also the heyday of the Second International, but ended in the notorious capitulation of the great majority of its member parties to the war objectives of their bourgeois governments. Thus the patterns in Europe and in North America were fundamentally similar. In both cases the white workers had elected to enter into alliance with their ruling classes, rather than with their working-class sisters and brothers descended from other lands.

Social Darwinism in the United States

The rising United States imported a ready-made doctrine to justify its expansionist practices. Hofstadter described the period in which social Darwinism came to be the dominant ideology in the United States:

> An age of rapid and striking economic change, the age during which Darwin's and Spencer's ideas were popularized in the United States was also one in which the prevailing political mood was conservative. Challenges to this dominant conservatism were never absent, but the characteristic feeling was that the country had seen enough agitation over political issues in the period before the Civil War, that the time had now come for acquiescence and acquisition, for the development and enjoyment of the great continent that was being settled and the immense new industries that were springing up.[8]

The writings of John Fiske constitute a synthesis of evolutionism, expansionism, and Anglo-Saxon superiority. In Fiske's writings the universality of conflict was accepted as a fact of savage society (outside family relations). Indeed, it was an element in selection. But for Fiske the superior, more differentiated and integrated societies had come to prevail in the hierarchy of societies by the process of natural selection. The power to make war on a grand scale consequently came to be concentrated in the hands of those communities in which predatory activity was at a minimum.[9]

In this view English victories over France in the eighteenth-century colonial struggles represented a "victory of industrialism over militancy."[10] For Fiske this was also the case in the American victory over Spain and the acquisition of the Philippines. Fiske held that the complete diffusion of the Aryan political system over the world would lead to the elimination of warfare and mark the final transition from barbarism and the arrival of a truly Christian world.

Expansionists argued for the annexation of the Philippines on the basis of the law of progress, the inevitable tendency to expand, the Manifest Destiny of Anglo-Saxons, and the survival of the fittest. In 1899 Albert Beveridge went before the U.S. Senate to claim that "God has not been preparing the English-speaking and Teutonic peoples for a thousand years for nothing but vain and idle self-admiration. No! He has made us the master organizers of the world to establish system where chaos reigns. . . . He has made us adepts in government that we may administer government among savages and senile peoples."[11]

But once the martial fever of the Spanish-American War had subsided, Hofstadter argues, the political psychology of the "American people" seemed to be quite defensive for a state rising so fast in stature as a world power. All around there was talk of racial degeneracy, race suicide, the decline of Western civilization, the Yellow Peril.[12] General Homer Lea warned that the Saxon races were courting disaster by allowing their militancy to decline. He saw a dangerous tendency to allow individual wants to take priority over the necessities of national existence. For Lea, this was the central threat to the United States, increasingly engulfed by a rising tide of non–Anglo-Saxon immigrants.[13]

The anti-imperialists of 1898 did not confront the theme of racial destiny advocated by the expansionists. The Democratic Party, the base of the opposition to imperialism, was strongest in the Solid South, so raising the question of racial destiny would threaten the anti-imperialist coalition. Instead they invoked the threat to traditional American values that would result from imperialist expansion.

Among the scholars of the time it was a commonplace that the development of the individual was a recapitulation of the race, that those groups below Anglo-Saxons in the racial hierarchy were at an arrested stage of childhood or adolescence.[14] This ideology was so widespread during this period that not only was it used to justify the position of the oppressed in the social system, it was also used to explain how oppressed groups could go about uplifting themselves. Nothing could be a better example of the use of this ideology in both ways than Booker T. Washington and the Tuskegee machine.

Booker T. Washington and the Tuskegee Machine

The political abandonment of the freedmen by the Republican Party in the 1870s, the strength of the counterrevolution in the South, and the reversal of the alliance with the southern populists enormously undermined the belief among African Americans and their leaders about the possibility of advancement through conventional political means. Within this context there occurred a revival of the ideas that had been popular in the 1850s concerning the importance of African American racial solidarity and Negro support of Negro businesses.[15]

With the end of radical Reconstruction the new ruling coalition sought to reassert its authority over the freedmen by disenfranchising them, gaining control over their schools, and, most important, gaining control over their leadership. Southern whites and northern philanthropists wanted a Negro leader who would symbolize the end of Reconstruction and represent moderate solutions to the race problem.

One of the main ideologists of the "New South," Henry Grady, advocated a policy of industrial cooperation between the North and the South, but asserted that the white people of the South knew best what would benefit the Negro. Grady argued that whites and Negroes in the South were best of friends, that Negroes were as much opposed to outside interference as whites, and that although the South stood for economic cooperation between the races, it emphatically did not believe in social equality. Grady even argued that the white southern leadership was prepared to use the "best" Negroes, the most gifted of them, to forestall the political aspirations of their own people. "We have no fear of [the Negro's gaining control in the South]; already we are attaching to us the best elements of that race, and as we proceed our alliance will broaden."[16]

It is in this context that we should assess Booker T. Washington's speech at the Atlanta Cotton States and International Exposition on September 18, 1895 (the year of Frederick Douglass's death). In the 1890s liberal arts colleges were temporarily eclipsed by the growing support for industrial education, including manual training, home economics, preparation for farming, and trades such as shoemaking, printing, carpentry, and bricklaying. Washington was president of one of the nation's best industrial schools for Blacks, Tuskegee Institute.

Industrial education among the Negroes was widely believed to eventually lead to a class of self-sufficient artisan-entrepreneurs. It was on behalf of this vision that Washington spoke.

Washington argued that Negroes should cultivate their relations with their southern neighbors instead of moving to a "foreign land." "Cast down your bucket where you are," he implored.[17] The South offered opportunities in agriculture, mechanics, commerce, domestic service, and the professions; it was in the world of business that the Negro had the best chance. However, "Our greatest danger is that in the great leap from slavery to freedom we may overlook that the masses of us are to live by the production of our hands."[18] Addressing white employers who were trying to make decisions about their labor force and wondering about the utilization of immigrant labor, Washington urged them to

> Cast down your bucket where you are. Cast it down among the eight million Negroes whose habits you know, whose fidelity and love you have tested. . . . Cast down your bucket among those people who have, without strikes and labor wars, tilled your fields, cleared your forests, builded your railroads and cities, and brought forth the treasures from the bowels of the earth, and helped make possible this magnificent representation of the progress of the South. . . . In all things that are purely social we can be as separate as the fingers, yet one as the hand in all things essential to mutual progress.[19]

Agitation about social equality is the extremest folly, Washington concluded; political progress will come to us as a result of the service we render. "No race that has anything to contribute to the markets of the world is long in any degree ostracized."[20]

The next day the *Atlanta Constitution* remarked that Washington's speech had been "a platform upon which Blacks and whites can stand and do justice to one another."[21] "The speech stamps Booker T. Washington as a wise counselor and safe leader."[22] James Creelman, a famous war correspondent, sent a story to the *New York World* that described Booker T. Washington as a "Negro Moses" whose oration marks "a new epoch in the history of the South."[23]

Initially Black people's response to Washington was mixed. T. Thomas Fortune, editor of the *New York Age*, called Washington the new Frederick Douglass. W. Calvin Chase, editor of the *Washington Bee*, described Washington's speech as death to Blacks and uplifting to whites. A.M.E. Bishop Henry McNeal Turner thought it would be a long time before Blacks would be able to undo the harm done by Washington's speech. The *Atlanta Advocate* condemned Washington's "sycophantic attitude."[24]

Washington's strength was that he blended an emphasis on self-help and racial solidarity designed to build a strong class of Negro landowners and businessmen with an ability to appeal to the "best" sentiments among the southern upper class and the northern philanthropists.[25] In Du Bois's estimate the "striking" "ascendancy" of Booker T. Washington was due to his mastery of the "speech and thought of triumphant commercialism."[26]

Despite his public and very studied role as an accommodator, however, behind the scenes Washington used his resources to fight for civil rights. In 1900 he obtained funds from white philanthropists to lobby against a racist election provision in the Louisiana constitution. From 1903 to 1904 he privately fought Alabama's disenfranchisement laws in the federal courts, and in 1903–4 spent at least four thousand dollars in cash to promote the struggle against Jim Crow.[27]

Washington thus was no "simple" Uncle Tom. While he acted as an apologist for the ruling class of his period, he also had his own agenda of building wealth and power. Booker T. Washington was not only the most powerful Black leader of this period (1895–1915), he was the most powerful African American leader in the history of the United States. His authority derived from his political influence and his popularity with the philanthropists. No Black schools received donations from Carnegie, Rockefeller, and various other donors without Washington's approval. He served as a political adviser to Presidents Roosevelt and Taft, and for the most part recommended all the Black appointees selected by these two administrations.[28]

William Monroe Trotter, editor of the *Boston Guardian* (the most militant of the anti-Washington forces), captured the irony of Washington's position most succinctly. Trotter asserted that Washington was a "self-seeker" whose antipolitical line was "a remarkable deception in view of the fact that Mr. Washington is claiming in private that he, and he alone, is responsible for the President's colored appointments, and his lily-white policy."[29]

Although Du Bois had previously been a supporter of Washington, he criticized Washington for condoning the caste system and assigning Black people the major responsibility for racial prejudice.[30] He was also concerned about the extent to which Washington was able to silence his critics through intimidation and revengeful acts. Du Bois held that Washington's accommodationism had brought together the South, the North, and the Negro in a monumental compromise that effectively accepted the alleged "inferior position of the Negro." Moreover, the period of Washington's ascendancy had seen an increase in segregation and in disenfranchisement laws, while philanthropic support for higher education had diminished. Du Bois held Washington personally responsible for these trends.[31] Black intellectuals by and large dissented from Washington's program. The Afro-American Council was the forum for the radical protest tradition from 1890 to 1908, and toward the end of the century began to level more and more severe criticisms against Washington. In 1902, however, Washington supporters took over the council, removed Ida Wells-Barnett from her position as secretary, and replaced Bishop Walters with T. Thomas Fortune as council president. Trotter accused Du Bois of not standing up to the Tuskegee takeover, and of showing evidence of jumping on the Washington bandwagon. One year later the Trotter forces were defeated in an attempt to regain control of the council from the Washington forces.[32]

Later that same month, Trotter and three other "radicals" attended a meeting of the Boston Business League at which Washington spoke, and attempted to get him to respond to questions about voting and education. In the resulting uproar the police were called and Trotter and his associates were arrested for their role in the "Boston Riot." Trotter spent a month in jail. Du Bois had not known about the plans to disrupt the meeting, but said that he agreed with Trotter's criticisms. This marked the definitive split between Washington and Du Bois.

It was from this point that Du Bois began to articulate his notion of a "Talented Tenth" who would be the vehicle of uplift for the Black masses. Unlike the Tuskegee machine, which was composed of businessmen, ministers, and politicians seeking to feather their own nests with appeals to racial solidarity, Du Bois's theory of the Talented Tenth held that Black professionals and intellectuals should transcend their narrow self-interest for the common good of all Black people.[33]

Later Du Bois admitted that neither he nor Washington "understood the nature of the capitalistic exploitation of labor, and the necessity of a direct attack on the principle of exploitation as the beginning of labor uplift."[34] In hindsight Du Bois believed Washington's role to have been even more malevolent than he had originally calculated. The philanthropists who supported Washington were capitalists and employers of labor. They supported Washington because he counseled Black workers of the South to accept their position as a cheap labor force and thus "restrain the unbridled demands of white labor, born of the North and now spreading to the South and encouraged by European socialism."[35]

For this group of capitalists, "One danger must be avoided and that was to allow the silly idealism of Negroes, half trained in missionary 'colleges,' to mislead the mass of laborers and keep them stirred up by ambitions incapable of realization." In Du Bois's view, then, to

> this school of thought, the philosophy of Booker T. Washington came as a godsend and it proposed by building up his prestige and power, to control the Negro group. The control was to be drastic. *The Negro intelligentsia was to be suppressed and hammered into conformity.* The process involved some cruelty and disappointment, but that was inevitable. This was the real force back of the Tuskegee Machine. It had money and it had opportunity, and it found in Tuskegee tools to do its bidding. (Emphasis added)[36]

From the Niagara Movement to the NAACP

By 1905 the tactics of intimidation and co-optation used by the Tuskegee machine forced Du Bois to stop attempting to play a middle role between Tuskegee and the *Guardian* radicals. Du Bois felt that the Negro press had definitely sided with Washington and had been attacking him by innuendos and jibes. He wrote an article for the Atlanta-based *Voice of the People* in which he charged that the Tuskegee machine had been funneling hush money to several Black newspapers, which meant that they were being dominated by Washington for political purposes. In the ensuing controversy Du Bois concluded that there was no longer a basis for co-operation with Washington, since "by means of downright bribery and intimidation" Washington was "influencing men to do his will . . . that he was seeking not the welfare of the Negro race but personal power."[37]

In 1905 Du Bois formed the Niagara Movement, with the support of William Monroe Trotter, A.M.E. Zion Bishop Alexander Walters, and the educator John Hope. The membership of the new organization represented diverse ideological strands. Some had previously been associated with the Tuskegee machine, some might be called Trotterites, others were socialists. Overall the Niagara Movement consisted of the most progressive fraction of the middle class, those willing to sacrifice their material and political security for the sake of advancing the general interests of Black people at all levels.

The new organization might have emblazoned upon its banners Du Bois's words from "Of Mr. Booker T. Washington and Others": "manly self-respect is worth more than land and houses, and that a people who voluntarily surrender such respect, or cease striving for it, are not worth civilizing."[38] This group followed in the tradition of Frederick Douglass and based itself on the tenet "Persistent manly agitation is the way to liberty."[39]

In sharp and vigorous language the Niagara Movement placed the blame for the race problem squarely on the shoulders of whites. The organization drafted a statement of principles, calling for, among other things, universal manhood suffrage, equal treatment in public places, equal opportunities in economic life, equal treatment in the court system, an end to the use of Negroes as strikebreakers, an end to discrimination against Negroes by trade unions, an end to racial discrimination, and an end to segregated churches.[40] The statement concluded in typical spirited fashion, declaring that "On the above grievances we do not hesitate to complain, and to complain loudly and insistently. To ignore . . . these wrongs is to prove ourselves unworthy of freedom."[41]

Although Niagara Movement members were actively engaged in fighting for various local reforms, the organization did not build up a large membership. Its publication, the *Horizon*, consistently lost money, and the organization's fund-raising capabilities were negligible; it raised less than $1,300 in its first two years. In addition members were often behind in their dues. Tensions developed between members and within the leadership, including a sharp conflict between Trotter and Du Bois in 1907. By 1908 many of the branches ceased to have regular meetings.[42]

The Tuskegee machine had set out to destroy the new organization from the beginning. One of Washington's lieutenants was able to get the Associated Press bureau in Buffalo to halt its coverage of the group's activities there. Washington's secretary, Emmett Scott, ordered the National Negro Press Bureau to suppress any information about the group.[43] Moreover, Washington also used the more vicious tactic of getting his enemies removed from jobs through the use of his political clout. This was used to intimidate actual supporters or potential supporters of Du Bois and the Niagara Movement radicals.[44]

Although the Niagara Movement failed organizationally, the opposition to the Washington program that it signaled was unmistakable, and over time would not be denied. Vincent Harding calls the Niagara Movement "the twentieth century's prototypical Black protest organization."[45]

However, its emergence at the turn of the century was premature. The times were not yet quite right for such an outspoken, Black-shaped, and Black-controlled organization.

Harry Haywood's view of what happened to the Niagara Movement is more ominous. Although the young, sincere, and idealistic leadership of the Niagara Movement was striking in the dark, seeking a way out of the morass of racist oppression that it could not fathom, there was a structural issue in the history and experience of the Niagara Movement we should not ignore. Haywood pointed out that "The overproduction of Negro intellectuals had already become a menace to the social peace and order." Negro businesses were far from able to absorb even a fraction of their number. The overproduction of Black intellectuals meant that many would be unemployed or underemployed and thus muchn more likely to develop a system of grievances that would bring them into the camp of the revolutionaries. The suppression of the Niagra Movement was thus an urgent matter for the defenders of the status quo. Haywood summarizes this point:

> The fear that this new Negro intelligentsia, thwarted by Jim-Crow barriers, debarred from opportunities for which it had been trained, might in bitter frustration fall back upon the restive and sullen Black masses, arousing them to struggle, and that such a contingency might well disturb the delicate equilibrium of the regnant social order—that was the problem posed before the dominant white ruling class.[46]

Nonetheless, Niagara with all its weaknesses—conflicts among its top leadership, lack of money, lack of an economic program for Black communities, especially in the South, lack of skill at the large-scale organizing it hoped to do—was the future. Although Tuskegee remained powerful, its power was clearly on the wane. Niagara's focus on the legal redress of grievances prefigured the approach of the National Association for the Advancement of Colored People (NAACP), which was founded in 1909, when, after a race riot in Springfield, Illinois, the white socialist William English Walling challenged white liberals to form a new movement for racial equality. Mary White Ovington contacted Walling and Dr. Henry Moscowitz, who decided to organize a conference. Oswald Garrison Villard (grandson of the famous abolitionist) was called in to the discussion and asked to issue a conference call.

The call was finally issued by a who's who of socialists and liberal reformers, including the pioneer social worker Jane Addams, and social reformer Florence Kelley, the writer William Dean Howells, and the educator John Dewey.[47] Although Villard, who had worked closely with Washington, requested the involvement of the Tuskegee machine, it quickly recognized a threat and called on Carnegie and other white philanthropists to boycott the new organization. During the course of the conference, however, Du Bois had an opportunity to modify the positions of some of the persons who had previously supported Washington in the Niagara-Tuskegee debate, especially Villard.[48]

Within a year a consensus had been reached to form a permanent organization to be called the National Association for the Advancement of Colored People. Most of the members of the Niagara Movement joined the new organization, although some individuals, such as William Monroe Trotter and Ida Wells-Barnett, played a lesser role because they feared that whites would control the organization. The membership of the Niagara Movement, however, made up the majority of the Black associates of the new organization.

Washington proceeded with a full-fledged attack on the new organization. He ordered the *New York Age* to attack Walling in an editorial. Tuskegee machine lieutenants were ordered to criticize Blacks who were joining the NAACP or creating new local chapters.[49]

In contrast to the all-Black Niagara Movement, however, the NAACP was interracial in composition; Du Bois was the only Black person among the national leadership of the organization. Du Bois was named director of publicity and research, the post from which he founded the NAACP journal, the *Crisis*.

The official purpose of the new organization as indicated in its incorporation papers was "To promote equality of rights and eradicate caste and race prejudice among citizens of the United States; to advance the interests of colored citizens; to secure for them impartial suffrage; and to increase their opportunities for securing justice in the courts, education for their children, employment according to their ability, and complete equality before the law."[50]

The new organization got off to a strong start. Within the first three months it had opened its first local office in Chicago and filed a petition of pardon for a South Carolina sharecropper who had been sentenced to the death penalty for slaying a constable who had burst into his cabin after midnight to charge him with breach of contract. In November 1910 the first issue of the *Crisis* was published. In this issue Du Bois stated that the *Crisis* would stand for "the highest ideals of American democracy, and for reasonable but earnest and persistent attempts to gain these rights and realize these ideals." The *Crisis* attained a readership of twelve thousand in its first year, and grew eventually to one hundred thousand.[51]

Within two years the NAACP had grown to twenty-four chapters, but violence and racial discrimination were increasing, not decreasing. The number of lynchings increased from sixty-three in 1912 to seventy-nine in 1913. Within another year the number of chapters had doubled to fifty, but the organization still faced the enmity of wealthy philanthropists, who gave no aid, and of conservative whites (and even some Blacks), who attacked the NAACP as being too radical. These groups took the position that the NAACP's demand for complete equality was impractical if not downright utopian.[52]

In the *Crisis* Du Bois had already begun to cast about for potential members of an alliance for racial equality. He called for a Black-Jewish alliance, repeatedly denounced anti-Semitism, and praised Jewish Americans as a tremendous force for good and for uplift in the United States. However, Du Bois also continued to argue for the need for racial solidarity (Black unity), and thus also argued that the abolition of lynching, political disenfranchisement, and Jim Crow required a race-conscious policy.[53]

Throughout this early period Du Bois had had an uneasy relationship with NAACP secretary Villard, who tended to be paternalistic toward Blacks. Villard saw his role as curbing the radical currents inside the NAACP and thus distrusted Du Bois's militancy. In 1913 there were a number of conflicts between Du Bois and Villard, and Villard finally resigned as chairman of the board of the NAACP, but remained as a board member. When he subsequently attempted to curb Du Bois's editorial independence on the *Crisis*, the majority of the board sided with Du Bois.[54] However, the question of a journal with an editorial policy which is independent of the organization did not go away. Eventually it would lead to a split between Du Bois and the leadership of the NAACP.

Although the tensions in the NAACP took somewhat the form of tension between Du Bois and the remainder of the leadership (all-white), beneath this or side by side with this was the tension between radical and liberal tendencies in the organization and across the broader movement for racial equality.

By 1915, when Booker T. Washington died, the conservatives were largely in retreat. It was now a different world. Black people were moving in increasingly larger numbers from the farms to the cities and from

South to North. With Blacks increasingly concentrated in the large cities in the North, the strength of numbers and the right to vote became a powerful weapon in their defense. However, in 1911 the National Urban League was founded by an interracial group ideologically close to Booker T. Washington to deal principally with the problems migrant Blacks, mostly from rural areas, encountered in their increasingly urban life. The National Urban League was strictly a service organization, not at all involved in protest or popular political action.

By 1915 the mantle of leadership was passing slowly from the conservatives associated with the Tuskegee machine to the radicals connected with the NAACP, who in the Black world were represented by W. E. B. Du Bois. Shortly following Washington's death the NAACP called a Negro leadership conference, which included all views, ranging from Trotter's to Emmett Scott's (formerly Washington's secretary), to try to reach a consensus on the principal goals for racial equality.[55] The Amenia Conference resolutions held that

> all forms of education were desirable for the Negro and should be encouraged, that political freedom was necessary to achieve highest development, that Negro advancement needed an organization and the practical working understanding of Negro leaders, and that old controversies were best forgotten. Finally, the conference "realizes the peculiar difficulties . . . in the South and the special need of understanding between leaders of the race who live in the South and those who live in the North. It has learned to understand and respect the good faith, methods and ideals of those who are working for the solution of the problem in various sections of the country."[56]

The sweet taste of victory was probably still lingering for the radicals when the United States declared war on Germany in 1917, thus entering World War I. In May a Negro leadership conference in Washington adopted a resolution written by Du Bois. This resolution traced the real cause of the world war to the fact that the dominant groups despised the "darker races" and were engaged in a fierce rivalry to "use darker people for purposes of selfish gain" regardless of those peoples' own wishes. The resolution stated further that "the only means of achieving a permanent peace is through the extension of the principle of government by the consent of the governed, not simply among the smaller nations of Europe, but among the natives of Asia and Africa, the Western Indies and Negroes in the United States."[57]

In the wake of this conference and also in response to a rebellion of Black troops in Houston in July and a similar rebellion of Black troops in Spartanburg, South Carolina, the War Department appointed Booker T. Washington's former secretary, Emmett Scott, special secretary to the secretary of war to be able to directly relate the complaints of the Negro community.[58]

Despite the strong statement in the May 1917 Negro leadership conference, the NAACP was rapidly drawn into a number of issues relating to the troop mobilization. This included seeking the creation of additional colored regiments and the establishment of two artillery regiments; attempting to get Blacks admitted to the regular officer training school, then failing that setting up a separate Negro officer training school; taking action to reassign Negro troops at Fort Meade to combat from non-combat jobs as stevedores and common laborers; and a number of other details.[59]

Du Bois argues that during the period of the war the NAACP retreated "from the high ideal toward which it aimed and yet [it was] a retreat absolutely necessary and pointing the way to future deployment of its forces in the offensive against race hate."[60] Later Du Bois recounted that at that time he was having "difficulty thinking clearly. In the midst of arms, not only laws but ideals are silent. I was, in principle, opposed to war. Everyone is." Yet despite his contention in 1915 about the African roots of the war, he wished to see German militarism defeated. The war was a fight for democracy, not just for Europeans but for "colored folks" as well.[61]

The NAACP had finally arrived. By 1919 it claimed 300 branches (155 in the South, formerly the turf of the Tuskegee machine) and more than 88,000 members. But the perhaps unasked question that now confronted it was whether the radical democratic idealism of its left wing would stay intact. At the moment of the triumph of the radicals, they were confronted with the most fundamental question of realpolitik. The left-wing Socialist Party leaders and IWW leaders went to jail during this period. But the members of the NAACP who were also in the Socialist Party were not associated with the left wing, and all of them supported the war.[62]

In pointing out that African Americans have always been critical of America's wars, Harding concludes,

> But war is war, and after America officially entered World War I Black people had to face the harsh realities of the government's power to conscript their sons and fathers, to imprison dissenters, to harass all opposition (and

to offer rewards bathed in the sweet perfume of patriotism to all who conformed their words and actions to the needs of the "white world"). Soon the soft-pedaling of Black struggle concerns was being justified, and criticism of America was discouraged.[63]

While many may today be alarmed that a militant like W. E. B. Du Bois might call for African Americans to close ranks with whites in fighting for democracy, we should keep in mind that Du Bois viewed this as a choice between two evils. Certainly this was a case of "civilized nations . . . fighting like mad dogs over the right to exploit and own darker peoples."[64] Yes, neither France nor England nor the United States was perfect, far from it. But the triumph of Germany would be the triumph of militarism, "autocratic and centralized government, and a studied contempt of everything" that is not German. Thus, Du Bois argued, we must choose. "If war comes, conscription will follow. All pretty talk about not volunteering will become entirely academic." Those who assume that the choice is between volunteering and not volunteering are making a mistake. "The choice will be between conscription and rebellion."[65]

Later Du Bois deplored the role he had played in asking the Negro to support the war. He acted narrowly, willing "to let the world go to hell" if the Negro could be free.[66] I think he very correctly noted the contradiction. But how many were ready at that time to rebel? This, however, would not always be the case.

4

World War I and the Deepening and Blackening of American Radicalism

War causes disruptions in the institutional fabric that allow oppressed social strata to make demands on their ruler. In some cases the state is so weakened that oppressed strata can be mobilized to attempt to seize control of the state. This is precisely what happened during the First World War and its aftermath, which profoundly unsettled the existing social order. Not only were the state structures of various members of the interstate system weakened and thus more open to challenge than during normal times, but also the mentalities of the populace were profoundly affected by the experience of the war. This far-ranging change in mentalities included, as is often the case in such truly world scale upheavals, an openness to the experience of other groups struggling for freedom, justice, and self-determination.

This was obviously the case in czarist Russia, where a government discredited by a costly war fell to a social movement that included a substantial number of soldiers returning from the war front. Many regarded the period following the First World War as the long-heralded proletarian revolution predicted by Marx, as the working class in various parts of Europe rose up in revolt (for example, the 1916 Easter Rebellion in Dublin, mass strikes in Germany and Austria, army mutinies in France, the Russian Revolution, the Shop Stewards' Movement in England, the establishment of a Soviet Republic in Hungary, a workers' rising in Berlin that was supported by soldiers, the occupation of factories by workers in northern Italy, and the establishment of an Independent Workers' Republic in Finland).[1]

Although the revolt of the European working class was ultimately suppressed, the social movements of this period (in particular the Russian Revolution of 1917) gave birth to the Third (or Communist)

International. The member parties of the Third International were far smaller than the mass workers' parties of the Second International, but the paramilitary structure of the parties and the International itself gave them a power far beyond their numbers.

In theory the Comintern seemed an efficacious instrument for central- ized direction of a world revolutionary movement. Unlike the Second In- ternational, it consisted of an executive body whose directives were bind- ing on member parties. Despite the inability of the Comintern to win the majority of the workers in any country to its member parties, the very idea of a general staff for world revolution was a terrifying specter for the defenders of the capitalist world-economy. And despite all the criticism of the Comintern about orders from Moscow, the Third International some- times played an important role in enabling member parties to see beyond their parochial national boundaries.[2] This was particularly the case, it is often pointed out, with the Communist Party of the United States (CPUSA), which became a powerful instrument for working-class unity and against anti-Black racism in part because of the urging of the Com- intern.

As with the Nation of Islam's white devil theory, it did not too much matter that the Black Belt nation theory promulgated by Harry Haywood and the Comintern did not resonate far and wide among Black intellec- tuals and in Black communities, given that it attempted to fit the African American experience into the mold of Stalin's ahistorical, tautological, and abstract notion of nationhood.[3] Much more important than the use- fulness of this theory as a guide to practice was the theory's role in di- recting the U.S. Communist Party to give special attention to the plight of the African American population in the United States, and to recognize the central role of that group in any fundamentally egalitarian thrust to- ward social change.

But the CPUSA was not the only organization that organized African Americans for justice and equality in this period. Far more fundamental in terms of the internal dynamics of social movement evolution was the Black nationalist trend led by the Universal Negro Improvement Associ- ation (UNIA) under the leadership of Marcus Mosiah Garvey. In addi- tion, a much smaller but historically important organization, the African Blood Brotherhood, combined the early revolutionary nationalism of the Garvey movement with the anti-imperialist and anticapitalist stance of the emerging world socialist movement. Another important organiza- tional tendency was represented by the *Messenger* group and later the

Brotherhood of Sleeping Car Porters led by A. Philip Randolph. We will be looking at each of these organizations, but we must always keep in our view the larger question, that is, the nature of the social movements that gave rise to and/or provided constituencies for these organizations. It is to this question that I now turn.

Imperialism and Social Struggle in the Industrialized Core of the Capitalist World-Economy

The character of social conflict within the core zones of the world-economy was transformed along with the social structures of the core states in the period following the rise of imperialism (actually the second phase of formal colonialism in the history of the capitalist world-economy). The interwar period can best be understood in the context of the history that preceded it. The very short historical sketch that follows is intended to illustrate the relationship between cycles of capitalist development and class and political struggle in the world-system.

According to Amin, the period of British hegemony and thus of informal empire was from 1815 to 1873.[4] It involved a twofold expansion, first internal and then external. The internal expansion was characterized by the development of new industries (still mostly family firms), which replaced the predominantly artisan system of production. The basis of this expansion could be an "internal" class alliance (for example, industrialists with the "peasantry" or with landowners) or an "external" class alliance (such as the one between English industrialists and U.S. farmers).

The external expansion was mainly toward the peripheral regions of America and Asia (particularly India). In this sphere British trade was dominant, and was based essentially on buying raw materials such as cotton and foodstuff relatively cheaply, leading to a rise in the rate of profit. The social basis of this external expansion was an international alliance between capital and latifundistas and comprador bourgeoisies of the periphery.

The reason for this twofold expansion was not the "need for external markets" (the Hobson and Lenin thesis), but the search for maximum profits, which, according to Amin, is made possible by hegemonic class alliances.

This was the period of British hegemony, one expression of which was a world monetary system based on the gold-sterling standard. Although there were other strong states in Europe, and the United States had declared the Monroe Doctrine in the Americas, they were, of course, not in a position to challenge the hegemonic power. This was the period of Pax Britannica. British hegemony thus constituted a period of stability in the world-system, and thus of peace among the core powers. This was also the period of the decolonization of the Americas and the rise of free trade policies from the 1820s to the 1870s.[5]

Periods of hegemony are rare in the history of the capitalist world-economy, and they are inevitably short-lived. Toward the end of the century British hegemony was in decline, under challenge by emerging core powers in Germany and the United States. This led eventually to a situation of chronic and acute rivalry among the major core powers. The great power rivalries were closely linked to shifts in core-periphery relations. During periods of hegemony the leading power insists on open access to markets, and is thus opposed to mercantilist activities of *other* states.

In this case the decline of British hegemony was coincident with the Great Depression of the nineteenth century, a B-phase of economic stagnation that lasted from 1873 to 1895. For Amin this contraction in the world-economy ensured the transition to what Hobson and Lenin called the imperialist stage.[6] The decline of economic viability of the hegemonic power was a consequence of the accumulation process itself. There were numerous factors: (1) the organization of the working class made it difficult for capital to lower wages; (2) competition between industrial firms and the rise in productivity that it entailed acted to lower prices; (3) the internal class alliances necessary to meet the threat from the organized working class lowered capital's profit margins; and (4) the United States and Germany, so to speak, ousted England from its technological monopoly.[7]

This evolution, however, laid the basis for a vast transformation of the social structure of the capitalist world-economy. Since the strength and organization of the working class and the workers' movement hindered capital's ability to expropriate maximum profits from the working classes of the core zones, capital proceeded to expand on an unprecedented scale, mainly in Asia and Africa. In this period the growing unity of the world market that took place during the Pax Britannica began to be undermined by the reemergence of "state protectionist/mercantilist" policies. Since this development displaced world capitalist competition from the realm of the enterprise to the realm of relations between states, we should not be surprised that Lenin advanced a conception of class conflict and class alliances that essentially fit very neatly into what might be considered an essentially "nationalist" framework.[8]

While Lenin argued for an antimonopoly coalition that would include the "popular" classes and even the nonmonopolist bourgeoisie, he also noted that imperialist bourgeoisie had used the superprofits obtained from the superexploitation of colonial and dependent peoples to win a section of the trade union leadership and labor aristocracy to its side.

The radical proletarian social movements that had emerged in Western Europe from the 1840s were faced in 1873–1914 with an internal social structure quite different from what they had previously known. The existence of a world division of labor allows for the higher real wages of the working classes in the core zones, as compared to the laboring classes in the periphery and semiperiphery. But they are also, as a consequence of this, threatened by the generic phenomenon of runaway shops.

While Amin argues that the Third International, if not Lenin himself, underestimated the effect of the social democratic integration of the working class into the imperialist alliance, I would argue, following the paradigm of imperialism presented by Hopkins and Wallerstein, that the position of the working class in the core is more ambiguous.[9] Amin, however, argues that the last gasp of proletarian insurgency in Western Europe and North America occurred during the interwar period. After this he offers (rather summarily) that the main body of the core zone proletariat conducted its business entirely within the framework of "the system."[10]

Amin's point is well taken. Imperialism transformed the social structures of the core zones of the capitalist world-economy. Class polarization was ameliorated by the expansion of the outer boundaries of the capitalist world-economy, which allowed core capital to incorporate new low-wage workers outside the core (and outside their national borders). Capital was thus able to raise the living standards, in tandem with productivity, for large sections of the working class and the middle strata in the core. Theoretically, he argues, the capitalist mode of production could operate as a closed system and dispense with "'external outlets,' but in reality it cannot; maintaining its power demands continued hegemonic class alliances."[11]

If it is true that this period saw a steady decline in insurgency among the industrial working class, the trajectory of social protest and mobilization among other sectors of the population was different, especially among African Americans, where the vector of struggle moved sharply upwards during this period. The previous period had witnessed the eclipse of the accommodationist but politically adroit Tuskegee machine by the civil rights radicals of the liberal/socialist group around the NAACP; in this period the radical Du Bois was to argue that the militance of the talented tenth radicals with which he was associated had been surpassed by a new radicalism, a new Negro who had emerged from the experience of war and revolution in Europe.[12]

The Sources of New Negro Radicalism

This new radical spirit came to be known as the New Negro movement. The term was treasured by people from different political currents: nationalists like Marcus Garvey, socialists like Randolph and Owen of the *Messenger*, Cyril Briggs of the African Blood Brotherhood, and militant young reformers like Roscoe Dunjee of the *Oklahoma City Black Dispatch*. The title was proudly claimed by those who fought to defend Black communities across the nation during the Red Summer of 1919.[13] The term was eventually co-opted by middle-class Blacks, who used the term to distinguish themselves as "new" aggressive individualists who would take advantage of the new opportunities offered by the North, in contrast to the more unobtrusive "old Negro" in the southern tradition.[14]

From 1910 to 1920 Blacks migrated in increasingly large numbers to northern cities to take jobs in industry. During World War I, 450,000 African Americans migrated to the North. Once there they met bitter opposition from whites who feared competition over jobs, housing, political power, and facilities for education, transportation, and relaxation.[15] From 1916 to 1923 there were more than four dozen race riots, mostly white against Black, and in the Red Summer of 1919 alone there were twenty-six.[16]

Tuttle relates the violence of the Red Summer to the conditions, values, and attitudes of the postwar world. There were clashes in areas of the former Hapsburg and Russian empires, between Poles and Lithuanians over Vilna; between Poles and Czechs over the Teschen district, and between Hungary and Austria over Burgenland, to mention a few.[17] But there was more than just interethnic rivalry. Nationalists in Egypt, Ireland, and India rose up in opposition to British overrule. Then of course there was the great civil war in the Soviet Union, and attempts at proletarian revolution in Germany and Hungary. The attempted seizure of power by the

Spartacists in Germany failed, but Hungarian communists established a short-lived government in March 1919. But the most significant event of this period in the minds of the U.S. ruling class was the establishment in March 1919 of the Communist or Third International.[18]

Economic conditions throughout Europe were very bad, with uncertain currencies and widespread fear of bankruptcy among states. Moreover, war demobilization dumped millions of soldiers onto the labor markets. Unemployment was widespread; general strikes paralyzed Winnipeg and Havana; riots or hunger strikes ensued in Spain, Germany, and Italy. Race riots also occurred in Johannesburg, Liverpool, London, and Wales as whites attacked Blacks.[19] By July 1919 in the United States, the army had discharged 2.6 million of its personnel at the rate of 15,000 per day. This is all the more significant in view of its coincidence with a time of decreasing employment. Labor strife soared to heights not seen since the 1890s, including a general strike in Seattle that the mayor of Seattle termed "an attempted revolution."[20] The coincidence of the Great Migration, the labor strife, and the ending of the First World War thus sets the context for not only the Red Summer, but the Red Scare as well.

Here I juxtapose the Red Summer and the Red Scare not simply for the sake of irony, but to illustrate the three points of struggle of this period. The Red Scare was partially an attack on radicals who opposed the war, but its more enduring target was the widespread labor unrest, which during these times was perceived with great concern. The sentiments of the mayor of Seattle were not too far from those of the economic and political elite of that period. Seattle's mayor argued that strikes and labor unrest of that intensity could very well have led to the overthrow of the "industrial system."

The Red Summer, on the other hand, was an attempt to control the African American, lower stratum of the working class, whose competition was viewed as a threat to the jobs, communities, and privileges (such as they were) of the white working class. This antagonism has been part and parcel of the relationship between white and Black (and other third world) labor from the beginnings of a system that identified whites as free labor and Blacks as coerced or slave labor. White labor first wished to contain slavery within certain territorial bounds, but when planters attempted to expand beyond those bounds, the attempts to contain slavery within that territory created the space in which enslaved Blacks could themselves intervene in such a way as to hasten the abolition of the slave system itself.

While the modern white working class had been able to increase its power from the middle of the nineteenth century in the United States, its attitude toward the forms of coerced labor within and outside the national borders of its home state was primarily defensive. Once slavery was abolished, the freedmen received partial enfranchisement and some of the rights of wage earners and property holders. But as Du Bois argues,

> long before they were strong enough to assert the rights thus granted, or to gather intelligence enough for proper group leadership, the new colonialism of the later nineteenth and twentieth centuries began to dawn. The new colonial theory transferred the reign of commercial privilege and extraordinary profit from the exploitation of the European working class to the exploitation of backward races under the political domination of Europe. For the purpose of carrying out this idea the European and white American working class was practically invited to share in this new exploitation, and particularly were flattered by popular appeals to their inherent superiority to "Dagoes," "Chinks," "Japs," and "Niggers."[21]

Here, then, are the rudiments of the analysis of the New Negro movement (although Du Bois himself was not considered one of their number), which developed into a torrent of resistance and rebellion far greater than anything seen heretofore among the African American population.[22] The potential constituency of radical movements in the African American population underwent an extraordinary growth during this period.

This seems to me to be the context for the rise of a multitude of organizational forms, from formal organizations to news journals, that raised the struggle for Black liberation to new heights. In addition to the large number of new organizations that came into existence in this period, African Americans began increasingly to enter into coalition with and even to join organizations of the traditional Left, the Socialist and later the Communist Parties.

In what follows I will attempt to sketch a broad trajectory indicating how these forms unfolded, interacted, conflicted, and attempted to fashion tactics and strategies far beyond the scope of the social movements that preceded them.

The Rise of New Negro Radicalism

It is of course well known that the major effort that emerged during this period was the Universal Negro Improvement Association (UNIA), founded by Marcus Garvey in 1917. But the UNIA was not simply a creation of Garvey's charisma, oratorical brilliance, or organizational genius. These personal characteristics were crucial to the kind of leadership he exerted, but proper analysis of the Garvey movement requires that we note that the UNIA came into being during a period when the relatively cohesive New Negro movement was in operation.

In 1914 Hubert Harrison, the dean of the Harlem radicals, had left the Socialist Party because he did not think the party was concerned with promoting the interests of the Negro.[23] By 1917 Harrison founded his own organization, the Afro-American Liberty League, which promoted the "race first" doctrine of the New Negro nationalists, such as John Bruce and William Bridges. In addition Harrison called for a new Black internationalism, which might be viewed as a revolutionary Pan-Africanism.[24] Harrison remained a socialist, but the race came first.

In opposition to the "race first" position of the New Negro nationalists, the Socialist Party launched the *Messenger* magazine under the leadership of two new young Black recruits, A. Philip Randolph and Chandler Owen. Randolph and Owen energetically propagated the "class first" view of the Socialist Party and subjected the views of other Black radicals to severe criticism. They described the *Messenger* as "the only Magazine of Scientific Radicalism in the world published by Negroes."[25]

Indeed in 1919, a very revolutionary year, the *Messenger* was very radical. It published a "Thanksgiving Homily to Revolution":

> First we are especially thankful for the Russian Revolution—the greatest achievement of the twentieth century.
>
> Second, we are thankful for the German Revolution, the Hungarian Revolution and the Bulgarian Revolution.
>
> Third, we are thankful for the world unrest, which has manifested itself in the titanic strikes which are sweeping and have been sweeping Great Britain, France, Italy, the United States, Japan, and in fact every country of the world.[26]

Manning Marable has argued that in Randolph's formative years his socialism was based on religious reformism, economic determinism, internationalism, and Second International Marxism. After the initial years of the *Messenger* Randolph moved closer and closer to reformist socialism. But the early Randolph leveled scathing criticisms of Du Bois, whose brand of socialism was too bland for him.[27] When Randolph broke with Du Bois over Du Bois's call for Blacks to unite with all Americans in favor of the war effort in his "Closing Ranks" editorial, this did push him to the left. Wilson's Justice Department deemed the *Messenger* the most dangerous of all Negro publications. During this period Randolph and Owen were known as the Lenin and Trotsky of Harlem.

While Randolph's opposition to Du Bois pushed him to the left, his opposition to Garvey and Black nationalism generally pushed him to the right. Initially Randolph had worked closely with the New Negro nationalists in Harlem. He broke with them over the formation of the Liberty Party in 1920, an all-Black party that used the slogan "race first." Randolph argued that a party that had no hope of attracting the support of the majority had no justification. Randolph was also concerned that the Liberty Party did not have an economic program.[28]

In December 1920 Randolph launched an all-out attack on Marcus Garvey as a menace to the Negro since he did not have an economic program. Randolph even argued that Africans were not capable of governing themselves.[29]

During this period the IWW collapsed. With the demise of this early beacon of racial egalitarianism, Randolph and the *Messenger* group were thrown back into organizing Blacks for entry into the AFL. To accomplish this Randolph acquiesced to the policy of AFL locals of placing Black workers into segregated "colored federal unions," which were decidedly of second-class status within the AFL. This practice led more militant Blacks to denounce the AFL in its entirety, while Randolph and the *Messenger* group moved closer and closer to the moderate civil rights leadership such as the NAACP's James Weldon Johnson and the even more conservative Robert R. Moten, Booker T. Washington's successor at Tuskegee.[30]

By the mid-1920s Randolph and the *Messenger* group had become advocates of class compromise rather than class struggle. They no longer supported the radical vision of the IWW, they denounced communism, and they announced open opposition to Garvey and Black nationalism. Randolph supported a Kautskyian brand of Marxist reformism wherein socialism would come about as a result of a series of economic reforms between management and labor, gradually increasing the decision-making role of labor in the workplace. Thus for Randolph the highest expression of working-class politics was the Socialist Party.[31]

In Randolph's view race and ethnicity played no part in the "scientific" evolution of class contradictions. He believed class to be an economic category without cultural or social limits. From this point of view nationalism was an obstacle both to the class struggle and to the Black freedom struggle.[32] In this context Randolph and the *Messenger* group moved closer and closer to the NAACP, with whom they collaborated in asking Attorney General Harry Daugherty for the conviction of Garvey on charges of mail fraud. As the *Messenger* group moved more to the right, it increasingly buried its socialist ideology.

The *Messenger* group played an important role in exposing Black people to socialist ideas and analysis, but it did not build a strong organization. And while it consistently emphasized the importance of building majoritarian political forces—for example, among the (white) working class—it was quite isolated, as was of course its parent organization, the Socialist Party.

The Universal Negro Improvement Association, on the other hand, was a very large organization during this period. It attracted large numbers of West Indians and Afro-Americans, especially those newly arrived in the North. The genius of Garvey's approach was that he correctly identified the need of the Black masses for self-respect.

Marcus Garvey and the Universal Negro Improvement Association

The preeminent organization among Black Americans during the post–World War I period was Marcus Garvey's Universal Negro Improvement Association. While the NAACP and the Urban League are widely recognized as advocates of the interests of Black people, they have never had anything like a mass constituency in the Black community itself.

E. David Cronon presents the central tenets of Garveyism as follows:

(a) Glory in all things Black; pride in the Black man's racial identity and an emphasis on racial purity.

(b) Rejection of the Black man's powerlessness in white societies (particularly the USA), while working for the attainment of power in the Black man's ancestral home, Africa.

(c) Preparation for the return to Africa by developing economic self-reliance and power.[33]

In Garvey's view the Black man was universally oppressed because of race, and therefore any program for liberation would have to be built around the question of "race first." In this sense the race had become a political entity that had to be redeemed. Although Garvey was only the most recent of a long line of Black nationalists (some of whom were also Pan-Africanists), he was the first Black leader in the history of the United States to advocate the idea in such a way as to capture the imagination and loyalty of the Black masses. All the previous advocates of Pan-Africanism, and indeed the official Pan-African Conferences (founded by the Trinidadian Henry Sylvester Williams in 1900, subsequently led by W. E. B. Du Bois), had relied on appeals to the good will of the colonial powers and the U.S. ruling class. Furthermore, there was no means by which people could be mobilized to implement a program of action.

Garvey's political perspective had been formed initially when he was a student of the Jamaican anticolonial radical Dr. Robert Love, best remembered for his militant journalism in the *Jamaica Advocate* (1894–1905). According to Lewis, Love was a Du Bois–type intellectual, a fighter who left a legacy of ideas and battles, but who had no mass following.[34] Garvey traveled and worked in Costa Rica, Panama, Nicaragua, Honduras, Columbia, Venezuela, and Ecuador. In all these countries he observed that white workers were treated better than Black workers. It was this experience that led him to interpret the workers' oppression in terms of color.[35]

In 1912 Garvey traveled to London and became associated with the Egyptian nationalist Duse Mohammed Ali, editor and publisher of the *African Times and Orient Review*. Garvey's association with Mohammed brought him into contact with various intellectuals who would later become active in the UNIA, including Hubert Harrison, John Bruce, William Ferris, and Arthur Schomberg. While in London Garvey also read Booker T. Washington's *Up from Slavery*, which led him to visualize his own destiny as a race leader.

When he called for the founding of the Universal Negro Improvement Association upon his return to Jamaica in 1914, Garvey explained,

> I was determined that the Black man would not continue to be kicked about by all of the other races and nations . . . as I saw in the West Indies, South and Central America, and Europe, and as I read of it in America. . . . I saw before me . . . a new world of Black men, not peons, serfs, dogs, and slaves, but a nation of sturdy men making their impress upon civilization and causing a new light to dawn upon the human race.[36]

In 1916 Garvey traveled to the United States. He had originally planned to meet with Booker T. Washington to discuss building a "Jamaican Tuskegee." Booker T. Washington had died, however, and thus Garvey made contact with some of the people he had previously met while working with Duse Mohammed Ali. He then traveled through the United States lecturing to Black audiences and meeting with Black leaders. The African American leaders disappointed him; he considered them opportunistic and lacking in a program that truly spoke to the needs of the common people in the Black communities they professed to lead. But the mood among the African American masses was more receptive.[37] In Garvey's view, Africans in America possessed a more developed sense of race identity than the Africans in the Caribbean.[38] In the United States Garvey's program changed from reformist to Black nationalist.

The conditions in the United States were quite different from those in Jamaica and throughout the Caribbean. The Caribbean states were still British colonies, and the colored middle class exerted quite an influence over the entire society.[39] The more overt racism in the United States and the particular structural conditions and political conditions discussed above meant that African Americans were ready for Garvey's message, whereas their counterparts in his native Jamaica were less receptive.[40]

From its establishment in 1917 the Harlem branch of the UNIA grew to two thousand members in two months. By 1919 the UNIA had established thirty branches in the United States, and additional branches in the Caribbean, Latin America, and Africa.[41]

In 1918 the UNIA founded a weekly newspaper, the *Negro World*, to communicate with its transnational membership. The *Negro World* appeared in Spanish and French as well as English. It focused on Black history, glorified Black heroes, and promoted African ("Negroid") physical features as a new standard of beauty. In the pages of the *Negro World* Garvey hammered home the major political goal of the organization, the political independence of Africa. The paper was banned by the European colonists in many of their territories, often with stiff sentences for violators of the ban.[42]

In 1919 and 1920 the UNIA established chapters in most of the urban centers to which Blacks had migrated from the rural South. In the spring of 1919 Garvey repeated an earlier nationwide tour through thirty-eight states, calling for Blacks to unite in one mighty organization, the UNIA. The race wars were in full swing (this was the year of the infamous Red

Summer), and many heeded Garvey's call. By 1921 Garvey was claiming a UNIA membership of six million. The most conservative estimate placed the membership at a minimum of one million.[43]

In August 1920 the UNIA held the First International Convention of the Negro Peoples of the World, which was attended by delegates from twenty-five countries (including Canada, most West Indian islands, Mexico, Venezuela, Colombia, Guiana, Surinam, Brazil, Sierra Leone, Liberia, and Nigeria).[44] More than twenty-five thousand people attended the opening session in Madison Square Garden. One outcome of this meeting, was the adoption of the Declaration of the Rights of the Negro Peoples of the World, which called for the redemption of Africa and demanded the right of self-determination. It also put forward the UNIA as the instrument of that redemption. But regardless of the primacy of the liberation of Africa, the UNIA program also demanded full political rights for Black people wherever they lived. Despite Garvey's remarks about the United States being a white man's country, the UNIA was opposed to segregation.

In 1919 in Pittsburgh Garvey spoke of a plan for a fleet of Black-owned steamships to carry African Americans back to their homeland. Garvey had in mind using the fleet to coordinate Black commercial enterprises throughout the world, but the UNIA office was flooded with calls requesting tickets to travel to Africa. In May 1919, therefore, the UNIA established the Black Star Line, and sold shares for five dollars each.[45]

By 1921 Garvey was unquestionably the leader of the largest organization of its type in the history of the Black race. As of August 21, 1921, the UNIA contained 418 chartered divisions (up from 95 a year earlier), and 422 not yet chartered. Together with the 19 chapters, this made for a total of 859 branches.[46]

These successes arrayed a goodly number of enemies against Garvey. Foremost among them was the U.S. government, which feared all Black radicals,[47] and European governments who felt that the Garvey movement was a threat to their colonies. Then there were other organized groups, such as the Communist Party USA, which fought with Garvey over the same constituency (Black workers), and the integrationists of the day, such as the NAACP.

In 1921 at the UNIA's second international convention, the African Blood Brotherhood (which Martin alleges was a Black auxiliary for the CPUSA) attempted to challenge Garvey's leadership of the UNIA. The

NAACP through Du Bois's articles in the *Crisis* continued its attacks on Garvey. British authorities banned the UNIA paper *Negro World* and prohibited UNIA officials from entering their colonies. The Black socialists (A. Philip Randolph and the *Messenger* group) also began to criticize Garvey.

By 1922, however, the Black Star Steamship Line had failed, and Garvey and his associates were being sued for mail fraud.[48] By 1924 the possibility of colonizing Liberia had fallen through, due in large part to the opposition of the European colonial powers, but also to the reluctance of the Liberian government, which viewed the Garvey movement as a potential threat. Initially the Liberian government had been receptive to Garvey's plan, which was to build colleges, universities, industrial plants, and railroad tracks. What it may have been less enthusiastic about was the UNIA's plan to use Liberia as a base of operation to rid Africa of the European imperialists. But Liberia's repudiation of the UNIA ended any possibility for the implementation of the UNIA's main goal in the immediate future.[49]

In 1925, after an unsuccessful appeal of his 1923 mail fraud conviction, Garvey entered the federal penitentiary at Atlanta. The sentence was commuted in 1927, but Garvey was deported to Jamaica as a "convicted alien felon." This deprived him of access to his main theater of operation, and although he continued to build the UNIA outside the United States, he split with some of his lieutenants in New York over whether the UNIA should be run from New York or Kingston.[50]

Garvey moved the remnant of the UNIA headquarters to London in 1935, where he appealed to the League of Nations for Black rule over the former German colonies in Africa, or if this was not possible then the establishment of a United Commonwealth of Black Nations in West Africa. This was quite a backward step for the man who in 1920 had declared that the UNIA did not intend to ask the colonial powers why they were in Africa, but intended to simply command them to get out.[51]

Garvey, Garveyism, and Critics

Critics of Marcus Garvey and the UNIA abound. In this section I will briefly survey and analyze them.

Cronon argued that an inherent weakness of the Garvey movement was its emphasis on racial solidarity at a time when the majority of "thoughtful men" were seeking to tear down racial barriers.[52] But such a statement simply reveals Cronon's liberal integrationist bias, which the UNIA and the Garvey movement sought to combat. These "thoughtful men" referred to by Cronon also shared this bias, a bias that appears to be the polar opposite of the more exclusionary views of the conservatives, but which will be shown to be actually complementary to it (from the point of view of specifically Black empowerment). Both Black and white adherents to this outlook believed that the only constructive solution to racial domination was to eliminate differences by incorporating everyone into the American "melting pot."

Garveyism was a complete break with the vision of (future) social and economic equality advocated by the NAACP and the Urban League. But Garveyism was also a break with the liberal and social democratic views of the white middle- and upper-class sympathizers with whom the NAACP and the Urban League were closely allied, and from whom they received substantial funds. In Garvey's view the supporters of the NAACP (if sincere at all) were a small minority; the strategies of the NAACP were based on a utopian detachment from the reality that the United States is "a white man's country."

Whether or not the white supporters of the NAACP were sincere (which Garvey strongly denied) in their belief in the social equality of African Americans, the UNIA's argument was posed on an entirely different plane. For these emergent African American or African nationalists, developing a separate and powerful Black society was more important than winning the right to participate in white American society. In Garvey's words,

"Do they lynch Englishmen, Frenchmen, Germans, or Japanese? No. And Why? Because these people are represented by great governments, mighty nations and empires, strongly organized. . . . Until the Negro reaches this point of national independence, all he does as a race will count for naught."[53]

More so than his opponents in the NAACP (Du Bois is a qualified exception), Garvey was influenced by the anticolonial revolts around the world, in Ireland, in India, in Egypt, in Poland.[54] For the whites who worked in the NAACP and similar organizations (sincerely or not), the specter of effective anticolonial sentiment among the people of the African diaspora must have seemed an intolerable (if scarcely understood) insubordination.[55] Today Garvey's suspicion may seem questionable, but in a period when public confidence about the continuity of their society was at once unstable and weak, a militant and defiant posture among those at the bottom of the social structure must have been quite disconcerting.[56]

Today the logic of their contention that Black people will never be respected as equal until they build an independent and strong Africa is no doubt much less controversial among middle-class African Americans. In fact Garvey's contention that "there is no justice but strength"[57] is little different from the stock assertion of today's liberal Black establishment that "Black people have no permanent friends, just permanent interests." It is thus today no more than a commonplace to assume that justice in America or anywhere else is a matter of power. This was decidedly not the case when the Garvey movement was in its prime. While there are many ways of obtaining power, one of the most effective ways of wielding power is through the control of a state. And for African Americans even today, when Africa is composed entirely of independent states, access to state power may be more likely in their African homeland than in the United States (even if it is not currently a popular political goal, given the economic devastation of Africa in the current conjuncture).

In the context of the debates among Black intellectuals and activists during this period, Garveyism had much more in common with the approach of Booker T. Washington than that of the NAACP and the Urban League. In fact the self-reliant approach of Booker T. Washington had been an inspiration to Garvey. But the similarities between Garvey and Washington have been overdrawn, leading some observers, such as Harold Cruse, to observe that Garveyism and, much later, Black Power are simply warmed-over Booker T. Washingtonism. To me, however, it seems obvious that despite their common emphasis on self-reliance, Garveyism's defiant anti-imperialism and aggressive anticolonial stance were far more distinct from Washington's accommodationist approach than were the timid liberalism of the NAACP and even that of Du Bois of this period.

The Garvey movement's criticism that the goals of the NAACP and the Urban League were unrealistic continues to ring true to a very large part of the Black working class.[58] In contrast to the "ideological" arguments of the U.S. Left (i.e., that the Garvey movement was a petty bourgeois movement), it was the Black working class that was overwhelmingly the constituency of the Garvey movement and of most nationalist movements since that time (Nation of Islam, Moorish Science Temple, Black Panther Party, League of Revolutionary Black Workers, DRUM).[59]

That this independent, anticolonial, and overwhelmingly proletarian organization acting outside the traditional spheres of the Black bourgeoisie did not have the intellectual respectability of the NAACP and the Urban League is understandable. The very radical tenor of its program was unprecedented for an organization with such a significant following. The reach of the UNIA has yet to be matched. The Communist Party in the 1930s, the Nation of Islam in the 1960s, and the Black Panther Party in the 1960s had significant followings in the Black working class, but they did not come close to matching the reach of the Garvey movement.

Thus the U.S. Left's attack on the Garvey movement as "petty bourgeois" seems myopic and istrumentalist. The attack stemmed in part from the fact that the Garvey movement rejected the ideological hegemony claimed by the Left, which itself reflected the power (class and ethnic/racial) relations of the larger social system.

As Tony Martin argued, Garvey's broad reach among the Black working class was due for the most part to his propagation of ideas not very different from those espoused by communists. While he took a strong position on the "race first" principle, as did the African Blood Brotherhood, there was a persistent class component in Garvey's thinking. Garvey consistently argued against class privilege, both among Blacks and in the wider world, though he did not often use the language of class, he had extensive experience as a labor organizer. The specifically racial character of Garvey's nationalism was a response to centuries of slavery, colonialism, and exclusion of Blacks by the white working class. Indeed, in 1921 the class appeal of the Garvey movement was recognized by Charles Latham, a State Department official who considered Garveyism more dangerous than communism: "Though he is certainly not an intellectual his particular propaganda and agitation is considered dangerous in that it will find a more fertile field of class divergence than Bolshevism would be likely to find in the United States."[60]

Garvey's hostility toward the white working class in the United States was based on its racist and exclusionary practices. The UNIA was no less working-class than the CPUSA, and both had their share of petty bourgeois leadership, although Garvey himself had a much humbler background than most of the leaders of the CPUSA.[61]

It is an oversimplification to brand Garvey an anticommunist, for despite his use of the "Bolshevist" epithet against the ABB, he urged Blacks to do the same thing for Africa that Lenin and Trotsky had done for Russia in overthrowing czarist despotism.[62] But Garvey also noted that communists were "fighting against one class interest for the en-thronement of *theirs*" (emphasis added). In the United States, in partic-ular, he was against the Communist Party because "In America it con-stitutes a group of liars, plotters, and artful deceivers who twist—a one third truth to a Whole big lie, and give it out to the unthinking clientele for consumption." His experience with people like Cyril Briggs and W. A. Domingo and their methods was, he said, "enough to keep him from that brand of Communism for the rest of his life."[63] Garvey further ar-gued that

> The danger of Communism to the Negro in countries where he forms the minority of the population, is seen in the selfish and vicious attempts of that party or group to use the Negro's vote and physical numbers in helping to smash and over-throw by revolution, a system that is injurious to them as the *white* underdogs, the success of which would put their majority group or race still in power, *not only as communists but as whitemen*. (emphasis added)[64]

Lewis has located the main weakness of the Garvey movement in the short time frame it set for the achievement of its goals.[65] Because of the short time frame, the movement was not able to attract the skilled people who could evaluate its business ventures and allowed no room for the evolution or maturation of world political forces that might have sup-ported its plan of New World Black migration to/colonization in Africa.

In addition, the UNIA failed to recruit from among the Black intelli-gentsia and the middle class, and thus was both deprived of their skills and set up in opposition to them. In this circumstance W. E. B. Du Bois, Chandler Owen, A. Philip Randolph, and George Schuyler were among the fiercest opponents of the UNIA.

A strength of Garveyism, however, was a mixture of the conventional American worldview (in its economic, political, and social vision) and a radical conception that Blacks could compete with whites as equals. This mix did not require grassroots Blacks to alter radically their conception of the world, except for their own place in it, which would of course be radically improved.[66]

The membership and the geographic scope of the UNIA remain un-surpassed. According to Martin, the UNIA was represented in thirty-eight states of the United States—and thus was the organization not only of the newly urbanized Afro-Americans but as well of the great mass of the Black rural working class and farmers all over the South and Southwest—

and in forty-one other countries. No area of significant Black population in the world was without a UNIA branch.[67]

In criticizing Garvey and Garveyism many scholars point to the *Messenger* group as a better model for African American social action. As we have seen above, Chandler Owen and A. Philip Randolph attempted to construct an alliance between urban Blacks and the white labor movement. But this movement was less than promising since the U.S. labor movement had long excluded Blacks, and Blacks had responded by accepting wages below union level in order to survive. Furthermore, Owens and Randolph's commitment to socialism was dogmatically antinationalist, and thus had no way to explain the deep experience of racism among African Americans.

The CPUSA, as we shall see below, did a much better job of appealing to the specificity of Black oppression. The CPUSA did attract a significant Black following, but its thesis about the right to self-determination of the Black nation in the Black Belt South failed to capture the imagination of many Blacks, even among its own cadre.

The organization that in my view came closest to developing a political line that was appropriate for building a revolutionary Black working-class movement during this period was the African Blood Brotherhood. This organization coexisted with the Garvey movement, but was not then and is not now well-known. It is very much worth our brief attention.

The African Blood Brotherhood

The African Blood Brotherhood (ABB) was a semisecret organization founded by Cyril Briggs, an immigrant from St. Kitts, some time between 1917 and 1919.[68] It had its headquarters in New York and chapters in various other cities in the United States and the Caribbean. According to its founders the ABB was the first secret organization to be formed in the Western world having as its purpose "the liberation of Africa and the redemption of the Negro race." Less than nine months after the *Crusader* announced the call for the ABB, the organization is described as numbering over a thousand men, in the United States, the West Indies, Central and South America, and West Africa.[69]

Cyril Briggs and the men who eventually became the leadership of the African Blood Brotherhood were part of the broader New Negro movement.[70] Post–World War I Black radicalism was distinct from the radicalism of previous periods because for the first time the movements took an explicit antisystemic stance. Briggs, a major spokesperson for this trend, and indeed one of the most radical of the New Negro leaders, played an important role in pushing the New Negro movement to seek alliances with other oppressed groups. He thought that successful coordination of effort was an essential ingredient of social transformations, and urged Blacks to ally "with the oppressed Irish, the oppressed Indian and all other oppressed peoples, *and* with the friend of the oppressed and enemy of our enemies, SOVIET RUSSIA."[71]

It seems to me that it is precisely the ABB's attempt to articulate radical nationalist, anti-imperialist, and anticapitalist views that makes it such an important group, despite its relatively short life. Some scholars who have studied the ABB seem preoccupied with its relationship to the CPUSA. I think this is an important issue (from a quite different perspective), but the ABB is of greater significance than the role it played in recruiting for the CPUSA. Its aggressive pursuit of the revolutionary implications of the "Negro Problem" in the United States and in the capitalist world elevated this question to a central position in the strategy of the world socialist movement and in the U.S. sector of that movement.

We can best appreciate the significance of the ABB by looking at how the organization came into being, evolved, and then declined. This will give us some idea of the potential reach of Black radicalism, both then and now. In contrast to those who argue that the ABB was simply a "front group" or "Black auxiliary" of the CPUSA, I argue that the ABB developed organically out of the New Negro or manhood rights movement, reflected the events, social structures, and mentalities of that time, and developed this thought to its logical "conclusion."

The ABB most likely had its origins in the early Afrocentric movement, represented by the Hamitic League of the World, of which Briggs was the vice president. This origin is suggested in the official statement of the "Aims of *The Crusader*" published in the November 1918 issue of the journal. Here the editors explained that their aim was to seek "an honorable solution to the 'Negro Problem', and to a renaissance of Negro power and culture throughout the world." Furthermore, since organized force is the only language intelligible to the whole world, there must be "self-government for the Negro and Africa for the Africans."[72]

In addition to the Hamitic League, the ABB probably derived some inspiration from John Bruce's Sons of Africa, a secret benevolent organization organized in 1912, on the basis of mutual self-help and paramilitary organizations. Hill believed that Briggs may well have been a member of this group since 1913.[73] From the Hamitic League the ABB carried on the tradition of racial vindication through study and propagation of the true facts about the race's past.

The masthead of the December 1918 issue of the *Crusader* indicated that it was the "Publicity Organ of the Hamitic League of the World." In the lead article in that issue George Wells Parker demanded that the peace negotiations grant full citizenship rights to all "people of Color," that all discrimination be made illegal, and that "self-determination be extended to all nations and tribes within the African continent and throughout the world" Briggs was listed as the vice president of the organization. In the same issue Parker put forward the task of the league. He contended that if you teach a nation that it springs from an inferior race, you have made it "an obedient servant, a community of slaves." Parker then pointed out,

> Ours is the greatest race that the world has ever known and will ever know. . . . When men speak of Anglo Saxon kings, they speak of men born just yesterday. It was as recent as the Twelfth Century that the barbarians of Europe stood before the cultured and swarthy Saracens of the East and wondered. When they returned home they awoke from their stupor of ages and birthed the Renaissance. It was the hamitic race who opened their eyes and later, these same barbarians, rising by brute force to world power and world domination, cast about for ideals and passions to sustain the minds of their children so that this power might be preserved. But their ideals of racial superiority were false and it has taken this world war to demonstrate that civilization is not safe in the hands of the white race. The Egyptians taught this ten thousand years ago, but mankind forgot.

According to Hubert Harrison, the entry of the United States into World War I, with Wilson's call for the right of those who submit to authority to have a voice in their own government, was one of the sources of the new manhood movement among American Negroes. Initially there was not much resistance to war mobilization among Blacks, but when in July 1917 a vicious race riot erupted in East St. Louis, the hope that Wilson's words would be applied to Blacks was dampened. It was precisely this era of violent atrocities against Blacks, culminating in the Red Summer of 1919, that gave rise to the demand for new leadership. The centerpiece of this new Black militancy was the idea that Blacks could and should fight back to defend their lives and communities. When the Black soldiers of the Twenty-fourth Infantry Regiment marched into Houston to avenge the brutalization of a Black woman, although they wound up killing fourteen white civilians, the national Black community was staunchly supportive of the group.

The imperialist war was the major event in the consciousness of the New Negro movements. On August 17, 1917, in response to the peace appeal issued by Pope Benedict XV, Wilson argued that "peace should rest upon the rights of people, not the rights of governments,—the rights of people great or small, weak or powerful,—their equal right to freedom and security and self-government and to participation on fair terms in the economic opportunities of the world."[74] In response, Cyril Briggs argued that the "race problem" in the United States could be solved by the establishment of an independent Negro nation within current U.S. borders. "As one-tenth of the population backed up with many generations of unrequited toil and half a century of contribution, as free men to American prosperity, we can with reason and justice demand our portion for purposes of self-government and the purpose of happiness, one-tenth of the territory of the continental United States."[75]

In Briggs's view this would be a plausible claim that Black people in the United States could make when peace was negotiated. However, after Wilson gave his Fourteen Points speech to Congress in January 1918, emphasizing the need to settle colonial claims, Briggs began seriously to entertain the idea of "Africa for the Africans," since the idea of forming an African American state on U.S. soil was unrealistic. Wilson's Fourteen Points speech, moreover, gave the entire New Negro movement official legitimacy.

The way Briggs took issue with Theodore Roosevelt in his January 1919 editorial in the *Crusader* clearly indicates the extent to which the imperialist war clarified the contradictions and allowed for the elaboration of consciousness that not only created the New Negro, but also framed the anticapitalist and anti-imperialist trend increasingly represented by Briggs. Roosevelt had said, "It is the fate of America as it has been the fate of England to govern subject races who cannot govern themselves. *We too have taken up the white man's burden.*"[76] Briggs thought such a statement revealed Roosevelt's true colors, so that even the most servile among Blacks could see that he not only condoned Western imperialism in Africa, but even praised it. Briggs also derided the British embassy in Washington, which claimed that the aim of Great Britain and France in "carrying on in the Near East the war let loose by German ambitions [was] the complete and final liberation of the peoples so long oppressed by the Turks and the establishment of Governments . . . deriving their authority from the initiative and the free choice of the native population."[77]

The Briggs editorial also commented on the fact that Moten (Booker T. Washington's successor at Tuskegee) had attended the peace conference; Briggs wondered whether he had been sent over to placate the Black troops. Then prophetically (or deliberately), Briggs hazarded that "The South has been greatly troubled of late with its guilty conscience and fear of what those Black Soldiers who have chased the white Huns, will do to murderous crackers when they get back home."[78]

In addition to the war, the rising resistance of people in the colonial and semicolonial world impressed the New Negro. Hubert Harrison, speaking in June 1917, had argued that Blacks should rise up against the government just as the Irish had against the English (no doubt referring to the Easter Rising of 1916. Briggs constantly referred to the Irish example in his assertions of the right of Blacks to self-defense.[79]

The Red Scare and the climate of repression it had unleashed led the publisher of the *Amsterdam News* to push for the severance of the paper's relationship with Briggs, who had been its editor. The severance, however, was not antagonistic, since the publisher of the *Amsterdam News* helped set up the *Crusader* as an independent paper.[80]

Briggs told Draper that his interest in communism was inspired by the national policy of the Russian Bolsheviks and the anti-imperialist orientation of the Soviet state. Thus it seems that the founding of the Third International and its March 1919 manifesto most influenced Briggs. The manifesto resonated with Briggs's own strong anti-imperialist views.

In the August 1919 edition of the *Crusader* Briggs's editorial derided the Lusk Committee, whose investigation of "Bolshevism" "has made the startling discovery that the Negro is adopting a radical frame of mind and is affiliating himself with the Socialists, the I.W.W.'s and other justice seeking organizations in this country." Briggs attributed the committee's surprise to its racist disregard of the humanity of Black people, who certainly having nothing to conserve, have everything in the world to gain by being radical. Furthermore, why shouldn't Blacks have the same aspirations for liberty and happiness as do other people?

The ABB program called for the creation of a worldwide federation of Black organizations for which it would provide the revolutionary cadre. In the colonies this federation would build a great Pan-African army. In the United States the ABB proposed that Blacks organize within the trade unions, build cooperatively owned businesses, and create paramilitary self-defense organizations to protect the Black community. In addition the program of the ABB called for a liberated race; absolute race equality—political, economic, and social; the fostering of race pride; solidarity with people of color around the world and with class-conscious white workers; higher wages and lower rents for Black workers; and a Black united front.[81] The ABB also discussed but never made specific plans for a separate Black state within the United States.

While the ABB pledged to fight for the liberation of Africa from the colonial powers, it took pains to make clear that it had no plans to set itself above the "chiefs and kings" of Africa. In this it differed from the Garvey movement, which was perceived as a threat by the government of Liberia. Moreover, the ABB believed in the possibility of a meaningful struggle for Black liberation within the United States itself, which would then constitute a decisive blow for the liberation of Africa.

Toward that end, around 1921 the ABB began to decrease its emphasis on being a secret organization, and began to organize openly in the North.[82] It began to emphasize its role as a Negro protective organization. In June 1921 the *Crusader* reprinted the constitution of the ABB, which asserted that the ABB was a propaganda organization, although highly centralized. The next issue of the *Crusader* (July 1921) carried a full-page advertisement for the ABB, "for immediate protection and ultimate liberation of Negroes everywhere." The ad claimed that the ABB was the only "effective" protective Negro organization in the world with the grandest lineage of any fraternal organization in history.[83]

While historical documentation of the work of the ABB is scanty, a key to its program was the need for armed self-defense, which it learned from the Irish Republican Brotherhood and its Sinn Fein. The ABB was catapulted into the national limelight when its Tulsa, Oklahoma, chapter, having defended a Black prisoner from a lynch mob, was said to have provoked whites to a riot that destroyed the Black residential area in Tulsa. The Black people of Tulsa resisted these attacks with arms, killing fifty of their white attackers. The headlines of the Tulsa papers accused the ABB of "fomenting" the riot. In a subsequent interview with the *New York Times* Briggs denied "fomenting" the riot, but emphasized that self-defense against white mob violence was indeed part of the program of the ABB.

Shortly after the articles appeared blaming the ABB for fomenting the riot, ABB leader W. A. Domingo argued that Blacks needed to dispense with white leadership in their organizations. Domingo argued that "instinctively whites will not permit Blacks who are under their leadership to bring the social problem to the fore. This does not mean that Blacks should not cooperate with whites who face the same exploiter, but that leadership should be in the hands of Blacks."[84]

The general line of the ABB printed in the June 1920 issue of the *Crusader* shows how close it was to that of the UNIA. There were of course also significant differences. No doubt Briggs and the ABB leadership believed that their politics coincided with the politics of the rank and file of the UNIA but also contained positions that would strengthen the hand of the UNIA and the workers' movement as a whole in the United States and internationally.

Harold Cruse has maintained that in this case the ABB was principally motivated in its split with Garvey by the viewpoint that the world revolution was right around the corner. It thus thought that if the UNIA did not follow the path trodden by the Russian communists, it was doomed to fail.[85] So to strengthen the hand of the revolutionary forces the ABB proposed a general line for ABB members and for the race in general:

1. "Affiliate with the liberal, radical, and labor movements." Don't be afraid of being called a Bolshevik. After all these are the same people who call us "niggers."
2. Patronize race enterprises, but distinguish between good and bad, honest and dishonest.
3. Encourage the UNIA, it's the biggest thing that has happened in terms of "surface movements."
4. Reject all allegiances which carry no corresponding rights and privileges. The latter should precede the former.
5. Make the cause of other oppressed people your cause, so that they may correspond in kind. This will make possible a single, coordinated blow against tyranny.
6. Study modern warfare.
7. Learn a trade.
8. Adopt the policy of Race First, but don't ignore alliances with other groups.
9. Kill the caste idea, of light and dark skinned Negroes with different interests.
10. Reject Uncle Tom leadership.
11. Demand a relevant education which tells the truth about our people.
12. Inculcate race pride in children.
13. Organize literary clubs to study Negro history and problems.
14. Ask ministers to teach race history from the pulpit.[86]

In 1921 Briggs sent a letter to Garvey making a formal proposal to affiliate the ABB with the UNIA. Garvey never answered.[87] Finally the ABB took the proposal to the floor of the 1921 UNIA convention, leafleting delegates with the ABB program so as to distinguish the ABB from the moderate socialists such as Du Bois, Randolph, and Chandler. They also had Rose Pastor Stokes, a white member of the CPUSA, address the convention, requesting an alliance with the world communist movement.[88]

Given the intensity of the state's attack on the Left during this period, Garvey decided to oust the ABB, declaring its members dangerous "Bolsheviks." In the October 22, 1921, issue of the *Negro World* Garvey contended that the UNIA was suspicious of "any secret organization such as the ABB claimed to be, and is not going to be tainted by personal or official contact with such a body."[89] Thus in this way unofficial cooperation was replaced with formal separation. From the time of this rupture between the ABB and the UNIA, according to Hill, the ABB set out to topple Garvey from the leadership of the UNIA.[90] According to Hill, Briggs began to probe the legality of Garvey's operation, particularly his use of the mail to solicit purchases for the Black Star Steamship Line's stock. This, according to Hill, provided the line of investigation that led eventually to the prosecution of Garvey.

Vincent has held that there was no official connection between the ABB and the CPUSA.[91] The ABB, he claimed existed before the formation of the CPUSA, and less than a dozen of the ABB's three thousand members joined the CPUSA. He noted that Briggs later said that leading members of the ABB executive council joined the CPUSA, but that the ABB maintained an independent existence. In Vincent's view members of the ABB contributed to the development of Garveyism as individuals and indirectly through their writings in the *Crusader*. The ABB helped to intensify the revolutionary militancy in the UNIA, which in turn helped the Brotherhood maintain a nationalist position. According to Vincent, as Briggs moved closer to the CPUSA he jeopardized his position as a spokesperson for Black nationalism.[92] Hill has concluded that the ABB was largely a propaganda organization and has questioned the membership figures issued by the organization's leadership at various times, ranging from three thousand to fifty thousand. This is a nonissue, since the ABB's programmatic statements themselves described the ABB as a propaganda organization. What is not clear is the class composition of the ABB rank and file. Foner and Allen point out that the ABB had a strong post of miners in West Virginia, and considerable support among

building workers in Chicago. Edward Doty, the Chicago post commander, was also the organizer of an independent union of Black workers in
Chicago.[93] What seems clearest about the ABB in terms of its membership, according to Harding, is that it included a large number of men who
were veterans of World War I.[94]

By 1925 Briggs and all of the ABB central leadership had left the organization to devote most of their time to the CPUSA. At this point, however, the ABB was being kept alive by infusions of resources and members
from the CPUSA. Naison notes that this is an ironic twist since the party
leaders who had recruited Briggs into the CPUSA had hoped that the ABB
would be a conduit for Blacks into the party.[95]

In contrast to Vincent, Robert Hill has argued that the evidence points
to the creation of the ABB as a Black auxiliary to the CPUSA from its inception, the first in a succession of such auxiliaries to be spawned over the
years.[96] Draper, on the other hand, argued that the CPUSA simply
claimed responsibility for organizing the ABB to bolster its image among
the African American population.[97] Former CPUSA general secretary
William Z. Foster claimed that the formation of the ABB was one of the
earliest expressions of the party's long interest in the "fight for justice of
the bitterly exploited and harassed Negro people."[98]

Briggs later told Harry Haywood that the reason for the decline of the
ABB was the unfavorable relations of forces: (1) Garvey had preempted
the leadership of the mass movement; (2) Garvey's hold was strengthened
by the anti-Black violence of the Red Summer of 1919 (which lent support in the eyes of the Black masses to Garvey's contention that the United
States was a white man's country in which justice for Blacks was not possible); and (3) the Black Belt South could not be projected as a Black state
because the masses were in flight from the area.

From a revolutionary nationalist perspective, Shanna and Seen deduce
that the real problem with the ABB, reflected in Briggs's response to Haywood, is that the ABB emphasized the external factor (relations with allies outside the Black nation) and neglected the internal factor (the
process of nation building itself).[99] Garvey was stronger, they argue, precisely because he emphasized the national element. Shanna and Seen
argue that the ABB failed because it did not understand that revolution in
America would be a consequence, not a prerequisite, of the New African
revolution. They cite the example of the relationship between the Por-
tuguese revolution and the national liberation movements in Mozambique, Angola, and Guinea-Bissau. This is why, in their view, the Ameri-

can ruling class fights to prevent New African independence, not integration. Shanna and Seen, who appear to be linked to the Black Liberation Army, assess the ABB in a much different way, than Robert Hill and Tony Martin, who obviously are more receptive to Garvey's nationalism than to the left nationalism of the ABB. However, the questions they raise about the ABB deserve a response. The ABB is a significant organization, not because it lasted for seventy years, but because of the potential it represented, as did the UNIA, which though still in existence is a very pale ghost of its old self.

Briggs and later the African Blood Brotherhood repeatedly cited the Russian Revolution as a source of inspiration, and the Soviet Union as a friend of oppressed people everywhere. This is most likely why there is so much controversy and confusion about the origins of the ABB and its relationship with the CPUSA. Garvey himself had taken the position that the ABB was a front for the Workers' Party (which later changed its name to the CPUSA). In my view this kind of confusion may be inevitable for propaganda organizations. The ABB admittedly was not a mass organization. In the issue of the *Crusader* in which the ABB was introduced, it was stated plainly that the organization's function was to provide the revolutionary cadre for mass organizations. The main mass organization to which it attempted to affiliate was the UNIA.

Theodore Vincent emphasized that the African Blood Brotherhood developed independently of the international communist movement and was nationalist at a time when some communists were deriding nationalism as right-wing ideology.[100] Briggs and the ABB, however, like revolutionary movements throughout the periphery of the world-system, were beginning to see what would later become the new line of the Communist International, "workers and oppressed people unite."

There is no need here to invoke a communist conspiracy, as do Robert Hill and Tony Martin, who charge that the ABB was always an auxiliary of the CPUSA. The major ideological influences on the ABB, the Irish Sinn Fein and the Russian Bolsheviks, are similar to the ideological influences on the Garvey movement, and the ABB's early pronouncements seem clear to me to be more a form of left Garveyism than communism. Clearly, over time the ABB came more and more to support the views of the CPUSA and the international communist movement, had overlapping membership, and was eventually absorbed by the CPUSA. But the history of the ABB is clearly different from that of the mass organizations that the

CPUSA had some hand in founding, such as the American Negro Labor Congress, the League of Struggle for Negro Rights, the National Negro Congress, and the Civil Rights Congress. However, what did happen is that in the mid-1920s the ABB retreated from Domingo's insistence on the necessity of Black leadership of organizations in the Black community. This was the downfall of the ABB.

Having said that, I think it is important to address the real question raised by Hill's and Martin's comments about the relationship between the CPUSA and the ABB. This is not just an issue for Hill and Martin, but a larger question of much more general interest: how African American activists and potential activists view the role of the CPUSA in the Black liberation movement.

The CPUSA and the Black Liberation Movement in the Twenties

Since the 1920s the CPUSA has played a vanguard role in the fight against racism. More than any other predominantly white organization it has contributed to the establishment of a tradition of commitment to interracial solidarity not only within the social movements but in U.S. society in general. While the tradition of interracial solidarity may be weak, the extent to which such a tradition exists owes much to the practice of the CPUSA.

While today we tend to take for granted the commitment of the Left to racial equality and solidarity (even if we are critical of the shortcomings), it has been the CP that has been most instrumental in establishing this tradition, with the prodding of the African Blood Brotherhood and the Communist International.

At the turn of the twentieth century racial equality seemed a remote possibility for most African Americans. The series of betrayals culminating in the betrayal of 1877, the draconian measures that overturned radical Reconstruction in the South and installed Jim Crow, and the betrayal of the southern Populists in the 1890s must have been central to the consciousness of African Americans contemplating means of advancing the race (to use the language of the day) during this period.

Until the 1920s the Left had little to offer African Americans and indeed saw no need for a special program to address the grievances of African Americans. Eugene Debs's statement indicates the official position of the Socialist Party of America at the turn of the century: "We have nothing special to offer the Negro, and we cannot make separate appeals to all the races. The Socialist Party is the party of the whole working class, regardless of color."[101] In 1926 the Socialist Party reiterated this position in its platform, warning that Blacks should not expect that their grievances can be met until the establishment of the "cooperative commonwealth." Norman Thomas added, "What the Negro wants and needs is what the white worker wants and needs; neither more nor less. This is what we socialists stand for."[102]

Not surprisingly, African American involvement in the socialist movement was scant. The *Pittsburgh Courier* ridiculed Thomas's and the Socialist Party's stand—that Black people would automatically achieve racial equality with whites with the establishment of socialism—as "pie in the sky."[103]

World War I, however, occasioned the transformation of international socialism. The central organizational thrust was relocated to the USSR and the Comintern succeeded the Second International. At the urging of Lenin and then Stalin, the Comintern interceded with the CPUSA, now the second most important section of the International, to insure that it addressed the "Negro Question."[104] The popularity of the Garvey movement among the African American working class was a clear indication of widespread antisystemic views and the possibility for the emergence of popular anticapitalist consciousness.[105]

Lenin had expressed surprise that the CPUSA reports made no mention of party work among Blacks.[106] He argued that Blacks should be recognized as a strategically important element in communist activity. From 1921 on, the Communist Party of the United States actively sought to recruit African Americans. This then became the occasion for the party's alliance with the African Blood Brotherhood.

The ABB articulated a left critique of Garveyism and sought to work in a cooperative manner with the CPUSA. The ABB, however, came to depend on the CPUSA for resources, and its leadership joined the CPUSA as an expression of its commitment to world revolution.

The ABB itself was a cadre organization, so it saw its policy of exchanging members with the CPUSA as a move that would strengthen both organizations. The ABB viewed its role as the cadre for mass organizations among African Americans, which in practice meant that the members of the ABB would work as the cadre of Garvey's Universal Negro Improvement Association. But the ABB was not able to win for itself a role as official cadre of the UNIA, although its members did function unofficially in this capacity over the life of the organization. When the ABB attempted to win the leadership of the UNIA in a clumsy maneuver at a UNIA conference, Garvey skillfully isolated them.[107]

But alas, the Garvey movement was not able to survive the concerted efforts of an unholy alliance whose members for different reasons wanted to see Marcus Garvey removed from the scene. The U.S. government, the ABB/CPUSA, W. E. B. Du Bois and the NAACP, and A. Philip Randolph and the *Messenger* group were for the most part mutually antagonistic, but they united in the effort to get Garvey. When Garvey was jailed and then deported, the UNIA gradually dissolved, with its cadres and members scattering among the various Black nationalist and communal groups in existence at the time.

In the 1930s the nationalist wave among African Americans subsided as the possibilities of the New Deal turned the Black dialogue outward. During this period of high unemployment and severe economic stagnation the CPUSA was provided with an arena in which the effectiveness of working-class unity could be clearly demonstrated. The combination of the lessons of the class struggle approach and the facade of progress represented by the New Deal pushed Black nationalism into the background. The UNIA continued to dwindle in size. But the memory of the Garvey movement remained.

The Communist Party USA discontinued its support for the ABB, and since most of the ABB leadership were now under party discipline, this meant the demise of the ABB.

In 1925 members of the CPUSA founded the American Negro Labor Congress (ANLC), but it met with little success. The NAACP and the Urban League thought the ANLC too separatist; prominent African American trade unionists led by A. Philip Randolph boycotted the organization.

Lovett Fort-Whiteman, national organizer of the ANLC, explained that the purpose of the ANLC was to gather, mobilize, and coordinate into a single fighting force the most militant, enlightened, and class-conscious Black workers. The objectives of the ANLC included the abolition of lynching, Jim Crow, industrial discrimination, political disenfranchisement, and segregation.[108] From an organizational perspective, Fort-Whiteman explained,

> The fundamental aim in calling the American Negro Labor Congress is to establish in the life of the American Negro working class an organization

which may serve as a medium through which the American Communist party may reach and influence the Negro working class and at the same time constitute something of a recruiting ground for the party.[109]

Although James Ford, an important Black party leader, was recruited from the ANLC, on the whole the ANLC cannot be counted as having been a successful conduit into the party.

The failure of the ANLC to draw Blacks to the Communist Party meant that the party had to go back to the drawing board. It was during this period that the party, under the influence of the Comintern and the Communist Party of the Soviet Union, adopted the position that African Americans constituted a nation in the sections of the Black Belt South where they were in the majority of the population.

While this was a rather questionable formulation, I do not doubt that it represented a serious attempt to come to an understanding of the basic social position of the Black population in the United States. However, this position reflects the party's distance from the problem it was attempting to understand. The position it arrived at is both mechanical analytically and ambivalent politically in its affirmation of the rights of Blacks to self-determination. As Harold Cruse was later to argue,

> American Marxism has neither understood the nature of Negro national-ism, nor dealt with its roots in American society. When the Communists first promulgated the Negro question as a "national question" in 1928, they wanted a national question without nationalism. They posed the ques-tion mechanically because they did not understand it. They relegated the national aspect of the Negro question to the "Black belt" of the South, de-spite the fact that Garvey's "national movement" had been organized in 1916 in a northern urban center where the Negro was, according to the Communists, a "national minority," but not a "nation," as he was in the Southern states. Of course the national character of the Negro has little to do with what part of the country he lives in. Wherever he lives, he is re-stricted. His national boundaries are the color of his skin, his racial char-acteristics, and the social conditions of his substructural world.[110]

Cruse was no doubt closer to the truth analytically. But the CPUSA was trying to change the world, and its analysis was intended to lay the groundwork for the practical tasks of building a revolutionary move-ment, principally among the African American people, and in that con-text among the U.S. working class. The CPUSA wanted to be able to re-cruit from among Black nationalist-leaning intellectuals and accommo-date the nationalist consciousness among the Black workers generally.

While it wanted to be able to build an anticapitalist and anti-imperialist foundation for this nationalist consciousness, it also wanted such movement as did emerge to be able to unite with the entire U.S. working class to oppose capitalism.

The purpose of its theory was also to justify its elevation of the importance of the struggles of the Black population in the United States. Eventually it abandoned the theory, arguing that conditions had changed, Blacks had migrated away from the historical Black nation in the Black Belt South, and furthermore that the main thrust of the Black population was for equality and justice within the United States.

But long before the party officially abandoned the theory of self-determination for African Americans in the Black Belt South in 1958, it gave only lip service to the theory while in practice it emphasized the struggle for equal rights. Moreover, the Comintern wording in the 1930 version of the resolution on self-determination for African Americans was ambiguous, so the CPUSA could give priority to the struggle for racial equality. What was not ambiguous in the Comintern resolution was the stipulation that Blacks would not be won to the revolutionary struggle until they saw the most conscious sections of the white workers fighting alongside them against all forms of racial discrimination and persecution.

Cultural Hegemony and Black Power

One need not be cynical about the sincerity of the Communist Party to raise questions about the issue of leadership in the struggle against racism, inequality, and injustice. While the question of whether the African Blood Brotherhood was an auxiliary group of the Communist Party of the United States is a legitimate question, the more important question that the history of the two organizations represents in this period is the question of Black leadership, control, and hegemony within Black social movements, within Black communities, *and* within U.S. society as a whole. Harold Cruse, who had been a dissident member of the CPUSA in the 1940s, raised this issue most forcefully in his monumental work *The Crisis of the Negro Intellectual*.

Since the issue of cultural hegemony has been a stock item in the social thought of Black nationalist intellectuals, leaders, and organizations since World War II, too little attention has been given to the predominance of a cultural assimilationist viewpoint in Black nationalism prior to World

War I, and a period of uneven transition from this cultural assimilationist view in the interwar period. Before World War I Anglo-Saxon cultural dominance and an equally suffocating political, social, and physical repression weighed heavily on Black folk. The ideology of the Black nationalism in the nineteenth century was based in part on the civilizational mission that was such a prominent component of Western imperial ideology. Ethiopianism, the ideology of early Black nationalism, emerged in the context of combating those who attempted to justify the enslavement of Africans and then the consignment of Blacks to secondary citizenship by denying the humanity of African people. Ethiopianism thus sought to redeem Africa and vindicate the humanity of African people. Ethiopianism held that Africa had had a glorious past, but had fallen victim to the slave trade because Africans had strayed from God. It was now the duty of those children of Africa who had been enslaved in the Western Hemisphere to return to Africa to carry Christian civilization to their thoroughly debased and humiliated ancestors. The redemption of Africa was the centerpiece of the attempt by Blacks, particularly in the United States and the West Indies, to create a sense of community and a rationale for cooperation initially among Blacks who had escaped enslavement to fight against slavery *and* be accepted as American citizens.

From the turn of the century Ethiopianism was gradually superseded by the more secular ideology of Pan-Africanism. The messianic themes of Ethiopianism as an ideology of deliverance in a racist society were subtly incorporated into Pan-Africanism. Moreover, there messianic themes remained central to Afro-Christianity and were deeply imbedded in African American culture, particularly that of the urban working class. Some came to view the suffering of the people of the African diaspora as a tool for the redemption not only of Africa, but also of the world.

These counterhegemonic ideas were articulated alongside the hegemonic ideas of Anglo-Saxon supremacy. World War I, the rise of nationalist movements in the periphery of the world-system, and the Bolshevik revolution of 1917 shattered Anglo-Saxon hegemony. While the Garvey movement borrowed some of the symbols of the British Empire, Cruse's claim that Garvey and the West Indian radicals of the African Blood Brotherhood were simply conduits of white hegemony over the Black freedom movement is much too one sided.

In the 1920s, according to Cruse, the African American intelligentsia entered onto the stage of American culture as a wedge against the overarching and deadening materialistic ethos that had increasingly overtaken the United States during its period of rapid industrialization. This materialistic ethos threatened to choke up the spiritual pores of the nation and smother its creative potential. After a ten-year stay in Europe Mabel Dodge had returned to the United States and sadly lamented that "America is all machinery and money making and factories."[111]

The vitally needed cultural renaissance came to be centered in the Harlem of the 1920s. Yet the Harlem Renaissance intellectuals had only a partial view of their own cultural movement, and Cruse's criticism of them was most incisive, if quite merciless:

> the trends of the 1920's had thrown the Negro intelligentsia onto the cultural stage in an intuitive and romantic outpouring of "soul," but without the depth of philosophical insight that would have enabled them to grasp the implications of their movement. It should have been the [Langston] Hugheses the [James Weldon] Johnsons and the [Claude] McKays who created the critical terms to be laid down on this movement—not the Michael Golds.[112]

For Cruse, Gold (of Jewish background, and an influential member of the CPUSA) and the communist Left had made no great original contribution to the Harlem Renaissance but instead had created confusion by injecting a foreign cultural and political ideology into a basically "American" cultural phenomenon.

> The essentially original and native creative element of the 1920s was the Negro ingredient—as all whites who were running to Harlem actually knew. But the Harlem intellectuals were so overwhelmed at being "discovered" and courted, that they allowed a *bona fide* cultural movement, which issued from the social system as naturally as a gushing spring, to degenerate into a pampered and paternalized vogue.[113]

For the largest portion of these Harlem intellectuals, their failure to articulate philosophical conclusions of their own meant that the leading literary lights in the 1920s adopted the communist philosophy of the 1930s and "thus were intellectually sidetracked for the remainder of their productive years."[114]

What was really at stake during the 1920s, Cruse argued was the issue of Black Power, since Harlem leaders were struggling over precisely those areas of economic, social, cultural, and institutional life where they exerted little power. This was then not only a cultural struggle, for cultural power was inextricably intertwined with economic and political power. According to Cruse, "In purely cultural terms, cultural arts expressions in

Harlem are controlled, discouraged, negated or otherwise stifled: the direct result of white ownership of properties and sites suitable for the housing, cultivation and encouragement of cultural expression (i.e., theaters, clubs, halls and film houses)."[115]

The integration of Black intellectuals and creative artists into the cultural arts thus resulted, in Cruse's view, in their participation on the basis of white standards, or as stepping stones to middle-class status using Negro art expressions. Harlem, the cultural mecca of the Black world, had thus been completely deracinated culturally, synchronous with the integration of members of the middle and upper strata of the Black communities into the larger white world. Integration, according to Cruse, led to cultural negation.[116]

> Harlem is a victim of cynical and premeditated cultural devastation. Harlem is an impoverished and superexploited economic dependency, tied to real estate, banking, business-commercial combine of absentee whites who suck the community dry every payday. In short Harlem exists for the benefit of others and has no cultural, political, or economic autonomy. Hence, no social movement of a protest nature in Harlem can be successful . . . unless it is at one and the same time *a political, economic, and cultural movement*.[117]

Cruse moreover believed that racial democracy could not exist without cultural democracy. He argued that the dominant white Anglo-Saxon Protestant group was profoundly antitheoretical, anti-aesthetic, anticultural, and anti-intellectual. Their forte, and the only position for which they had any respect, was the application of practical values in the pursuit of materialistic ends. This ethos, Cruse argued, they pressed upon other groups, including even the Negro.

While the lost generation of North American artists (Hemingway, Sinclair Lewis, T. S. Eliot, Ezra Pound) had to leave for Europe so that they could be artists, away from the cultural suffocation of the United States, it was the Negro creative intellectuals who tried to create art in their own native "American" way. Consequently Negroes were the only group with the capacity for democratizing American culture.

Yet the "crisis of the Negro intellectual" was precisely its acceptance of a subaltern position in relation to the dominant Anglo-Saxon ethnic group, to Jewish intellectuals, and to West Indian intellectuals (who, Cruse argued appropriated Marxism as right because it was white, and thus became conduits for white hegemony in the radical wing of the Black freedom struggle). Cruse held that Negro Marxists were essentially integrationists, differing from the NAACP only in the use of "revolutionary" rhetoric.

Cruse's rhetorical brilliance brought into sharp relief the issue of cultural hegemony, but the very intensity of his polemic has tended to preempt debate about the issue. While Cruse was devastating in his critique of the middle-class aspirations of the Harlem intellectuals, he did not himself properly recognize the effect of the African American working class on the overall culture of Black North America. While he was correct in his analysis of the militant protest tradition of the early W. E. B. Du Bois and the economic nationalism of Booker T. Washington as representative of two factions of the Black middle class, he did not properly explain the role of the working class in the creation of what has come to be known as Black culture. Cruse argued that the militant protest tradition was based among the educated strata of Black professionals—doctors, lawyers, ministers, teachers. Their demands emphasized immediate assimilation, political agitation, and the demand for civil rights. The economic nationalists emphasized race pride, solidarity, self-help, intergroup moral improvement. This fraction of the Black middle class was centered in the rising entrepreneurial strata.[118]

Ernest Allen and William Eric Perkins note that Cruse did not give appropriate credit where due. He did not credit the Black working class for the role it played in the creation of its own culture. Allen notes that there is a sense of group identity and collective Black culture that exists among the Black "working masses" apart from that of the dominant American identity and culture.[119] This sense of group identity among the common people of the national Black community (despite some regional variations) served to cohere into a collective African American consciousness. The institutional expression of this consciousness was manifest in various cooperative enterprises such as mutual aid or insurance societies, or other all-Black institutions such as churches and lodges. The core of this collective consciousness, despite the administrative role of the Black middle class, was the African American working class.

Cruse performed an important service in raising the issue of cultural hegemony to such a high theoretical position. This issue is too often overlooked, but it forms the context for the constant rebirth of nationalist trends in the Black freedom struggle.

5

From the Great Depression to World War II

The Recomposition of White-Black Alliance

The Great Depression of the 1930s made the generally bad economic situation among African Americans even worse. No group was harder hit by the depression. By 1933 most Blacks could not find jobs of any kind nor contract for their crops at any price.

The heaviest toll came in the rural South, where over half of African Americans lived in 1930. Cotton prices had dropped from eighteen cents to less than six cents per pound from 1929 to 1933, devastating some two million Black farmers who depended on the crop. Over two-thirds of this number made no profits from the crop in the early thirties, and thus had to make ends meet by hunting, growing what they could, scavenging, and begging. Many moved to the cities, even if there were no immediate prospects for jobs there.[1]

In the urban South the "Negro jobs" disappeared, as desperate whites clamored for Black removal from jobs until all whites were employed. In the urban North unemployment ran between 40 and 50 percent in cities like Harlem, Chicago, Detroit, and Philadelphia. In general the Black jobless rate was twice that of white unemployment. Since domestic workers depended on the prosperity of others, this group, which was largely Black, was devastated by the depression; it accounted for 43 percent of those on relief in the North in 1934.[2]

Outright discrimination by employers and unions added to the burden that Blacks bore during the depression. In New York City two-thirds of the hotels in Manhattan hired no Blacks. Gimbel's department store did not hire Blacks, nor did Metropolitan Life Insurance. Many companies hired only a relatively small proportion of Blacks, and all at the lowest occupational levels.[3]

Despite the severity with which Blacks were impacted by the Great Depression, the Black leadership responded not with militant action but with requests for more charity, more jobs, and more food and clothing collections. Most observers have noted that the onset of the Great Depression virtually ended all support for the Garvey movement. Religious nationalism persisted, and many former Garveyites joined these movements, the most well known of which were Noble Drew Ali's Moorish-American Science Temple and Elijah Muhammad's Nation of Islam.[4]

In addition to these two explicitly nationalist organizations a number of ex-Garveyites joined some of the emerging "Holiness" cults, some of which were nationalistic (e.g., the Church of God, or Black Hebrews), and some of which were interracial (e.g., Father Divine's Peace Mission Movement and Bishop [Daddy] Grace's United House of Prayer). The Holiness cults differed from Holiness churches in their emphasis on leadership, economic activities, and the church community.[5] While not always nationalistic, the Holiness cults seem to have provided a refuge from the oppressiveness of a racist society, a place where African Americans could "do for self."

The hard times of the Great Depression seem to have made it more difficult for most African Americans to pursue what was of necessity a protracted struggle, if more immediate gains could be obtained by an alliance with labor, liberals, and radicals (mostly communists). During this period white trade unionists and communists sought allies in the Black community. Black intellectuals such as E. Franklin Frazier, Ralph Bunche, and Abram Harris wrestled with problems of Black people's relationship to the New Deal, the role of trade unions in advancing the interests of Blacks, and the relevance of Marxism to the problems of Blacks.

The CPUSA and the Black Working Class in the 1930s

Most of the Black leadership adopted very conciliatory stances during the early part of the Great Depression. Only the CPUSA organized militant action to improve the quality of life of Blacks in Harlem. The CPUSA organized the Workers' Alliance, which focused on the problems of unemployed workers. The party also developed a repertoire of tactics to address the depression conditions in Harlem. These included hunger marches to the mayor's office and to the Board of Estimates to demand relief; eviction resistance to put furnishings back into dwellings where the landlord had had them removed; and Relief Bureau sit-ins, in which unemployed councils would refuse to leave until all had been granted relief.

Richard Moore and Cyril Briggs, formerly members of the ABB, played a central role in elaborating the party's strategy and leading the party work in Harlem. It is thus possible to argue that the demise of the ABB was not a unilateral loss to the Black community if these two men were more effective in their role as direct party organizers.

In March 1931 the CPUSA admitted the failure of its analysis of African American oppression in the United States. However, it now emphasized that it had to prove in deed, not in words, that white workers would fight beside Blacks for racial equality and justice. First of all the party had to make it clear to its own militants that white chauvinism would no longer be tolerated in its ranks. It thus initiated an antichauvinism campaign. On several occasions during the early 1930s party members were brought to trial before a workers' court. While some have derided this practice as show trials, they demonstrated to its members that the party was serious about eliminating white chauvinism from its ranks.[6]

In addition to the trials, the party decided it was important to make Blacks visible in the party, on its leadership bodies and in its electoral campaigns. Until 1929 no Black person had served as a full member of the party's central committee. After 1932 no central committee was complete without African American membership. In 1932 James Ford was the vice presidential running mate of William Z. Foster.[7]

At the same time the party instructed its members that the highest degree of fraternization both inside and outside the party was an imperative. All party social functions were to be interracial; white female communists were to fraternize with Black males. While this practice drew fire from conservatives it won a considerable amount of good will among Black leaders. However, when Black women communists protested that the startling number of marriages between Black men and white women in the party was an insult to Black women, they were criticized for nationalism.[8]

Criticisms such as this—that Black women in the party were committing a nationalist deviation—highlight the CPUSA's lack of depth in its understanding of racism. While Party leaders' commitment to eliminating white chauvinism in their ranks seems clear, they did not seem to grasp the more sophisticated racism of the intellectuals, which assumed the universality of European and North American civilization, and how such views generated a healthy assertive reaction among oppressed strata insisting on the validity of their own identity.

The CPUSA played a key role in organizing the CIO despite the history of stormy relations with the CIO's president and founder, John L. Lewis, and most of its other top leaders. Lewis knew that the upstart CIO needed organizers, and despite his dislike of communists and communism he was ready to use the organizing experience, discipline, and energy of the communists.

Their acceptance in the CIO placed party members in a position where they were able to exert leadership over large numbers of noncommunists for the first time, since party members for the most part played leadership roles in CIO locals. According to Klehr, this new situation called for the party to develop new relations with its trade union members.[9] Gone were the days when the Trade Union Unity League leaders (who were party functionaries) would simply carry out party orders. These new union leaders could not simply be party functionaries, for if they were really to function in their new roles they had to have some degree of power and responsibility. And the party gave these militants wide leeway. Sometimes, however, this so loosened the ties between the party and the militant that a militant's loyalty to the trade union took priority over his or her loyalty to the party and sometimes led to separation from the party. But for the most part the CIO experience vastly increased the influence and power of the party, even while it loosened the party's control over some of its cadre. The party even abandoned its union fractions and shop papers because the existence of a fraction created distrust within the union, and party members should be able to exert influence by the power of their arguments and by their exemplary practice. Communist labor leaders were challenged to be able to persuade their membership in the day-to-day struggle to see the importance of some of their core values: racial equality, democracy, and peace.

In a number of the industries (e.g., packing and stevedoring) where the party played a key role in the organization of the CIO, Black workers were employed in large numbers. These Black workers had to be brought into the union if the CIO was to succeed. The special role the party played in facilitating this process greatly strengthened the party's influence among Black workers, and placed Black workers in a position to fight for antilynching legislation, anti–poll tax legislation, and fair housing. In fact it was the Black Communists in the CIO who became the key organizers in the National Negro Congress, as we shall see later.[10]

However, the party's experience in the CIO did have its negative side. Since the party desired to maintain the peace in the CIO, it not only abandoned its fractions but also did not object to "pro forma" anticommunist statements. One party member even introduced a resolution in the 1940 CIO convention denouncing policies that emanated "from totalitarian dictatorships and foreign ideologies such as Nazism, Communism, and Fascism."[11] This sort of stance put the party in a weak position. Because of the precedence that the party had set in not standing up to so-called pro forma anticommunist attacks, what would it do when the anticommunist attacks became more than merely pro forma? In 1938 and 1939 the CIO leadership took several steps to reduce the party's influence by restricting the influence of some of the party's high-level leaders in the CIO (Harry Bridges, John Brophy, and Wyndham Mortimer). Party members were under orders to support the decisions of the CIO leadership even when, as in 1949, the CIO expelled eleven "progressive" unions from its ranks on the basis that they were allegedly "communist dominated."[12]

In addition to its role in the CIO, the CPUSA played a key role in organizing the unemployed councils around the country, which in turn organized hunger marches to put pressure on the government to take some action about the plight of the unemployed. Angelo Herndon, a young Black communist organizer, led one of these marches in Atlanta. When he was arrested for attempting to incite an insurrection the party organized a national campaign to free him. Herndon's lawyer was Benjamin Davis, whose work with the CP in this case led him to become a member. Later Davis, as a communist, was elected to a seat on the New York City Council.

The party's influence in organized labor and its control of the unemployed councils secured an influential position for the party in the New Deal. It had specific influence in the Works Progress Administration.[13]

But it was the Scottsboro case that built the reputation of the CPUSA as a fighter for racial equality. On March 25, 1931, nine Black youths and two young white women who had hopped a freight train southbound from Chattanooga were removed from the train near Paint Rock, Alabama, after the Black youth had clashed with several whites, forcing them off the train. The women accused the Black youth of raping them at knifepoint. After a change of venue to Scottsboro, the youths were quickly convicted and sentenced to death, despite the conflicting testimony given by the women. On the day of the sentencing the CPUSA issued a statement condemning the "legal lynching," and within twenty-four hours had initiated the mobilization of many of the groups in which it had influence to protest the case.

The party organized marches and demonstrations in every major city in the country. In Chicago it held fourteen protest marches in a three-month period; members marched in Harlem, Washington, Atlanta, and Birmingham. They persuaded hundreds of internationally known authors, labor leaders, politicians, and scientists to sign petitions demanding the freedom of the Scottsboro Boys. The CPUSA turned the Scottsboro case into a searing indictment of Jim Crow. Dozens of authors close to the party, including Sherwood Anderson, Theodore Dreiser, John Dos Passos, Lincoln Steffens, and Langston Hughes wrote and lectured on the racial oppression that the Scottsboro case epitomized.[14]

The CPUSA's International Labor Defense (ILD) pressed the legal campaign to reverse the verdict for the Scottsboro Boys. Once won, it returned to the courtroom, and the militants and supporters hit the streets, staging demonstrations and interracial rallies. After 1933, however, the ILD did not work alone; it welcomed lawyers from the NAACP. The latter were hesitant, but after laying down very carefully a set of ground rules, the NAACP agreed to work with the ILD on this case. Later the ACLU, the Methodist Federation for Social Action, and the League for Industrial Democracy worked as well on the case along with the NAACP and the ILD. The Communist Party, however, antagonized the NAACP and W. E. B. Du Bois, who had their own ideas about how the case should have been pursued.[15]

In 1935 the case of two of the Scottsboro Boys went to the Supreme Court, which overturned the conviction since Negroes had been systematically excluded from Alabama juries and that constituted a clear denial of due process. This decision was the most progressive decision won before the Supreme Court to date, and facilitated the entry of the CPUSA into the mainstream of the civil rights movement.[16]

By 1935 the Communist International and its member parties had developed the strategy of the people's united front explicitly in order to combat fascism. A great many communists recognized the value of building a broad unity to achieve their goal of a just and egalitarian social order, as opposed to a class-against-class approach based on a working-class majority, which was proving slow to materialize (if it ever would). This change in approach set the basis for the revision of the CPUSA's approach both to reformist organizations and to the Black middle class. However, old habits and beliefs are not transformed overnight, so it seems obvious to me that there continued to be tension between the new direction and those who continued in their hearts to hold to the old, class-against-class position. While the new policy would enable the CPUSA to work with reformist organizations of the Black middle class such as the NAACP and the Urban League, the party felt that these organizations were too narrow in scope. The party felt that it was necessary to assist in the building of an overall Black organization that could unify the various Black organizations around the immediate problems Black people faced.

It was in this context that the party lent its support to a special committee to organize a National Negro Congress (NNC), which had emerged out of a conference called by Ralph Bunche, chairman of the Division of Social Science at Howard University, and John Davis, chairman of the Joint Committee on National Recovery. The party assigned James Ford to be a member of the NNC's sponsoring committee.[17] By the time the NNC held its organizing meeting in Chicago on February 14–16, 1936, 585 organizations with a combined and unduplicated membership of 1.2 million had sent delegates. Among the groups represented were churches and religious organizations, fraternal societies, trade unions, youth organizations, civic groups and societies, women's organizations, and political groups and parties. The congress proposed unified action to protest war and fascism; build a more powerful and inclusive civil rights organization among Blacks; improve the conditions of sharecroppers and tenant farmers; draw Blacks into the labor movement; build a consumers' union among Blacks; and develop an independent working-class political party.[18]

Although party members worked untiringly for the NNC and party-led CIO locals provided much of the financial base, the organization did not make substantial progress in its first year. The 1937 congress, however, included more labor support among its delegates, and included the participation of a number of notables, including Philip Murray of the Steel Workers' Organizing Committee, Norman Thomas of the Socialist Party, Thomas Kennedy of the United Mine Workers, and Walter White of the NAACP. After the 1937 congress the NNC was able to work more closely with NAACP branches, became more labor-oriented, and attracted a number of Black intellectuals for whom the gradualism and conservatism of the NAACP and the Urban League were unsatisfactory. Gunnar Myrdal observed in his travels that local councils of the NNC were established in many cities and as late as 1939 and 1940 were the chief Black organization in some western cities.[19]

According to Record and Myrdal, however, the NNC lost its widespread support when party members assigned to work with the organization attempted to force it to take an antiwar and anti-Roosevelt stand, which was consistent with the party's position at the time of the Stalin-Hitler pact.[20] A. Philip Randolph strongly opposed the NNC taking a position that tied it to the CPUSA and the USSR. He resigned from the chairmanship of the organization when the CP members and their supporters (who had packed the meeting, according to most observers) threatened to bring the matter to a vote.[21] The party's change in line, according to Naison, deeply disillusioned its important allies in Harlem and undermined its ability to serve as a catalyst for community action. For the most part individuals who had developed united front relations with the party stopped working with it. For the first time since the early part of the depression a strong anticommunist current developed in Harlem politics, led by A. Philip Randolph. Indeed, Randolph and his supporters would later press for the exclusion of communists from the March on Washington Movement.

This was the beginning of some changes in the fortunes of the party. The thirties had been an exhilarating period from the perspective of the development of communist influence among a number of strata of the population. But the most lasting and durable influence was in the Black community. In the 1930s literally thousands of Blacks had been recruited into the party. Even today David Montgomery remarks that "Only in the civil rights movement were there significant continuities of personnel and styles of thought from Marxist movements of the thirties."[22]

The dramatic loss of support for the NNC can be seen as a local symptom of difficult times for the world communist movement. The Stalin-Hitler pact was clearly an example of the member parties of the Comintern subordinating their own interests to the defense of the world's lone socialist state. When the USSR later established the Yalta pact with the United States and Britain, and the Comintern was disbanded, the CPUSA disbanded to form the Communist Political Association, which would work within the two-party system for progressive change.

When the party was reconstituted in 1945 it needed to build a new organization that could work in the field of civil rights. The Civil Rights Congress was formed in 1946, according to Gerald Horne, out of a merger of the NNC, the International Labor Defense (ILD), and the National Federation for Constitutional Liberties (NFCL).[23] Horne argues that the NNC was the heart of the CRC. The Civil Rights Congress, however, faced a more difficult situation than that of its predecessors. According to Harry Haywood, during this period lynching and Ku Klux Klan activity were on the increase throughout the South.[24] While this terror was specifically directed against the African American population, it was accompanied by federal and state government policies that in effect promoted an anticommunist hysteria targeted at the communist and noncommunist Left, socialists, liberals, and militant labor.

The Civil Rights Congress faced the formidable task of formulating political and legal defense campaigns to protect oppressed Blacks, the working class, and their political supporters from repression. The magnitude of the repression—and practically all the groups on the Left were under surveillance—was such that the CRC was wracked by repeated fights over the allocation of its increasingly slim resources. The highest leadership of the CPUSA, itself under attack, constantly pressed the organization to do more. The CRC simply could not do it all.

The harassment of the CRC was of course part and parcel of the harassment of the CPUSA and affiliated organizations. The U.S. government sought both to repress communists and to intimidate anyone who would work with them. Horne cites countless examples of official harassment and several instances of notables terminating their relationship with the organization because of the official and unofficial pressure they were under. Mary McLeod Bethune and Benjamin Mays are examples of prominent persons who broke their relationship with the CRC because it was under investigation by the attorney general.

The CRC combined imaginative and sometimes brilliant courtroom litigation with mass action in the street to publicize legal injustices and put pressure on the courts. The CRC's tactics were an example of what the NAACP's might have been, but the CRC with its association with the CP faced the full brunt of McCarthyite repression. In 1951 the CRC submitted a document to the United Nations entitled *We Charge Genocide*. The document sought U.N. relief for African Americans from the crimes of the United States against them. Clearly the CRC viewed the repression to which Blacks were subjected as U.S. government policy, not as the doing of merely local or regional interests. By 1956, however, the CRC was forced to close down its operation as the federal government brought its full weight to bear on suppressing the organization. This ended the role of the CRC as a militant advocate of civil rights and civil liberties in a period when these rights were under severe threat.

Despite the role the Communist Party played in support of the Black people's fight for equality and social justice through basic civil rights, its participation remains problematic for many African American activists. The basic charge raised by African American political activists of varying beliefs is that the party proved to be an unstable ally, that its line changed according to the dictates of the international communist movement (in turn dictated by Communist movements in state power), and that the party used Black people to obtain its goals, which were often viewed as propaganda goals (whether against the United States or against the capitalist system).

While there has been much criticism of the CPUSA's participation in a world movement centered in Moscow, such criticism should be obligated to spell out why movements should *not* so participate, why there is something inherently wrong with being a part of an international movement that collectivizes and attempts to coordinate its strategies and tactics. While it seems possible to decide upon analysis that it is "problematic" in some (many) regards, one should not a priori rule out this type of approach. The tradition of international solidarity has a long history, not only in the Pan-African movement but in the worker's movement as well (although the relations among the local affiliates varied from one "international" to another).

In any international or transnational organization the question of relations between the local and the international body must be decided. One model might be that the international leadership considers the input of local affiliates in its decisions. There is no simple answer to the dilemma posed by such an approach. Whether or not this constitutes collective decision making, which is central to the democratic component of revolutionary ideology, depends partly on the organization of the central leadership of the international, how it is determined, and the role local affiliates play in selecting the central leadership. There is in addition the question of how much autonomy affiliates can assume, while still allowing for the coordination of strategies and tactics, if this is what all deem essential to the success of the international organization. It is not necessarily the case that coordination requires centralized control. The Third International, however, assumed that this must be the case if the international working class was going to be able to overthrow a world bourgeoisie by revolutionary means. Today we may question whether democratic centralism was the best strategy, but it was the basic assumption of all the socialist and nationalist movements of the time (both "revolutionary" and "reformist") that sought to make change by seizing state power. If groups decide that the use of state power is the (sole) means of effecting change, then democratic centralism is the most effective strategy (whether or not the specific terminology is utilized).

Today many groups are questioning the efficacy of democratic centralism, but in the period now under discussion democratic centralism, or something like it, was the strategy of most bureaucratic organizations. As a means of coordinating the operations of a widely dispersed body it was unsurpassed.

In the context of democratic centralism, it seems that local affiliates must have some autonomy to accept or reject the counsel of the international (this was the democratic aspect), but the international must have the power to assess whether a local is keeping to the internationalist spirit of the organization. If a local is judged to be departing from this internationalist spirit, there must be some means to change the course of action or sever that particular local from the international organization.

Furthermore, over and above the relations that different individuals, organizations, and social forces had with the CPUSA itself, the role the CPUSA played in support of the Black movement and in opposition to certain other movements has been key in defining the relationships between Black and white social movements on a national scale. The CPUSA's role in the Black movement has also prescribed the approach of Black-led social and political movements toward working with whites. This brings us to the crux of the issue. Despite the sincerity of the CPUSA in attempting to create a model of interracial cooperation and unity in its ranks, punishing its members for white chauvinist behavior, and being willing to place its resources into the struggle for racial equality alongside Blacks, it was not in its power to make of the white working class a revolutionary class—nor, a fortiori, to make of the Black movement a revolutionary force. The political stance of the various strata of the capitalist world-economy is much more dependent on their own social position than the CPUSA and others have been willing to admit. It is not that classes or groups are static and frozen into a deterministic "role" to be carried out for all time. Groups develop in relation to other groups, and obtain a social role in the context of the overall relationship of the different groups in the social system. The white working class did not develop as a "revolutionary" class vis-à-vis the capitalist world-system as a whole, although it fought very militantly for its own (limitedly perceived) rights vis-à-vis those immediately above it. Its attitude toward those immediately below it was primarily defensive. This defensiveness is not a "betrayal" of its historic mission in any sense, but a reflection of the actual social relationship between the two groups in the capitalist world-economy. Many have committed the error of voluntarism because their class analysis lacked the depth to gauge a group's actual social position.

While I do not agree with Du Bois's 1933 argument that the white working class is the cause of most of the suffering of the Black working class, his analysis of the class structure of the imperialist system seems to me an excellent statement of the problem. In contrast to some "Marxist" arguments about a so-called false consciousness among working-class whites who identify their interests with their own ruling class instead of their class brothers and sisters across national borders and ethnic lines, Du Bois argued that the problem of the times was not that the white workers were ignorant. "William Green and Matthew Wolf of the A.F. of L. have no excuse of illiteracy or religion to veil their deliberate intention to keep Negroes and Mexicans and other elements of common labor, in a lower proletariat as subservient to their interests as theirs are to the interests of capital."[25] In the capitalist world-economy of the twentieth century, the white working class no longer occupied a "proletarian" position within the social structure. Since capitalistic production had now gained worldwide organization, there has developed within the American working class a large petty bourgeoisie. According to Du Bois,

> A new class of technical engineers and managers has arisen forming a working class aristocracy between the older proletariat and the absentee owners of capital. . . . [They] form a new petty bourgeois class, whose interests are bound up with those of the capitalists and antagonistic to those of common labor . . . common labor in America and white Europe far from being motivated by any vision of revolt against capitalism, has been blinded by the American vision of the possibility of layer after layer of the workers escaping into the wealthy class and becoming managers and employers of labor.[26]

This new class structure of the capitalist world-economy means that in the United States we have witnessed a "wild and ruthless scramble" of labor groups seeking to obtain greater wealth on the backs of Black and immigrant labor. However, immigrant labor adopted the same stance toward Black labor, eventually resulting, in my view, in the creation of a "white working class" that by 1945 occupied an essentially intermediate status in the capitalist world-economy.

On the one hand this arrangement has spawned a "new proletariat" worldwide of colored workers toiling under conditions equivalent to those of nineteenth-century capitalism. On the other hand "capitalists have consolidated their economic power, nullified universal suffrage, and bribed the white workers by high wages, visions of wealth, and the opportunity to drive 'niggers.'"[27] "Soldiers and sailors from the white workers are used to keep 'darkies' in their 'places' and white foremen and engineers have been established as irresponsible satraps in China, India, Africa, and the West Indies, backed by the organized and centralized ownership of machines, raw materials, finished commodities and land monopoly over the whole world."[28]

While this same process has given rise to a petty bourgeoisie among Blacks in the United States, West Africa, South America, and the West Indies, the opportunity for upward mobility of the petty bourgeoisie in these different locales varies. The group in the United States is particularly weak, having little opportunity or no ability to exploit the labor power of Black workers. Furthermore, any significant hope of enlarging this group is an idle dream because, as Braverman points out, those individuals who in earlier times might have become small businesspersons for the most part only have opportunities to become employees of capital, that is, a part of the new petty bourgeoisie.[29]

If Du Bois's analysis is correct for that time, as I believe it is, then the CPUSA's problem was not that it failed to mobilize Black workers. According to Record, the CPUSA had 2,500 Black members out of a total of 24,536 in 1934.[30] Given the practices of racial exclusion among the white working class during that period, it seems remarkable that a predominantly white organization was able to attract such a large proportion of Blacks to its membership.

I think that a much more serious problem for the CPUSA was its inability to attract Black intellectuals to the party. Several Black intellectuals did join the ranks of the party (e.g., Richard Wright) or were closely allied fellow travelers (e.g., Claude McKay, Paul Robeson). But the party needed to attract more of the nationalist-oriented intellectuals to be able to truly understand the depths of racism and understand how the Black working class itself perceived its position in the social structure. It was precisely Garvey's genius to be able to do this. This is the issue that Harry

Haywood had raised with regard to the missed potential of the Niagara Movement.[31]

The CPUSA's mechanical position on the African American national question reflects, inter alia, the party's attempt to appeal to this group and at the same time the lack of any input from the Black intelligentsia. If there had been substantial input from this group, the CPUSA would have developed a different position, Blacks would have composed a more substantial section of its leadership, and the party would have been stronger and more capable than it proved to be. Black intellectuals could have assisted working-class Blacks in expressing their experiences and articulating a clear culture of resistance.

On this matter Stalin was right. Otto Hall recounts that when he and a delegation of Negroes were selected by the CPUSA to attend the Communist University of Toilers of the East, Stalin had requested a meeting with them. During the meeting Hall recalls Stalin as saying that "The Negroes represented the most oppressed section of the American working class. Therefore, the American party should have more Negroes than whites."[32]

Part of the party's difficulty in recruiting African American intellectuals stemmed from the class-against-class approach that it used as its model of organizing. I do not think that a revolutionary movement can be built without the significant participation of the lower working class, but it is necessary to mobilize other sections of the population as well. When the lower working class is an ethnic subproletariat, nationalist-oriented intellectuals have to be involved in the struggle. And as Cruse pointed out, it is illusory in such cases to want a "national question" without nationalism (or national consciousness). I do not claim that it is easy to bring all these groups together, but it is essential to the construction of a revolutionary movement based in the most oppressed section of the working class.

The attacks on the middle-class membership of the NAACP and the Urban League were, it would turn out, counterproductive. They established a legacy the Party never lived down and developed habits that were hard to eliminate from the party's repertoire, since they became so deeply ingrained. When the Communist International called for a united front against fascism, the party was able to formulate tactics that did not isolate it from the progressive middle class. But it had a history that was hard to overcome. Many of the Black middle-class political organizations were by now set in their opinion of the party, and the party's history of changing its line to suit the needs of the international movement (or the USSR), its instrumental attitude toward the middle class, and the popular notion spread by J. Edgar Hoover that the communists were "masters of deceit" made it hard for them to believe that any change in the party's attitude was sincere.

However, the question remains: even if the party had been able to recruit large numbers of the nationalist intelligentsia and hence develop a position on the national question that resonated with the experience of the African American working class, would it have been more successful in building a revolutionary movement in the United States? I think it is indisputable that the party would have built a stronger movement. Could it have remained the official representative of international communism in the United States? Maybe not. Stalin seems to have thought so, but the party would have had to abandon some of the Third International's dogma on the African American national question and its focus on the necessity of a "national territory" in the Black Belt South.

But the key question is, could the party constituted in this way—with much greater representation of the African American subproletariat—have mounted a more successful challenge to capitalist rule in the United States? Probably not in the short run, but certainly the working class would have been incomparably stronger. The barrier of course is the real social structure, which has been constructed along certain lines, quite independently of the ability of a particular organization to alter it.

As Du Bois argued, the period of radical Reconstruction was the only time that there was an opportunity for the United States to eliminate race instead of class as the principal stratifying process. As the United States became a contender for the hegemonic position in the capitalist world, as capital expanded to incorporate the African, Asian, and Latin American peripheries more securely under its control, as the core ruling classes consolidated their rule through a social democratic alliance with sections of the organized working class, racism became pervasively integral to the structures of authority (as an open/tacit form of legitimation) and to the structures of rule (to which matters of "legitimacy" are strictly incidental). These relations of rule and authority are complemented within the world-scale social system of production by the increasing coreness of the core via the increasing peripheralization of the periphery, itself a reflection of the ordinary working of the capitalist world-economy. "Wage structures" followed suit everywhere; white workers received higher wages and people of color, lower wages. But in the core during this period the United States was the only principal locale of "nonwhite workers." Since inequality was a given, this racial distinction anchored the principal social arrangements of structures of rule (government, within organizations and by organizations) and structures of production (as administered and developed by increasingly large-scale, that is, centralized, concentrated capital.

The world-scale scope of racism, as fundamental to rule and to the determination of wage scales, made equality a historical impossibility in the United States. No matter what the CPUSA did, inequality between white workers and people of color would have remained a central feature of the society. Only a successful revolution, which would have to have been a world revolution, could have changed this situation.

Nonetheless, an American Communist Party made up disproportionately (not necessarily predominantly) of Black and Latino workers and intellectuals would have seriously altered the relations of force between capital and labor in the United States, and would have been a much more serious obstacle to the consolidation of the social democratic alliance in the United States.

The social democratic alliance accepts both the hegemony of capital and implicitly a racially structured capitalist world-economy, which allows white workers to assume a more intermediate position in the social division of labor. If the most radical organization of the working class had truly reflected the structure of the working class, it would have had a better chance of building a united front based on unity with the most oppressed section of the working class, rather than itself becoming more and more ambivalent about that section—so much so that in the 1960s it would find itself in the rather curious position of having some members brand one of the most exemplary revolutionary leaders in the history of the African American working class, Malcolm X, a CIA agent.

Here we have, dare I say, a repeat of the Garvey debacle, wherein the unity paradigm (that is, the presumption that all the correct strategies and revolutionary consciousness would be captured, or mostly captured, in one organization, the vanguard party) leads ineluctably to sectarian behavior. The CPUSA presumed the need for unity, but did not seek to develop a genuine united front. This prevented it from being able to learn from the experiences of the nationalist mobilizations among African Americans in the twentieth century, which of course would have been extremely enriching for the party's analyses of the world, its political culture, and its development of political line.

I will return to the wider implications of the united front approach and how it relates to strategy as well as tactics.

Communists and Nationalists in Harlem

In the summer of 1933 a former Garveyite, Sufi Abdul Hamid, organized a "Don't Buy Where You Can't Work" campaign. According to Naison, the leadership of the CPUSA feared that Sufi's campaign would become the focal point of a nationalist upsurge, aimed at driving all whites out of Harlem. This led the national leadership of the party to remove Briggs and Moore from the leadership of the Harlem branch and bring in college-educated James Ford, who was a competent administrator rather than an agitator. The party also assigned a number of its top Black organizers from all over the country to the Harlem branch. Benjamin Davis came from Atlanta, Abner Berry came from Kansas City, and James Ashford came from Detroit. The national leadership also assigned a small group of white communists to work behind the scenes, tightening administration and coordinating party activities more efficiently. This new leadership was expected to expand the party's Black membership dramatically, minimize internal dissension, and prevent the emerging community protest from assuming a nationalist direction.[33]

In the summer of 1934, when a coalition of Garveyites and church and civic leaders initiated a boycott of Blumenstein's department store, the CP leadership was dismayed by the nationalist tone on the picket lines, from which white communists were regularly excluded. They thought boycott leaders should demand that no whites be fired, welcome whites on the picket lines, and warn that Black neighborhoods alone could not solve the problem of Black unemployment.[34] The leaders of the "Don't Buy Where You Can't Work" movement viewed the boycott as a step toward Black control of the Harlem economy. Instead of directly taking on the nationalist character of the campaign, the party organized parallel campaigns to win jobs for Blacks through the joint efforts of community groups and workers in those enterprises in which discrimination was practiced.

In 1934 the party initiated a boycott of a huge Harlem cafeteria and won the full support of its white unionized employees. But the implicit bargaining chip with this group was the more nationalist boycotts. Later that year the CP organized the Relief Employees Association to fight against discrimination in the relief system. This campaign forced the promotion of several Blacks to supervisory positions and substantially increased the number of Black investigators and clerks.

These victories won the respect of Black church and civic leaders, who were themselves coming into increased conflict with the nationalists over who would control jobs. These leaders viewed the party's strategy of linking Blacks with white allies as a more effective strategy. Under Ford's leadership the Harlem branch grew from seventy to three hundred members by January 1935, and to seven hundred by the summer of 1935. The party developed a range of community leaders, which enabled them to communicate with everyone from the Elks to the followers of Father Divine. While the party branches were interracial as a matter of principle, the Harlem branch was predominantly Black, and increasingly dealt with other Harlem organizations as one Harlem organization to another, rather than as an outsider.[35]

The party was able to count on a number of successes during this period. It was able to turn the investigation of the Harlem Riot of 1935, in which it was alleged to have played a role, into an indictment of discrimination. It was able to organize mass protests against the Italian invasion of Ethiopia, bringing in Italian communists who denounced Italian fascism and called for the overthrow of Mussolini. Here the party aimed to define the issue as an antifascist struggle rather than one of Blacks against whites. Harlem merchants had attempted to organize against Italian merchants, but did not receive wide support.[36]

Throughout 1937 communists in Harlem engaged in rent strikes, campaigns to improve local schools, efforts to lower meat and milk prices, and organizing drives for support of the CIO. The *Amsterdam News* declared in August 1937 that practically all the social and economic gains of the New Deal stemmed from sustained agitation by radicals and liberals.[37]

But as communists gained leadership positions in the trade union movement, they moderated their zeal against racial discrimination for fear of alienating their white members and jeopardizing their positions in the CIO and the New Deal coalition. The party's prestige was also damaged by its attempts to gain support among Harlem Blacks for the Hitler-Stalin pact.

While the nationalist trend was weakened during the Great Depression by the successes of the CP's strategies, the more moderate and sometimes controversial actions of the party toward the end of the 1930s meant widespread loss of support for the party, and for some a feeling (certainly reinforced by decades of anticommunist propaganda) that communists could not be trusted.

This assessment of the activities of the Communist Party in Harlem during the Great Depression now allows us to gauge its impact on the Black nationalist movements that had been dominant during the twenties. It seems to me that Black nationalism declined in the 1930s because an alliance with labor and liberals became possible during a time of "crisis." However, when the New Deal reforms incorporated labor and the liberals into the "establishment," Blacks were again not included. The reradicalization of the Black movement took forms expressly antagonistic to these groups, including the CPUSA.

The CP's weakened position resulted from a number of factors that impinged on its work. But principally it was because its strength, the ability to bring a wide range of resources and personnel into the struggle, became its weakness as it increasingly had to conciliate the diverse groups within its orbit. And its status in the Black community was undermined by its attempts to placate the white working class, which often adopted a defensive stance toward the demands of the Black working class.

These lessons were not lost on other social forces seeking to appeal to the same constituency. The March on Washington Movement picked up on the mass protest tactics initiated by the CP and used them to gain concessions from the U.S. government.

The March on Washington Movement

The March on Washington Movement (MOWM) emerged in the early 1940s when the government was in the midst of war preparation. It differed from the Garvey movement and the Black Muslims in its limited and reformist goal of opening up the defense industries to Black workers. It was also cross-class in composition, and very loosely organized.

The brainchild of A. Philip Randolph, president of the Brotherhood of Sleeping Car Porters, the MOWM was especially significant in its timing in the midst of war preparations, when all were being urged to put aside special interests for a show of national unity. In addition, it was organized against a president who had very deep support in the Black community.

The Roosevelt administration had to consider how such a demonstration would look in the arena of world politics, occurring against a government that was preparing to go to war in defense of democracy and human equality. In addition this would be an indication that national unity did not exist at a time when it was necessary to prosecute the war effort. Roosevelt entered into a process of collective negotiations with Randolph and other leaders. As a result, Roosevelt was forced to issue an executive order establishing a Fair Employment Practices Committee (FEPC) to deal with the problem of equal opportunity in the defense industries.

The MOWM deemed the establishment of the FEPC a great victory (for some, equivalent to a second Emancipation Proclamation), but a report issued by the Bureau of Employment Security in March 1942 indicated that many defense employment opportunities remained closed to Blacks. This led the MOWM leadership to reactivate the movement, leading to spectacular events during the summer of 1942 in Madison Square Garden and in Chicago. In September Walter White of the NAACP and Lester Granger of the Urban League withdrew their support for the MOWM, leaving Randolph as the principal leader. This allowed Randolph to press the MOWM to take a more militant stance. His proposals were widely criticized. He held that the MOWM should be an all-Black organization so that Blacks could show what they could accomplish with their own resources and strength, and he argued that a strategy of nonviolent resistance might be employed with some effect.[38]

Alkalimat points out that for Randolph the purpose of the MOWM was to guarantee that when the war was over people would get something other than the dispersal of equality and power among individual citizens within a political democratic framework. That is, Randolph wanted to target specific grievances of the Black community. He wanted an economic, social, and racial equality, which is the heart of democracy. He demanded for Blacks "full works of citizenship with no reservations. We will accept nothing less."[39]

The key to the importance of this movement, however, was Randolph's insistence that these goals would be achieved through struggle by the masses: "Therefore, if Negroes secure their goals, immediate and remote, they must win them and to win them they must fight, sacrifice, suffer, go to jail and if need be die for them. These rights will not be given. They must be taken."[40]

The MOWM demonstrated that a broad-based Black constituency could be mobilized. The broadness of the MOWM was probably due to its focus on a specific issue around which all Blacks could unite.[41] The tactics used in this campaign also indicated the effectiveness of a strategy of mass mobilization. The FEPC became a reality only when governmental authorities perceived that thousands of angry Blacks would demonstrate in Washington and thus interfere with the pursuit of national (government) objectives.

Although Harding somewhat derisively deemed the MOWM a "marching movement which did not march," in the minds of many historians the MOWM was the model for the postwar civil rights movement, and even for the Black Power movement's moderate wing. Randolph's genius was to parlay potential criticism of U.S. foreign policy into gains for African Americans. This has become a standard tactic of a whole generation of Black leaders, who use U.S. sensitivity about its image as the leader of the "free world" to gain concessions for Blacks.

In this sense the MOWM *was* the model for the modern civil rights movement. From 1944 to 1950 Black initiatives led to several concessions by the executive and judicial branches of the federal government. The white primaries were struck down in the courts; President Truman formed the first presidential civil rights commission; segregation in interstate bus travel was legally prohibited; segregation in the army was attacked; literacy tests for voting were declared unconstitutional; and border states began the token desegregation of graduate schools, dining cars, and so forth.[42]

Some historians have been wildly enthusiastic about the MOWM and its alleged demonstration of the power of mass protest. But when compared to the more serious empowering tactics utilized by the CPUSA in Harlem, the Randolph tactic can be seen as a somewhat opportunistic use of threats to gain concessions by tacitly condoning the imperial activities of the U.S. state.

Randolph and the moderate civil rights leadership who followed his lead were concerned that the anger and frustration among the masses of Black people might lead them to take increasingly radical measures to redress their grievances and that they would therefore be more open to the agitation of communists. Furthermore, since there was open support in the Black community for the Japanese, as an example of standing up to white domination, leaders like Randolph and Walter White (of the NAACP) feared that the movement would be open to charges of sedition.[43] The March on Washington Movement thus can be viewed as an attempt to recast the possibility of formidable mass dissidence into a more conciliatory mold, one that aimed not at power, but concessions.

To place this skepticism about the March on Washington Movement in context, we should spend some time examining alternative movement sites of enduring significance: the rise of the Nation of Islam, the Italo-Ethiopian crisis, and the radicalizing impact of World War II.

The Nation of Islam

The Nation of Islam drew on two traditions that engaged the hopes and aspirations of the Black working class in a desolate and hopeless waste-land: the Black Islamic tradition of Noble Drew Ali's Moorish-American Science Temple, founded in Newark, New Jersey, in 1913 by Timothy Drew of North Carolina; and the Black nationalist tradition of the Universal Negro Improvement Association (or Garvey movement), founded and led in the United States in 1916 by the charismatic Jamaican Marcus Mosiah Garvey.

Noble Drew Ali's movement, the Moorish-American Science Temple, supported Garvey but its emphasis was more on establishing the contention that Black people were children of Allah. The Moors established centers in Newark, New York, Philadelphia, Pittsburgh, Detroit, and Chicago. Their work in Detroit and Chicago is believed to have sown the seeds for the emergence in the 1930s of W. D. Fard and Elijah Muhammad's Nation of Islam.

Fard first appeared in Detroit in 1930, presenting himself as a merchant of silks and trinkets. He soon began to proselytize among his customers, entreating them to convert to Islam, the religion of their ancestors. The Black man was the original man, the white man no more than a usurper, who had enslaved the Black man, exploited him, and deprived him of his true heritage. Within a short time Fard had a following in the thousands. Members renounced Christianity and totally committed themselves to the goals and values of Islam. As the movement grew, Fard receded more and more into the background; finally he disappeared altogether in June 1934.

Fard had appointed Elijah Poole the supreme minister and had given him the Muslim name Kariem. Before his departure he designated Poole his heir and named him Elijah Muhammad. Some ministers resented Poole's appointment, and in 1935 dissented from Temple No. 2 in Chicago and threatened Elijah Muhammad's life. Muhammad fled to Milwaukee and them took up residence on the East Coast, primarily in

Washington, D.C., for seven years. During this period Muhammad organized congregations in a number of cities on the East Coast.

In 1942 Elijah Muhammad returned to Chicago to assume leadership of the national office. But when the United States entered World War II he was imprisoned for refusing military service, counseling others to resist the draft, and maintaining relations with the Japanese government (which was being presented as the champion of the darker races). The imprisonment imparted to Elijah Muhammad a sense of martyrdom, which reinforced his claim of leadership. He returned to Chicago in 1946, after his release from prison as undisputed leader of the Nation of Islam. He then proceeded to spread the movement throughout Black communities across the country. Under Muhammad's leadership the Nation of Islam became a highly disciplined national community that was for a time the concrete manifestation of the ability of Black people to resist continued victimization. Under the leadership of Elijah Muhammad, the Nation of Islam distinguished itself by its ability to propagandize among the Black working class and to sustain the loyalties of talented functionaries in a hierarchy whose discipline was (and is) matched by few organizations in the contemporary United States. The Nation of Islam succeeded where the Garvey movement failed at being able to demonstrate concrete achievements in the economic realm while avoiding commitments that would overextend it and thereby expose its weakness, its inability to deliver on the claim for a separate territory, and its lack of any serious strategy to gain reparations from the United States government.

The cornerstone of the Nation of Islam's ability to propagandize among the Black working class was the sensitivity of Elijah Muhammad to the needs and conditions of life of the urban Black working class of that time. But it was not until the fifties, when Malcolm X joined the Nation and the environment was more favorable, that the Nation was able to reach out more broadly to the Black community.

The rigid parochialism that had been the source of the NOI's internal cohesion tended to weaken its ability to mobilize the Black masses. During the early period the emphasis was on the creation of a sacred community, which totally removed members of the Nation of Islam from the communities in which they lived. They formed their own self-contained communities, and did not move aggressively out into the rest of the community. Yet the strict discipline of the movement sustained them and enabled them to endure over a long period.

Members of the Nation were restricted in their dietary intake (for example, they could not eat pork or corn bread); they could not be alone with members of the opposite sex except for their spouses; men had to accept familial responsibility as providers and leaders of their families; women had to be modest and obedient in their self-presentation. Conversion to the Muslim faith was not something one did lightly but a commitment of one's total life to a series of exceptionally stringent demands. The demands imposed a limit on the extent to which the Nation of Islam could aspire to a mass following.

Lewis argued that the secret of Garvey's success was that in spite of his rejection of the social order, he did not challenge the basic parameters of the potential convert's experience.[44] The mass movement is the child of the society it is intending to replace. The goals of the movement and the existing state of affairs, no matter how antithetical they may seem, are said to be derivatives of a common social grammar. In Lewis's view, sacred legitimation simply runs counter to the normative experience of the majority of Americans, Black or white.[45]

If this is the case, however, then how do we explain the great significance of the Black church in African American life, and the role that the church has played in the nurturing of social movements in the Black community? That so many political movements have taken a religious form should be instructive.

Lewis conflated different types of organizations—mass organizations like the UNIA and more disciplined organizations like the Nation of Islam. While it is not possible to build a disciplined organization without some form of social glue, a mass organization cannot grow if membership in it is too demanding and restrictive. For a disciplined organization, religious belief and eschatology may very well be the social glue. This has been the case time and time again not only among African Americans but among all people.

Black Nationalism and the Italo-Ethiopian Crisis

While some insist that the economic devastation of the Great Depression forced African Americans to abandon the "luxury" of "romantic" Black nationalism and focus on the bread and butter issues of survival, the response to the Italo-Ethiopian crisis indicates that the flame of Black nationalism continued to burn throughout this period of daunting socioeconomic stress. In the large northern cities such as New York and Chicago, African Americans rallied to the cause of the defense of the Ethiopian motherland because of its symbolic importance for the people of the African diaspora. Moreover, African Americans linked the defense of Ethiopia to their own struggle against racism and imperialism.[46]

Indeed, as has been argued elsewhere in this volume and in other works, the awareness of the historic and contemporary importance of Ethiopia was central to the development of a theory of Black liberation.[47] St. Clair Drake traced the origins of Ethiopianism to the debates in the eighteenth- and nineteenth-century United States over what to do with the slaves. Colonization societies emerged from the manumission movements promoted most persuasively by Thomas Jefferson, who argued that prudent men would not wait to have their throats slit, but would free their slaves voluntarily. Jefferson did not think it possible for Blacks and whites to coexist as equals and therefore favored emigration to the Far West, the Caribbean, or Africa. While most Black abolitionists opposed the program of the colonization societies, the latter found allies among Quakers and other antislavery leaders who wished to see American Blacks go to Africa as teachers and missionaries.

These abolitionist leaders articulated a notion of providential design, which argued that God allowed Africans to be enslaved in Christian North America so that they could return to their homeland and uplift their kinsmen in Africa. The colonization societies split the Afro-American leadership over the issue of emigration. As a result of this split, Black people ceased referring to themselves as "Africans" because it was felt that use of this designation implied being in favor of emigration.

In this case nomenclature does not tell the whole story, for within the straits of bondage, cultural suppression, and the "acceptance" of "the white man's religion" there emerged a doctrine of hope that in time came to be known as Ethiopianism. This doctrine, woven from the fabric of biblical prophecy, presaged the global deliverance of people of African descent. According to Psalms 68:31, "Princes shall come out of Egypt and Ethiopia shall soon stretch forth her hands unto God."

In contrast to many latter-day assumptions (most notably of Noble Drew Ali, Elijah Muhammad, Malcolm X, and the Black Muslim movement generally), the embrace of Christianity by enslaved and free Africans in North America did not include for the most part an acceptance of those theories that justified slavery or racial oppression (e.g. the curse on the sons of Ham; they argued that Noah was drunk so the curse was invalid). Further, they interpreted the Bible in a way that made it clear that African people had a role in the history depicted.

This worldview was embraced in the last part of the eighteenth century by notables such as Richard Allen, founder of the African Methodist Episcopal Church; Prince Hall, founder of the African Masonic Lodge; and the poet Phillis Wheatley.[48] The theme of universal Black brotherhood, redemption, and resurgence is thus not a product of the twentieth century but emerged and evolved over a period of two centuries.

Ethiopianist themes ran deep among African Americans. Ethiopianism explained how the ancient glory of African civilization was lost. When a people forget God and sin, he will bring them down. When they turn back to God they will be redeemed. Africa would return to its ancient glory when its people came back to God. And it was in God's own inscrutable way that Africans were taken as slaves into the Americas, and these same people would return to Africa to take the word of the Lord.

While this ideology often took an emigrationist (back to Africa) posture, it was also the viewpoint of the missionaries of the African American Methodist and Baptist churches. It is thus a phenomenon of the grassroots, of the blood and the bone of the African American people.

Edward Wilmot Blyden, one of the major architects of Ethiopianism, likened the redemptive promise of Black people to Jesus of Nazareth. He held that the path to advancement is through suffering, as we learn not only from the Bible but from all history. In Blyden's view the suffering of the people of the diaspora would redeem all Black people. Later leaders would broaden the scope of redemption to all of America and indeed all the world.

Drake has pointed out that with the increasing number of college graduates who were not trained in theology, the vindication of the race passed from theologians to historians, anthropologists, and archaeologists. Thus in the early twentieth century Pan-Africanism began to replace Ethiopianism as a social and political philosophy among African American intellectuals, but Ethiopianism remained strong among the people as a whole; it was at the base of Marcus Garvey's UNIA, the Moorish-American Science Temple, the Nation of Islam, and the popularity of Afrocentric notions in the Black inner cities of the 1990s.

One can best understand Ethiopianism as an expression of the ever latent and often militant nationalist consciousness that exists among the common people of the African diaspora. Ironically, this consciousness is perhaps strongest among those who live in societies that are structurally and discursively deeply racist but adhere to a public ideology of universalism and equal rights. The tension between racism and universalism is undoubtedly strongest in the United States.

I believe that Bracey, Meier, and Rudwick's classic study of Black nationalism in the United States reflected this phenomenon as they took pains to construct a dialectical notion of nationalist consciousness among African Americans. They pointed out that nationalist consciousness and integrationist consciousness are not absolutes, nor are they mutually exclusive. They produced a periodization that shows the waxing and waning of nationalist consciousness in accordance with the ups and downs of the struggle for inclusion and democracy in the United States. Despite the care with which their position was constructed, this formulation includes an element of reductionism.

The pervasiveness of Ethiopianism is a testament to the endurance of nationalist consciousness among the Black working class. With regard to those who argue that Garveyism collapsed after Garvey was deported from the United States, it should be considered that the organizational decline of Garveyism did not necessarily also entail philosophical and ideological decline. Thus any periodization of nationalist consciousness should reflect the fact that such consciousness is always latent, and is evoked by particular circumstances or historical events, not simply by the mood of whites. The response of African Americans to the Italian invasion of Ethiopia demonstrates the depth and the breadth of nationalist consciousness among African Americans and among the other peoples of the African diaspora.

In the spring of 1935 the newly founded Negro Fraternal Council of Churches met in Cleveland, Ohio, to plan an ecumenical program of racial uplift. But the conferees possessed a striking sense of a troubled world situation, and of the impending decline of the world prestige of the West. They envisioned a decline of Western hegemony over the darker peoples of the world, and considered the implications of the possibilities of economic decline throughout the Western world. Bishop James Bray of the CME Church in Chicago warned that Mussolini's ambitions in Abyssinia would intensify racial antagonisms and provoke worldwide revolt of the darker races against the master race. "In Asia, the islands of the sea, America, and all over Africa," proclaimed Bray, "the dark races were organizing to save Ethiopia from white conquest and restore colored civilization to its pre-Columbian glory." Italy's ungodly assault on Christian Ethiopia, the conferees argued, excited sentiments passionately hostile to the entire white race. These churchmen viewed the conflict in Ethiopia as the fulfillment of biblical prophecy concerning the redemption of Ethiopia.[49]

These messianic notions took secular forms as well. DuBois's analysis of the crisis detected a similar mentality. Among that vast sea of colored humanity who had suffered the abuse, exploitation, and insult of the white world he detected "a swelling tide of hostility and mutiny."[50] People of color no longer believed it was the destiny of the white nations to rule the world.

New Negro radicalism continued to exert an influence over the style and substance of Black politics during the depression years. Along with Garveyism as a more specific form of New Negro radicalism, the 1930s constituted a continuation of the radical 1920s in more ways than is usually considered.

In some ways the movement to stop the Italian invasion of Ethiopia recapitulated the ideological struggles of the 1920s. One example is the controversy about boycotting Italian American merchants. Grassroots activists of various ideological hues (liberal integrationists, socialists, and nationalists) were concerned about the impact of such a strategy on domestic race relations, although many Italian Americans supported Mussolini's invasion of Ethiopia.

Although only two African Americans (both pilots) were able join the ranks of the Ethiopian combatants against Mussolini's invaders, it is estimated that nearly fifty thousand volunteered for active duty in Ethiopia.[51] These volunteers were strictly prohibited by U.S. law from serving in any foreign military forces. Violators of the law faced heavy fines and possibly imprisonment. Most ultimately accepted this stricture, but some protested it vigorously. An example is the International African Progressive Association (IAPA) of Beckley, Virginia, which claimed that African Americans had a legal right to fight in their African fatherland. This right, it argued, flowed from the peculiar historical circumstances of the African American people. The IAPA argued that the Black man in America is neither alien nor foreign to any part of the African continent, having been "carried away by violence into the American continent."[52]

Representatives of the Ethiopian government stated that they appreciated the numerous offers of Black American military assistance, but what they really needed was financial assistance. In addition, there were practical considerations involving the organization, funding, transport, and deployment of troops, which when combined with the legal strictures mitigated against any significant involvement of Black U.S. volunteer forces.[53]

Scott points out that by the time of the October 1935 invasion, Ethiopia's survival was the topic of angry debate in poolrooms, barbershops, taverns, and street corners in Harlem. The topic was also hotly debated in the boardrooms and salons of the local elites. Some of the key Harlem leaders involved in the mobilization in support of Ethiopia included Adam Clayton Powell, Jr., Garvey stalwarts such as A. L. King and Willis N. Huggins, ardent race nationalists such as Arthur Reid and Ira Kemp, and Black communist leaders such as James Ford and Abner Berry.

One of the most important organizations in the Harlem mobilization was the Provisional Committee for the Defense of Ethiopia (PCDE), a united front that included Black communists, the UNIA, the African Patriotic League, the Harlem YMCA, the local Elks lodge, and the League of Struggle for Negro Rights. Some of the communist elements in the PCDE later collaborated with several Harlem physicians to form the Medical Committee for the Defense of Ethiopia. The purpose of this organization was to secure and forward medical, dental, and pharmaceutical supplies to Ethiopia. According to Robinson, this organization shipped two tons of medical and surgical supplies to Ethiopia.[54]

At about the same time that the medical committee was being formed, the PCDE decided to appeal directly to the League of Nations. The noted Africanist scholar Willis Huggins was selected to carry out this mission. Huggins met with Waqneh Martin, the Ethiopian minister to Great Britain, who authorized Huggins to organize activities on Ethiopia's behalf in the United States.

When Huggins returned to the States he organized the all-Black Friends of Ethiopia. In two months the organization is reported to have established 106 branches, and shortly thereafter to have affiliated with a variety of national and international organizations, for the most part Black organizations. These included the Association for the Study of Negro Life and History, the Ethiopia Research Council, the American Pro-Falasha Committee, the Universal Ethiopian Students' Association, the International African Friends of Ethiopia (London), la Revue de Monde Noir (Paris), the Women's International League for Peace and Freedom (Geneva), and Jeunes Ethiopenes (Addis Ababa). The Friends of Ethiopia came to be considered the most important of the Ethiopian support organizations, but is said to have generated little in the way of material aid for Ethiopia.[55]

In December 1935 Lij Tasfaye Zaphiro, the private secretary to the Ethiopian minister in London, persuaded fifteen Harlem Ethiopian support organizations to come together and form the United Aid for Ethiopia.

The NAACP was also involved in the attempt to prevent Mussolini's invasion of Ethiopia. On March 20, 1935, it sent a letter of protest to the U.S. secretary of state, insisting that the people of the United States had an interest in maintaining peace in the region. NAACP officials felt that the NAACP was the advocate of universal Black freedom, and was thus obliged to take a strong position on this issue.

The NAACP did not have much faith in the League of Nations but thought that the Soviet Union, given its anti-imperialist and anticolonial stance, could be persuaded to intervene on behalf of the Ethiopians. But when Maxim Litinov, the Soviet envoy to the League of Nations, carefully avoided the issue of Ethiopia in his address to the council and assembly on May 21, it was clear that the USSR placed a higher priority on retaining Italy in its united front against Nazi Germany. Unable to explain why the Soviets did not support the Ethiopians, numerous Harlem communists quietly resigned their membership in the Communist Party of the United States.

An NAACP editorial in its journal, the *Crisis*, deemed Mussolini's invasion of Ethiopia as the League of Nations and the white world stood idly by a sorry spectacle. As Haile Selassie laid the blame for the invasion of his country and the murder of his people on the League of Nations, they hung their head in shame. the *Crisis* editorialized that "The perfidity of the world's white idealists and peace-and-justice lovers had been revealed for all to see. The white powers displayed their indifference to the rights of Black Ethiopia and, by implication to Negro justice everywhere."[56]

But the anger of the NAACP is of course only the tip of the iceberg. The fact that such strong reactions extended even to a nominally integrationist organization like the NAACP is an indication of the depth of nationalist consciousness.

Italian American support for the invasion was widespread, although there was also significant antifascist sentiment among Italian Americans. A popular Italian American newspaper, *Il Progresso*, launched a drive to raise half a million dollars for the Italian Red Cross and to aid their compatriots fighting in Africa "to write another epic page of glory in the history of civilization."[57]

When news of an Italian massacre of Ethiopian patriots reached Harlem in May 1936, a full-scale riot broke out. Ira Kemp of the African Patriotic League led an angry mob of four hundred people down Lenox Avenue attacking Italian-owned stores and battling with the police.

The Italo-Ethiopian crisis generated extensive support for Ethiopia among the Black people of the United States and throughout the African diaspora. This illustrates that nationalist consciousness is a complex phenomenon, not simply a product of domestic race relations.

World War II and the Black Revolution

Just as World War I served as a context for the political education and radicalization of large numbers of Black people, which came to be expressed in the various forms of the New Negro movement, World War II juxtaposed the realities of U.S. racism to the government's slogan of a war for democracy against an enemy that preached the doctrine of a master race. The democratic rhetoric used by the government in the war provided a context in which Blacks could use the same logic to strike for their own freedom. Many Blacks had learned the bitter lesson that support for U.S. goals in World War I had *not* led to federal opposition to white supremacist practices.

Thus most Blacks shunned the "closing of ranks" position advocated by W. E. B. Du Bois in World War I. As a matter of fact, when war broke out in Europe in 1939 many Blacks adopted an isolationist position. Columnist George Schuyler wrote that this was a "white man's war." "So far as the colored people of the earth are concerned," he wrote, "it is a toss-up." For him there was little to choose between German rule in Austria and British rule in Africa. Some Black columnists thought it a blessing that white people were killing each other rather than people of color.[58]

The NAACP noted the striking hypocrisy of the U.S. claim to be waging a war in defense of democracy:

> THE CRISIS is sorry for brutality, blood, and death among the peoples of Europe, just as we are sorry for China and Ethiopia. But the hysterical cries of the preachers of democracy for Europe leave us cold. We want democracy in Alabama and Arkansas, in Mississippi and Michigan, in the District of Columbia—*in the Senate of the United States.*[59]

After the bombing of Pearl Harbor in 1941 this position evolved into the Double V slogan adopted by most prominent Black leaders, calling for victory against international fascism and victory against domestic racism. The sense of militancy that pervaded Black America in the face of the recalcitrance of the federal government under Franklin Delano Roosevelt led to agitation for mass pressure, leading eventually to the March on Washington Movement. In calling for this protest Randolph argued, "Only power can effect the enforcement and adoption of a given policy. . . . Power is the active principle only of the organized masses, the masses united for a definite purpose."[60] Randolph's statement is indicative of the mass militancy that was characteristic of Black people during World War II.

So we see that Black participation in World War II internationalized the Black experience as had previously been the case with World War I. In this context the collective memory of Black people in the United States meant that a radical Black consciousness would be inflamed by any repeat of the debacle of World War I.

It is also important to note that the war created a demand for Black labor, which was increasingly filled by southern Black immigrants. The industrial boom stimulated by the war in fact created a situation of relative full employment, which reduced the intensity of job competition and thus the opposition to Black entry into some sections of the labor force. This situation bolstered the self-confidence of the Black working class vis à vis white society, despite the continued existence of a racial division of labor that relegated Blacks to the lowest rungs of the labor force.

This period of increasing militancy on the part of the Black working class formed the context in which Malcolm X grew up. During this period interracial violence increased, leading finally to the bloody summer of 1943.

One Harlem leader argued, "If we don't fight for our rights during the War, while the government needs us, it will be too late after the war."[61] The Black press highlighted evidence of Black exclusion from defense jobs, blood plasma segregated by the Red Cross, abused Black soldiers, and white hostility and violence. With its circulation increased by 40 percent during the war, the Black press served to encourage increasing militancy and racial solidarity, and embarrass America's "war for democracy" by publicizing its Jim Crow practices and policies. The NAACP membership increased tenfold. CORE was formed in 1942, stimulating sit-ins and other forms of direct action.

On the intellectual front there was a steady stream of articles, books, letters, and speeches by people like Pearl S. Buck, Eleanor Roosevelt, Wendell Wilkie, and Henry Wallace disputing scientific racism and condemning America's hypocrisy. This reached its peak with the publication of Gunnar Myrdal's book *An American Dilemma* in 1944. Myrdal sidestepped the socioeconomic issues around which racism revolved and highlighted instead the moral issue of the conflict within the American creed generated by the practice of racial discrimination.

Interracial strife in the military was common during this period, including sporadic conflict and outright rioting. Thousands of spontaneous and individual rebellions went unreported and unnoticed by the public. But there was an unusually high number of casualties suffered by white officers of Black troops.[62] There were in addition numerous riots around military facilities, including facilities at Alexandria, Louisiana, New Orleans, Vallejo, California, Flagstaff and Phoenix, Arizona, Florence, South Carolina, Fort Dix, New Jersey, and Tuskegee, Alabama.

In 1943 the Social Science Institute at Fisk University reported 242 racial battles in 47 cities. Racial gang fights took place in Newark, Philadelphia, Buffalo, Chicago, Cambridge, and Brooklyn. Zoot suit riots occurred in many cities, the most severe in Los Angeles, where a thousand white sailors and soldiers roamed the streets stripping zoot suits from Black and Chicano men. There were in addition two quite notable riots of 1943, in Detroit and Harlem. FBI chief J. Edgar Hoover announced plans to arrest communist agitators.

Liberals urged Blacks to go slow as a means of averting violence. White liberals had joined the movement against racial injustice in large numbers, reflecting the popular consensus about the need for racial reform, but at the same time pushed the movement increasingly into a more conservative, nonconfrontational, legalistic stance. The NAACP urged its members to get out of the streets and into the courtrooms and voting booths.

But the sense of mass militancy far exceeded the reach of the mainstream civil rights organization such as the NAACP. This sense of mass militancy was also reflected among the most alienated and impoverished members of the Black community and was reflected in part in their support for the isolationist position on the war. By 1940 a number of organizations, such as the Ethiopian Pacific Movement, the World Wide Friends of Africa, and the Brotherhood of Liberty for the Black People of America, explicitly preached a doctrine calling for the unity of the darker people of the world, including the Japanese.[63] In 1942 and 1943 the federal government arrested members of several pro-Japanese Black organizations in Chicago, New York, Newark, and East St. Louis who were alleged to have been in contact with Japanese agents.[64]

In 1942 when Detroit Red (a.k.a. Malcolm Little), later to be known as Malcolm X, received his draft notice, he went around Harlem saying that he wanted to fight for the Japanese to kill some crackers. For this talk Malcolm was rejected as unfit for military service as a psychopathic personality. At the same time Elijah Muhammad, leader of the Nation of Islam, was doing time in prison for counseling young Black men that they should resist the draft and not fight "our Asiatic brother."[65]

6

The American Century
Labor Peace, Hegemony, and Civil Rights

At the end of World War II the long struggle for hegemony of the capitalist world was finally over, and the United States was the clear victor. Hegemony not only held out the promise of sure prosperity to large sections of the domestic population, it demanded their cooperation in the social peace and the defense of their state's dominant position in the state system. For the capitalist class, for the new petty bourgeoisie of managers, professionals, and technocrats, for the upper working class of skilled and white men, the post–World War II era undoubtedly seemed to inaugurate a regime of unending and unlimited prosperity.

Although Blacks had won some benefits (e.g., the desegregation of the armed forces and of defense industries), they were clearly demarcated from the segments of the population that were the main beneficiaries of American power and prosperity in the world (along with women as a whole and the increasing numbers of Puerto Ricans and Chicanos). In order to obtain social peace in its home base, the U.S. ruling class had embarked on a policy of extreme repression of the U.S. Left, driving the major part of the CPUSA leadership underground and utterly decimating its rank and file and its mass base. At the same time it effectively incorporated the leadership of the labor movement into the ruling coalition.[1]

It was in this context that the Black movement became the central force for a just and egalitarian social order within U.S. borders. This movement took two forms: (1) the civil rights movement, marked indelibly with the aura of U.S. hegemony, and (2) the Black Power (or Black liberation) movement, partially a response to the limits of the civil rights movement, and partially a response to a change in conjuncture, the crisis of U.S. hegemony.

From the end of World War II to the early 1960s integration was the dominant ideology among Black protest movements. The goals of integration coincided with the interests of the new Black middle class that was developing as a result of the rise in trade union membership and lower-level white-collar jobs in the expanding postwar economy, particularly in the federal, state, and local governments.

These protest movements coincided thus with wide-ranging structural and socioeconomic changes. There was in addition a conscious promotion of integration among some of the economic and political elites. Bracey has argued that the most significant conclusion of Myrdal's *American Dilemma* was that the existence of the Black community was "pathological" and should be eliminated through integration.

The Civil Rights Movement

Improved economic conditions, the eviction of the Left from the unions, and the growth of industrial unionism moderated unrest among the industrial working class by the late 1940s. One significant group that continued to be excluded from the benefits of affluence were Blacks, who were largely located outside or at the bottom of the industrial working class, and who lost employment in the postwar rehiring of white veterans.

The Black movement sought to gain formal political rights in the South and to secure economic advance. With the passage of a series of civil rights bills between 1957 and 1965 Blacks were no longer denied formal political rights in the South. Economic advance, however, accrued only to those Blacks who were able to enter middle-class occupations and thus take advantage of "integration" and the liberal employment practices that the turbulence of that era had produced. For the lower stratum of the Black population the main benefit was liberal welfare practices, which enabled them to survive despite widespread unemployment and underemployment.

In the view of many observers racism was a product of the need of the cotton planters to secure a cheap and reliable workforce for the difficult job of growing cotton. This was no less true after the emancipation of the slaves than before. A workforce was needed that could be made to work on terms that were not much different from those that had prevailed during slavery. After the Reconstruction period and the Tilden-Hayes compromise of 1877, the southern elite developed a system of political domination that returned Blacks to servitude.

The methods used were mob and police violence, legislative measures, and court rulings. Of these methods mob violence was most fundamental. As indicated above, the North did not become a model of a more open society that should be pursued in the South; instead the social arrangement of the South (the Jim Crow system) became the model for U.S. relations with the people of color of the third world who had begun increasingly to come under U.S. tutelage from 1898 on.[2]

While the imperial ambitions of the United States were seen to have led to widespread acceptance of racist ideology from 1898 on, the rise of communism to power in several countries after the Second World War forced the United States, now the hegemonic power in the capitalist world-economy, to shift to the profession of an ideology of freedom and democracy. In this context the existence of Jim Crow in the South constituted a national embarrassment to the United States.

Furthermore, since northern capital had acceded to the demand for the right to organize trade unions, it no longer used Black workers as a pawn in its battle with white labor. These changes in relations of force eroded the support for the southern social system among the economic elites of the North.[3]

Black people's resistance to subordination first emerged in the urban North, since they were protected to some extent by northern capital, which had encouraged them to migrate. In the Black ghettos of the urban North, segregation provided Blacks with the security and concentration of numbers. In that sense segregation could be viewed as a source of strength.

As we have seen above, the first indication of this was the phenomenal success of Marcus Garvey's Universal Negro Improvement Association (UNIA). At the same time Blacks began to fight back against white mob violence (riots) in cities around the United States. Although they were cast in the role of scabs, Black workers fought whites for the right to work. During the depression they confronted police in eviction actions and joined the struggles of the unemployed against the relief system. Blacks participated in the great strikes of the 1930s that led to the building of the CIO and organized a march on Washington to protest discrimination in war industries and segregation in the armed forces. Black troops took up arms against whites who attacked them in the communities surrounding southern military camps.

Concentration and segregation also generated an economic base, despite the poverty of the individual members of the community. Churches acquired mass memberships, small businesses were sustained, segregated union locals were formed, and a Black press was nourished. Piven and

Cloward argue that these institutions provided the vehicles to forge solidarity, define common goals, and mobilize collective action. The fact that the Brotherhood of Sleeping Car Porters, without white participation, was able to mobilize the March on Washington Movement to press for the establishment of the Fair Employment Practices Commission is an example of the impact of concentration and segregation on the emergence of Black protest.

An example of the impact of economic modernization on Black protest was the social disorganization created by rapid urbanization, detaching some men from employment and thus giving rise to a volatile segment of the Black population from which civil disorder could erupt. One form that such disorder took is rioting, which broke out in Harlem in 1935 and again during World War II.[4]

The economic trends that led to the migration to northern cities also led some Blacks to migrate to southern cities. For the most part these Blacks lived under the same conditions as northern Blacks, except that they were not free from caste relations.

Preceded by a similar action a year earlier in Baton Rouge, the Montgomery bus boycott was initiated by the heads of the Women's Political Council (formed when the local League of Women Voters refused to admit Blacks) and E. D. Nixon, an influential member of the Brotherhood of Sleeping Car Porters. The Black ministerial alliance joined the meeting of the Black leadership called to respond to the arrest of Rosa Parks on December 1, 1955.

As we know, Rosa Parks refused to give up her seat. E. D. Nixon called for the boycott and for a leadership that came to be known as the Montgomery Improvement Association. The association mobilized some forty thousand people, who held frequent rallies in churches, carpooled or walked instead of taking the bus, and eventually brought the bus company to its knees. This was an astounding show of strength and courage, given the intimidation methods that had been used by white racists in the South for many years.

The Montgomery bus boycott attracted attention throughout the United States, and indeed around the world. Funds for the operation came from the NAACP, the UAW (with its large Black membership), and individuals in the North. The Alabama legal system was used to restrain the boycott, but finally the U.S. Supreme Court declared Alabama's segregated bus system unconstitutional. The Montgomery boycott had been followed by a similar boycott in Tallahassee; boycotts spread to other southern cities as well.

Southern elites, with their Declaration of Constitutional Principle (the so-called Southern Manifesto), encouraged whites to resist the Supreme Court's infringement on states' rights. Many organizations were formed across the South, the most important of which was the White Citizens' Council, which at its height in 1956 claimed 250,000 members. The council issued large amounts of propaganda in favor of segregation, denounced and intimidated whites who spoke up in favor of compliance with the law, and instigated systematic retaliation against Black activists. Piven and Cloward have remarked that in the late 1950s the South was in a state of economic warfare.

In the electoral arena the Democratic Party's strategy of proceeding cautiously on the civil rights issue for fear of antagonizing its white base in the South had led by 1956 to massive African American defections from the Democratic presidential nominee. Adlai Stevenson, who had received 80 percent of the Black vote in 1952, received only 60 percent of the Black vote in 1956. The upward trend of Black support for the Democratic Party, begun in 1936, was broken.[5]

This defection, and not the rise of substantial Black voting blocs in the North, set the stage for civil rights concessions. The Democratic Party could no longer conduct business as usual by conciliating the southern white vote. Now the Black vote, like the southern white vote, was unstable.

The Republican Party was encouraged to break from its alliance with the Dixiecrats to resubmit a mild civil rights bill, which Lyndon Johnson had previously defeated. This time Johnson, who had national ambitions, prevented a filibuster, and the Civil Rights Bill of 1957 was passed, seventy-two to eighteen. The significance of this symbolic bill was that it signaled the end of the era of avoiding regional divisions within the Democratic Party by avoiding the civil rights issue. Now the fight was over the substance of these concessions.[6]

On February 1, 1960, four students from North Carolina A&T sat in at a "whites only" section of a Woolworth store in Greensboro, North Carolina, and refused to move until the store closed. The next day thirty additional students joined the protest; their numbers increased to fifty on the following day. Although this was not the first sit-in, it sparked a massive sit-in movement in five southern states among already developed forms of community organization, based mainly in the churches, the Black colleges, and local civil rights organizations.[7]

This was a decisive turn for the civil rights movement. The direct action strategy broke the dominance of the legalistic leadership of the national NAACP over the movement. New young leaders like Julian Bond, Diane Nash, Marion Barry, and John Lewis emerged. By April 1960 over fifty thousand Black and white students had participated in protests.[8] SCLC officials in Atlanta were quick to offer financial and moral support to the movement. In April with SCLC aid and Ella Baker's oversight, students from dozens of universities assembled at Shaw University in Raleigh, North Carolina, and formed the Student Nonviolent Coordinating Committee (SNCC).[9]

SNCC, like all the direct action organizations that came into existence during this period (e.g., CORE and the SCLC), was a cadre organization and thus did not concentrate on building formal membership. The cadre first engaged in exemplary actions; they were the most active demonstrators. These exemplary actions inspired a mass mobilization. Mobilizations usually took place through segregated institutions, which ironically had helped Black people in the South achieve a degree of organization and discipline, which now became useful for the conduct of the civil rights struggle.

The initial perspective of the young student activists was that of militant reformers. They wanted to make a place for themselves in the system. Unlike the moderate civil rights leadership, however, they were very critical of the system (although their criticism was not yet systematic).

The early civil rights period also stimulated the growth of the Congress of Racial Equality (CORE), which had almost ceased to exist in the early 1950s at the height of the cold war. From 1958 to 1960 the number of CORE chapters increased from eight to nineteen, and financial supporters increased from 4,500 to 12,000. On February 12, 1960, just twelve days after the Greensboro demonstration, CORE locals across the country picketed drug and retail stores that allowed segregated services in their southern-based facilities. Floyd McKissick, a CORE activist in North Carolina, led workshops on nonviolence across the state.

In the 1960–61 period SNCC and CORE were very successful in mobilizing Black college students throughout the South. The cadres of the direct action organizations were also very successful in mobilizing middle-class and poor Blacks throughout the South for civil disobedience. Within a year of the Greensboro sit-in over 50,000 people had been mobilized for demonstrations in more than one hundred cities, and 3,600 people spent some time in jail.

The arrests, mob violence, and police brutality that were provoked by the protest activities created major dilemmas for national political leaders. When Martin Luther King was arrested and sentenced to four months at hard labor just before the 1960 presidential election, President Eisenhower and candidate Nixon decided not to take the political risk of taking any kind of action. Kennedy did take action, and gained strong support from the Black community. The Democratic Party's proportion of the Black vote in 1960 increased from 60 percent to 68 percent, providing Kennedy with the margin of victory in eight large states (New York, Illinois, Pennsylvania, Michigan, Maryland, Missouri, Minnesota, and New Jersey), all but one (Missouri) of which had gone to Eisenhower in 1956.[10]

Although Black people could legitimately expect aggressive action on civil rights from Kennedy, the narrow margin of victory, attributed to defections from the South, made Kennedy move cautiously. He thus chose to get his social legislation through Congress before breaking his coalition with any civil rights legislation. In the meantime he attempted to move through executive action so as to forestall demands for immediate legislative action.

Kennedy also issued an executive order against discrimination in federal employment and hired more Blacks than any previous president. He instructed all departments to systematically upgrade all Blacks, leading to an increase of 36.6 percent in the number of Blacks in middle grades of the civil service.[11]

Shortly after the U.S. Supreme Court ruled that segregation on interstate buses and trains and in the stations was illegal in December 1960, James Farmer, as new national director of CORE, called for another journey of reconciliation (CORE had been formed out of the Chicago-based Fellowship of Reconciliation in 1942).[12] The Freedom Riders were attacked at several stops during the route, the buses were burned, and the activists were arrested for disturbing the peace. During the summer of 1961, four hundred Freedom Riders were arrested, and three were murdered.[13]

The Freedom Rides reestablished CORE's reputation in the civil rights movement, and its membership climbed from twenty-six thousand in May 1961 to fifty-two thousand in December 1962. However, given the intensity of the violence against the Freedom Riders, CORE decided to call off the Freedom Rides. Despite the danger, some thought that the Freedom Rides had to be completed at all costs. In that spirit Diane Nash, coordinator of student activities for the Nashville Christian Leadership Council, and other Nashville students quickly organized a group to continue the Freedom Rides. The group was told that at least one of them would be killed if they participated. Not one of them backed down.[14]

When attempts were made to stop this group from continuing the Freedom Rides by denying them a bus, they were able to gain the support of the Kennedy administration to get a bus. One of the key tactics of the civil rights movement was to create situations that would force or cajole the federal government to intervene to enforce the law of the land.

The mob violence and police harassment against the Freedom Riders continued. The intensity of the violence and the confrontations of the courageous Freedom Riders against lawless and brutal mobs in full public view dramatized the issue of civil rights to the nation. National attention was riveted on the Freedom Riders, gaining the civil rights movement considerable public support, and leading the Justice Department to get the Interstate Commerce Commission to prohibit separate facilities in bus and train stations.

In the early years of SNCC's organizational life, there emerged two opposing political tendencies, the "moralists," who emphasized direct action, and the pragmatists, who emphasized voter registration. Ella Baker had recommended that SNCC have two wings. However, James Forman was able to gain the trust of both groups.[15]

In Albany, Georgia, a coalition of SNCC, the NAACP, and several groups organized to bring about the end of segregation in their town. Their target was the Trailways bus station. When members of the coalition were arrested for attempting to enter the whites-only waiting room, the Albany movement initiated a week of mass protests and rallies, leading local officials to call for negotiations. Martin Luther King, who had been invited to speak by the Albany movement, was arrested as he participated in one of the demonstrations. After a series of false starts, local officials finally agreed to comply with the ICC ruling and to release the demonstrators who had been arrested. While these concessions allowed for the demobilization of the movement, the local officials did not deliver on their promises, and the movement was only revived when King and Abernathy returned to Albany to be sentenced for the December protests. A series of demonstrations was sparked when King and Abernathy were sentenced to forty-five days in jail. So many demonstrators were arrested that authorities had to send some prisoners to nearby cities. After repeated requests by Albany Black leaders, President Kennedy finally made a statement urging Albany officials to negotiate a settlement.

Civil rights activists view the Albany protests as a turning point for the civil rights movement. The Albany movement demonstrated the limited effect of appealing to white conscience. From this point the pragmatic wing of SNCC came increasingly to predominate in the organization. They also drew the lesson that patient suffering was not sufficient to bring about federal intervention. But despite its failures, the Albany movement was a model for techniques of sustaining mass militancy over long periods. Julian Bond pointed out that the significance of SNCC's approach is that when it completed its mission in any particular locale, it left behind "a community movement with local leadership, not a new branch of SNCC."[16]

One important lesson of the Albany movement was that SNCC workers became aware of the cultural dimension of the Black struggle. They learned, for example, the value of freedom songs, often based on Black spirituals, to convey the ideas of the southern movement and sustain the movement's morale. Bernice Reagon described the Albany movement as a "singing movement." The songs used in Albany came to be used in SNCC's work throughout the Deep South. Two of the key songs that originated in Albany were "Ain't Gonna Let Nobody Turn Me 'Round" and "Oh Freedom."[17]

Overall the Albany experience reinforced SNCC's confidence in its organizing approach. For the first time it had organized large numbers of Black adults for a sustained struggle. Patient efforts to win the confidence of local residents and calculated acts of disobedience had unleashed the dormant militancy of Albany Blacks. On the other hand, SNCC activists learned that sporadic acts of nonviolent resistance were not enough. More was needed to dismantle the enduring structures of racism in the Deep South. It was necessary for SNCC to become a political organization with full-time, politically sophisticated staff and some means of coordination.

Jim Forman played an important role in moving SNCC toward a more sophisticated approach. While maintaining SNCC's traditional emphasis on flexibility, creativity, and innovation, Forman also emphasized discipline and political sophistication as essential to an organization of "professional revolutionaries." Furthermore, SNCC needed specialized skills and a division of labor that would greatly enhance the organization's effectiveness. Forman was very good at convincing people to take on responsibilities and to commit themselves to implementation through routine work (office work and fund raising), instead of only through the more exciting work of protest.

He recruited several full-time staff members, including Julian Bond, Dotty Zellner, Casey Hayden, Mary King, Dinky Romily, and Ruby Doris Smith. Fannie Lou Hamer joined SNCC in 1962 after hearing Forman and Bob Moses speak in Rulesville, Mississippi. SNCC salaries were very low (ten dollars per week) so staff members did not develop a vested interest in the survival of the organization solely as a means of making a livelihood.

SNCC was unique in its belief that its role was to encourage local Blacks to direct their local movements regardless of their educational level. SNCC cadres should not and could not do the work themselves. Only if local people became involved in the movement could any campaign be judged successful.

In the spring and summer of 1963 protests exceeded in intensity and size anything seen up to that point. There were 930 demonstrations in 115 cities in 11 southern states.[18] This militant mood among African Americans forced SNCC to reassess its views on nonviolent protest. The Birmingham campaign displayed the violence of the southern racists, as marchers were clubbed and beaten on national television and vicious dogs were released on children six to sixteen years old as they knelt to pray. When eight moderate white ministers denounced King for his impatience with the pace of change, King eloquently rebutted them with his famous "Letter from Birmingham City Jail." In it he argued that the greatest foe of desegregation is not the Ku Klux Klan, but the moderates who agree with our goals, but not our methods, who are more devoted to order than to justice, who agree in principle but disagree in fact.[19]

The bombing of Black homes and businesses by white racists finally led Senator Jacob Javits to demand that the Justice Department intervene. There were demonstrations in San Francisco and Detroit in support of the Birmingham campaign. Tens of thousands of whites were recruited into the movement. Thousands of telegrams were sent to the White House demanding action. The beating of children finally forced the Kennedy administration to take action.[20]

In discussions about a march on Washington initiated by A. Philip Randolph (leader of the 1940s March on Washington Movement) SNCC and a few CORE militants argued that the march should become a massive display of civil disobedience that would paralyze Washington, DC. White liberals from labor and religious groups strongly disagreed with such a radical approach. The SCLC, the NAACP, and the Urban League wanted an orderly demonstration that would receive the full support of the federal government. Kennedy convinced the civil rights leadership to use the march to support his civil rights bill. John Lewis, who spoke for SNCC at the 1963 march, delivered the most militant speech, although it had been sanitized for the sake of maintaining the united front. Lewis criticized the civil rights bill as too little, too late; he called for "one man one vote," which was not addressed by the bill. He urged Black people to stay in the streets until the great unfinished revolution of 1776 was completed.[21]

King's speech was the highlight of the march. It evoked deep sentiments for white Americans; it was the ultimate tribute to the American dream. It was the ultimate expression of American hegemony.

After Kennedy's assassination in November 1963 Johnson accelerated the implementation of civil rights reforms; he was very skilled at dealing with Congress, and peace in this domain was indispensable to war abroad. The passing of the civil rights reforms is often viewed as the end of the official civil rights movement in the South. The end of de jure segregation meant it was now illegal to practice racial discrimination, but outside of the South discrimination had long been institutionalized in labor markets, real estate markets, police practices, and other arenas. The ensuing shift of Black protest to the North, the rise of the Black Power movement, and the entrance into the war in Vietnam, was to galvanize the nation. However, it also represents a transitional period in which the cadres of the movement and the people who were beneficiaries and allies of the movement underwent wrenching changes in their thinking, as they struggled to draw correct conclusions from the years of struggle that the civil rights movement represented.

The Mississippi Summer Project might be seen as one important turning point. Initially there were very few whites directly involved in SNCC's work in the Deep South. Bob Moses thought that white participation would be counterproductive, given the massive white resistance to the movement. In addition Moses thought that white participation would detract from SNCC's efforts to develop local Black leadership. But the Mississippi Summer Project, of which Moses was an architect, consciously sought to recruit large numbers of white students to come to the Deep South to do voter registration, which had heretofore been routinely disrupted by local authorities. They did not believe that the national authorities would tolerate assaults on white students from leading colleges and prominent families. Thus part of this strategy involved provoking a confrontation between the Mississippi authorities and the federal government so that the federal government would have to enforce the law of the land.

Although a white volunteer was killed in Philadelphia, Mississippi, the strategy did not bring about massive intervention by the federal government. But the anticipated tensions between Black SNCC workers and the white volunteers did materialize. This was to deepen the tension within the organization about the participation of whites.

Another key turning point was the Mississippi Freedom Democratic Party, which was established by SNCC to challenge the Mississippi regulars who excluded Blacks and for the most part supported Republican candidate Barry Goldwater anyway. Prior to going to the Atlantic City convention SNCC workers had lobbied strongly to gain support for their strategy, and indeed obtained support from nine state delegations and twenty-five congresspersons.

Johnson, for his part, was determined to avoid any action that would weaken his southern support; he put the MFDP under FBI surveillance at the Democratic national convention, and only after Fannie Lou Hamer gained considerable national support with her speech at the convention did he offer a compromise. At first Johnson offered the party an opportunity to come to the floor but without voting rights. When they refused he came back with an offer to seat two members of the delegation along with the Mississippi regulars. He then assigned Hubert Humphrey to get Martin Luther King and Bayard Rustin to convince the MFDP to accept the compromise, but the members of the MFDP stood their ground.[22]

The MFDP experience greatly embittered SNCC, and deepened the militant mood that gripped the organization. Bob Moses argued that Black people should set up their own government and declare the other one null and void. SNCC and the MFDP's refusal to accept the compromise offered by Johnson and Humphrey at the Democratic national convention represented the beginning of SNCC's final break with the liberal center.

In the aftermath of the MFDP experience SNCC accepted Harry Belafonte's invitation to send a delegation to Africa. In Africa they met with Sekou Toure, who encouraged them to take a broader view of the struggle and relate it to the struggles of Africans on the continent. John Lewis and Donald Harris met with Malcolm X, who was also in Africa during that period. After the meeting Malcolm attempted to forge links with SNCC. In fact the increase in racial militancy among some SNCC workers resonated with Malcolm's views. In February 1965 Malcolm traveled to Selma to address demonstrators at the invitation of SNCC. But Malcolm was assassinated on February 21, 1965, shortly after his speech at Selma, and the conjoining of the revolutionary nationalist and militant protest tradition was temporarily halted.

SNCC was increasingly stymied by unresolved tensions and problems in the organization. In 1965 a split developed between James Forman, who wanted SNCC to become a more centralized organization, and Bob Moses, who wanted it to remain an informal community of organizers. As the split deepened, one group, called floaters, insisted on moral purity, deference to the masses, and anti-authoritarianism. A second group, called hardliners, wanted a more disciplined and pragmatic organization. The tension between these two positions remained unresolved, although Bob Moses resigned as chairperson of COFO, the SNCC umbrella organization in Mississippi.

The formation of the Lowndes County Freedom Organization (LCFO) in Alabama was an important element in the development of the Black Power position in SNCC. LCFO was formed as a consequence of repeated difficulties with the Democratic Party in voter registration efforts. LCFO was independent but not actually nationalist in ideology. The main purpose of the organization was to bring political power at the county level to the poor and excluded. LCFO, however, was not intended to be an all-Black organization, it is just that whites did not want to join. The attitudes of the SNCC workers were profoundly influenced by the core of militant and self-reliant residents who formed the backbone of LCFO. The symbol of LCFO, the Black Panther, was also significant, for as LCFO chairman John Hulett explained, the panther will back away when it is pressured, but when it is cornered it will come out fighting. "We felt we had been pushed back long enough and that it was time for Negroes to come out and take over."[23]

The Black Power position was further developed by the deliberation about the Atlanta Project. The Atlanta Project consisted of persons more nationalistic in orientation than any of the SNCC veterans at that time. The members of the Atlanta Project argued that SNCC would be stymied in its development as long as it included whites, since the mere presence of whites was intimidating for most Blacks. They argued that white radicals were always trying to escape reality by organizing in the Black community, but refused to take on the more demanding task of organizing whites. Most of the SNCC veterans, including Carmichael, disagreed with the position of the Atlanta Project, but the discussion of the paper submitted by the project allowed SNCC to clarify its position. The Atlanta separatists demanded that all white staff be forced to leave, but in the spring of 1966 only a few white staff members remained in SNCC. The SNCC veterans overwhelmingly rejected the demand, even those with strong nationalist tendencies. Willie Ricks, one of the leading nationalist-oriented militants, was skeptical of the Atlanta separatists: "We would always say, 'Mr. Say ain't the man, Mr. Do is the man.' They talked about nationalism and that kind of thing on the inside of SNCC, but they did not have an organization in the community."[24]

While Carmichael agreed with some of the ideas enunciated by the Atlanta separatists, he thought that their paper was an opportunistic power play, and did not support them. However, the debate had clarified his ideas and made him believe that it was time to challenge John Lewis as chair. Lewis's soft-spoken commitment to nonviolence, continuing participation in the planning of the White House Conference on Civil Rights, and relationship with the SCLC made him seem out of step with the mood of most of the other SNCC staff.[25]

Carmichael emerged the victor in the contest with Lewis, since his views were more representative of the majority of the SNCC staff. But Carmichael's subsequent announcement of the Black Power concept created a furor in the civil rights movement. At a meeting with the SCLC, SNCC, and CORE at Yazoo City, Mississippi, Floyd McKissick spoke out in favor of the Black Power concept. King attempted to convince Carmichael and others that they should not use a slogan that would "confuse our allies, isolate the Negro community and give many prejudiced whites, who might otherwise be ashamed of their anti-Negro feelings, a ready excuse for self-justification."[26] Carmichael and McKissick responded that there was nothing wrong with the concept of Black Power, since it was the same kind of group power that other ethnic groups had sought.

At this meeting it must have been clear to all that the civil rights era had come to an end. King symbolized the moral high ground that the civil rights movement had so long commanded. The utter desperation revealed in his remarks spoke volumes about Black people's dependence on liberal "allies" and the naked power relations behind it. Carmichael and

McKissick could do little more here than state the obvious. It was time for a reassessment of direction.

Through a logical extension of his moral vision, King ceased to be concerned about "allies" and moved in an essentially antisystemic direction until his assassination two years later. The Black Power movement then relocated from the South to the North, since it articulated the conscience of the urban Black subproletariat more clearly and viscerally than had been done since the death of Malcolm X in 1965.

Economic Transformation

In part the transition from civil rights to Black liberation (to use a phrase popularized of late by William Sales, Jr.) follows an internal logic based on the evolving experiences and understanding of the activists and militants.[27] But we are in danger of missing the whole picture if we focus only on the efforts of human subjects to effect social change. We must always also keep in view the evolving social structures of the capitalist world-economy.

Piore explained the social unrest of the late 1960s and early 1970s in terms of the manner in which the mass production economy met its demand for labor.[28] Because of the rigid wage structure in the United States, the demand for labor at a level lower than the prevailing wage was met by the use of labor reserves consisting of Blacks from the rural South, women, and youth.

The smooth operation of the labor market, and of the fixed-price allocative system as a whole, depended on the "willingness" of the above mentioned labor reserves to move in and out of the factory labor force on demand. Such conditions of employment were acceptable to these socially defined labor reserves so long as they saw themselves as outsiders to industrial society, and their industrial income as a means of establishing or defending a place in the extra-industrial world. According to this analysis, rural Blacks wanted money from factories to support rural life and to buy and enlarge farms at home. Women wanted factory money to pay off a mortgage and then return full-time to homemaking. Youth wanted money for college expenses.

These workers were not interested in obtaining factory skills or job security since this work was not central to their long-range plans, that is, they were not *of* the industrial working class subjectively, only temporarily there objectively. Proletarianization, thus, had a ways to go. As these workers became increasingly drawn into full participation in the industrial workforce, their expectations began to resemble those of the regular workforce. They wanted high-status, well-paying jobs, and would no longer tolerate the substandard conditions they endured when they did not view themselves as permanent members of the industrial labor force.

In this context, then, Piore viewed the social unrest of the 1960s as a parallel to the Roosevelt electoral coalition and the industrial union movement of the 1930s, rather than as a response to high levels of unemployment, welfare dependency, and other problems related to their status as poorly educated and ill-adapted rural southern migrants. Piore implied that we should differentiate between different components of the unrest. Further, although "riots" were one form that "protest" took, young Blacks also rebelled against the quality of existing employment opportunities. The press and the government, however, took special pains to suppress news about conflict and violence on the job for fear of jeopardizing efforts to expand further employment opportunities for Blacks and encouraging similar incidents elsewhere.[29]

Piore pointed out that numerous incidents of resistance on the job, although not reported by the press, were circulated orally in the Black communities by the Black workers employed in the plants, among employers, and in white working-class neighborhoods by white workers employed in plants with Blacks. This period of labor unrest and turmoil of the 1960s and 1970s is said to have signaled to employers that the Black labor force could no longer be relied on to fill secondary jobs. Piore contended that Black youth were known to be insulting and insubordinate, and had high turnover rates. Piore cited one story in which a Black worker shot his foreman. While this is not by and large information that is available from formal sources, Piore seemed to believe strongly enough in it to conclude that as a consequence of these activities, since the late 1960s employers in the secondary labor market have turned increasingly toward undocumented workers from the Caribbean and Latin America.[30]

I do not agree with Piore's assertion about the comparability of all the groups he listed under labor reserves, but his assessment of the 1960s and 1970s is onto something. I think that the African American working class has always been used as both a labor reserve, as Piore argued, and a source of low-wage labor.

This position of large segments of the African American working class stems in part from the fact that for some of them their capacity to labor is deemed to be nil, and others consciously render themselves redundant in the labor market by refusing to do "shitwork."[31] In contrast to the more traditional Marxian-inspired vision of the proletariat, I will argue that it is here where you find the most "class-conscious" workers, although this consciousness may not appear on the surface in class terms. It is here that we have the real analog to that social group that has nothing to lose but its chains, and a world to gain.

Malcolm X spoke very directly to this group. His capacity to articulate their feelings and clarify their thoughts endeared him to this social group and to others who shared to some extent or were sympathetic to their plight. It was their situation that most forcefully contradicted the triumphalism of the American century, called into question its moral authority and benevolence, and pointed out the limitations of its contribution to the public good.

The Rise of the Nation of Islam: The Revival of Black Nationalism

The modern civil rights movement captured center stage in the drama of race relations in the United States, and dominated civil society for much of the 1950s and 1960s. To the extent that it appealed to white Americans on the basis of the American dream, so long as it sought to complete the great American Revolution of 1776, it was extremely flattering. But the civil rights movement was not the only show in town. Not all Black people held to these integrationist dreams.

The masses of Black people of the urban North did not suffer from lack of citizenship rights, yet many of them were in more difficult straits than their Southern brothers and sisters who labored under the yoke of Jim Crow racism. For them there was no veil of segregation that concealed from them the brutality and callousness of the white man's world. For these sons and daughters of Black America the American dream was a fraud, a nightmare. American democracy applied only to whites, regardless of the formal rights to which one was entitled.

It is from this population that the troops of resurgent Black nationalist movements were drawn. In the 1950s currents of Black life in these ghettoized communities gave rise to a revival of Black nationalist consciousness among the population, and various organizations surged to the fore to articulate and embody these feelings.

The Nation of Islam was by far the largest of the Black nationalist organizations that flourished during this period. It had been in existence since the 1930s, but in the mid-1950s, with the help of a dynamic and popular young minister named Malcolm X, it grew into a powerful organization that challenged the civil rights movement for the allegiance of urban Blacks in the North.

In 1959 the award-winning Black author and television commentator Louis Lomax attempted to do a story on the street corner nationalists he had encountered while walking in Harlem one day. They told him that he really should try to see Minister Malcolm X of the Nation of Islam. Lomax approached Mike Wallace about doing a series of five-minute specials on the Nation. These reports ultimately expanded into an hour long documentary called *The Hate That Hate Produced*. Elijah Muhammad had not wanted to do the show, but was persuaded by Malcolm X that it would be beneficial to the Nation of Islam. Whites were shocked that some Black people felt so strongly and disliked their world so intensely.

The documentary opened with a scene from a morality play entitled *The Trial*. In this play the rest of the world places the white man on trial for his crimes against Black people. The prosecutor charges the white man with being the greatest liar on earth, the greatest drunkard on earth, the greatest murderer on earth, the greatest robber on earth, and more, in a seemingly endless list of charges. The jury finds the white man guilty and sentences him to death.

Then Mike Wallace appeared on the screen, explaining that the Nation of Islam was a Negro group that called itself Muslim but was disavowed by orthodox Muslims. However, Wallace continued, it had fifty temples and 250,000 members around the country. The Nation of Islam was the largest of the Black supremacist groups, Wallace maintained, yet incredibly, whites knew almost nothing about them. Wallace wanted to alarm white America. He emphasized the Nation's hatred of whites, their discipline, and their influence in the Black community. He then cut to Louis Lomax, who interviewed the Honorable Elijah Muhammad and then Minister Malcolm X.[32]

The Nation of Islam had only four hundred members when Malcolm Little joined in 1952. With Malcolm's help the Nation had grown to some forty thousand members (according to C. Eric Lincoln), and many more sympathizers. Membership is estimated to have doubled as a result of the broadcast.

Soldiers of the Nation of Islam became familiar fixtures on the streets of Black inner cities across the United States. There were hundreds of members of the Fruit of Islam (FOI) on the streets of all the largest cities. These were often the baddest, cleanest brothers to be found. The FOI, of course, attracted significant police attention. But FOI members were exceptional in their discipline and adhered stringently to the admonition to always obey the law but defend themselves when attacked.

Despite the law-abiding posture of the FOI, there were inevitably clashes with the police. In 1957 in Harlem a member of the NOI, Hinton Johnson, attempted to stop police officers from beating another Black man, and the police turned on him. A fellow Muslim quickly alerted Malcolm X and the Fruit of Islam of Temple Number 7 about the incident. Malcolm X went to the police station to inquire about the whereabouts and condition of Hinton Johnson, while hundreds of FOI and other Muslims gathered outside the police station in rank formation.

The police initially took a hostile attitude toward Malcolm X's inquiries, but upon seeing the crowd assembled outside, allowed him to see Hinton Johnson and then acceded to his demand that Johnson receive medical attention immediately. While Malcolm was getting assurance that Johnson was being cared for properly, a police official attempted to dismiss the crowd. No one moved. Only when they were assured that Johnson was receiving the proper attention did Malcolm X wave his hand and the Muslims quietly slipped away. As they walked away, an editor of the *Amsterdam News* overheard the white police captain say, "No man should have that much power." Of course he is believed to have meant "no Black man." This incident has become a folk legend in Harlem. It gave the Black Muslims a status in Harlem like no other organization. From this time on, mused Robert Mangum, a deputy commissioner of the NYPD, police and political figures realized that they had a significant force to deal with.[33]

The Nation of Islam provided Black people with a sense of pride not seen since the heyday of the Garvey movement. The ongoing presence of the Fruit of Islam on the streets of large cities across the United States increasingly attracted the attention of law enforcement officers. Both the police and the powerful elites to whom they were most accountable were increasingly nervous about the presence of a disciplined paramilitary force, entirely alienated from their world. Observers believe that both the elite and the police felt that the Black Muslims had to be tamed.

In the spring of 1962 police attacked an NOI temple in Los Angeles; the attack resulted in the shooting death of an unarmed member of the temple named Ronald Stokes. Several other members of the temple were injured by shooting and beating. Stokes had been unarmed but the police officer argued that he moved in a menacing way. It took an all-white grand jury all of twenty-three minutes to rule that Stokes's death was justifiable homicide.

Stokes had been a protégé of Malcolm in Boston, and Malcolm traveled to Los Angeles to deal both with Stokes's funeral and the very tense situation there. At a press conference after the funeral Malcolm had accused the police of committing a "Gestapo type atrocity, a crime against any society which professes to be civilized, religious and God-fearing." He waited for instructions from Chicago to avenge their dead. However, Elijah Muhammad counseled nonviolence, arguing that Allah would bring the killers to justice. Later Elijah Muhammad argued that Malcolm himself was responsible for Stokes's death.[34]

This was of course an ongoing struggle between Mr. Muhammad and Malcolm, an issue we will analyze in more detail as we turn our attention to the overall significance of Malcolm X for the Black liberation movement. The differences between Malcolm X and Elijah Muhammad highlight the rise of a specifically revolutionary nationalism rooted in the New Negro movement of an earlier period, the popular front of the 1930s, the labor radicalism of the 1930s and 1940s, and the oppositional culture of African American youth during the 1940s.

Malcolm attempted to be philosophical about his differences with the Honorable Elijah Muhammad. Mr. Muhammad, he argued, has been with Allah, so he has the patience to say that Allah will take care of our enemies. But those of us who are younger, Malcolm continued, do not have so much patience. We need to see some action.

The differences persisted. Malcolm was increasingly in conflict with various members of the Chicago leadership, especially John Ali, the national secretary of the NOI. In addition to Ali, Raymond Sharrieff, supreme commander of the Fruit of Islam, Herbert Muhammad, and Elijah Muhammad, Jr., were hostile toward Malcolm. Mr. Muhammad's youngest sons, Wallace and Akbar, remained friendly toward Malcolm.

After the attack on the Los Angeles mosque and the murder of Ronald Stokes, Malcolm began to talk less about Allah's divine retribution on the white devil and more about obtaining justice through their own efforts, through their impact on public opinion, through their impact on societal institutions. Yusef Shah (Captain Joseph) told Strickland that during this period Malcolm had changed from religious talk to nationalistic talk. He told Malcolm that his new focus did not give him chills like the old truths he had told.[35]

A few months after the police murder of Ronald Stokes, Malcolm made his monthly visit to Chicago to deliver funds from Mosque Number 7. He encountered two of Mr. Muhammad's former secretaries, who implored the Messenger to give them money to support their children. He had been hearing rumors about Elijah Muhammad's sexual indiscretions for a number of years but discounted them. He confirmed the story with Wallace Muhammad. Malcolm was shocked, but he was discreet with the Messenger. He attempted to do damage control by discussing how this might be handled with some of the ministers on the East Coast, including Louis X (now Farrakhan) and Captain Joseph (later Yusef Shah). They already knew about it. The word got back to the Honorable Elijah Muhammad that Malcolm was laying the grounds for attacking his leadership. Malcolm confronted Mr. Muhammad, but was told that he was no different from other prophets who engaged in these kinds of activities.

From this time on Malcolm began to increasingly lose faith in Mr. Muhammad's moral and spiritual leadership. He began to focus more on the political and economic plight of the African American population. In addition, he was further alienated from some NOI ministers and the Chicago leadership. He turned increasingly toward the civil rights movement.

Nineteen days after the August 1963 March on Washington, a bomb exploded in the Sixteenth Street Baptist Church in Birmingham, killing four young girls. Many members of the NOI were distraught that the NOI could not or would not do anything to defend Black people from this type of brutalization. Malcolm noted that President John F. Kennedy did nothing about the Birmingham situation until Black people rose up in revolt.

At the same time, according to Yusef Shah, there were increasing rumblings of dissatisfaction and opposition to Malcolm within the Chicago leadership. When Malcolm made the "chickens coming home to roost" statement about President Kennedy's assassination, John Ali was in the audience. Malcolm was silenced for ninety days.

During the suspension, the FBI fed stories to the press to try to deepen the rift between Malcolm and the Chicago leadership of the NOI. Malcolm told John Henrik Clarke that his enemies in the Chicago leadership were taking money from funds to be used for the NOI and buying expensive clothes and fancy cars. Clarke argued that if Malcolm took over the leadership of the NOI after Mr. Muhammad's death, he would throw the money changers out of the temple. That is why they wanted to get rid of him before Mr. Muhammad died. They could use Mr. Muhammad as a powerful ally and as a shield against Malcolm.[36]

On March 8, 1964, Malcolm announced his resignation from the Nation of Islam. Articles in *Muhammad Speaks* denounced Malcolm as the chief hypocrite and said that he was worthy of death. Wallace Muhammad told Strickland that it occurred to him that they were trying to get Malcolm killed.

When the NOI took Malcolm to court to evict him from his house, legally owned by the Nation of Islam but informally given to Malcolm by Elijah Muhammad, Malcolm revealed publicly that Mr. Muhammad had fathered eight children by six teenage girls who had worked for him as secretaries.

While the conflict between Malcolm X and the Nation of Islam was intensifying, a crisis in the civil rights movement was drawing Malcolm closer to the more radical elements who were emerging as a result of that crisis. Indeed, William Sales argues that Malcolm's increasingly radical and independent leadership developed largely as a product of the crisis in the civil rights movement and the forces that were pushing him out of the Nation of Islam.[37]

In 1963 the Birmingham working class had exploded in response to the brutalization of civil rights workers in the SCLC and the NAACP. The Revolutionary Action Movement (RAM) was formed, one of the first of the explicitly revolutionary organizations of that period. At some point it was said that Malcolm became a nonpublic member of RAM. During this period Robert Williams, president of an NAACP branch in Monroe, North Carolina, took up arms to defend himself against violent attacks by the Ku Klux Klan. The Deacons for Defense organized to protect nonviolent protesters in Louisiana. When Malcolm visited the radicals in the Detroit-Cleveland area, he was constantly pushed to clarify and deepen his positions.

In addition, Malcolm's contacts with revolutionaries in Africa and the Middle East intensified his anti-imperialist stance and moved him in-

creasingly in an anticapitalist direction. Louis Lomax argued quite forcefully that people's focus on Malcolm's changed attitude toward whites
cause them to miss the much more important and consequential issue of
his new understanding of capitalism, imperialism, and the worldwide
struggle of oppressed peoples and classes for freedom, justice, equality,
and socialism.[38] Malcolm's increasing ideological sophistication about
the nature of white world supremacy, imperialism, and capitalism; his development of a dense network of ties to revolutionary states and movements in Africa, Asia, and Latin America; and his skills as a teacher, re-
cruiter, and speaker brought him increasingly into the crossfire of what
John Henrik Clarke calls that "invisible, international cartel of power
and finance which deposes presidents and prime ministers, dissolves par-
liaments, if they refuse to do their bidding."[39]

Lomax argued that Malcolm was clearly supported by the Ben Bella-
Nkrumah axis, which arranged for his eighteen-week stay in Africa.[40]
They also arranged for Malcolm to be an observer at the meeting of the
Organization of African Unity (OAU). Malcolm's task was to rally U.S.
Blacks against CIA antigovernment activity in Algeria and Ghana.
Lomax held that there is no doubt that Malcolm X was involved in in-
ternational intrigue in what he believed to be the best interest of the
American Black man.[41] Nearly thirty years later Brenda Gayle Plummer
made a strikingly similar argument.[42] Indeed, Ben Bella had invited Malcolm to be a keynote speaker along with Che Guevara at an international
conference of liberation movements to begin on February 28, 1965, a
week after Malcolm was assassinated.[43]

Malcolm was clearly moving in the direction of the Black united front
strategy. Later Martin Luther King indicated support for Malcolm's strategy of taking the United States before the United Nations because of its
racist actions toward its Black citizens. According to Ossie Davis, Juanita
Portier set up a meeting in January 1965 in which Malcolm met with
leaders of the civil rights movement to establish a common platform.[44]
The meeting was attended by A. Philip Randolph, Dorothy Height, Whitney Young, and several others. King could not attend, but he sent a representative. They spent the day discussing Malcolm's philosophy, his mistakes, and how he could become a part of the civil rights movement.

Malcolm was invited to speak at a meeting in Selma, Alabama, on February 4, 1965. At this meeting he argued that the nation should listen to
Martin Luther King, because if King stumbled, there was another faction
in the wings, waiting to do things another way. Jack Newfield said that

Malcolm met with Coretta Scott King and Andy Young at that meeting. The following week, according to Newfield, King sent his lawyer, Clarence Jones, to meet with Malcolm X and work out a common agenda. They agreed to disagree about self-defense, but agreed generally that Malcolm would work in the northern cities and King would continue to work in the South. Newfield noted that the coming together of these two leaders must have been J. Edgar Hoover's worst nightmare.[45]

In the meantime NOI leaders had created a climate of fierce antagonism toward Malcolm, who they now branded as the chief hypocrite. According to Clarke, Louis X (now Farrakhan) and the FOI contributed to Mr. Muhammad's increasing suspicions of Malcolm. Benjamin Karim (formerly Goodman) argued that the Boston mosque, headed by Louis X, was actually plotting against Malcolm's life.[46] This does not in and of itself implicate Farrakhan, since the Boston FOI chief, Clarence X Gill, took orders directly from Raymond Sharrieff and Elijah Muhammad, Jr., the FOI commanders in Chicago. However, FBI files show that two weeks after Malcolm resigned from the NOI, Elijah Muhammad told Farrakhan in a telephone call that hypocrites like Malcolm deserve to have their heads cut off.[47]

Karim claimed that Captain Joseph, under direct orders from Sharrieff and John Ali, constantly urged Mosque Number 7 officials to speak out against Malcolm X during the time that he was on suspension. During this period, Karim was told that Captain Joseph instructed Brother Luqman to wire a bomb to Malcolm's car. Brother Luqman reported this plot to Malcolm and quit the NOI. It was at this time that Karim brought these inappropriate activities to the attention officials of Mosque Number 7, and took his leave of the NOI to join Malcolm.

In June 1964 Leon Ameer was at a meeting of the Fruit of Islam when Elijah Muhammad, Jr., castigated Captain Joseph for failing to kill Malcolm. Elijah Muhammad, Jr., said that Malcolm's tongue should be cut out and sent to him. He would stamp it approved and forward it to the Messenger.[48] Leon Ameer also related how Clarence X Gill from the Boston mosque and the FOI captain from Springfield approached him about getting a silencer to use on Malcolm.

Although Malcolm was out of the country for more than half of his last year, the NOI made several attempts on his life. Elijah Muhammad is said to have directly ordered the firebombing of Malcolm's house, although NOI officials and police claimed that Malcolm must have firebombed his own house in order to get publicity. Before he died in 1993,

Yusef Shah (Captain Joseph) admitted that he participated in the fire-bombing of Malcolm's house.[49]

Malcolm's assassins finally caught up with him on February 21, 1965, at a regular meeting of the Organization of Afro-American Unity (OAAU) at the Audubon Ballroom. When Malcolm began his opening greeting with the customary "Asalaam-Alaikam," a man in the audience yelled out, "Get your hand out of my pocket, Nigga!" As Brother Malcolm attempted to calm the dispute, security moved toward the fracas. Everything happened very fast. One man threw a smokebomb; three men in the front row started shooting. The first assailant unloaded two shotgun blasts into Malcolm's chest. The second and third gunmen fired their pistols into his fallen body.

Talmadge Hayer was caught at the scene by Malcolm's followers. But there is a great deal of controversy over who his coconspirators were. Norman 3X Butler and Thomas 15X Johnson, known FOI enforcers at Mosque Number 7, were later arrested by the NYPD. Although Hayer confessed and exonerated Butler and Johnson, they were found guilty, since he refused to name the people who were his actual coconspirators. In 1978, three years after the death of Elijah Muhammad, Hayer changed his mind and named his coconspirators. He retained William Kunstler to arrange a new trial for him. The request for a new trial was refused on the grounds that Hayer's story was not substantially different from the one he told at the original trial. Yet Hayer's new affidavit contained minute details of the assassination and the names and addresses of the co-conspirators. Hayer identified members of the Newark Mosque as his co-conspirators: Ben Thomas, assistant secretary of the Newark mosque, was the man who recruited Hayer. William Bradley, a known stickup man, brandished the shotgun during the assassination. Wilbur McKinley and Leon Davis were the remaining members of the assassination team named by Hayer.[50]

More than likely the lack of interest in pursuing justice in this case is related to attempts to cover up the role of federal and local law enforcement authorities in this matter. Numerous Malcolm X scholars have argued that the FBI played a role in "developing" the antagonism between Malcolm X and the Chicago leadership of the NOI. Indeed, the FBI files show that the Chicago office bragged about the success of this operation.

William Sales argues that there may be a CIA connection as well. He points out that Benjamin Read of the State Department asked the CIA's Clandestine Services Division to take covert action against Malcolm X to penetrate his foreign connections before his U.N. petition became a crisis for the Johnson administration. Read indicated that such action might damage the image of the United States as a cultural and racial melting pot.[51]

The State Department worried that Malcolm's contacts among third world leaders and at the United Nations might pay dividends for his U.N. strategy. Especially troublesome would be the radical Casablanca states that Malcolm was closest to. Malcolm was friends with Kwame Nkrumah of Ghana and with Alex Quaison-Stuckey, Ghana's ambassador to the United Nations, who was about to be elected president of the U.N. General Assembly.[52]

The State Department took up the matter with President Johnson, who asked J. Edgar Hoover for more information on Malcolm X. Hoover asked Burke Marshall of the Justice Department's Civil Rights Division to investigate Malcolm's foreign ties and financial resources. When Marshall was not able to turn up anything, Read again asked the CIA to take covert action against Malcolm X. While there is no record that the CIA took any action, FBI documents indicate that the FBI's Newark field office reported attempts to develop new assets in the Newark mosque in the months just before Malcolm's assassination. The Newark mosque was known as a center for enforcers. As we saw above, Talmadge Hayer and his team of assassins were all from the Newark mosque.

Baba Zak Kondo argues that two forces, the U.S. government and the Nation of Islam, were primarily responsible for the assassination of Malcolm X. Kondo places five Chicago officials at the center of the conspiracy: Elijah Muhammad, Raymond Sharrieff, Elijah Muhammad, Jr., John Ali, and Herbert Muhammad.[53] There were in addition a number of secondary assassination teams. Other major actors in this drama included Minister Louis X (Farrakhan), Clarence X Gill of the Boston FOI, and Captain Joseph of the New York FOI.[54]

But why did the FBI and the CIA side with the Chicago establishment and its main supporters against Malcolm X? Was there something especially significant about Malcolm X as a person or a social type that helps us understand the transformations of that period, which fundamentally and profoundly deepened the radicalism of the forces arrayed for Black liberation and joined them with the larger forces seeking human emancipation on a world scale?

The Significance of Malcolm X

Malcolm's autobiography is viewed by friends and antagonists as a story of an individual's triumph over a life of poverty and spiritual decadence. He cited Elijah Muhamad's revelations as the catalyst for his evolution from dope peddler, pimp, and burglar, and of course that is factually accurate, but there was more.

Malcolm X's biographers have too often focused almost exclusively on the personal and organizational experiences thought to have been influential in his emergence as a historical figure. I will argue that to understand the significance of Malcolm X we must also consider the social forces operative at the time that he came to maturity, the broad historical forces that impacted him, and the traditions from which he learned. The major exception to this overall tendency is of course William Sales, Jr., *From Civil Rights to Black Liberation: Malcolm X and the Organization of Afro-American Unity.* Robin D. G. Kelley's briefer treatment of Malcolm X in *Race Rebels: Culture, Politics, and the Black Working Class* also takes a broader view of the development of Malcolm X as one of the most important organic intellectuals in the twentieth century.[55] Louis De-Caro's *On the Side of My People: A Religious Life of Malcolm X* is also an important contribution to our understanding of the life and meaning of Malcolm X.

Robin Kelley takes exception with Malcolm's depiction of his lifestyle prior to his acceptance of Islam. In *The Autobiography* Malcolm uses a "narrative of degradation" as a rhetorical device to highlight the extreme contrast between his early life and his later years as a Muslim minister. Kelley argues, however, that the Black youth culture of the war years was not simply an agglomeration of fads (the Lindy hop, the zoot suit, the conk) but a central component of wartime social, political, economic, and ideological transformations.[56] Thus in contrast to Malcolm's own assertion, Kelley argues that Malcolm's participation in the underground wartime subculture was not a detour on the way to political consciousness, but an essential element in his radicalization.

According to Kelley, the language and culture of zoot suiters represented a subversive refusal to be subservient. The language was fast-paced and improvisational, in sharp contrast to the slow, stuttering style of the Sambo. Zoot suiters mocked existing styles, and pointedly used the term "man" in addressing each other in a world where a Black man was commonly referred to as "boy." After the War Production Board forbade the sale and distribution of zoot suits in March 1942 because of war rationing, zoot suiters were viewed as clearly un-American. Zoot suiters were doubly un-American in their disproportionate presence among those seeking to avoid the draft. Cosgrave argues that the zoot suit riots of the summer of 1943 had a profound impact on a whole generation of socially disadvantaged youth, including Cesar Chavez and Malcolm Little.[57]

Yet dressing up was also a means of collapsing distinctions between themselves and higher-class people and of becoming something other than just low-wage, dirty workers. The dance halls were sites of leisure and pleasure, in sharp contrast to the back-breaking work that most were required to do. While hustling may be viewed as an activity on the margins of the dominant capitalist economy, an activity that requires a capitalistic mentality, Kelley argues that hustlers held an antiwork, anti-accumulation mentality. Hustling was a means of avoiding wage work and negotiating status through the purchase of prestigious commodities.[58]

There was a spirit of mutuality in the hustlers' inner circle, but outsiders were subject to mistreatment and misuse. Particularly subject to mistreatment and exploitation were women. To the extent that the social psychology of these networks was reproduced in the proletarian nationalist movements led by this stratum, this was one of the major weaknesses of the movements. In the 1950s the constituency represented by this social stratum was to expand with the continuing migration of southern Blacks to the cities. It is this group that provided the social base for the emergence of a massive nationalist thrust among African Americans in the post–World War II period. There has been too little attention devoted to this group.

But we would be amiss if we attribute the essential character of this group just to economic marginalization. These young people grew up in the Afro-Christian cultures of the early twentieth century. During slavery and Reconstruction the churches were centers of resistance to slavery and racial oppression. But during the repressive era that followed radical Reconstruction the churches turned inward, their culture grew more conservative, and they often failed to meet the needs of young Black males, who in turn defected from the churches in droves. The second generation of Black intellectuals, those associated with the New Negro, often tended to identify with these disaffected youth and themselves strayed from the church. But the cultural impact of Afro-Christianity remained a moral anchor in Black communities, and often influenced the conscience and values of those who did not participate in the life of the church because of the lure of the streets.

Louis DeCaro does an excellent job of reconstructing the religious life of Malcolm X as a key to his effectiveness and his commitment to the Black liberation movement.[59] DeCaro points out that we cannot understand Malcolm without understanding his family, particularly their religious background. The Littles were ecumenical in their religious beliefs. They were anything but the Black Christian stereotype that Malcolm imposes on them in his autobiography. Louise Little was particularly ecumenical in her religious beliefs, and had had some exposure to Islam. Malcolm's father, Earl Little, constantly preached the gospel of Garvey's Black nationalism from the pulpit, but he was not a Baptist preacher.

Thus Malcolm grew up in a climate that was deeply religious, but flexible. This was an all-important element in opening him up to experiences that would make such a dramatic change in his life. This is why Malcolm's deep appreciation for education and knowledge, dampened by Ostrowski, could be so dramatically rekindled by his prison mentor Bimbi (John Elton Bembry).

DeCaro argues that Malcolm and the Nation of Islam consciously sought to Christianize and whitenize all of Malcolm's sins prior to his rehabilitation by Elijah Muhammad, the Messenger of Allah. But Malcolm conked his hair not because he wanted to be white, but because he identified with the Black vanguard of the urban underworld and the stylish and hip masculinity of Black entertainers.[60]

Malcolm's Black nationalism did not come entirely from the honorable Elijah Muhammad, but owed much to the Garveyite heritage bequeathed to him by Earl and Louise Little. His friends from the streets of Harlem recall incidents when Malcolm took political positions or intervened in situations to help people on the basis of a sense of racial unity. While in prison Malcolm followed Paul Robeson's activities through the newspapers and radio. Karl Evanzz argues that aside from Elijah Muhammad, Robeson was Malcolm's only living hero.[61]

On the day before Malcolm's letter to President Truman, Robeson had vigorously protested Truman's decision to send U.S. troops to Korea and urged Blacks to resist being drawn into the conflict. Robeson argued that today it's Korea, tomorrow its Africa. Black people's fight for freedom is right here in the United States. Malcolm's letter to Truman reflected these very same sentiments.

Thus Robeson, closely linked to the communist world in the public mind, was one of Malcolm's heroes, despite his well-known differences with Garvey's separatist outlook. Robeson argued that unless the white man was kicked out of Africa and Asia, the nonwhite races would end up like the "decadent Westernized Negroes," bereft of their culture and subjugated to a self-inflicted form of mental slavery.[62]

Malcolm's efforts to internationalize the struggle for freedom, justice, and equality for Black people was at odds with Elijah Muhammad's antipathy for foreigners and his focus on the Lost-Found Nation in the wilderness of North America. The effort to make the struggle for civil rights a struggle for human rights to be adjudicated in the World Court got Malcolm in trouble with the U.S. government as it did Garvey and Robeson, not to mention Du Bois and King. These views cannot be attributed to Elijah Muhammad; they start from Malcolm's pre-Muslim period. But they also to some extent derive from his period on the streets, when he listened and learned while he hustled.

John Henrik Clarke has provided the most incisive, if brief, commentary on the movements of this period.[63] Harlem had long been the incubator of Black nationalism in the United States, but a major characteristic of the collective experience of these groups was the splintering of Black nationalist efforts by too many groups with conflicting programs. Among the groups Clarke counted in Harlem were the Nation of Islam; the Muslim Brotherhood; the United African Nationalist Movement, founded in 1948 by James Lawson; the Universal African Nationalists, led by Benjamin Gibbons, formed after the breakup of the UNIA; the Cultural Association of Women of African Heritage, headed by Abby Lincoln; the African Nationalist Pioneer Movement, led by Carlos Cooks, the most influential of the former followers of Marcus Garvey; United Sons and Daughters of Africa; the Garvey Club; and the First Africa Corps. New groups catalogued by Clarke included the Liberation Committee for Africa, the On Guard Committee for Freedom, and the Provisional Committee for a Free Africa.

Clarke thought it quite significant that unlike the middle-class–led African nationalist movements, the Afro-American nationalist movements were proletarian-led. He pointed out that there was little participation of the Negro leadership class in these movements. Yet these proletarians, he noted, learned a great lesson that still eluded the Negro leadership class, namely, the value of history and culture in stimulating the spiritual rebirth of a people.

With perhaps more sensitivity to the surging integrationist civil rights movement than he might muster today, Clarke argued that this kind of spiritual rebirth was absolutely necessary in order for African Americans to be able to live together optimally with other people. He did not think that the "smug middle class" leadership of the NAACP and the National Urban League could begin to comprehend the need for such a spiritual rebirth, and thus could in no way provide leadership to the masses of the urban Black proletarians outside the southern United States. No people are really free, Clarke contended, until they become the instruments of their own liberation. This is the only hope not only for Afro-Americans, but for people of African descent everywhere. Thus the issue of self-determination not only affected the internal cohesion of Black people, but also was the foundation upon which they built mutually respectful relations with others.

The Nation of Islam, though the largest, was one of many groups that existed in an atmosphere of debate and contention. Malcolm X was at the forefront of these debates, and thus grew in political understanding and scope as a consequence.

William Sales, Jr., has provided perhaps the most incisive overall assessment of the role of Malcolm X in the Black liberation movement. First of all he identifies the key ideological role Malcolm X played in the development of the Black liberation movement in the 1950s and 1960s. Sales does not regard Malcolm's leadership as one based on charisma or mystical allure. Sales argues persuasively—and, I believe, correctly—that the secret of Malcolm X's leadership was that he was able to give back to people in a highly refined and clarified form ideas and insights that were rooted in their *own* experiences. Malcolm X was not a man on a pedestal who bedazzled people with oratorical brilliance and held the status of a remote quasi-deity. Malcolm X was most of all a man of the people, a man who deeply and profoundly loved his people, a man who was constantly in the process of discovering just who his people were. Malcolm X did not lead from on high, but was able to obtain and sum up the sense and wisdom of the people on the basis of very personal and intimate relationships that he established with ordinary people in one-on-one encounters.

Sales argues that Malcolm's ideas also reflect the ongoing street debates characteristic of Harlem political and social life. These debates took place around and about Africa Square (125th Street and Adam Clayton Powell Boulevard) with important historical figures such as Carlos

Cooks, Eddie "Pork Chop" Davis, Elombe Brath, Ahmed Basheer, and George Reed. Malcolm was also influenced by Harlem-based intellectuals such as John Henrik Clarke, Sylvester Leeks, and John Oliver Killens.[64] Outside Harlem Malcolm was influenced by the radical nationalists in the Cleveland-Detroit area and by Max Stanford (now Muhammad Ahmed), then of the Revolutionary Action Movement (RAM). Later Malcolm X, who had long been influenced by the spirit of Bandung, of Afro-Asian solidarity, came under the influence of African revolutionaries and some heads of progressive African movements that had achieved state power.

According to Sales, the significance of the Nation of Islam was that it articulated a mission of racial redemption similar in many ways to that of the Garvey movement of the 1920s. The Nation of Islam sought to rehabilitate Black people from self-hatred and their corresponding antisocial behavior; this approach was also similar to the strategy of Booker T. Washington. Like Washington they did not engage in agitation, but emphasized "doing for self." The Black Muslims under Elijah Muhammad did not engage in social protest; Allah would deliver the Lost-Found Nation from the "white devils."

Malcolm's approach was in general much more secular than the theocracy under Elijah Muhammad, and increasingly so over the years. Elijah Muhammad himself admonished the ministerial body: "I will never get any where with people like you. All you do is teach the same old thing we taught in the thirties. . . . Look at this young man; . . . he's in modern times, he knows how to help me."[65] While Malcolm's views coexisted with Mr. Muhammad's views for a time, they clashed increasingly as the Nation of Islam attained more and more prominence.

Malcolm X related the rising nationalist consciousness of the Black urban populace to the spirit of Bandung, which occasioned the rise of independence movements and nations in the third world, the countries primarily of Africa, Asia, and Latin America. Thus while Malcolm remained faithful to Elijah Muhammad's theology up through 1962, according to Sales, he exploited the political implications by relating the situation in the United States to the larger world of dark humankind.

Despite the overall conservatism of the Nation of Islam's theology, it fundamentally challenged the basic tenets of white world supremacy, which were not challenged by liberal integrationism (and this is why, parenthetically, Minister Louis Farrakhan today enjoys such popularity). In this task the Nation of Islam was the major organization of this period, but the Black nationalist tradition was carried forward more faithfully if less effectively by a number of other much smaller nationalist organizations, which criticized the Black Muslim program because it had no role for Africa and because it advocated a political policy of nonengagement. At the same time Sunni Muslims in the Black community questioned the authenticity of the Nation of Islam's Muslim credentials. The tough talk of the Nation of Islam carried it only so far. The people of the Black inner cities wanted to see and be involved in some action. Malcolm came to identify more and more with the critics of the Nation of Islam.

While the Nation of Islam started as an organization with few members scattered over several cities, it grew in the early 1960s to an organization with two hundred temples with at least fifty thousand members and many times that many sympathizers in nearly every large city in the United States with a significant Black population. By the early 1960s the organization had come to be a significant power in most Black communities, with a relatively strong financial base. This power and financial strength often supported an affluent lifestyle for the national leadership in Chicago and many of its ministers.[66]

Precisely because of the success of the Nation of Islam, those leaders who received the material benefits and perks sought to tone down the militancy of the organization. Increased scrutiny by the U.S. government and its police agencies threatened a stratum of the organization that now had quite a bit more to lose than its chains. NOI leaders now objected to Malcolm's injection of Black nationalism into the Black Muslim movement, and argued that they preferred to keep the organization religious in nature.

Here again we must keep our eye on the larger picture, for as Sales argues, and as Elombe Brath and others have stated on a number of occasions, Malcolm X was not the original Black nationalist thinker who brought this ideology to the Black Muslim movement. He learned Black nationalism from the long-standing nationalist tradition of Harlem. In this sense it was the people who lived this tradition who brought it to the Black Muslim movement. Malcolm's contribution, as Sales argues, was to clarify and refine these ideas, which were based on Black people's historical experience and common culture.

Malcolm X articulated this Black nationalist tradition into a new common sense, the logic of which resonated deeply with the sons and daughters of Afro-America. Whereas the logic of the integration of Black people into American society led Black people to view themselves as an isolated minority dependent on the goodwill of their oppressors, Malcolm was able to change Black people's frame of reference. For Malcolm it was clear that the U.S. stage was a white stage. If one looked at the plight of African Americans as a problem of human rights and not civil rights, then one moved to the world stage, where Blacks were a part of the dark majority of humankind. And while the white world had been hegemonic for what the longer view reveals as a short time, the pendulum was clearly on the swing back. Many now felt that just beyond the horizon was the end of white world supremacy, as the Afro-Asian world began to challenge this hegemony directly.

Malcolm argued not for an actual physical return to Africa but for a cultural identification with Africa. This identification was not for Malcolm an end in itself, but a means whereby African Americans could reclaim their psyches and their self-respect, and thus be better able to fight within the belly of the beast.

The assumption implicit in locating African Americans in the belly of the beast is that the struggle for Black liberation is part of a worldwide struggle against Western imperialism, a worldwide system of exploitation and oppression overseen and protected for the most part by the United States of America. Defining the struggle in terms of the world scale meant that the concept of Black nationalism continued to have some utility for the political self-definition of Malcolm X and the OAAU, but it was limited in its ability to define relationships with genuine revolutionaries who were not Black, as was implied in the discussion Malcolm had with the Algerian ambassador to Ghana (below).

Malcolm X and Elijah Muhammad had profound differences in strategy. Muhammad preached that Allah would deliver the Lost-Found Nation in the wilderness of North America, and that Muslims should not involve themselves in the white devils' political institutions. Malcolm argued on the other hand for a policy of engagement in the social and political struggles of the masses of Black people. These views coexisted for a time, but clashed as the Muslims achieved more and more prominence.

By the 1960s the Nation of Islam had come into a measure of visibility, wealth, and power, based largely on Malcolm's ability to attract converts, gain widespread publicity in the media, and inspire admiration and respect among Black people at large. But these successes, according to Goldman, could also be seen as his undoing.

The Kingdom of Allah had passed into that condition identified by the sociologist Max Weber as the routinization of charisma—a time when the fires cool, when commitment becomes vested interest and the conservatism of the bureaucracy gradually supplants the passion of the street. The nation in the 1960s had got clotted at the top with men who, as one well-informed outsider put it, had grown "fat and comfortable" in the service of Allah— "and when you become comfortable . . . there is no point in making a big noise."[67]

The men at the top of the Black Muslim hierarchy included a large number of yes men and opportunists, more interested in the perks of leadership than in the cause to which they were all committed. According to Goldman, Malcolm complained that "Those guys are on Easy Street." Revenue collections and newspaper sales became the central preoccupation of many temples. There were stories of a special FOI squad that roughed up those who did not pay their dues or who were lagging in their sales of *Muhammad Speaks*. These men increasingly resented Malcolm's preeminence in the public eye, and feared the direction that Malcolm might take the Nation if he were to ascend to the top leadership after Elijah Muhammad's death.

Although he argued for engagement in the struggle of the masses of Black people, Malcolm was not interested in the civil rights movement as it was, nor at all in liberal integrationism. Civil rights were something the United States could grant or withhold. The movement had to be recast as a struggle for human rights, which were the inalienable rights of all people, everywhere. Malcolm argued,

When you are begging for civil rights you are putting it in Uncle Sam's lap. You're taking it to Uncle Sam's courts. You're taking the criminal to the criminal—asking the criminal to solve the crime. Whereas when you are attacking this thing at the level of human rights, you can take it to the United Nations. You can take Uncle Sam, the one who's really guilty, to the U.N. and accuse him or charge him with violating the UN Charter on Human Rights.[68]

Malcolm was intrigued by the arithmetic of the United Nations, in which the nations of Africa, Asia, and Central and South America held a numerical majority, but he understood the power of the Yankee dollar within that body. His objective was to expose whites to themselves and to Blacks in the United States as a minority in the world—a minority with great power, but a group that was irrevocably in decline. If Black people understood the vulnerability of the white man in this context, they would be emboldened and would gain increased confidence in their own viability as an independent force against the white world. Whites might be inspired to a new sense of compassion and humility; indeed, he already perceived in some young whites "a sense of collective guilt and rebelliousness against their parents."[69]

When Malcolm departed from the Nation of Islam, he sought to affirm his belief in Islam by seeking knowledge of orthodox Islam. Malcolm sought out Dr. Mahmoud Youssef Shawarbi, a professor at the University of Cairo who was on leave to direct the Islamic Center of New York. The Saudi Arabian government required a letter from Shawarbi certifying any American wishing to make the hajj, or pilgrimage to the holy city of Mecca. Shawarbi's first point was to show Malcolm a verse in the Qur'an that stated, "Muslims are all brothers regardless of their color and race."[70]

Malcolm was struck by the apparent lack of color consciousness among the Muslims of every shade who made the hajj with him. When one becomes a Muslim, he concluded, color ceases to be a determining factor in one's worth or value. White Americans, on the other hand, were consciously racist, resulting in an antiwhite sentiment among Blacks in the United States, which Malcolm himself shared and for which he would never apologize. But this also meant that there was some possibility of redemption of whites, and thus they could not be called devils by nature.

Some have argued that both religious and political motivations drove Malcolm's changing public view of whites. He wanted to broaden his appeal among Blacks, as well as provide a means of exerting leadership and motivating young whites to organize and effectively engage in the struggle against racism and colonialism.

In traveling to Africa Malcolm sought to revitalize the age-old dream of Pan-Africanism, which had enjoyed strong support among some Blacks in the United States at various points in history. Malcolm enjoyed an enthusiastic reception among various strata of the African population. The old anticolonial revolutionaries loved him, according to Goldman, although some (e.g., Kwame Nkrumah) who now had responsibilities for governing in a world still dominated by Western capitalism were cautious. The out-of-power radicals, the national liberation movements, and students adored Malcolm. A student association in Nigeria gave Malcolm the name Omowale, which in Yoruba means the son who has returned home.[71]

Malcolm sought to counter the notion among many Africans that Blacks in the United States were merely U.S. citizens, a view that was promoted by the U.S. Information Agency. He argued that Blacks in the United States were a subject people, colonized by white men and racially oppressed. The issue for Black people in the United States should not be primarily civil rights, but human rights. He stressed that Blacks in the United States considered themselves inseparably linked to Africa in origins and destiny, and that the separation had been maintained for much too long.[72]

The African American expatriate community was of great importance to Malcolm's work in Africa. Members of the expatriate community in Ghana, in particular Julian Mayfield and Maya Angelou, were instrumental in assisting Malcolm in the development of a Pan-African internationalist agenda. These expatriates, who, Sales argues, were sensitive to the charge that they had abandoned the struggle against racism in the United States, constantly sought ways to reaffirm their kinship with the struggle. According to Sales, they were central players in the conceptualization of the Organization of Afro-American Unity.[73]

While in Ghana Malcolm also solidified his ties with representatives of radical third world nations such as China, Cuba, and Algeria. The Algerian ambassador was a Muslim and a revolutionary, but would have been classified as a white man in the United States. When Malcolm argued that he followed the social, political, and economic philosophy of Black nationalism in the United States and Africa, Kaid asked where that left him. Malcolm, who was so often ready with a retort, was not sure what to say. He wondered whether Black nationalism might not be too narrow, cutting him off from the non-Black nations of the third world. He did not wish to alienate the revolutionaries dedicated to overturning the system of exploitation on the earth by any means necessary.[74] He commented, "We nationalists used to think we were militant. We were just dogmatic . . . it's smarter to say you are going to shoot a man for what he is doing to you than because he is white. . . . He can't stop being white. We've got to give the man a chance."[75]

I have not focused very much on the Organization of Afro-American Unity (OAAU) because of time and space limitations. The definitive work on that period is William W. Sales, Jr., *From Civil Rights to Black Liberation: Malcolm X and the Organization of Afro-American Unity*. The

OAAU made contributions both to the theory of Black liberation and to our collective understanding of the most appropriate organizational forms for the pursuit of our collective liberation, though it could not survive as an organization after Malcolm's assassination.

Malcolm X's detractors have thus argued that Malcolm X made no (or little of) lasting contribution to the Black freedom struggle. I think nothing can be further from the truth. Malcolm X's contribution is on a much larger stage. From 1965 to 1980 a Black revolutionary movement of unprecedented scale and intensity was set loose in the United States.[76] This movement was expressed through a number of organizations and cadres within organizations. The Revolutionary Action Movement, the Black Panther Party, the League of Revolutionary Black Workers, the Black Workers Congress, the Student Organization for Black Unity (which later became the Youth Organization for Black Unity), the National Association of Black Students, the Student Nonviolent Coordinating Committee after 1965, the African Liberation Support Committee, the Congress of African People, the African People's Socialist Party, the Republic of New Africa, Malcolm X Liberation University, the Young Lords Party, the Brown Berets, the Young Patriots are only some of the most prominent national organizations. Malcolm X's influence was similarly felt among numerous local organizations, among Black student unions at every white university with more than a dozen or so Black students, and in the Black university movement among the traditionally Black colleges. Malcolm X's influence was deeply felt among youth in predominantly white Old Left organizations, and among the more youthful radical New Left organizations.

The children of Malcolm X were in fact counted among untold numbers of the 1960s generation. Today we have the 1990s generation counting themselves or being called by the pundits the children of Malcolm X. It is thus urgent that we struggle to communicate across the generations about our understanding of the contributions of this pivotal figure in modern African American, U.S., African, third world, and world history.

7

The Crisis of U.S. Hegemony and the Transformation from Civil Rights to Black Liberation

After 1966 the revolutionary Black nationalist tradition, renewed and invigorated by Malcolm X, caught fire. The example set by the Black Panther Party and the League of Revolutionary Black Workers led to a proliferation of revolutionary nationalist organizations, such as the Congress of African People, the Youth Organization for Black Unity, Malcolm X Liberation University, Peoples College, the African People's Socialist Party, and the African Liberation Support Committee.

However, the power of the nationalist position during this period was so strong that the nationalist fever also extended to the right. The once militant CORE began to interpret Black power as a demand for Black capitalism. Even Jesse Jackson's Operation Breadbasket used the slogan "It's nation time!"

In the 1970s the deepening economic crisis intensified competition among the various segments of the labor force. During the unprecedented expansion of the 1960s, there seemed to be room to bring more and more people into the labor force. This led to a tight labor market and, from capital's viewpoint, a lack of discipline in the workforce. As the profitability of capitalist enterprises began to be squeezed, they sought cheaper workforces outside the core zones. This attack on the working class was focused on the most militant and vulnerable segment, the Black and Latino working class.

In addition, given the gains of the civil rights movement, room had been created for a significantly enlarged Black middle class. This resulted in a move to the right among the major civil rights organizations, and also the establishment of a conservative segment of the Black body politic to the right of the liberal civil rights establishment.

But overall the central theme of this era was the crisis of U.S. hegemony, represented by the military and political challenge in Vietnam, and spearheaded by the increasing competitiveness of Japanese and German enterprises vis à vis U.S. enterprises. The global liberalism of the post–World War II era was no longer adequate; the political and economic elite sought a way to reverse the declining fortunes of the United States. Eventually the backlash started in the 1970s.

This is the context for the rise and decline of one of the most powerful African American organizations of the post–World War II period, an organization that had the potential to bring unity to the diverse social movements of the time: the Black Panther Party.

The Black Panther Party

The Black Panther Party was founded in October 1966 by Huey P. Newton and Bobby Seale, who had met while they were students at Merritt Junior College in Oakland, California. Newton and Seale had been working with an organization called the Afro-American Association (AAA) at Merritt, but both were critical of its middle class membership and its debating-club and cultural nationalist orientation.[1] A clear example of the Afro-American Association's conservatism was its failure to support Seale and Newton after an altercation with police, who had accosted the two during a street rally. This incident led Newton and Seale to break with the student group. They were interested in action—not just any action, but action guided by a clear strategy and a conception of what the community needed. They turned to the Black community, going out knocking on doors to find out what people needed and wanted. This was the source of what later became the Black Panther Party's ten-point program.

While Newton and Seale had broken with the AAA, they still wanted to understand why the debating-club mentality predominated in student groups. One of the main problems that they perceived was the inability of these organizations to relate to the brothers and sisters on the street. They felt that Malcolm's Organization for Afro-American Unity had the right approach, but Malcolm was killed before it could implement its program.

They also read Fanon's *Wretched of the Earth*, Mao's *Selected Works*, and Che Guevara's *Guerrilla Warfare*. Newton argued that Fanon, Mao, and Che saw that people had been stripped of their dignity, not by philosophy, but at gunpoint.[2] They were particularly impressed by Fanon's observation that not only is revolutionary violence a necessary weapon against the violence of the system, but fighting back is a means of transforming the personalities of the oppressed. More than any other organized political group in the United States at that time, the founders of the Black Panther Party understood the naked violence that undergirded U.S. power, in particular in its relations with the lower strata of society (both in the United States and abroad).

Since they rejected the debating-club approach of the student organizations, they emphasized the need for a concrete program that spoke to the deepest needs of the people. Among the demands of the party's initial ten-point program were calls for self-determination of the Black community, full employment, decent housing fit for the shelter of human beings, the exemption of all Black men from U.S. military service, and an immediate end to police brutality and murder.

Since they set out to get the community's attention, they started by focusing on point 7 of their ten-point program, the opposition to police brutality. They initiated armed patrols, which monitored arrest situations with unconcealed guns and law books. Newton made it clear that it was perfectly legal for their militants to carry guns, and that the purpose of the guns at this point was political, not military.

The Oakland police were outraged by the armed patrols, but the community was deeply impressed. The reputation of the Panthers was enhanced when Newton and Seale and a half dozen other members of the party faced down a carload of police officers in a confrontation in front of the Black Panther Party headquarters.

Eventually the California state legislature set out to revoke the statute under which the Black Panther Party was able to carry out these armed patrols. The Panthers countered by sending a contingent of thirty armed Panthers to demonstrate against the legislation at the capitol building. The resulting scene caused a media uproar, but the brothers and sisters on the street around the country were impressed by the courage and audacity of the Black Panther Party. Within a few months, according to Foner, Black Panther Party branches were established in Los Angeles, Tennessee, Georgia, New York, and Detroit.[3] Hundreds of Black youth were attracted to the party.

While the BPP was receiving a great deal of attention because of its self-defense work, it was engaged in work on a number of other fronts. It was protesting rent evictions, informing welfare recipients about their legal rights, teaching classes in Black history, and demanding and winning traffic lights. But as these community activities increased and its reputation expanded, so also did police harassment. Party members were routinely stopped and arrested for petty traffic or other violations. On October 28, 1967, Huey Newton himself was stopped, and in an ensuing shoot-out was wounded. One police officer was killed, and a second police officer wounded.

On April 6, 1968, seventeen-year-old Black Panther Party member Bobby Hutton was gunned down by the Oakland police. Hutton was the first member to be recruited to the party by Seale and Newton, and the first to be killed. Over the next year and a half, according to Charles Garry, twenty-seven additional members of the Black Panther Party were killed.[4]

The Black Panther Party's militance, its serious analysis of the structures of U.S. imperialism and the forces that could be allied against it, its skill at speaking to the lower strata of the working class and to members of the intelligentsia and middle class as well, and its conscious attempt to use a mass line process to maintain its sense of unity with and leadership of the people were all too much to be tolerated by the ruling elite.

Huey Newton explained that the Black Panther Party grew out of the Black Power movement, but through its struggle came to understand the international character of the bourgeoisie, and thus the necessity for the international character of the struggle for liberation.[5] While Black people in the United States as a colonized people have a moral right to claim self-determination, in reality this is not desirable because of the necessity to destroy U.S. imperialism. Once this is accomplished, Newton argued, nations will no longer be needed because they will not need to defend against U.S. aggression.

Of all the Black militant organizations of the 1960s it was the Black Panther Party that most effectively carried on the legacy of Malcolm X. When Huey Newton heard Malcolm X speak in Oakland, he remarked that here was a man who combined the wisdom of book learning with the wisdom of the streets. In Newton's view Malcolm had the cool style of a prison man. More important, he knew how to reach people and identify the cause of their condition without blaming them. Newton and Seale believed that Malcolm had been on the right road when he established a Black organization, the Organization for Afro-American Unity, that would speak to the brothers on the block in language they understood.

For Alprentice (Bunchy) Carter, Huey Newton was the personification of what Malcolm talked about. What was notable about the Panthers in Carter's view was that the rank and file were not born in the South, but were the first generation of Blacks who had grown up on the West Coast. Rather than the suffocating racism of the South, these youth experienced a degree of freedom within an oppressive system. They were free enough in Carter's view to produce a Huey Newton, "a cat who . . . would say, 'well motherfuck the police.'"[6]

Carter explained that street brothers were not afraid, because they had "been down in these ghettos, and they knew that to live they had to fight." For Carter the genius of Huey Newton was that he was able to tap the vast reservoir of revolutionary potential among Black street people, "really TAP IT, to ORGANIZE it and direct it into an onslaught, a sortie against the power structure."

> Huey Newton was able to go down, and to take the nigger on the street and relate to him, understand what was going on inside of him, what he was thinking, and then implement that into a PROGRAM and a PLATFORM, you dig it? Into the BLACK PANTHER PARTY—and then it spread like wildfire across this country. . . . This is the genius of Huey Newton . . . the establishment of the first vanguard party in the liberation struggle in the Western hemisphere.

If, as Eldridge Cleaver stated, Malcolm had "mastered language and used it to slash his way through the veil of lies that for four hundred years had given the white man the power of the word,"[7] it was Huey Newton who built on Malcolm's achievement by mobilizing those most willing to fight to enlist in an army of Black liberation.

Cleaver argued that one of Huey Newton's greatest contributions was that his formulation of Black Panther ideology was free from ideological flunkeyism and thus opened the road to the future. In this way ideological formulations could be developed to fit an ever changing situation. What was most important in Cleaver's view was that Newton had provided an ideology and methodology for organizing the Black urban lumpenproletariat.[8]

The focus on the so-called Black lumpenproletariat derived from the party's understanding that this group had been locked out of the labor force, and thus had no institutional input into the system. Since in the Black Panther Party's conception these individuals were not a part of the labor force, they were not represented by organized labor. As a consequence this group had been forced to create its own forms of rebellion, which were consistent with its relations to the means of production and to the institutions of the larger society in which they lived.

If we keep in mind that social movements respond to the institutional arrangements that compose their day-to-day experience, we can see the reason for the BPP's emphasis on control of the police, and on the community survival programs. No amount of dogmatic lecturing about the role of the working class and the importance of work at the point of production can alter the reality of the groups to which the Black Panther Party appealed.

The Black Panther Party propounded a bold theory of revolutionary intercommunalism, which can be seen as a consequence of its practice, which fostered class unity,[9] and its ability to develop its practice to a higher level. Like other organizations the Black Panthers learned from the practice and theoretical deliberations of the world revolutionary movement. But they did not codify these deliberations into a rigid and ossified dogma. They attempted to analyze the world as it evolved before their eyes.

Huey Newton argued that since the United States was an empire that economically dominated the entire world, the concept of the nation no longer applied. What once were nations are now interrelated communities, tied together by economic interdependence created by U.S. imperialism. Newton described the U.S. monopoly of the resources of the world and the allocation of these resources according to U.S. ruling-class economic interest as reactionary intercommunalism.

Newton opposed revolutionary intercommunalism to this reactionary intercommunalism. Revolutionary intercommunalism was the process by which the people seized the means of production and distributed the wealth justly among the countries of the world.

In explaining the concept, Newton pointed to Washington's description of the war in Vietnam as a police action as similar to the attacks on urban rebellions in places such as Newark. The Black Panther Party was thus acting in concert with revolutionary movements all over the world. While FRELIMO and the ANC battled U.S. imperialism in Southern Africa, and the Vietnamese NLF battled it in Southeastern Asia, the Black Panther Party attacked the nerve center of the empire. What distinguished the Black Panther Party from groups with similar claims was that the BPP was not merely a group of intellectuals; it had a mass base from which it recruited troops.

In articulating the theory of revolutionary intercommunalism the Black Panther Party rose above its revolutionary nationalist ideological beginnings. From this perspective Newton argued that although peoples legitimately fight for nationhood, nations cannot exist for long anywhere because all nations fall somewhere on a scale from liberated to nonliberated territories.

Newton viewed the American empire as being everywhere, even in China, a fact dramatically illustrated by Nixon's visit. In the struggle against the empire, communities must be able to produce, educate, and defend themselves. The revolutionary process is advanced when these communities reach across national borders to forge linkages with one another.

In Newton's view millions of white Americans lived not in communities, but as atomized individuals and in households. Newton concluded that the Black Panther Party could no longer take its stand as nationalists, because the closer one is to the center of the empire, the more illusory is the idea of nationhood for any people.

The Black Panther strategy involved a model of organization of communities similar to that of the Chinese Communist Party in its Yenan period. This approach was based on the elemental belief that the community can develop by utilizing the strengths of the people themselves. For the Black Panther Party self- determination was not simply a slogan, but a goal that it took concrete steps to achieve. BPP members believed that with hope and resources they would be able to succeed in the long run. As long as people have the desire for change, they would unite with those who had both a vision and a practical program. However, they did not see the struggle for self-reliance as a struggle for autarky. They not only skillfully utilized external forces, they were able to inspire people to undertake struggles in their own interests. Thus they were able to get wealthy liberals such as Leonard Bernstein to assist them in raising funds, and were able to develop alliances with organizations such as the Puerto Rican Young Lords in Chicago, the Chicano Brown Berets, the white working-class Young Patriots, who had moved from Appalachia to the northside of Chicago, and the Chinese American Red Guards.

Indeed, it was the young leader of the Illinois Black Panther Party, Fred Hampton, murdered in his sleep along with Mark Clark by Chicago police, who originated the concept of a rainbow coalition. This coalition, according to Bobby Rush, included the Black Panther Party, the Young

Lords, and the Young Patriots.[10] The Black Panther Party viewed itself as the vanguard of the U.S. front of the world revolution, and consciously constructed a united front that accentuated the role of subproletarian sectors of the population but drew from other sectors as well. These subproletarian communities were the center of the revolution, but could only play that role by being converted into liberated zones. This was viewed as a protracted process.

In order to carry out the program of the development of a liberated area through the Black community survival programs, the Black Panther Party under Newton's leadership conscientiously practiced correcting mistaken ideas and learning from past mistakes.

In criticizing Eldridge Cleaver's defection from the Black Panther Party, Newton argued that

> The original vision of the Party was to develop a lifeline to the people by serving their needs and defending them against the oppressors, who come to the community in many forms, from armed police to capitalist exploiters. We knew that this strategy would raise the consciousness of the people and also give us their support. Then if we were driven underground . . . the people would support us and defend us.[11]

Newton argued that the Black Panther Party would survive because of its survival programs, developed to meet the true needs of the people. These programs were based on the party's ten-point program "What we want" (showing its emphasis on practice) and "What we believe" (which showed the ideological basis of the practical programs). Newton stressed that revolution was a process, not a particular action. Cleaver had been attracted to the party because of particular actions that were functional (in terms of the need to establish an image that would allow it to recruit among the people it wished to be the party's constituency), and had occurred at a given time (e.g., the confrontation with the police at the Ramparts office), but that had no revolutionary content in and of themselves—and could not have had.

Newton did not limit his criticism to Cleaver. He admitted that the Black Panther Party as a whole also defected from the Black community. It needed to reassess Black capitalism, the Black church, and the Black middle class, because all these groups had a potential role to play in the creation of a liberated community.

For example, the Black Panther Party had initially taken an implacable stand against the Black capitalist. But members came to see that not only did this tend to isolate them from certain sections of the Black community, it was not consistent for them to rely on white corporate philanthropists while being antagonistic to the much smaller (and much less powerful) Black capitalist. In rectifying this situation they were able to get Black businesses to play a key role in donating food, clothes, supplies, or a percent of their profits. This process was naturally not without some coercion, since these donations cut into the small profit margins of these businesses. Thus these businesses often submitted under threat of boycott and leafleting.

But once relationships between the Black Panther Party survival programs and these enterprises had been established there were benefits for each party, as well as for the survival programs per se. The businesses were a source of skills that the party desperately needed in its administrative and fiscal operations. The businesses were able to claim tax deductions, and were given ads in the *Black Panther Paper*. Supporters of the Black Panther Party and its survival programs were also urged to patronize businesses that supported them.

The Black Panther Party developed a number of specific programs.[12] The free breakfast program was initially set up by Bobby Seale. It was probably the most successful of all the Black Panther Party survival programs. In October 1968 the Black Panther newspaper advertised for volunteers to prepare and serve free breakfasts in Berkeley. The program spread quickly to churches, community centers, and auditoriums in San Francisco, Berkeley, and Oakland. By the end of 1969 breakfasts were being served in nineteen cities under the sponsorship of the national headquarters organization and twenty-three local affiliates. More than twenty thousand children received full free breakfasts before going to their grade school or junior high school.

From the beginning the program sought to recruit welfare mothers, grandmothers, and guardians in the Black community to prepare and serve the breakfasts. Members woke up early to prepare food. The program was very organized, which facilitated its speedy delivery so that children could get good, wholesome breakfasts. Generally the programs started off in churches, although they occasionally got started in schools. Citizen advisory committees were created to increase community support. The party aimed ultimately to turn the programs over to the community.

Although many of the breakfast programs were located in predominantly Black neighborhoods, the program also fed children of other ethnic groups. One program in Seattle operated in a white middle-class neighborhood.

Seattle had three free breakfast programs weekly for children, a medical clinic twice weekly, and a free clothing store open daily. There was no rhetoric and no shoot-outs. The free breakfast program fed over six hundred children daily, over three thousand weekly, at five different locations. These programs spread to Kansas City, Detroit, Philadelphia, Oakland, New York City, and Des Moines.

The Black Panther Party also built liberation schools, which were free educational facilities for Black and other oppressed children to promote a correct view of their role in the society.

The Black Panther Party maintained a large number of other survival programs, which were an essential part of its strategy of building a liberated zone as part of the world class struggle. The following is a brief overview:[13]

The Samuel Napier Youth Intercommunal Institute in East Oakland was an accredited alternative school. In this facility licensed teachers taught conventional basic skills and also political awareness. When students graduated from the institute, it was expected that they would become the political organizers in the high schools to which they were assigned.

Oakland Community School's 150 students from two and a half to twelve years of age consistently scored one to two years beyond grade level in an area of the city where reading scores were usually among the lowest in the nation. Most students who were accepted into the school reading below their grade levels achieved grade level within two years. Class size ranged from seven to twelve. The school also provided before- and after-school child care, three meals a day, complete medical and dental treatment, and overnight care at a Panther-run dormitory when parents requested it. All of this was provided free to parents who could not afford the twenty-five-dollar-a-month tuition. Most were single mothers. Parents contributed twelve hours a month as classroom aides, cafeteria workers, or office personnel. The Oakland Community School won an award from the California legislature for its achievements.

Two of the most successful nationwide programs were aimed at improving the quality of health care in the Black community. The George Jackson's Free Medical Research Health Clinics provided medical treatment and preventive medical care to those in need. In the Bay Area twenty-five doctors and medical students pledged time, free of charge.

The People's Sickle Cell Anemia Research Foundation was established to test individuals for traits of the disease, to create better educational programs about the disease, and to coordinate research of physicians already working in the area.

A medical program sent people out to test the elderly for high blood pressure, take them to hospitals for appointments, and help them with agencies and with voting.

The Black Panther Party survival programs also included a Free Busing to Prisons program, which achieved a considerable amount of success because virtually everyone in the Black community had either a relative or a friend in prison, and frequently they were unable to provide their own transportation for visits.

Along those same lines the party established a Free Commissary for Prisoners, which provided money for imprisoned men and women to purchase necessities from prison commissaries.

These services to the imprisoned and their families only highlighted the need for programs that could keep community residents out of entanglements with the legal system. To do this the party set up legal aid educational programs and provided free legal assistance and classes. Under this program both civil and criminal cases were handled.

The survival programs also attempted to meet the need for clothing by the distribution of free shoes and clothing to the needy in the Black community. The People's Free Clothing Program and the David Hilliard Free Shoes Program were examples of this type of program. The party opened a free shoes factory to support these programs.

In addition Black Panther Party members went out and asked businessmen to donate sets of clothes for children and teenagers. They tried to get new clothes because people were tired of hand-me-downs. Some of the clothing distributed through this program was from unclaimed clothes at dry cleaners. Although they were able to obtain a considerable amount of clothing for this program, their primary objective was to get free clothing for the people by asking the businessmen to donate two complete changes of clothes for children. Special emphasis was placed on getting clothes before school in September and January. When the Free Clothing Program got kicked off, some five hundred to six hundred people in Harlem got clothing for their kids.

The Black Panther Party started a community center in Oakland and a Teen Diversion program with $100,000 LEAA funds, and hired teenagers to take senior citizens on errands to protect them from muggings (hire the mugger to protect the muggee).

In addition to these survival programs the party maintained the *Black Panther* as its principal organ. The paper included information about Black Panther Party campaigns and activities, analysis of some local and national events, communications to the party and its supporters, and international information. Over thirty thousand copies of the Black Panther paper were distributed regularly.

Despite the breadth of the party's programs and the skill of its leadership, it was not able to survive the repressive apparatus of the U.S. state, which clearly understood the party's promise and the danger it posed to the status quo. While one might say the party had an exaggerated sense of its own importance, it indeed put together the pieces of revolutionary strategy and analysis as no other organization had in the history of the United States.

Its approach to the revolutionary process was open, and most important, it strove to understand how people it had to deal with could be used (were the only reliable weapon that could be used) to transform themselves and in the process the world around them. Picking up the gun was not the key to revolution, the Black Panther Party emphasized, for the "fascists" had guns, indeed many more guns than the Panthers or any other revolutionaries.

However, the de-emphasis on the gun led to some loss of support for the party. Eldridge Cleaver and his supporters are a clear example of this, but there was a whole wing of the Black liberation movement that believed that a correct military strategy was the most important element of revolutionary strategy. Some individuals had been attracted to the party primarily because it legitimated their desire to project themselves as gun-toting toughs.

While there are some who say that the primary contradictions of an organization are always internal, I would only say that there are always the limits of human ability. My intent here is not to provide a complete analysis of the Black Panther Party, but to indicate in what way it illustrates the point that social movements reflect both the institutional arrangements existent in their loci of struggle, and the larger social structure of the capitalist world-economy.

I agree with George Katsiaficas, who pointed out that when the Black Panther Party convened the Revolutionary Peoples' Constitutional Convention, "they had developed a new conception of the organization of society . . . a decentralized society of self-governing institutions and communities."[14] The continuing power of this conception was that it looked beyond the fragmentation produced by the present system. But at the same time that this convention sought to negate the social divisions of capitalism, attendees sought to preserve their unique cultural diversity by calling for the self-determination of Blacks, women, students, and gay people.

I take sharp exception to Katsiaficas' contention that the disintegration of the Black Panther Party was in any way simply a result of its reversion to the gangsterism of the past. This is much too facile (and arrogant) an explanation for the fate of a group that had so much promise, but faced such overwhelming odds.

The power of the Black Panther Party was in its example. Toward the end of his autobiographical portrait in *Revolutionary Suicide*, Newton noted that "Camus wrote that the revolutionary's 'real generosity toward the future lies in giving all to the present.'" For Camus this commitment stemmed from an "intense love for the earth, for our brothers, for justice." In Newton's view the Black Panther Party fully embraced this principle. "By giving all to the present we reject fear, despair and defeat. We work to repair the breaches of the past. We strive to carry out the revolutionary principle of transformation, and through long struggle . . . 'to remake the soul of our times.'"[15]

While the Black Panther Party's activities were oriented toward the community, and thus it recruited from a wide range of social strata, including the permanently unemployed, another wing of the movement appealed more to young Black workers entering employment in the industrial proletariat for the first time. This organization was the League of Revolutionary Black Workers.

The League of Revolutionary Black Workers

The 1967 African American rebellion in Detroit was met by particularly vicious repression. Given the order to "shoot to kill," national guard and police left thirty-four African Americans dead in the streets of Detroit.

Geschwender argued that the Detroit rebellion was "one of the bloodiest and most violent urban insurrections in American history."[16] Despite the murderous repression to which their community was subjected, the optimism of the time lived in Detroit as elsewhere. The insurrection stimulated a new burst of pride and increased conviction that through united and militant effort, Blacks could bring about social change in Detroit and in the nation at large. The form the movement took in Detroit was strongly influenced by the fact that here there was a large concentration of young African American workers entering the labor force at the same time that radical ideas were being propagated in the Black community by young intellectuals associated with the *Inner City Voice*. These young Black intellectuals—John Watson, Mike Hamlin, Ken Cockrel, General Baker, and John Williams—were influenced by revolutionary intellectuals and leaders such as Mao Tse-Tung, Che Guevara, Frantz Fanon, and Malcolm X. In their view Black workers would take the lead in the socialist transformation of the United States.

It was largely due to the influence of the *Inner City Voice* that many Black workers joined with white coworkers in a wildcat strike for better wages and improved working conditions. According to league member Ernie Allen, "the issue was the incessant, nerve-destroying, and accident-causing speed-up of the line."[17] In the aftermath of the strike, however, punitive measures were launched at some of the Black workers, including General Baker of the *Inner City Voice*. Despite the role these workers played in uniting these traditional antagonists, the UAW did not defend the workers who were fired.

Since the UAW leadership tended to be alienated from the young and militant Black workers (this despite the fact that Blacks were 30 percent of the UAW membership),[18] there was growing feeling among some Black workers that they needed to build their own organization. This was the context for the formation of the Dodge Revolutionary Union Movement (DRUM) at Dodge Main.

For Chuck Wooten and eight other Black workers who formed DRUM the issues were clear. Blacks had been kept out of the auto plants until World War II. In the 1960s Black workers held the most dangerous, poorly paid jobs and had the least seniority and job security. Despite the aging plant and the uncomfortable and unsafe conditions, the auto companies pushed to produce more cars with fewer workers. The Black workers bore the brunt. They called this process "niggermation."[19] According to Allen, DRUM was organized to fight discrimination in both the plants and the union, and to attack the power of the company to determine working conditions. The founders of DRUM invited the editors of the *Inner City Voice* to help build the union. It was felt that this group would serve an important function by articulating revolutionary ideology.

In May 1968 DRUM led a wildcat strike in which Chrysler's production dropped by 1,900 cars.[20] This strike gained considerable publicity for DRUM and led to the proliferation of Revolutionary Union Movements throughout the Detroit area, at Ford and General Motors plants, and at the United Parcel Service. According to Grigsby, the most important new RUM was ELRUM at Chrysler's Eldon Avenue gear and axle plant. Other RUMs included FRUM at Ford's River Rouge plant, CADRUM at Cadillac, UPRUM at UPS, and HRUM among health workers.

But by 1969 the wave of popular discontent symbolized by the 1967 insurrection had begun to subside. This discontent was a major part of the political psychology that had been the context for the formation of the RUMS. The waning of the wave of popular discontent undermined the spontaneous energy that had been much of the force behind the RUMs. In addition the RUMs faced increased repression from the plants, the UAW, and the state.

The leadership of the RUMs and the *Inner City Voice* believed that a central organization was needed to coordinate the plant struggles, link them with community-wide support, and develop a base for financial resources. This was the rationale for combining the RUMs to form the League of Revolutionary Black Workers (LRBW).

In response to charges that the UAW, local police, and white workers had conspired to prevent DRUM organizer Ron March from being elected to a union office, the league demanded that the UAW have a Black president and vice president, and that 50 percent of its staff be Black. It also demanded that the UAW recognize the league, provide financial support for the league's community work, and invest strike funds in Black banks. The league called for an end to the war in Vietnam, and argued that corporate profits be taxed at a higher level to provide funds to be used in Black and poor communities.

By 1969 the league had hundreds of members in auto plants in Detroit, New Jersey, and California, and thousands of supporters. The league was not only a Black workers' organization with a focus on the plants, it had extensive ties throughout some Black communities, but especially in Detroit. Like the Garvey movements it established independent enterprises like the Black Star Publishing Company and the Black Star Bookstore. It also articulated what was considered at the time an important anticolonial strategy with its Parents and Students for Community Control. To deal with all the ferment on campuses and to recruit and train future intellectuals for the movement, it established several Black student unions. In fact league leaders Luke Tripp and John Williams were instrumental in forming the Detroit branch of the Black Panther Party, whose major work was supporting Black worker organizations.[21] The league played an important role in switching the focus of the National Black Economic Development Conference from Black capitalism to soliciting donations from white churches and synagogues for reparations to the Black community. The Black Manifesto, developed under the leadership of ex-SNCC leader James Forman, led to substantial fund-raising in Detroit and elsewhere. Some of the funds went to the league and were used in some of the programs mentioned above.[22]

According to the league, conditions in the United States meant that one could not usefully envision a "pure" class struggle as the road to socialism. Black workers were considered the vanguard because, as Mike Hamlin argued, "Whites in America don't act like workers. They don't act like proletariat. They act like racists. And that's why I think blacks have to continue to have black organizations independent of whites."[23]

By 1971 a split had emerged in the leadership of the league: one trend was more revolutionary nationalist (General Baker and Chuck Wooten); the other was more Marxist (Mike Hamlin, Ken Cockrel, Luke Tripp, John Williams, and John Watson). Below the league's Executive Board (EB), the second level of the organization's leadership tended to defer to the EB; its cohesiveness, according to Ernie Allen, was a shared nationalist sentiment, and thus a specific commitment to the struggles of Black workers.[24]

Much of the leadership associated with the Marxist trend (Hamlin, Cockrel, and Watson) resigned from the league in 1971 to join the Black Workers Congress (BWC) along with James Forman. Initially the entire EB had endorsed the idea of building a national Black workers' organization through the formation of a Black Workers Congress, of which the league would be the showcase. However, the in-plant leadership of the league became more and more reluctant to play a subordinate role to the BWC, with its out-of-plant orientation. The BWC supporters, on the other hand, argued that the league could not be built worker by worker, plant by plant, but by bold leaps forward, making massive and simultaneous gains in various sectors of public work. These operations, it was argued, were not peripheral but absolutely essential to maintaining organizational momentum.[25]

The BWC advocates resigned from the EB when their position was not accepted. After Hamlin, Cockrel, and Watson's departure the remaining portion of the leadership and the greatest part of the membership considered continuing with the league along more nationalist lines. But in the ensuing six months, more and more workers drifted away from the league, and the bulk of the remaining cadre decided to affiliate with the then California-based Communist League (later the Communist Labor Party).[26] The Black Workers Congress fell far short of its goal, and in no way matched the successes of the league. James Forman had insisted that the BWC be a mass party organized around a cadre core. This notion was challenged by those who felt that opening up the organization to persons who were not committed and developed Marxist-Leninists would lower the level of the organization, and its work would come to focus on mass antiwar activities.

Although the concept of the BWC seemed to be of great potential since it brought together so many experienced cadres, in the end the organization was stymied, despite Forman's efforts to link together his former SNCC contacts, new workers' groups, and local Black militants.[27]

By 1974 the BWC executive body, headed by Mike Hamlin, had purged Forman from the BWC, and the organization had come to believe that it was no longer proper for a communist organization to organize along strictly national lines.[28] This was not an anomaly, however, since this was pretty much the trend throughout much of the African American radicalism of the 1970s.

Black Radicalism in the 1970s

During the 1970s the struggle against the war in Vietnam, the Black rebellions throughout the United States, and the birth of oppositional movements of great variety severely undermined the legitimacy of the government, and indeed of U.S. civil society. The Chinese Cultural Revolution was fashioning an image of what the power of the people could do. Maoist ideas influenced the New Left throughout the United States, as in other core countries.

The Maoist movement that emerged from the New Left visualized reconnecting the revolutionaries to their revolutionary heritage in the Third International, through the prism of Mao Tse-Tung Thought. Maoism was envisioned to be a truly radical critique of reformism and "revisionism," a means of continual social transformation carried out through class struggle under the dictatorship of the proletariat in the socialist countries, the most superexploited sections of the working class in the core countries, and the radical national liberation movements in the periphery. Some of these organizations envisioned the creation of a new international under the leadership of the Chinese Communist Party, although others thought such an international body would inevitably lead to the same lack of national rootedness that the CPC fought against in the Third International. Those who were skeptical about the formation of a new international often cited Mao's own contention that all movements had to develop their strategies according to their own conditions. Some of these organizations took the major lesson of the Chinese Cultural Revolution to be the significance of proletarian socialism versus petty bourgeois socialism or "liberal socialism" (the socialism of the experts).

While there was a range of political sophistication within the movement, on one issue there was considerable unanimity: through a voluntarist effort utilizing the correct line, revolutionary transformation could be undertaken. There was a great deal of variety among these organizations. Some had exceptional strengths in some areas, and utilized the ideology in creative ways. The story of this movement has not been told, and I cannot tell it here. What follows is an attempt to simply illustrate the evolution of certain African American nationalist organizations into Maoist organizations, and the extent to which they followed the trend set by the Black Workers Congress.

In the 1970s a variety of Black nationalist organizations expressed variants of the ideas articulated by the Black Panther Party, the LRBW, and the BWC. One of the most important of these organizations was the Congress of African People (CAP), headed by Imamu Amiri Baraka. CAP was initially strongly "cultural nationalist" in orientation. It was the force behind the National Black Assembly in Gary, Indiana, in 1972. Under Baraka's leadership it had developed an exceptional united front approach to organizing, which was clear at the conference itself, and had been made manifest in the organization's successful electoral work in Newark.

Their experience with Black politicians (Newark Mayor Kenneth Gibson and elected officials in the National Black Assembly), however, led CAP and Baraka to increasingly question their "cultural nationalist" perspective, and led eventually to an embrace of revolutionary nationalism by 1974. CAP's radicalization was also related to the debates in the Black liberation movement at the time, specifically in the African Liberation Support Committee, which had been profoundly influenced by the liberation movements in Mozambique. Since CAP's initial embrace of revolutionary nationalism was strongly influenced by Maoism, it moved rapidly from a revolutionary nationalist stance to a more or less orthodox Maoist stance, changing its name to the Revolutionary Communist League (M-L) in the process. In 1978 Baraka and the RCL merged with the Asian American I Wor Kuen and the Chicano August Twenty-Ninth Movement to form the U.S. League for Revolutionary Struggle.[29]

Another organization that followed a similar trajectory during the late 1960s and early 1970s was the Youth Organization for Black Unity, initially a student organization (the Student Organization for Black Unity— SOBU), started in Greensboro, North Carolina, by some of SNCC's secondary leadership. YOBU initially presented its perspective as Pan-Africanist, nationalist, and socialist. For YOBU the Black liberation struggle was national in character, international in scope, and scientific (socialist) in principle. By 1972 YOBU had moved toward Marxism. By 1974 it was in the process of forming a Maoist pre-party formation to include Peoples College, Malcolm X Liberation University, Lynn Eusan Institute in Houston, and the Marxist Leninist Collective in San Francisco and Detroit. These organizations formed the left wing of the African Liberation Support Committee, a united front–type organization. The merged organization, called the Revolutionary Workers League (M-L), later merged with a Young Lords Party offshoot, the Puerto Rican Revolutionary Workers Organization (PRWO), to form the Revolutionary Wing. The Revolutionary Wing articulated extremely ultraleft and anti-nationalist positions, in a movement where ultraleftism was the rule rather than the exception. It embarked on a campaign of expulsions, which decimated an organization that had some of the most able cadres in the movement. When the Revolutionary Wing folded, much of the YOBU leadership in the RWL cadre joined with the predominantly Chinese American Workers Viewpoint Organization to form the Communist Workers Party.

Although there had been much debate within the movement, for example, between the Black Panther Party and Maulana Karenga's US Organization in the late sixties and early seventies, the emergence of the African Liberation Support Committee in the early seventies as a united front of radical Black and Black community organizations and individuals provided the first opportunity for sustained debate about strategy and ideology in the Black movement of this period. The debate took the form of whether race or class constituted the most important analytic variable for understanding the Black condition. The debate between cultural nationalists, revolutionary nationalists, and Marxists took the form of various position papers circulated within the ALSC.

Finally in 1974 the African Liberation Support Committee organized a debate at Howard University in which the major ideological trends in the Black liberation movement became explicit. The theme of the debate was "Which Direction for the Black Liberation Movement." Abdul Alkalimat, speaking for Peoples College, articulated the most developed Marxist position. Owusu Sadaukai, representing Malcolm X Liberation University, and an extremely popular leader of the Black liberation movement, renounced nationalism and said he was taking up the study of scientific socialism. Amiri Baraka shocked many in the audience by starting out with a quote from Lenin. He was showing a clear sympathy with the left wing of the ALSC. Muhammed Ahmed, formerly chairman of RAM, but at this time of the African Peoples Party, articulated a clear revolutionary nationalist position, more of a synthesis than any of the other views presented. Kwadjo Akpan from the Pan African Congress of Detroit articulated the cultural nationalist position. Stokely Carmichael advocated a position he called Nkrumahism, which emphasized uniting Africa, and denigrated any form of struggle in the United States, which properly speaking was the business of the Native Americans.

The cards were stacked in this conference. The program favored the Left.[30] The nationalists and some Pan-Africanists were driven out of the ALSC, and there were bitter recriminations from cultural nationalist intellectuals such as Haki Madhubuti (Don Lee), whose later book *Enemies: The Clash of Races* denounced the "Negro Communists" who had taken over the ALSC. The bitterness of the debate polarized the two ideological camps in the Black liberation movement, driving them to take extreme positions in opposition to one another, and thus losing sight of the subtlety of the real world, in which both class and race must be analyzed correctly. In the aftermath of the conference, a large proportion of the left forces in the Black movement took increasingly antinationalist positions, which later fed into the establishment of white left ideological hegemony over the left forces in the Black liberation movement. The cultural nationalists took increasingly isolationist, anti-Marxist positions, which essentially closed them off from taking the path that Baraka and CAP had taken from cultural nationalism to the Left. Over time this tendency adopted the isolationist position in the Afrocentric movement, as opposed to the African internationalism of groups like the African People's Socialist Party, the Republic of New Africa, the New African People's Organization, and the Community Self-Defense Program of Brooklyn.

The point of this short historical excursion is to show that the movement of the BWC toward a "multinational" form of organization was typical of the radical African American organizations of that time. The resulting formations were in principle multinational, but most of the organizations that were formed as a result of the merger of the Black Marxist-Leninist Mao Tse-Tung thought organizations were predominantly composed of people of color. The story of these organizations as well as the predominantly white Maoist organizations deserves much more serious treatment than it has thus far been accorded, but that will have to be the focus of a future project.

8

The Future of Black Liberation and Social Change in the United States

The repression of the Black liberation movement and the political failure of its most radical organizations during the 1970s were one component of the overall repression of the New Left. The organizational manifestations of the world revolution of 1968 were defeated everywhere, but its impact on American society and on the world has been profound, and has set the stage for a much more profound transformation in the years to come, although this may not at all seem likely from the more general short-term perspective, a catastrophic sense of defeat.

I would hold that the first breakthrough on the U.S. front of this world revolution occurred with the mobilization of the civil rights movement. This is not an extraordinary conclusion; none other than FBI director J. Edgar Hoover held a similar point of view. According to Kenneth O'Reilly, Hoover decided to destroy the civil rights movement after the 1963 March on Washington, when it became clear that after decades of intermittent conflict and then three years of continuous skirmishes over voting rights responsibilities and Freedom Ride failures, the movement was not going away.[1] By 1963, O'Reilly argues, Hoover had concluded that the nation was in the midst of a social revolution, and the racial movement was at its core. In one sense Hoover did not believe that the civil rights movement was an authentic expression of Black people's dissatisfaction with the racial status quo. He fundamentally agreed with the die-hard segregationists who argued that the southern Negro was satisfied and sought integration only at the urging of communists.

But Hoover, like some of his more sophisticated conservative associates, did indeed have his finger on something. The fear of the red menace was not entirely feigned, although it had nothing to do with the rhetoric about democracy versus godless communism. The red menace was deemed a powerful and effective adversary of Western capitalist dominion over the world. The U.S. communists opposed this system of domination and were some of the most effective fighters for democracy for all on the domestic front. But they were far from a threat to U.S. society at this time. By the 1950s the CPUSA had dwindled from its power and authority in the 1930s and 1940s. So now Hoover used the imagery of the red menace to intimidate any force that might disrupt the privileges of the social, political, and economic elites of the United States. Deep down they no doubt had some inkling that the rebellion of the bottom layers of the social structure, whose grievances were irrefutable, could in fact be a threat to the whole structure of social privilege that it was Hoover's job to defend. The threat of the red menace was a perfect means by which to keep this movement contained, and to destroy it if and when necessary.

Hoover's FBI conducted extensive surveillance of civil rights leaders in the guise of looking for communist infiltration and influence in the movement. He then attempted to use derogatory information gained from this surveillance to discredit or destroy civil rights leaders. As the civil rights movement became more radical after 1965, the FBI adopted tactics of disrupting radicals by fomenting discord and antagonism within their ranks and between various organizations. These activities often had murderous results.

The Iron Fist

Conflicts between the Black Panther Party and the US Organization were the prototype of this kind of operation. Although the operations covered over three hundred other activist organizations, the Black Panther Party bore the brunt, according to extensive research conducted by Ward Churchill and James Vander Wall.

According to an FBI memorandum by J. Edgar Hoover dated March 4, 1968, the long-range goals of COINTELPRO were to

1. Prevent the *coalition* of militant Black nationalist groups. In unity there is strength; a truism that is no less valid for all its triteness. An effective coalition of Black nationalist groups might be the first steps toward a real "Mau Mau" in America, the beginning of a true black revolution.
2. Prevent *the rise of a "messiah"* who could unify and electrify the militant black nationalist movement. Malcolm X might have been such a "messiah;" he is the martyr of the movement today. Martin Luther King,

Stokely Carmichael and Elijah Muhammad all aspire to this position. Elijah Muhammad is less of a threat because of his age. King could be a very real contender for this position should he abandon his supposed "obedience" to "white, liberal doctrines" (nonviolence) and embrace black nationalism. Carmichael has the necessary charisma to be a real threat in this way.[2]

No direct evidence that we are aware of proves that the FBI or the CIA played a direct role in the assassinations of Malcolm X and Martin Luther King, although the FBI is known to have played a clear role in establishing the atmosphere that allowed both assassinations to proceed. There is little doubt that it was seeking to create a situation in which someone would assassinate these two leaders. In the case of the assassination of Fred Hampton, chair of the Illinois chapter of the Black Panther Party, the FBI played a very direct role. Hampton was an extremely effective organizer and diplomat. In December 1968 FBI informant William O'Neal reported to his superiors that Hampton was on the verge of pulling off a merger between the BPP and the Black Stone Rangers, a southside street gang with several thousand members. This merger would have doubled the size of the national BPP. The FBI sent anonymous letters to Hampton and Black Stone Ranger leader Jeff Fort to create antagonism between them. At the same time O'Neal was on the inside turning the Panthers against the Rangers. Not only did the merger halt, but the two groups became actively hostile to one another. In November 1969 Hampton traveled to California to speak at UCLA and meet with BPP national leadership. They informed Hampton that he was being selected to serve on the Central Committee as chief of staff and main spokesperson for the national BPP.[3]

To prevent this enhancement of the BPP national leadership, the FBI agents responsible helped arrange an arms raid on Hampton's apartment, on the basis of information supplied by William O'Neal about weapons located in the apartment. O'Neal had supplied them with a floor plan of the premises, showing the bed in which Hampton would be sleeping.

The raiding team invaded the apartment in a torrent of gunfire. The Panthers got off one shot when the dying Mark Clark discharged a round in response to being shot. All the gunfire had converged where the floor plan had indicated Hampton's bed was located. Hampton, who had been drugged by O'Neal so he would not awaken during the raid, had been wounded by one of the shots. When one of the officers saw that he was still alive, he put two bullets at point-blank range through

Fred Hampton's head. One of the officers commented, "He's good and dead now."

On January 17, 1969, the antagonism that the FBI had been "developing" between the BPP and the US Organization in Los Angeles bore fruit. Alprentice "Bunchy" Carter and John Huggins were ambushed after a tense meeting of the UCLA Black student union in which they were in contention with members of the US Organization over the direction of the Black studies program at UCLA.

Carter, like Fred Hampton, was one of the rising stars of the Black Panther Party. He had been a member of the Slausons street gang and was a master of diplomacy with the youth gangs that operated in the Black and Latino inner city of Los Angeles. He spoke eloquently about the art of the correct handling of contradictions among the people. He joined the party as deputy minister of defense of the Southern California branch of the BPP.[4]

The assassination of Carter and Huggins is generally thought by the informed public to be a case of the FBI simply exacerbating existing tensions between the two groups. This was an unethical act in and of itself, given the anticipated deadly consequences, but it allowed the FBI to deny any direct responsibility for the violent and deadly assaults that its instigations led to. But there is much more to this action.

An FBI informant who had infiltrated the Black Panther Party had left the scene of the meeting to take a walk in the parking lot outside. The agent, D'Arthard Perry (also known as Othello), heard gunshots, and shortly afterward saw three men run out of the building and get into an automobile. Perry recognized all three of the men who ran from the scene as fellow FBI informants. The three men, George Stiner, Larry Stiner, and Claude Hubert, were all working for the FBI in the US Organization. The car was driven by Brandon Cleary, one of the FBI agents that Perry himself reported to. Perry later found out that Jomo Shambulia, the security chief for the US Organization, had parked the car for Cleary to use.[5]

Carter had met with Karenga and Jomo Shambulia on the day before the meeting and agreed that despite their differences, they should not treat each other as enemies.[6]

On August 21, 1971, the BPP field marshall and celebrated prison author George Jackson was assassinated at San Quentin Prison in California while allegedly trying to escape. Stephen Bingham, his lawyer, was the last person from the outside to see George Jackson alive during a visit just minutes before the alleged escape attempt. Bingham is thought to have given Jackson a gun that had been concealed inside a tape recorder that Bingham brought into the visiting room. But Bingham only carried the tape recorder in because it had been passed to him by Vanita Anderson, a BPP member who had seen Jackson earlier in the week and who the prison authorities would not let in. So why did the authorities assume that Bingham passed the gun to Jackson and did not pursue Anderson, not even as a witness?

Paul Liberatore, a journalist working on a book on George Jackson, located her and found that she is now a professor at a community college and is primarily involved in recruiting and training students to be prison guards. Liberatore concluded that she had been an undercover agent in the BPP who was part of a police conspiracy to murder George Jackson. Neither the defense nor the prosecution called her as a witness. The defense had pragmatic reasons for not doing so. If she was not called, Bingham could not be convicted.[7] Others argued that within the BPP there were tensions between those members inside the walls and those outside, and that Jackson's escape, though originally planned with the assistance of BPP members outside the walls, faltered when Newton withdrew the outside assistance. Some speculate that Newton withdrew outside support because he had learned that the ultimate purpose of Jackson's escape was to enable him to take over the leadership of the party from Newton.[8]

When Geronimo Pratt assumed leadership of the Los Angeles branch of the BPP after the assassination of Bunchy Carter and John Huggins, he was almost immediately targeted for neutralization by COINTELPRO. On April 23, 1969, he was arrested with FBI informant Julio Butler on suspicion of having kidnapped another BPP member, Ollie Taylor. He was acquitted. On June 15, 1969, he was arrested along with several other Panthers for suspicion of having murdered BPP member Frank Diggs. Of this too he was acquitted.[9]

The FBI did not give up. Four days after the raid in which Fred Hampton and Mark Clark were murdered, on December 8, 1969, a similar raid took place in Los Angeles. Since an FBI informant by the name of Melvin "Cotton" Smith had provided the raiding team with a floor plan, the firepower had been directed into Geronimo Pratt's bed. He was sleeping on the floor, however, because of back injuries he had sustained while in Vietnam.

Pratt remained in jail for two months while the $125,000 bond was being raised, but once he was out he was "bad-jacketed" by FBI informant Cotton Smith; Smith raised suspicions about Pratt's loyalty to the party in the BPP national office. Although he passed the loyalty test in June 1970, his open alignment with Cleaver in the Newton-Cleaver split did not rest well with the national leadership. When Newton was released from jail on August 5, 1970, he ordered that all Cleaver supporters be expelled from the party.

After Jonathan Jackson's aborted attempt to free his brother, George Jackson, from prison, Pratt (who had become close to the Jackson forces, often called the People's Army) left for Texas to think things over. In the meantime federal agents sought Pratt for crossing state lines to avoid prosecution. They did not tell him, however, that he had also been accused of murder by two witnesses, who it would later be shown were FBI informants. On this charge Pratt was convicted and sentenced to twenty-five years to life, although the FBI knew that at the time of the murder Pratt was at a BPP meeting in the San Francisco-Oakland Bay Area, four hundred miles away. Geronimo Pratt had finally been removed from the scene, and the internecine warfare in the Black Panther Party promoted by COINTELPRO isolated him from outside forces that could support him.[10]

The FBI's secret war against the Black freedom struggle netted many more victims than we can discuss here: Dhoruba bin Wahaad, a Panther 21 codefendant previously known as Richard Moore, served twenty years for being in possession of a weapon allegedly used to fire into the home of one of the Panther 21 prosecutors, wounding two police officers. This was a complete fabrication, but Dhoruba was kept in jail for twenty years.[11] Similarly, the New York 3 (Herman Bell, Anthony Bottom, and Albert Washington) received twenty-five years to life for the shooting of two New York police officers on the basis of a weapon found in their possession said to be the murder weapon (it was not), and the testimony of a witness who had been tortured by the police (and subsequently recanted). But the New York 3 remain in jail.

Assata Shakur had left the Black Panther Party because of disagreements with Huey Newton's expulsions of valuable party members such as Geronimo Pratt and the New York Panther 21. She joined with a loose grouping of people who constituted the underground collectively referred to as the Black Liberation Army (BLA). She had been sensationalized in the press as the soul of the Black Liberation Army, and was wanted in connection with a series of cold-blooded murders of police officers.[12]

On May 2, 1973, Assata Shakur, BLA founder Zayd Malik Shakur, and Sundiota Acoli were stopped on the New Jersey Turnpike in what seemed to be a routine application of the notorious principle of stopping people who are "driving while Black." When the state troopers realized who they were, the troopers opened fire, incapacitating Assata Shakur with the first shot. When she awoke, one of the state troopers, Werner Foerster, and one of her comrades, Zayd Malik Shakur, were dead. Sundiota Acoli and the other officer were both injured. She was later charged with the shooting of the police officer, despite having been incapacitated with the first gunshot. She was not, however, charged with the "cold-blooded murders" of police officers that had previously earned her such notoriety and made her a fugitive. She was charged with a host of bank robberies, the murder of a heroin dealer in Brooklyn, and a failed ambush of two cops in Queens on January 23, 1973. She was acquitted of all charges in a series of trials lasting till 1977, while being held in isolation without bond in miserable prison facilities. On March 25, 1977, she was finally convicted of the murder of officer Werner Foerster, despite the fact that Acoli had long since been convicted of firing the fatal shot. Shakur was set free by the BLA's Multinational Task Force on November 2, 1977, and made her way to Cuba, where she was provided sanctuary.[13]

Republic of New Africa member Mutulu Shakur had established the Lincoln Detox Center in the Bronx, using the methods developed by Malcolm X and the Nation of Islam to cure heroin addicts. Some found the politicization of drug rehabilitation hard to accept, and the fact that the Detox Center championed the Black Panther Party's agenda of community control was anathema to government officials. The government withdrew funding and evicted the center from the facility on November 29, 1978. Shakur reestablished a treatment center in Harlem known as the Black Acupuncture Advisory Association of North America (BAAANA). According to the Joint Terrorist Task Force (JTTF), an organization called the Revolutionary Armed Task Force, associated with the Black Liberation Army, emerged out of BAAANA and robbed banks and armored trucks to provide a funding base for the heroin clinic. Shakur and other RATF members were arrested and convicted for an attempted armored truck robbery in West Nyack, New York.[14]

Mumia Abu-Jamal had been a member of the Black Panther Party in Philadelphia. After the party collapsed around 1975 he continued to carry out the kinds of activities he had carried out in the Ministry of Information of the Black Panther Party. He worked as a journalist, on community radio, and as an independent political activist who supported the MOVE community. This work earned him the enmity of the Philadelphia police department, whose abuses were the subject of some of his work. When he was shot while attempting to stop a police officer from beating his brother on December 9, 1981, the police took the opportunity to put him away, although all the witnesses who testified against him have questionable motives, the physical evidence is at odds with the claims of the witnesses, and there is substantial evidence that was not solicited in the trail and that contradicts the testimony of the witnesses.[15]

The repression of the Black Panther Party and other militant organizations by federal agents during the late 1960s and early 1970s was a far-reaching, comprehensive, and vile effort. J. Edgar Hoover put the full resources of the FBI into destroying the Black Panther Party, which he argued was the most dangerous threat to the national security of the United States since the Civil War. The intent of this repression was not only to destroy the Black Panther Party as an organization, but to destroy the spirit of the African American people and undermine their will to resist.

The federal security agencies recognized that the political threat of the Black radicals of this period was much more significant than the military threat. The willingness of the BPP and similar groups to organize and mobilize among people considered to be outlaws had enormous political significance. But the brutal repression meted out by the security agencies and the police forced a response among those who were subject to or likely to be subject to repression in the near future. The Black Liberation Army developed less as an instrument of immediate urban guerrilla warfare than as a brave and daring attempt to defend against FBI and police terror. After the 1969 assassination of Bunchy Carter and John Huggins, BPP chief of staff David Hilliard wrote, "Bunchy's murder terrifies me. Bunchy isn't simply a beloved brother. He's Bunchy—invincible, beyond death! I've seen him control gangbangers, dominate people who would scare me. If this can happen to Bunchy, what will happen to us?"[16]

That sector of the movement that embraced some elements of Third International Marxism was also subject to neutralization, but this is a story that has yet to be told. As I indicated in an earlier work about the new electoral activism in Black communities, the neutralization of the Black Panther Party proved to many African Americans that the United States was not a democracy for Black people.[17] The Black Panther Party and others from the radical protest tradition began to view the possibilities for social change afforded by participation in the electoral arena in new ways.

The New Black Vote

Thus between 1975 and 1980 the bright flame of Black liberation flickered and died in the United States. The radical organizations that had galvanized so many social groups since 1965 were almost totally spent. Some observers point out that the Black Panther Party devolved into electoral activism. But Huey Newton did not regard the party's entry into electoral activism as a retreat; he regarded it as just one additional tactic to build the power of the people in Black communities. He thought that some of the leadership had misunderstood or misinterpreted the overall scope of the BPP project that he had initiated in 1966, or that his long period of separation from the cadres of the party had led them to move imperceptibly in directions that he had not intended. At any rate when Newton got out of jail in July 1970 he began to question what he felt to be the overemphasis on militarism in the BPP and began to place more emphasis on the survival programs.

The survival programs were central to Huey Newton's plan for the BPP to lead the people in taking over the institutions of the communities in which they lived and develop a political machine that would focus less on control of offices than on insuring that the needs of the people were met. Capturing political power in these areas was viewed as one component of establishing control of these communities, which would effectively establish them as liberated zones. In January 1972 Newton announced the involvement of the BPP in voter registration in Oakland. In a November 1972 speech Elaine Brown explained their electoral campaign as "part of a revolutionary process—to build a base of operation in Oakland, New York, Texas." Shortly thereafter Bobby Seale announced his campaign for mayor of Oakland.[18]

This involvement in an electoral strategy did not constitute an incorporation of the revolutionaries into the U.S. political system as just another special interest group seeking reforms. This was not a simple move from protest to politics, as Bayard Rustin claimed. Unfortunately, too many saw this as a retreat, but it was a broadening of the revolutionary struggle in Huey Newton's mind. There was nothing intrinsically revolutionary about "picking up the gun." For Newton, picking up the gun was an organizing tactic. But the party could not remain fixated on armed resistance because that would surely lead to defeat. "The fascists have guns," he told Elaine Brown and David Hilliard.[19] Indeed, they have more guns.[20] The survival programs in and of themselves were neither revolutionary nor reformist, but if properly used they could educate the people beyond the issue of "pigs with guns." The survival programs could make people begin to ask how the party can do so much with so little and the capitalists do so little with so much.[21]

Newton held that since the Black Panther Party grew out of the conditions and needs of oppressed people, it was interested in everything that the people were interested in despite the party's view of whether such participation was the "revolutionary" answer to the needs of the people. Participation in electoral politics, therefore, was a means of trying to bring the will of the people to bear on the quality of governance that they were subjected to.[22]

Revolution, Newton argued is a process; the party strives to remain connected to the people, to serve the needs of the people, so that the process can develop. Acts that disconnected the party from the people, such as a one-sided emphasis on picking up the gun, were nonrevolutionary. In this way, Newton argued, Cleaver gave the people an ultimatum, either pick up the gun or you are part of the problem, and not part of the solution. In this way the Black Panther Party defected from the Black community and became a revolutionary cult. The correct approach, Newton held, was to serve the needs of the people, and "when the people are ready to pick up the gun, serious business will happen."[23]

The maturation of the Black Panther Party was part of a general maturation of the radical forces in the Black community, which learned from their experiences and attempted to fashion strategies that made sense in view of the collective experience of the Black liberation movement and the overall movement for social transformation and human emancipation.

We have seen that the politics of cultural nationalism in Newark, New Jersey, led to the radicalization of Amiri Baraka and his comrades in the Committee for a Unified Newark (CFUN). Baraka's ideological conversion from cultural nationalist to Marxist-Leninist is legendary. At a national level the politics of cultural nationalism was manifest in the activities of the National Black Political Assembly (NBPA), which grew out of the 1972 National Black Assembly in Gary, Indiana. The NBPA was an attempt on the part of cultural nationalists to unite with Black elected officials around a common Black agenda. The driving force behind this strategy was Baraka's articulation of the concept of the Black united front, following the teaching of Malcolm X. This was an ill-fated coalition, sabotaged by the elected officials, who deserted the coalition as the mobilizations of the 1970s cooled.

This was a sign of the times. The epicenter of Black activism had passed from the radicals to the elected officials, who fancied themselves the champions of real Black Power. The conservative faction in the Black Power movement was now center stage; even Richard M. Nixon declared himself in favor of Black Power (by which he meant Black capitalism).

Nonetheless, activists across the country attempted to enter the electoral arena in a revolutionary way. This was indeed a daunting task, given the overwhelming tendency of all politicians to give priority to getting elected and reelected. This priority tends to pull all politicians in the direction of compromise, that is, to become a part of the good old boys' club and operate according to its rules and norms.

Yet in several cities activists sought to participate in electoral politics in such a way as to transform and empower the powerless instead of simply getting a piece of the pie for themselves and a few crumbs for their constituents. The following examples indicate that one cannot simply dismiss the Black Power militants as middle-class hustlers who promoted only their own interests. I have attempted to show that the Black Power movement was much more complicated.

In 1977 Ken Cockrel, a veteran community activist in Detroit, had been elected to the Detroit city council under the auspices of a radical multiracial organization called DARE, the Detroit Alliance for a Rational Economy. Cockrel had also been associated with the Dodge Revolutionary Union Movement (DRUM), the League of Revolutionary Black Workers (LRBW), and the Black Workers Congress (BWC). He was a radical lawyer who had been engaged in numerous community campaigns, especially around police brutality. While Detroit with its history of industrial trade unionism was no stranger to leftist and progressive ideas, the emergence of the LRBW and the BWC, as we argued in the previous chapter, constituted a more radical leftism associated with the radical wing of the Black Power movement and proletarian socialism. It represented a political tendency much closer to the Black Panther Party than the more traditional communists and social democrats who had been associated with trade union movements in metropolitan Detroit and left-leaning political figures such as the young Coleman Young and Judge George Crockett.

In Boston the forces supporting the African American mayoral candidate Mel King in 1979 and 1983 articulated an explicitly progressive message and sought to create a rainbow coalition that was anchored in the egalitarian sentiments of the African American community but reached out to other progressive constituencies as well.

Perhaps the most dramatic example of the power of this new black vote was the 1983 mayoral campaign of Harold Washington. Washington had been a popular congressman from the Chicago area, but he would not run unless his supporters could demonstrate some electoral muscle. The Chicago Democrats are the ultimate urban political machine; without competent supporters there would not be a ghost of a chance against them. But Chicago Black and Latino neighborhoods consisted of a dense network of grassroots organizations that had been built on the basis of popular opposition to the austerity politics of that period. These community organizations were not simply an ideological opposition; the network was based on what Alkalimat and Gills call the construction of a political movement from concrete instances of organized protest. This dense network of grassroots organizations in Black and Latino communities was the basis of the Harold Washington victory over the Democratic machine in 1983.

To recapitulate the Chicago example at the national level would take some doing indeed. It was Chicago's own Jesse Jackson and his conception of a Rainbow Coalition that came to symbolize this radical challenge to the political status quo on a national level. Jackson's Rainbow Coalition is not quite the same as the revolutionary rainbow coalition envisioned by Black Panther leader Fred Hampton, but it was a realistic program for the establishment of a racially egalitarian social democratic program in one of the stingiest welfare states on the face of the planet.

The Jesse Jackson Phenomenon

Jackson had been in the mainstream of the civil rights movement as a member of the SCLC and a lieutenant of Martin Luther King. His base in the urban North meant that he was properly located to take on the next stage of the civil rights movement. Yet as an individual he was not trusted by several of the southern-based ministers who were closest to King, nor by the radicals who either were associated with the SNCC and CORE radicals or identified with them. Nor was Jackson trusted by members of the white social democratic Left, since they felt that a Black candidate would be divisive and would antagonize further the Reagan Democrats who had become realigned with the Republican Party. But Jesse Jackson was a man of tremendous ability and drive. He was not to be so easily denied.

Jackson came late to the SCLC. He was a seminary student in Chicago when King put out the call for people to come to Selma. Jackson answered the call, and traveled to Selma to help with the voters' rights campaign. While there for only three days, Jackson was able to obtain an interview with King and pleaded for a staff position.[24]

He was not successful in this bid, but the following year, when King chose Chicago as the northern city in which to extend the nonviolent protest movement, Jackson was selected to become a part of the SCLC staff. Although nonviolent protest was a dismal failure in Chicago, King established a program he called Operation Breadbasket to open up jobs in the private sector to Black people. Jackson overwhelmed many of the white companies doing business on the southside of Chicago. In two years Breadbasket won contracts for black sanitation firms and black exterminators. They convinced the white firms on the southside to advertise in the Black media. They won three thousand jobs for Chicago Blacks.[25]

In the meantime King was moving beyond racial politics. He now saw U.S. power as a triple-headed monster: militarist, racist, and economically unjust. He wanted to go to Memphis in support of striking sanitation workers. Some SCLC staff members thought King was spreading them too thin. Jesse Jackson refused to go. Later King called the staff to Atlanta for a meeting and strongly rebuked them, especially Jackson. He admonished them all, however, that these problems were not just his problems, they were not Jesse's personal problems, or Andy Young's problems, or any individual's problems. These were America's problems and the only solution was to work together to redeem the soul of America.[26]

This was King's legacy to Jesse Jackson. A few days later he was dead, shot by an assassin in Memphis, Tennessee. Ralph Abernathy succeeded King as chairman of the SCLC and Jackson returned to Chicago to Operation Breadbasket. Although Breadbasket was the major fund-raiser for the SCLC, antagonisms between Jackson and Abernathy continued, and in 1971 Jackson left the SCLC to form Operation PUSH (People United to Save Humanity). An ambitious title? Hadn't King told him to redeem the soul of America?

Jesse Jackson labored away in Chicago and wherever else he got the call. While his initial thrust with Operation Breadbasket had been primarily on economic issues, he increasingly focused on political issues. Jackson presented the keynote address at the National Black Political Assembly. He was swept along in the nationalist rhetoric of the time. He called for a Black party. He did not trust white Democrats or white Republicans. At his Saturday morning liturgies with his congregation in Chicago he began to ask, "What time is it?" The resounding answer: "It's nation time!"[27]

But the corollary to this nationalist approach was a quite conservative social outlook:

> "Black Americans" he argued, "must begin to accept a larger share of responsibility for their lives. . . . We don't need to carry chips on our shoulders. . . . " But Jackson's point was quite different from that of white conservatives. "In spite of yesterday's agonies, liberation struggles are built on sweat and pain rather than tears and complaints. . . . We black Americans can rebuild our communities with moral authority. . . . Parents, teachers, superintendents, school boards have all failed to impose discipline.". . . Rich Barber, an editor at Viking indicated his interest in Jackson was based on Jackson talking the language that whites want to hear."[28]

Nonetheless this was also the language of Black nationalism, long familiar to Black Chicago, which for fifty years had been the national headquarters of the Nation of Islam. The message of moral uplift and self-reliance preached by Jackson was also the message of Louis Farrakhan and the Nation of Islam.

The alliance that developed between Farrakhan and Jackson was ironic. While Jackson was moving away from the sort of organic Black nationalism of the urban North, Farrakhan was riding the wave of the social and economic devastation of inner cities to a revival of Black nationalism. Yet the Jackson campaign, especially his talk about the establishment of a Rainbow Coalition, attracted many of the former cadres of the radical organizations of the 1960s and 1970s, and of course the support of the few radical organizations that still existed. This was not an unusual arrangement. The Left has often found its niche in mainstream politics by providing the foot soldiers and intellectual workers for left liberal political campaigns. These campaigns frequently find the discipline, commitment, and political sophistication of the labor almost always freely donated by leftists to be a godsend.

These campaigns provided an opportunity for the Left to demonstrate its usefulness and elevated some individuals into prominence in the political mainstream. But the few remaining organizations of the Black Left (nominally multinational) often split over the strategy to be taken in regard to the National Rainbow Coalition, which was carefully controlled by the interest of candidate Jesse Jackson, rather than allowed to grow as a progressive political force in its own right.

On the other hand, Minister Louis Farrakhan rose to national prominence (or notoriety) in his role as a supporter of Jesse Jackson and as his defender against threats and harassment by the Jewish Defense League. Can we say that we have a repeat of the late 1960s when, according to William Julius Wilson, the Black Power militants sabotaged the rise of an authentic social democratic program by aggressively polarizing Blacks and whites?

This is questionable in my view. It seems that most whites are by and large distrustful of both social democracy and Black Power. Yet as economic difficulties jeopardize the life chances of large parts of the white population, interest in a social democratic strategy may revive. Furthermore, in the wake of the Farrakhan phenomenon, Jesse Jackson seems to be more popular among whites, including some Jews, than he was in the 1980s.

The Rediscovery of Black Nationalism

The civil rights revolution of the 1960s outlawed segregation and discrimination, and affirmative steps were taken to undo the harm done by the historical exclusion of Blacks and others from the benefits of our society. The civil rights revolution inaugurated a new spirit of inclusion throughout large segments of the white mainstream, and inspired egalitarian revolts among the lower stratum of society and among many groups that had been historically excluded. Among the general white public, the period seemed one of progress, but increasingly large numbers of them believed that the government had overstepped its bounds by catering to Blacks and other groups to such an extent that it now discriminated against whites.

The civil rights movement had peaked just as the capitalist world-economy entered a long B-phase of economic stagnation and U.S. world hegemony began to unravel. The ruling political coalition of this period was built largely on antagonism toward the gains of the Black and Latino populations, and the alleged misdeeds especially of the poorer sector of the Black and Latino communities. The exclusionary political psychology reflected the nation's declining economic fortunes and the decline of U.S. dominance of the world-system. This was in stark contrast to the political psychology of the 1960s, the high point of U.S. world hegemony, morally symbolized by King's "I Have a Dream" speech.

The change in the economic fortunes of the nation, at the same time that large numbers of inner-city youth became increasingly marginalized, led large segments of the white population to conclude that those Blacks who could not succeed given the preferences now lavished on them were simply lazy, pathologically criminal, or irredeemably incompetent. Moreover, as an abstract principle detached from our moral and historical circumstances, "preferences" were clearly unfair. Not surprisingly for a white public given to ahistorical, self-justifying worldviews, opposition to "preferences" for "minorities" became the unifying ideology for a color-blind racism posing as fairness. There would be no more talk about equality of results. Blacks and Latinos, they argued fiercely, get the results they deserve.

In this context it should not be surprising that this generation was so strongly attracted to larger-than-life images of Malcolm X, whose militance and clarity of vision resonated profoundly with their own sense of justice denied. A culture of opposition that took shape among inner-city youth as a counter to public humiliation and disdain was deepened by insights from Malcolm's revolutionary nationalist perspective. Notwithstanding its negative features, the egalitarian elements in hip hop culture cut sharply against the grain of the prevailing selfishness and greed of the dominant white culture. This egalitarian ethos cemented the solidarity between inner-city Black and often Latino youth and their more middle-class sisters and brothers. For these youth, so scathingly demonized in public discourse, Malcolm X was a model of Black dignity, standing up to the racist system, telling it like it is. He was viewed as a prophet who articulated their righteous anger against white society's racism and hypocrisy.

Contrary to the claims of official class analysis, the nationalist form of this trenchant working-class critique of the modern world was not an anomaly. The tradition of field Negro revolt that Malcolm X articulated so well has long been an autonomous form of Black struggle that did not derive from the inspiration of the European and North American Left.[29] This tradition has long been the wellspring of radical ideologies among the Black working class and its organic intellectuals. Malcolm's unique contribution is that he articulated this tradition in an international context. Unlike some Black nationalists with narrower horizons, Malcolm X was a living and dynamic manifestation of the spirit of Bandung. Not only did he understand the rebellion of Black people in the United States as part of the rebellion of the overwhelming majority of the world's people of color against Western domination, but with the gift of second sight so burned into the souls of the Black residents of the United States, he understood better than almost anyone else that this revolt heralded the end of white world supremacy. When in 1963 Mao Tse-Tung argued that the evil system of colonialism and imperialism had grown up with the enslavement of the Black people and that it would surely come to an end with their complete emancipation, he could very well have been paraphrasing Malcolm X.[30]

But the movement of which Malcolm X was a central figure had been militarily repressed from the late 1960s, and the favorable relations of force that signaled white supremacy's vulnerability had been tempered (but not entirely reversed). The repression of the radical wing of the Black Power movement was accompanied by the co-optation of its more moderate elements, who were opposed to the system's racism but thought the system could be reformed if Blacks were admitted to the system commensurate with their qualifications.

In the complex and confusing conjuncture in which the 1990s Black nationalist revival occurred, Malcolm X's legacy was reinterpreted or nullified (most notoriously by Spike Lee's film). Black nationalism as an ideology was increasingly appropriated as the sole intellectual and political property of proponents of a more elitist and conservative social praxis, associated with some Afrocentric scholars and elements in the Black Muslim movement who favored a spiritual rather than a revolutionary opposition to white supremacy.

J. Edgar Hoover and the FBI had made their point rather well. Those Black people who identified with and attempted to unite with the ideals, sentiments, and practices of the revolutionaries of the three continents should realize that they would be subject to the same lethal disincentives that U.S. imperialism's iron fist offered to its third world opponents. We have seen some of the examples: Malcolm X, George Jackson, Fred Hampton, Alprentice Bunchy Carter, Jonathan Jackson, and even Martin Luther King.

I should emphasize here that this is not merely a scholastic question. When Betty Shabazz viewed a film clip of Farrakhan's speech at a February 26, 1993, closed meeting of Nation of Islam members in Chicago, she was asked by WNBC reporter Gabe Pressman if she thought Farrakhan was involved in the assassination of her husband, Malcolm X. She replied that she had no doubt that he was involved. "Everybody talked about it . . . it was a badge of honor."[31]

In the film clip Farrakhan argued that every nation has a band of zealots who protect the honor of its prophets. If someone defames or threatens to harm that prophet, the zealots will kill him. He was not a killer, he said, but "I loved Elijah Muhammad enough so I would kill you yesterday, today, and tomorrow. . . . We don't give a damn about no white man's law when you attack what we love." Farrakhan argued that every nation has to be able to deal with traitors. Then he asked rhetorically, "Was Malcolm your traitor or was he ours? And if we dealt with him like a nation deals with a traitor what the hell business is it of yours?"[32]

After the furor over Betty Shabazz's accusation, her daughter Qubilah was apparently entrapped by FBI informant Michael Fitzpatrick into entering into discussions about a plot to assassinate Farrakhan. In May Farrakhan and Betty Shabazz appeared on the stage of the Apollo Theater for a public reconciliation. Farrakhan was now magnanimous, arguing that the FBI had set Qubilah up, and seeking reconciliation, in the interest of Black unity. Farrakhan said, "our zeal, our love and hatred, our ignorance was manipulated by powerful outside forces. . . . We cannot deny whatever our role was, but we cannot let the real culprit get away."[33] Then he talked about calling one million men to Washington, DC, for a day of atonement.

A diversion?

According to Karl Evanzz, an FBI tap on Elijah Muhammad revealed that on March 8, 1964, the day Malcolm X declared his independence from the Nation of Islam, Muhammad called Farrakhan and broached the idea of evicting Malcolm X from the Queens home legally owned by the Nation of Islam. Mr. Muhammad said that once Malcolm was out, the house would be given to Farrakhan. On March 19, 1964, FBI wiretaps recorded Elijah Muhammad telling Farrakhan that Malcolm X had to be silenced before he revealed too many scandalous secrets. Muhammad told Farrakhan, when you find a hypocrite, you have to cut their heads off. According to Evanzz, the FBI documents do not show any reaction from Farrakhan.

In September 1964 Mr. Muhammad assembled a select squadron of two hundred men to Chicago and again said that Malcolm X had to be stopped at any cost. In the December 4, 1964, issue of *Muhammad Speaks*, Farrakhan, under the byline Brother Lewis, said, "Only those who wish to be led to hell, or to their doom will follow Malcolm. The die is set, and Malcolm shall not escape. Such a man as Malcolm is worthy of death."[34]

According to *New York Post* columnist Jack Newfield, Charles 37X Kenyatta told him that Fruit of Islam Captain Yusef Shah (Captain Joseph) admitted to him before he died that Farrakhan was personally involved in planning the assassination of Malcolm X. Shah had also admitted that he was involved in the firebombing of Malcolm's house on February 14, 1965.[35]

In the CBS documentary *The Real Malcolm X*, well-known civil rights attorney Clarence Jones says he has no doubt that the FBI and/or the CIA were involved in the assassination of Malcolm X. So who are the real culprits? Did the FBI and/or the CIA have an interest in ensuring the hegemony of rhetorically militant but otherwise conservative leadership of the Black nationalist movement in the United States?

This is a question worthy of pursuit. But more broadly, the assassinations of key Black leaders represent only a few of the best-known casualties of the 1965–85 revolution against the U.S. social system. Many of the intellectuals who came of age during this period became full-time cadres in the movements, and did not pursue more traditional academic interests or a career in mainstream politics. As a consequence of these choices their impact on the politics and intellectual life of the larger society was moderated.

Thus in the 1990s we moved very quickly from the revolutionary political discourse of Malcolm X, discovered by a new generation seeking to address their situation in U.S. society, to the controversial but nonrevolutionary discourse of Louis Farrakhan and Leonard Jeffries. These conservative Black nationalists opposed racial domination and degradation but lacked a structural or systemic critique of U.S. society. They injected verbal militance and rhetorical bombast into an already superheated public discourse, forming a perfect target for a white racist backlash that had gained the upper hand in the nation's polity since the Reagan counterrevolution of 1980. The Reaganites cynically exploited the liberal premises of individual rights. They called for a color-blind policy against racism, but deftly shifted to an attack against a phenomenon that they identified as reverse discrimination (against white men), which was implicit in the color-conscious remedies (like affirmative action) that had emerged from the struggles of the 1960s.

Nationalist consciousness is ever present among the racially oppressed. The centrality of racism to the rightward political realignment fanned the flames of nationalism not only among the poorest and less fortunate in the Black communities, but also among members of the Black middle class who, though at the height of their fortunes, were themselves tarnished by the sheer weight of the degrading myths about the Black underclass. The middle class was pushed not only to express its resistance to these degrading stereotypes in nationalist terms, but also to identify strongly with the less fortunate members of the Black community and even elevate them to heroic levels.

The initial manifestations of nationalistic sentiment in the 1990s were strongly influenced by the egalitarian views and revolutionary sentiment of Malcolm X and took a decidedly ghettocentric form. But since the political and ideological tendency that Malcolm X and the radicals of the 1970s represented had been destroyed, the more conservative tradition survived and grew in the academy and in Black communities. Thus when nationalist consciousness began to grow among the broader Black community, these conservative nationalists were in place to insinuate themselves as the *only* legitimate voices of Black nationalism. The important point is not so much that conservative Black nationalists have become a part of the popular discourse and social praxis in the Black community, but that they view themselves as the *only* legitimate voice. This allows the conservative nationalists to play a prosystemic policing function in the Black community, which the representatives of the white establishment can never do.[36] The attack on the memory of Malcolm X and the actual removal of Malcolm X from the scene are inextricably related to this phenomenon.[37]

Conservative Black nationalists have claimed the mantle of leadership in the Black community because they correctly identified and acted on some of the internal barriers to Black success and unity. They sympathized with the militance of youth but focused on the need for responsibility, self-respect, Black pride, and respect for one another. But the emphasis on self-improvement and internal cohesion has meant that much of their focus has been on exhortation, often substituting inspiring rhetorical militance for substantive programs and strategies for destroying the power of white capitalist hegemony and domination. They tell it like it is to whites and Blacks, no matter how unpleasant their truths. But we should be clear that this is not the basic challenge to the system that is needed. This is a plea for entry into the system. Its boldness stems from its potential for success as a strategy for increasing the competitive position of *some* Blacks within the system by making use of Black solidarity and racial uplift as resources for advancement. This is basically the strategy of Booker T. Washington, but with an important element of Black pride as a form of social cohesion.

The ascendancy of conservative nationalists and conservative white racists in the political arena in the 1990s pushed the so-called culture wars to the front pages of public discourse about race, while the systemic racism that is the heart of the U.S. social, economic, and ideological structure proceeded without significant critique except from the radical fringe.[38] This radical fringe was outraged by the cynical posturing of the conservative Right. But there were tensions among Black radicals as well.

As I indicated above, many of the Black intellectuals who came of age during the 1960s and 1970s were first of all militants in the movement for social change whose intellectual work sought to serve that movement. Politically and temperamentally their orientation was closer to that of the better-known activists of that time, such as Huey P. Newton, George Jackson, Bunchy Carter, Fred Hampton, Elaine Brown, and Erika Huggins.

After the military defeat of the revolutionaries of the 1960s and 1970s and the retreat of the popular mobilizations, a new generation of Black intellectuals came to increasing public prominence. This group of Black intellectuals were mostly left and left-leaning, but mostly rejected the extremism of the radicals of the 1960s and 1970s.[39] While their prudence has ensured them a positive reception among progressive and left-leaning whites, they have been much less successful than the more vociferous conservative nationalists in getting the attention of Black youth both in the academy and on the streets.

The left liberal or social democratic intelligentsia often soft-pedaled its critique of white supremacy or balanced its critique of white supremacy with a corresponding critique of the nihilism of Black youth and the alleged follies of neonationalism. These essentially liberal measures simply added momentum to the white racist backlash that had increasingly characterized U.S. political culture since the 1970s. Indeed, the white racist backlash lent a great deal of credence to militant but relatively conservative Black nationalists who undermined their trenchant and correct critique of white supremacy by indulging in the anti-Semitic language of Euro–North American culture and by adhering to that culture's masculinist and homophobic values.

Ironically, the marginalization of the Black Left took place while the conditions of the Black masses worsened and the attitude of the white public changed from disdain to contempt. The politics of the white backlash, which perhaps appeared ineffectual to the liberal elite in the 1970s, had moved to center stage throughout white America. The oppositional stance of the revolutionaries clashed violently with the deeply racist and conservative culture of the white majority. The radicals had sought to change the terms of the debate from the need for tolerance to the need for the transformation of the structures and values of the entire U.S. society. This fundamental challenge evoked a defensive posture among many whites, and deeply antagonized the conservative true believers, who then sought to stampede both the Black radical interlopers and their supplicant liberal friends in the public discourse.

Does this mean that the militance of the Black community was responsible for the ensuing ideological polarization, as has been charged by a chorus of left liberal intellectuals from William Julius Wilson to Jim Sleeper? This is a highly suspect accusation. Clearly more than tolerance is required if we are to deal effectively with the legacy of racial oppression in our country. In truth the white backlash was simply an elaboration on the basic cultural framework of historical capitalism, which explained inequality in cultural/racial terms.

Contention between deeply racist and pro–civil rights views among whites, sometimes within the same individual, is not an anomaly. As Wallerstein argues, racism and universalism are complementary ideologies that relate to different parts of the process of class formation in the capitalist world-economy.[40] Racism is the ideology that justifies the allocation of some groups to lower positions in the social division of labor of the working class. In contrast, the intermediate strata are assimilated to a neutral universal culture. The ideology by which the intermediate strata are controlled is thus called universalism. If indeed racism and universalism are applied to two different classes, then the existence of racist ideas and pro–civil rights ideas in the same individual makes much more sense.

Liberals, on the other hand, believed that racism is a moribund ideology, a holdover from slavery, which would wither away under the processes of rationalization in the industrial society. Many on the Left held to a variant of the liberal position, emphasizing racism as a superstructural phenomenon, a product of the false consciousness of the working class, which lost sight of its real interests by partaking of the psychological salve of racial superiority.

But the evolution, deepening, and intractability of the white backlash shattered the traditional liberal optimism about the inevitability of progress. The declining significance of race that William Julius Wilson had triumphantly observed in the late 1970s was by now an obvious fiction, much to the embarrassment of Wilson and the liberal establishment. Even Nathan Glazer, who had split with the liberal establishment and joined the neoconservative camp, was later to say that America had not proved to be receptive to the humanity of Black people and that the only way forward is to declare that we are all multiculturalists now.

But what about the Black nationalist project? When Boston's Reverend Eugene Rivers criticized the alleged failure of Black intellectuals at elite white universities to address the pressing needs of the Black community,[41] he was assailed by some Black liberal and social democratic intellectuals for reviving a chimera of Black nationalism at a time when processes of globalization are increasingly rendering nations superfluous, and when nationalist struggles have led to increasingly narrow visions and fratricidal wars all over the world.[42]

This points to a weakness in our understanding of Black nationalism in the contemporary United States. While Carmichael and Hamilton's *Black Power: The Politics of Liberation in America* was an important historical document of the Black Power movement of the 1960s, it was not a work of sociohistorical analysis. It represented an attempt to come to grips with the situation of Black people in the current U.S. realities. A primary objective of the work was to conceptualize a way forward that transcended what an increasing number of activists and members of the national Black community saw as the limited horizons of the 1960s civil rights movement. Despite the Black nationalist rhetoric of the 1960s Black Power militants in SNCC, the biographies of its members were only a faint reflection of the much broader Black nationalist tradition represented by Malcolm X and the Nation of Islam. Elombe Brath, one of the most prominent representatives of the Black nationalist tradition, has noted the irony that the Black Power militants who were associated with Black nationalism by the white public had been integrationists whose historical and ideological ties to Black nationalist movements were weak.[43]

I follow William Sales, Jr.'s very important observation that the revolutionary tradition in Black nationalism evolved out of the tradition of field Negro revolt, which Malcolm X reinvigorated.[44] Thus the urban rebellions of the 1960s, the armed resistance of the New Negro period (the African Blood Brotherhood), and the self-defense tradition among the Black rural working class of the South are all part of the immediate historical legacy of revolutionary Black nationalism. These revolutionary nationalist trends can be traced back to the maroonage tendency in the resistance and opposition to slavery. But these cultural and political legacies were not theorized by Carmichael and Hamilton, although the Lowndes County Freedom Organization was a clear example of this tendency.

Carmichael and Hamilton sought to problematize the current U.S. realities and legitimate the concept of Black Power as a reasonable and logical approach to Black realities, similar to the strategies that other ethnic groups had followed. In this sense the concept of Black Power was quite unextraordinary. But Carmichael and Hamilton also viewed Black Power as a politics of liberation, and this was outside the ordinary. Despite the manifold left-wing critics of Black Power, Carmichael and Hamilton were themselves quite aware that Black Power was a broad-based ideology that could be a means of pluralist integration as well as Black liberation.

It is thus true, as some critics have claimed, that the conservative strand of the Black Power movement reinforced the system, despite the very real militance of the exponents of that position. Too often the debate about the Black Power movement has been diverted by a misplaced focus on whether or not its adherents were truly militant. But the political significance of the Black Power movement does not revolve solely around its militance. A more important question (but one that is frequently confused with the question of militance in the minds of grassroots activists, people in the community, and scholars) is whether they were truly antisystemic, whether they opposed the logic of capitalist exploitation and oppression, the foundation of the system of white supremacy and racism.

Despite its spurious claims to represent a universal program, nothing could be clearer than the fact that the trade union movement long practiced exclusionary policies toward Blacks and other people of color. So since the very process of working-class formation was intertwined with the distinction between free white labor and enslaved African labor, the trade union movement itself was founded on these exclusionary bases. Opposition to the logic of exclusion (itself central to the maintenance of a low-wage labor force) developed not primarily in the so-called universal organizations such as the trade union movement, but in organizations that were often national in form. Thus whether or not one adopts a formal position on the national question, national forms of organization have been key to the elaboration of strategies for Black liberation.

Furthermore, it was the debate over the African American national question within predominantly white organizations that allowed those organizations to broaden their perspectives by examining the full range of strategies for Black liberation, even though they tended to shy away from certain options.

The African American national question is not a national question of the old type in nineteenth-century Europe. The African American national question has traditionally been posed as a question of a nation within a nation. But the 1930s formulation tended toward dogmatism by freezing the Black Belt South as the homeland of the Black nation in the United States. But the relocation and concentration of Black people throughout the urban centers of the United States deepened rather than weakened the national aspect of their struggle. It did not solve the African American national question as many Marxists claimed.

Despite the relocation of the African American people, their relationship to the United States has remained fundamentally similar, although the new petty bourgeoisie has followed the trend toward integration, as has been the case of the new petty bourgeoisie worldwide. But the integration of the African American petty bourgeoisie is still weak. They are still suspect because they maintain an allegiance to their sisters and brothers from the lower stratum. And this lower stratum is hardly integrated.

The recent emphasis on the phenomenon of social isolation of inner-city Blacks by William Julius Wilson and others points precisely to this issue. But in contrast to an alleged declining significance of race, it could not be clearer that race is all too important as the United States enters the twenty-first century. Does this portend a movement toward fratricidal warfare such as that which exists in parts of Europe and Africa?

I do not think so, because the African American national question occupies a crucial position in the structuring of power both within the United States and on a world scale. The African American people are indeed a consequence of a process of class formation that gave rise to racial capitalism as the cultural foundation of the capitalist world-economy. The process by which the African American people constructed their own sense of peoplehood is intimately intertwined with the class position that most occupy. Thus what St. Clair Drake described as the Black perspective in social inquiry and social thought is notable for its identification with the poor and the dispossessed.

Today the radicals of the 1970s have mostly abandoned the organizations they promulgated. Many have moved into the academy. Some have continued to work in other organizational forms. The revolutionary nationalists work mainly in small organizations that come to public attention in some crisis situation, such as the African People's Socialist Party, which gave leadership to the National People's Democratic Uhuru Movement in the rebellion against police repression in St. Petersburg, Florida; and the December 12th Movement, which has organized disruptive civil actions in response to acts of official (police) violence or white mob racial violence in New York City.

Most of the high-profile individuals and organizations of whom the public has some knowledge represent the more moderate and mainstream segments of the movement. Many of the radicals now largely work within these movements, but not on their own terms. The most urgent task that the radicals face is to begin to discuss with each other how they are going to organize on their own terms. These are tumultuous times; radical solutions are needed.

Radicals should also discuss what is to be done in light of the lessons of the past. They should strive to develop a means of working among the broad masses of the people, helping to form grassroots initiatives, proposing means of addressing the larger issues, and addressing the need for radical solutions in a manner that makes sense to the masses of seriously aggrieved people in our sorely oppressed inner cities.

To this end a discussion began in the wake of the Million Man March among Abdul Alkalimat, Leith Mullings, Manning Marable, Bill Fletcher, and Barbara Ransby about reestablishing a visible and vibrant Black radical tendency in U.S. society. This current, envisioned as multi-tendency, would include religious radicals, communists, socialists, feminists, and revolutionary nationalists. The discussion led to the establishment of the Black Radical Congress, which will hold a founding congress in Chicago on June 19–21, 1998. The purpose of this meeting, according to BRC literature, is to set a Black liberation agenda for the twenty-first century.

While the BRC at this point consists mainly of cadres of the 1960s and 1970s Black Left, its agenda is broader than that of similar organizations from that period. The Black Radical Congress calls for unity against all forms of oppression, including "class exploitation, racism, patriarchy, homophobia, anti-immigration prejudice and imperialism."[45] The Black Radical Congress has also proposed a Black Freedom Agenda, which, though still under discussion, is a remarkable statement of democratic sentiment that should be able to gain broad support not only among African Americans but among all people who are victims of corporate capitalism's vicious assault on our livelihood, communities, and well-being.

There are additional indications of efforts toward unity in the formation of the New Afrikan Liberation Front and the ongoing work of the Campaign to Free Political New African Prisoners. The defeat of the police by the insurgents under the leadership of the National People's Democratic Uhuru Movement in St. Petersburg is an indication that the Black liberation movement is on the rebound from the defeats of the previous period. Most important the united front character of much of the work that is being done is an indication that the movement has accepted the challenge of handling contradictions among the people in order to effectively mobilize them to overcome the dead weight of corporate capitalism and the culture of white supremacy.

We live in a time of great uncertainty. In my view capitalism has certainly entered its moment of structural crisis, a crisis that over the next fifty to seventy-five years will bring capitalism as we know it to an end. The intensity of the culture wars that are raging in the United States and increasingly in other countries where the third world within is a growing proportion of the population is a symptom that the capitalist system is approaching its bifurcation point. The growth of the third world within in most of the core zones of the capitalist world-economy indicates a fundamental demographic transformation that will deplete capital of the reserves it has historically used to add new sources of cheap labor to the workforce. This is one secular trend of the system that is not reversible or cyclical. As it takes effect, the ability of the system to function will be increasingly undermined.

But these culture wars should not be confused with the ethnic wars raging in the areas of the collapse of the Old Left (communist and national liberation movements). The ethnic wars represent the failure of liberal universalism, which is a strategy of co-optation of the upper strata of subordinate peoples into the capitalist world-economy and its system of Euro–North American hegemony. Despite their ultimate aims, the socialist, communist, and national liberation movements of the twentieth century were all fatally infected with this liberal bias (although ideology was not the only problem these movements faced; there were insurmountable structural issues, as well as the related issue of rapports de force). The integrationist strategy of the African American civil rights movement was buoyed by this ideology, which is a part of the process of class formation of the petty bourgeoisie on a world scale (what I referred to above as bourgeoisification). The culture wars reflect a fundamental demographic transformation of the capitalist centers, and the African American population—the crucible of one of the oldest, most politically conscious, and strategically located subproletariats on earth—can be the source of a truly egalitarian solution to the long impasse that is upon us. This structural crisis of capitalism will bring the five hundred years of historical capitalism to an end.

To have this kind of impact the African American freedom struggle must finally transcend its radical nationalist moorings, but it will most certainly start from this historical crucible of Black radicalism. Radical nationalism does not stand alone. It has always been a component of a more general nationalist mobilization. In the 1920s the African Blood Brotherhood was one component of the larger New Negro movement of which the Garvey movement was the largest component. In the 1950s and 1960s Malcolm X and the Black Panther Party were associated with the Black pride movement, of which the largest organized component was Elijah Muhammad's Nation of Islam.

Conservative Black nationalism is an expression of the competition within the existing system. Yet it should be clear that such a movement is legitimate in its own right, as much as any other nationalist movement or any attempt to use ethnic politics to bolster a group's position within the status quo. In contrast radical Black nationalism is essentially an antisystemic movement pressing for the unity of all the oppressed and exploited in the United States to come together for an egalitarian response to the collapse of capitalism. Thus we must beware of any type of knee-jerk antinationalist positions, for within the social movements of the United States these have almost always (but not always) served reactionary purposes, moving progressive movements and people to the right and away from the most rebellious and potentially revolutionary constituencies.

It should be kept in mind that both radical Black nationalism and conservative Black nationalism derive from an extensive and profound nationalist consciousness that exists throughout the African American population. It is the deep egalitarian culture of this population that gives radical Black nationalism (or what most of its adherents call revolutionary Black nationalism) its significance as a transformative force.

Class consciousness in and of itself does not ensure an antisystemic thrust. Classes cannot simply be viewed in the context of their national borders. The reality of class is determined by the social structure of capital accumulation on a world scale. Thus one must assess what role a particular group plays in the world-system as a whole.

I hold that the radicalization of social movements in the United States was in large part a consequence of the impact of radical Black nationalist movements. The development of seriously antisystemic (revolutionary) strands within the North American Left can be clearly related to the impact of the African Blood Brotherhood in the 1920s, Malcolm X in the 1960s, and the Black Panther Party and its descendants in the 1970s. All these organizations attempted to go beyond radical nationalism, but finding themselves in uncharted waters, either attempted to rely on old formulas (the leadership of the African Blood Brotherhood liquidated its leadership responsibility and joined the Communist Party USA on the assumption that we were on the verge of a world socialist revolution; the Black Marxists of the 1970s became part of the new communist movement and unsuccessfully attempted to synthesize the traditions of the Third International and Maoism, while often undervaluing the tradition of the Black liberation movement); or were not able to make the turn before they were destroyed (Malcolm X and the Black Panther Party).

Where Do We Go from Here?

Giovanni Arrighi and Andre Gorz stress the role played by the two sections of the working class, the skilled workers whose social power can challenge capital, and the unskilled workers whose misery delegitimizes the capitalist system.[46] Arrighi argues that cost-cutting has led to the spread of mass misery to the core zones, which partially involves the substitution of cheaper for more expensive labor. Thus while there has historically been a geographical separation between those sections of the working class experiencing growing social power and those sections of the working class experiencing mass misery, the two groups are increasingly being consolidated in one location.

But there is more to it than simply class position. Historical capitalism's development of an ideological framework of "oppressive humiliation"[47] via racism and sexism has sparked the rise of the lower strata within the antisystemic movements and reinforced the egalitarian thrust in Marxism, thus providing us with an ongoing pressure, along with the struggle on the ground, to rethink our strategies.

I believe that one of the main political achievements of the movements of the 1960s was the elevation of the so-called minorities to a strategic position coequal to the industrial proletariat as agents of transformation of the U.S. social system. Among large sections of the social movements there has increasingly been the realization that there is no easy or final resolution of the minority issue, and thus no real process whereby the "proletariat" and "oppressed nations" are transformed into uncontested majorities within nation-states.[48]

For this reason I would argue that a more adequate model of societal transformation in the United States may be precisely the specter brandished by the multiple movements of the 1960s, which everywhere made claims on the system that it could not meet. Thus rather than calling for everyone to unite under one big tent, we will find it more effective to call for a broad inclusiveness among the movements for equality and social justice. There is a need to coordinate among the various groups, but each group has a right to its own autonomy.

In the twentieth century the nationalism of oppressed groups has been the most significant opposition to world capitalist imperialism. But, alas, these movements are inherently limited in their ability to transform the world structure of capitalist accumulation. Nationalist and national liberation movements (like their communist and social democratic siblings) have relied almost exclusively on a strategy of seeking or seizing state power to achieve their goals. But once in power they found that control of a state does indeed give them a great deal more power than they had previously, but less than they had hoped for. This is because the processes of the capitalist world-economy are beyond the control of any one state, even the strongest states, even the hegemonic state in a phase of hegemony. Thus the nationalism of oppressed groups has been an important factor in increasing the political strength of particular oppressed groups, but it is not enough to transform the competitive and zero-sum nature of the capitalist world-economy into a just and egalitarian social system.

I think that a major task of the social movements (all of them) is to deal very seriously with the question of the correct handling of contradictions among the people. Arrighi's analysis enables us to see the potential for the unity of the oppressed and exploited majority of the world's population, but his inattention to the issue of consciousness (particularly of racism and racial consciousness) does not allow him to fully articulate the manner in which (racial) consciousness has both strengthened and weakened antisystemic movements, especially in the United States.[49]

Nevertheless, his projection about the spread of mass misery to the core sets the condition for solidarity among the working classes, which had previously been divided by their contrasting experiences of growing social power and growing mass misery. However, it is also important to note that the ruling groups of the core are pushing heavily for an inter-class solidarity among the upper and middle strata of the capitalist world-economy as a whole, while leaving the lower strata, worldwide, the victims of a "culture of poverty," which, if eradicable at all, will only be so in the very long term. But we all know that tomorrow never comes.

Political conflict is an ongoing reality of the capitalist world-economy. We would be naive if we did not recognize that whenever a powerful minority is opposed by a potentially powerful but divided majority, it will always seek to exacerbate the divisions. We would also be naive to think that those who have privileged positions within our ranks will concede these privileges without pressure from those who may have a little more to lose than just their chains, but not much more.

Therefore, so long as racism remains the main ideological pillar of historical capitalism, the Black liberation movement will continue to play a vanguard role in the United States, as was indicated by the promise of the Black Panther Party. Such a movement will have to deal effectively with the correct handling of contradictions among the people, and elaborate a social vision capable of mobilizing the lower strata of the United States as well as their relatively more advantaged allies.

Notes

NOTES TO THE INTRODUCTION

1. See Lerner 1992.
2. Horne 1987b.
3. Leid and Buesing 1987.
4. See Pollack 1987; Horne 1987a; Wadsworth and Burnham 1987a, 1987b. Also available in pamphlet form as *Race, Class, and Howard Beach*, from *Frontline*, P.O. Box 2729, Oakland, CA 94602.
5. See Horne 1987b; Burnham et al. 1987.
6. From Carmichael and Hamilton 1967, 44–45.
7. I am of course fully aware that some intellectuals from the white Left attempted to understand the concept and elaborate on the implications raised by Black Power activists and idealogues. Most notable here is Blauner 1972.
8. See Cruse 1968, 201.
9. I do not think it is accidental that Rustin's claims, or Cruse's recapitulation of Rustin's claims, have been so often referred to in the literature on the Black Power movement. Perhaps there is an appearance of greater legitimacy when criticisms of "nationalist" deviations come from other Blacks. I do not doubt that the practice of using some Black intellectuals to criticize nationalist politics stems from both cynical and "politically correct" motivations. In either case this is a needlessly divisive practice, and confirms for nationalist-oriented Black intellectuals the arrogance and unprincipled (racist) nature of the white Left.
10. This concept can be found in the work of Omali Yeshitela, chairperson of the African People's Socialist Party.
11. The concept of antirevisionist Marxist came to be used in the 1960s and 1970s to distinguish between revolutionary Marxist heritage of Marx, Lenin, and Mao (some also included Stalin) and the reformist Marxist of the Communist Party of the Soviet Union and its allied parties since Khrushchev's 1956 revelations about Stalin's crimes and the CPSU's subsequent articulation of a peaceful road to socialism.
12. Indeed, this is Adolph Reed's judgement; see Reed, ed., 1986. The Third, or Communist, International was an attempt to organize a disciplined world revolutionary force in the wake of the refusal of the member parties of the socialist

(or second) international to adhere to the organization's position in opposition to involvement in World War I. Lenin argued that the socialists' capitulation to their own ruling classes in favor of an imperialist war constituted a class collaborationist strategy that was essentially counterrevolutionary. He thus called for a new Communist (or Third) International.

13. Harry Braverman's analysis (1974b) in a special issue of *Monthly Review* strikes me as a more balanced criticism of this phenomenon.

14. See Wilson 1987, 125.

15. Wilson 1987, 126–27.

16. Wilson 1987, 128.

17. Harrington 1972, 163.

NOTES TO CHAPTER 1

1. Owen 1994, 43, 72.

2. West 1991.

3. See Glastris and Thornton 1994, 38–39.

4. This is the thesis of Arrighi, Hopkins, and Wallerstein 1991. An interesting popular statement of the thesis as it relates to what is happening in the United States is provided by Katz 1992, 33–34, 75.

5. See Arrighi, Hopkins, and Wallerstein 1991.

6. The famous French historian Fernand Braudel (1972) speaks about the need to understand that there are three time frames with which one works in the study of history. They are the short term, or the time frame of the event; the medium term, or the time frame of the conjuncture (twenty-five to thirty years), and the long term (or *longue durée*), the time frame of structures.

7. At a news conference on February 3, 1994, Farrakhan said that he found Khallid Muhammad's remarks at Kean College to be "vile in manner, malicious, mean-spirited and spoken in mockery of individuals and people, which is against the spirit of Islam." However, Farrakhan stood by the truths that Khalid Muhammad spoke, but condemned in the strongest terms the manner in which these truths were represented (by which he meant the charges that Jews, Catholics, Arabs, and whites in general participated in the enslavement of Blacks and benefited from both the enslavement and the system of racial oppression that grew out of slavery). By and large the mainstream white media (at least in New York City) claimed to have not known what Farrakhan meant by "truths" and accused him of making a two-faced retraction (or "a poisoned message," according to a *Daily News* editorial, February 4, 1994, 38). See *New York Amsterdam News*, February 12, 1994, 12; *City Sun*, February 9, 1995, 5.

8. See Lipsitz 1988b.

9. In Sellers, May, and McMillen 1981, 1.

10. Wilson's *Declining Significance of Race* (1978) was awarded the Sidney

M. Spivak Award of the American Sociological Association (ASA), prompting the Association of Black Sociologists (ABS) to issue a statement denouncing both Wilson, for undercutting the struggle for racial equality, and the ASA, for cynically making the award to a Black sociologist who mouthed the views of the white sociological establishment.

11. Clarke 1992.

12. Quoted in Douglas 1994, A31.

13. These are the precise words of Daniel Patrick Moynihan (1968), 21.

14. See Lewis 1968. Oscar Lewis, like Daniel Patrick Moynihan, should be distinguished from the neoconservative camp, but it should be revealing how their views have been used for purposes for which they were at least not originally intended.

15. See Sales 1994, a pathbreaking study of Malcolm X and the Organization of Afro-American Unity.

16. Wynter 1992, 13.

17. See Franklin 1991, esp. 89–116.

18. See Hall 1993, 109.

19. Farrakhan 1994, 24–25.

20. In *The Jesse Jackson Phenomenon*, Adolph Reed (1986) argues that the Jewish/African American relationship has been mediated through elite formal advocacy organizations such as the NAACP and the National Urban League on one side, and the American Jewish Congress, the American Jewish Committee, and the Anti-Defamation League of B'nai B'rith on the other. Since the interaction has been governed by an ideological commitment to interracialism, Jews have been able to impact the dialogue from both sides, as representatives of autonomous Jewish organizations and as prominent members of interracial civil rights organizations. But Jewish organizations do not have an imperative to be interracial. Black advocacy organizations have historically depended on private philanthropy, access to which runs through or can be vetoed by elites of Jewish interest organizations.

21. Steinberg 1993.

22. See Steinberg 1993.

23. Quoted in Epps 1968, 132–33.

24. Sales 1994, 41–48.

25. Bennett 1964, 21–48.

26. Sales made these remarks at a February 16, 1994, presentation at Seton Hall University, "A Tribute to Malcolm X and Martin Luther King, Jr.," summarizing arguments made in his book *From Civil Rights to Black Liberation* (1994).

27. See Kelley 1993.

28. Summarized in Sales 1994, 41–48.

29. Sales 1994.

30. See Wacquant 1994.

31. See Piven 1981.
32. See Piven 1981; Piven and Cloward 1992.
33. Ucelli and O'Neil 1990.
34. Ucelli and O'Neil 1990, 6.
35. Robinson 1988, 4–5.
36. West 1991, 224.
37. See Anderson 1994.
38. West 1991, 224.
39. West 1991, 224.
40. Cornel West indeed has come a long way since a 1986 presentation at the Socialist Scholars Conference, when he quoted Patrice Lumumba about why Africans have such revolutionary longings: "We can never forget these scars."
41. West 1991, 226.
42. Katz 1992.
43. This argument is elaborated in Arrighi, Hopkins, and Wallerstein 1991.
44. Arrighi, Hopkins, and Wallerstein 1991, 235.
45. Arrighi, Hopkins, and Wallerstein 1991, 235.
46. Marable 1993.
47. See Puddington 1994.
48. Meyers 1994.
49. See Gilmore 1993.

NOTES TO CHAPTER 2

1. Exceptions include Harding 1982
2. See Robinson 1983 and 1997.
3. See Sales 1994.
4. Kazin 1988.
5. See Arrighi, Hopkins, and Wallerstein 1989 for a recent explanation of this concept. But the concept can also be found in Wallerstein 1974, 1979, 1980, 1984b; in Hopkins and Wallerstein 1982; and in Amin et al. 1990.
6. Wallerstein 1984c, 20–21.
7. While the attempts to make facts fit a doctrine is the essence of dogmatism, a focus on facts without any context or framework is an error of empiricism. I am aware that arguments against doctrine are often used to defend the status quo against someone who attempts to draw systemic conclusions about any set of data.
8. Michels 1962, 79.
9. Michels 1962, 337–338.
10. This is an argument Samir Amin has made in many of his writings. The

African People's Socialist Party also makes this argument, based on Lenin's analysis of the aristocracy of labor.

11. Moynihan 1967.

12. See Arrighi 1978, 1982, 1990; and Arrighi and Silver 1984.

13. These issues are also discussed in Arrighi, Hopkins, and Wallerstein 1991; and Wallerstein 1991f.

14. Quoted in Harding 1982.

15. This argument is elaborated in Meier, Rudwick, and Broderick 1971, xix–xxi.

16. See Meier, Rudwick, and Broderick 1971, xxiii–xxiv.

17. See Wallerstein 1991a, 23.

NOTES TO CHAPTER 3

1. Here I follow Hopkins and Wallerstein's 1982 usage.

2. Wallerstein 1991c, 3–4.

3. Wallerstein 1991a, 22.

4. Wallerstein 1991c, 3–4.

5. Du Bois 1979, 87–88.

6. Wallerstein 1979, 215–16.

7. Herbert Hill 1987, 43.

8. Hofstadter 1955, 5.

9. See Hofstadter 1955, 176–77.

10. Hofstadter 1955, 176.

11. Quoted in Hofstadter 1955, 180.

12. Hofstadter 1955, 185.

13. Hofstadter 1955, 190–91.

14. Hofstadter 1955, 193.

15. See Meier 1962, 258.

16. Quoted in Cox 1950, 238.

17. Washington 1971, 5.

18. Washington 1971, 5.

19. Washington 1971, 5–6.

20. Washington 1971, 7. These comments reflect the popularity of the natural selection arguments of the predominant social Darwinist outlook of the time.

21. Quoted in Cox 1950, 239.

22. Quoted in Marable 1986, 42.

23. See Washington 1965, 157.

24. See Marable 1986, 42.

25. This interpretation is shared by Meier (1971, 104) and Marable (1986, 41–43).

26. Du Bois 1961, 42–43.

27. Marable 1986, 43.

28. Meier and Rudwick 1976, 222.

29. Quoted in Meier 1971, 174.

30. The details of Du Bois's criticism are spelled out in Du Bois 1961, 42–54.

31. In his famous "Of Mr. Booker T. Washington and Others" (Du Bois 1961, 42–54) this is not spelled out clearly, although it is certainly intimated.

32. See Meier 1971, 171–89 for more details of the struggle within the Afro-American Council, and to get a sense of Booker T. Washington's methods of political conflict with his Black opponents.

33. This story is told in Marable 1986, 45–51.

34. Du Bois 1969, 236.

35. Du Bois 1969, 239.

36. Du Bois 1969, 240.

37. Quoted in Marable 1986, 55.

38. Du Bois 1961, 48.

39. Quoted in Allen 1970, 96.

40. See the Niagara Movement's Declaration of Principles in Grant 1968, 206–9.

41. Grant 1968, 209.

42. Marable 1986, 68.

43. According to Marable (1986, 56).

44. Marable 1986, 58–59.

45. Harding 1982, 90–91.

46. Haywood 1976, 177.

47. Marable 1986, 72.

48. Marable 1986, 72.

49. Marable 1986, 72–73.

50. Quoted in Hughes 1968, 212.

51. Hughes 1968, 213. Hughes does not know when the *Crisis* reached the one hundred thousand mark. Du Bois (1969, 269) indicates that by 1918 the circulation was sixty-eight thousand.

52. Hughes 1968, 213–14.

53. Marable 1986, 79.

54. Marable 1986, 80–81.

55. Broderick 1969, 366–72.

56. See the selection from Du Bois's summary, "The Amenia Conference: An Historic Negro Gathering," in Meier, Rudwick, and Broderick 1971, 73–74. Summarized in Broderick 1969, 371–72.

57. Du Bois 1970, 248.

58. This story is related in Du Bois 1970, 248, and in Meier and Rudwick

1976, 238, but in both books in an extremely elliptical way for such an important point.

59. See Grimke 1977.
60. Du Bois 1970, 247.
61. Du Bois 1970, 252–53.
62. Marable 1986, 94–96.
63. Harding 1982, 96.
64. Quoted in Moon 1972, 246.
65. Quoted in Moon 1972, 250.
66. Du Bois 1970, 255.

NOTES TO CHAPTER 4

1. See Abendroth 1972, 69–76, for a good overview of this period.
2. See Naison 1971; Hill 1983; Record 1971; Padmore 1972; Solomon 1988.
3. See Robinson 1983, 301–11 for an analysis of the Black Belt nation thesis.
4. See Amin 1982.
5. Bergesen 1980, 121.
6. See the previous chapter for a brief description of the Hobson-Lenin paradigm, and how I differ from that position along the lines of the paradigm suggested by Hopkins and Wallerstein 1982.
7. Amin 1982, 172–73.
8. "Nationalist" is my terminology. Arrighi, Hopkins, and Wallerstein (1989, 12–13) make a similar analysis, but they focus on how Lenin's conception of class analysis and class conflict constitutes a reversion to the Smithian paradigm of political economy. See also Wallerstein 1991c, 146.
9. See Hopkins and Wallerstein 1982, 51; and Wallerstein 1980, 21.
10. Amin 1982, 173–74.
11. See Amin 1982, 175; 1977, 103–17.
12. Quoted in Harding 1982, 104.
13. See Vincent 1973, 62–76; and Waskow 1966, 10.
14. This distinction is pointed out in Vincent 1973, 63.
15. See Tuttle 1985.
16. Vincent 1973, 44.
17. Tuttle 1985, 14–15.
18. Tuttle 1985, 15; Zinn 1980a, 371.
19. Tuttle 1985, 16.
20. Quoted in Zinn 1980a, 370.
21. Du Bois 1970, 140–41.
22. I do not mean to sound too absolute about this. Resistance to slavery was sometimes revolutionary, but it was always resistance. The relations of force

among the slave plantations of the U.S. South did not allow the expression of out-right revolutionary resistance as was the case in the Caribbean and South America. Further, the goal of the abolitionists was the abolition of slavery; any critique of the society as a whole was more implicit than explicit.

23. Foner 1977, 217–18, 266.

24. Harding 1982, 98.

25. Harding 1982, 99.

26. Partially reprinted in Vincent 1973, 46–47.

27. See Randolph 1919.

28. Marable 1980, 70–71.

29. Quoted in Marable 1980, 71.

30. Vincent 1973, 66.

31. Marable 1980, 66.

32. Marable 1980, 66.

33. Cronon 1959, 13–15.

34. Lewis 1988, 25–34.

35. See Vincent 1971, 93.

36. In Jacques-Garvey 1968, 126.

37. See Hollis Lynch's introduction to Jacques-Garvey 1968.

38. Wilson 1982, 30.

39. Note here that "colored" means mixed race or mulatto. In the Caribbean the mulattos were the middle class, while Blacks were the working class.

40. Wilson 1982, 31.

41. See Lynch's introduction to Jacques-Garvey 1968.

42. See Lynch in Jacques-Garvey 1968.

43. See Lewis 1970 for the conservative estimate. Michael Lewis's treatment of Garvey is in general more critical than most of the contemporary treatments. More recently Ernest Allen has located a citation from Du Bois that cites the West Indian radical and former editor of the *Negro World*, W. A. Domingo, as a source for a membership estimate of around 100,000 (Allen 1991).

44. Vincent 1971, 111. Vincent argues that representation from African countries may have been higher since African UNIA members were forced to use false names and work clandestinely.

45. Vincent 1971, 101.

46. Cited in Martin 1976, 13, from *Negro World,* August 21, 1921.

47. For details see chapter 9 in Martin 1976, 174–214, entitled "U.S.A. versus UNIA."

48. This charge stemmed from the representations they had made while soliciting stock purchases.

49. See Lynch's introduction to Jacques-Garvey 1968.

50. This story is related in Lynch's introduction to Jacques-Garvey 1968.

51. See Lynch's introduction to Jacques-Garvey 1968.

52. See Cronon 1959.

53. Jacques-Garvey 1968, Vol. 1, p. 52.

54. Jacques-Garvey 1968, Vol. 1, pp. 40–41.

55. Garvey certainly thought that the white liberals in the NAACP were insincere, and were simply seeking to distract the Negros from the real solution: building their own nation (see Jacques-Garvey 1968, Vol. 2, pp. 70–71). Harry Haywood argued similarly that liberals and philanthropists associated with the Tuskegee machine joined forces to form the NAACP when they witnessed the militant defiance, and came to suspect the potential of the Niagara Movement. For the details of this argument see Haywood 1976, 177–79.

56. Higham 1975, 270–77.

57. In Jacques-Garvey 1968, Vol. 2, p. 13.

58. This description may not apply as much to the NAACP today, which is in the process of renaissance and a return to the Du Boisian vision under the leadership of the Reverend Benjamin Chavis.

59. It is a fairly common observation among those who have studied African American nationalist movements that they are predominantly working-class in composition. See Bracey 1971; Bracey, Meier, and Rudwick 1970; Essien-Udom 1962; Lincoln 1973; and Pinkney 1976, among others.

60. Quoted in Martin 1976, 232.

61. Martin 1976, 231–36.

62. Martin 1976, 240.

63. Jacques-Garvey 1968, Vol. 2, pp. 333–34.

64. In Jacques-Garvey 1968,Vol. 2, p. 69.

65. See Lewis 1970.

66. Lewis 1970, 170–71.

67. Martin 1976, 15–17.

68. For some time there has been considerable controversy about the founding date of the African Blood Brotherhood. Originally many observers thought that the ABB had been founded in the fall of 1917, based on information from Carl Offord's interview with Cyril Briggs dated July 27, 1939. Draper (1960), Robert Hill (1987), and Solomon (1988) all reject the contention that the ABB was founded in the fall of 1917. Robert Hill and Solomon date the founding of the ABB with its announcement in the September 1918 issue of the *Crusader*.

69. "The African Blood Brotherhood," *Crusader* 2, no. 10 (June 1920); 7.

70. See Robert Hill 1987.

71. In Robert Hill 1987, xxxi. Grigsby (1987, 90) argues that Briggs's observation of the militancy of the interracial IWW and the example of the Bolshevik revolution convinced him that revolution was both possible and necessary.

72. "Aims of *The Crusader*," *Crusader*, November 1918, 1.

73. Robert Hill 1987, xxx.

74. Robert Hill 1987, xiii.

75. Quoted in Draper 1960, 323.
76. Quoted in *Crusader*, January 1919, 6.
77. *Crusader*, January 1919, 7.
78. *Crusader*, January 1919, 14.
79. See Robert Hill 1987, xii.
80. Robert Hill 1987, xvii.
81. These points were summarized by Draper (1960), who argued that this was not the original program of the ABB, but one that evolved from its later connection with the CPUSA. Draper noted that the ABB program was not reproduced in any of the fifteen issues of the *Crusader* available at the time Draper wrote, 1958. The program Draper saw was taken from Whitney 1924, 190–93. According to Whitney, the ABB program was one of the documents seized in the Bridgeman raid on the underground communist convention in 1922. The general line of the ABB appeared in the June 1920 issue of the *Crusader*.
82. See Briggs's letter to Garvey, reprinted in the *Crusader*, November 1921, 5.
83. In the *Crusader*, November 1921, inside front cover.
84. See Foner 1978.
85. Cruse 1967, 134.
86. *Crusader*, June 1920, 7, 22.
87. In the November 1921 issue of the *Crusader* Briggs claimed that Garvey turned his letter over to Justice Renaud in the 12th District Magistrate Court on October 20, 1921, with the statement that "Briggs sent me this letter asking me to co-operate with him in the overthrow of white governments." *Crusader*, November 1921, 1.
88. See Vincent 1971, 81–82.
89. Reprinted in *Crusader*, November 1921, 22.
90. Robert Hill 1987, xliv.
91. See Vincent 1971.
92. Vincent's claim here may indeed be true. But there is a tendency to mystify a situation that simply reflects the contradictions in real life. In some sense the preoccupation with communist fronts is misplaced, Domingo's position regarding the necessity of Black leadership notwithstanding. The relationship between the two organizations seems straightforward, although perhaps shrouded by security concerns, which were of course real at the time. Both the CPUSA and the ABB were revolutionary organizations operating in what they believed to be a revolutionary period. What is more natural than for them to work together to try to maximize their chances for success, provided they established the proper trust and respect between the two groups?
93. Foner and Allen 1987, 16–18. Harry Haywood describes how in the ABB (in Chicago) he forged his first active experience with Black industrial workers, who he found to be "literate, articulate, and class conscious, a proud and defiant

group which had been radicalized by the struggles against discriminatory practices of the unions and employers" (Haywood 1978, 131).

94. See Harding 1982.
95. See Naison 1983.
96. Robert Hill 1987, xlvii.
97. See Draper 1960.
98. See Foster 1968, 268. However, there is no mention of the ABB in Foster 1970, although he mentions Briggs as part of the *Messenger* group, which Briggs denies.
99. See Shanna and Seen 1986.
100. See Vincent 1971.
101. Quoted in Draper 1960, 316.
102. Quoted in Sitkoff 1978, 141.
103. See Sitkoff 1978.
104. Robinson 1983, 291.
105. Wilson Record (1971, 39–42) seems to agree with this assessment.
106. See Draper 1960.
107. Robert Hill 1987, xlii-xliv.
108. See Foner and Allen 1987.
109. Quoted in Draper 1960, 331.
110. Cruse 1968, 78.
111. Quoted in Cruse 1967, 28.
112. Cruse 1967, 51.
113. Cruse 1967, 51–52.
114. Cruse 1967, 63.
115. Cruse 1967, 84.
116. Cruse 1967, 83–85.
117. Cruse 1967, 86.
118. See Allen 1991.
119. See Allen 1991.

NOTES TO CHAPTER 5

1. Sitkoff 1978, 34–35.
2. Sitkoff 1978, 35–37.
3. Sitkoff 1978, 37–38.
4. See Bracey 1971.
5. Frazier 1974, 54–71; Fauset 1971, 1–13.
6. Klehr 1984, 328–29.
7. Klehr 1984, 330.
8. Sitkoff 1978, 156–58.
9. See Klehr 1984.

10. Record 1971, 143–46.
11. Quoted in Klehr 1984, 243.
12. Klehr 1984; Alkalimat 1985, 137.
13. Klehr 1984, 297–302.
14. Sitkoff 1978, 145–47.
15. Sitkoff 1978, 148–49.
16. Sitkoff 1978, 149.
17. Record 1971; Sitkoff 1978; Cruse 1967.
18. Record 1971, 156.
19. See Myrdal 1944.
20. Record 1971; Myrdal 1944.
21. See Naison 1983, 295–98 for the details of this meeting.
22. Montgomery 1987, 123.
23. Horne 1988.
24. Haywood 1978.
25. Du Bois 1973.
26. Du Bois 1973, 213–14.
27. In Du Bois 1973, 214.
28. Du Bois 1973, 214.
29. Braverman 1974a, 403–9.
30. Record 1971, 116.
31. See Haywood 1978, 177.
32. Quoted in Draper 1960, 334.
33. Naison 1978, 27–29.
34. Naison 1978, 28–29.
35. Naison 1978, 30–31.
36. Naison 1978, 32–33.
37. Naison 1978, 35.
38. Many were astounded that Randolph, who had opposed Garvey's nationalism in the 1920s, could now advocate an all-Black organization. Manning Marable (1981b) points out that people forget that Randolph worked in coalition with Garvey against Du Bois and the NAACP from 1916 to 1919. Marable thus argues that Randolph's break with Garvey did not represent a strategic repudiation of all-Black organization. Sitkoff (1978), however, argues that the nationalist-sounding rhetoric of Randolph with regard to the MOWM was designed to forestall a takeover by white communists who had achieved substantial influence over the National Negro Congress.
39. See Alkalimat 1985, 255–56.
40. Quoted in Alkalimat 1985, 256.
41. See Lewis 1970.
42. Harding 1982, 143–44.
43. Harding 1982, 132–33.

44. See Lewis 1970.

45. Despite the apparent religiosity of Blacks, they live in a secular society. However, this very religiosity is viewed as one reason for the success of the Nation of Islam. See Laue 1964.

46. This topic has not been accorded significant scholarly investigation, with the exception of William R. Scott's majestic work, *The Sons of Sheba's Race: African-Americans and the Italo-Ethiopian War, 1935–1941* (1993). Another excellent treatment of this topic is Robinson 1985.

47. See especially Drake 1970

48. Scott 1993, 15–17.

49. Scott 1993, 5.

50. Scott 1993, 87.

51. Scott 1993, 62.

52. Quoted in Scott 1993, 66.

53. See Scott 1993, 62–68.

54. See Robinson 1985.

55. Scott 1993, 110–16.

56. Quoted in Scott 1993, 135.

57. See Scott 1993, 142.

58. Dalfiume 1969, 301–2.

59. Quoted in Dalfiume 1969, 302. From "Lynching and Liberty," *Crisis*, July 1940, 209.

60. Quoted in Dalfiume 1969, 305.

61. Quoted in Sitkoff 1971, 662.

62. Sitkoff 1971, 668.

63. Dalfiume 1969, 302. For a more extensive treatment, see Allen 1994a and 1994b.

64. Dalfiume 1969, 303.

65. Strickland 1994, 38.

NOTES TO CHAPTER 6

1. Wallerstein 1984c, 72–73.

2. See Piven and Cloward 1979.

3. Piven and Cloward 1979.

4. Piven and Cloward 1979, 205–6.

5. Piven and Cloward 1979, 214–15.

6. Piven and Cloward 1979, 217–19.

7. As Aldon Morris 1984 points out, the sit-in had been used in sixteen cities from 1957 to 1960. Morris emphasizes the role of preexisting movement centers in planning or encouraging the massive sit-in movement that followed.

8. See Carson 1981 and Marable 1985b.

9. Carson 1981, 19.
10. Piven and Cloward 1979, 225–26.
11. Piven and Cloward 1979, 228.
12. Marable 1985b, 25.
13. Marable 1985b, 25–28.
14. Carson 1981, 34.
15. Carson 1981, 39–42.
16. Quoted in Carson 1981, 62.
17. Carson 1981, 63–64.
18. Marable 1985b, 76–77.
19. King 1991, 289–302.
20. Marable 1985b, 79–81.
21. Carson 1981, 94–95.
22. Carson 1981, 123–28.
23. Quoted in Carson 1981, 166.
24. Quoted in Carson 1981, 199.
25. Carson 1981, 202–3.
26. Quoted in Carson 1981, 210.
27. See Sales 1994.
28. See Piore 1979.
29. Piore 1979, 161.
30. Piore 1979, 163.
31. See Gus John in Alkalimat 1991, 79–80.
32. Lomax 1968, 65–76.
33. Strickland 1994.
34. Strickland 1994, 81–83.
35. Strickland 1994, 134.
36. See Strickland 1994.
37. See Sales 1994.
38. See Lomax 1968.
39. Clarke 1990, xxiv.
40. Lomax 1968, 181.
41. Lomax 1968, 252.
42. See Plummer 1996.
43. Lomax 1968, 288–89.
44. In Strickland 1994.
45. See Baxter and Aalmuhammed 1994.
46. Karim 1992; Baxter and Aalmuhammed 1994.
47. Kondo 1993, 170.
48. Malcolm X 1989, 136–37.
49. See Baxter and Aalmuhammed 1994.
50. Kondo 1993, 203–5.

51. Sales 1994, 156.
52. Sales 1994, 157.
53. Kondo 1993, 173.
54. Kondo 1993, 195.
55. See Kelley 1994, chap. 7, "The Riddle of the Zoot: Malcolm Little and Black Cultural Politics during World War II."
56. See Kelley 1992a.
57. Cosgrave 1984, 78–81.
58. Kelley 1992a, 168–69.
59. See DeCaro 1996.
60. DeCaro 1996, 66, 56.
61. Evanzz 1992, 15.
62. Evanzz 1992, 16–17.
63. See Clarke 1961.
64. Sales 1994, 59–60.
65. Quoted in Sales 1994, 66.
66. Sales 1994, 68.
67. Goldman 1979, 108.
68. Quoted in Goldman 1979, 157.
69. Goldman 1979, 163.
70. Quoted in Goldman 1979, 164.
71. Alkalimat, ed., 1990, 31.
72. Sales 1994, 101.
73. Sales 1994, 101.
74. See Malcolm X 1966, 212.
75. Quoted in Malcolm X 1966, 213.
76. Unfortunately the story of this movement has yet to be presented and analyzed in sufficient detail.

NOTES TO CHAPTER 7

1. See Foner 1970.
2. See Newton 1973.
3. See Foner 1970.
4. Garry 1970, 258.
5. Newton 1972.
6. All quotes from Carter are taken from Carter 1969, reprinted in Foner 1970, 27–28.
7. Quoted in Blair 1977, 87.
8. This position was elaborated in Cleaver 1970.
9. This is not a satisfactory formulation. The Black Panther Party was able to foster unity across class lines as well. Like Malcolm it appealed to the Black

intelligentsia, but unlike Malcolm it was able to appeal to oppressed groups throughout the United States, and the white intelligentsia as well (both liberal and radical).

10. See Hampton and Fayer 1990, 528.

11. Newton 1972, 45.

12. I am indebted to an unpublished manuscript by Melanie Bush for this chronicle of the party's survival programs.

13. See Withorn 1978b; Foner 1970.

14. Katsiaficas 1987, 203.

15. Newton 1973, 370.

16. Geschwender 1977, 83.

17. Allen 1979, 71.

18. According to Georgakas and Surkin 1975, 40.

19. This process is described in Allen 1979 and in Georgakas and Surkin 1975.

20. See Grigsby 1987.

21. Geschwender 1977, 142.

22. Geschwender 1977, 143–45.

23. Quoted in Foner 1974, 422.

24. Allen 1979, 92.

25. Georgakas and Surkin 1975, 160–64.

26. Allen 1979, 102.

27. Georgakas and Surkin 1975, 166–69.

28. Geschwender 1977, 204.

29. Baraka 1984, 312.

30. Baraka 1984 concurs with this view.

NOTES TO CHAPTER 8

1. O'Reilly 1989, 355.

2. Reprinted in Churchill and Vander Wall 1990, 110.

3. Churchill and Vander Wall 1988, 64–69.

4. Hilliard and Cole 1993, 238–39.

5. Newton 1996, 79–80.

6. Newton 1996, 78–81.

7. Liberatore 1996, 243–47.

8. Hilliard and Cole 1993, 378–82.

9. Churchill and Vander Wall 1988, 79–80.

10. Churchill and Vander Wall 1988, 85–87.

11. Churchill and Vander Wall 1990, 157.

12. Shakur 1987.

13. Churchill and Vander Wall 1990, 308; Acoli 1995, 6.

14. Churchill and Vander Wall 1990, 309.

15. Weinglass 1997, 4–6.

16. Hilliard and Cole 1993, 239.

17. See Bush 1984.

18. Bush 1984, 323.

19. Brown 1992, 248.

20. Newton 1972, 48.

21. Brown 1992, 248–49.

22. Newton 1972, 50.

23. Newton 1972, 51.

24. Frady 1996, 8.

25. Frady 1996, 9–10.

26. Frady 1996, 13.

27. Frady 1996, 286.

28. Frady 1996, 295.

29. For a detailed elaboration of this issue see Robinson 1997 and 1983.

30. See Mao Zedong 1969.

31. Baxter and Aalmuhammed 1994.

32. Evanzz 1996, 4.

33. Evanzz 1996, 1.

34. Evanzz 1996, 3.

35. Telephone interview with Jack Newfield, January 5, 1998; Newfield 1994a, 1994b.

36. Thus Jack Kemp's praise of Louis Farrakhan makes perfect sense. For an elaboration of this theme, see Reed 1991a, 1991b, 1996; and Lubiano 1997.

37. The complicity between the state and conservative nationalists in the murder of Malcolm X has been alluded to, but too much emphasis has been placed on attempts to disrupt the Black liberation movement by fishing in troubled waters. More attention should be paid to the fact that the state invariably sides with the more conservative elements. See Madhubuti 1994 for a discussion of this issue.

38. The publications of the radical fringe are now less numerous than in the 1970s, but they include the *Black Scholar, Third World Viewpoint,* the *Nation,* the *Progressive, Monthly Review, Social Justice, Race and Reason, People's Tribune, New Politics,* the *Burning Spear,* and *New Left Review.*

39. See Cornel West's critique of Black Marxists in *Prophesy Deliverance* (1982) and his critique of Black nationalists in *Race Matters* (1994). However, if he is to take his choice of nationalists, it is Elijah Muhammad over Malcolm X. See West 1992.

40. See Wallerstein 1983, 1991e.

41. Rivers 1994/95.

42. See in particular Martin Kilson's (1995) and Glenn Loury's (1995) response to Rivers 1994/95.

43. Telephone interview with Elombe Brath, October 1995.

44. See Sales 1994.

45. Black Radical Congress 1997.

46. Arrighi 1990; Gorz 1982.

47. I take this term from the concluding chapter of Wallerstein 1983, 102.

48. See Wallerstein 1991d.

49. Arrighi 1990.

Bibliography

Abdel-Malek, Anouar. 1981. *Nation and Revolution*. Albany: State University of New York Press.

Abendroth, Wolfgang. 1972. *A Short History of the European Working Class*. New York: Monthly Review.

Abraham, Kinfe. 1991. *The Politics of Black Nationalism: From Harlem to Soweto*. Trenton: Africa World Press.

Abron, JoNina. 1986. "The Legacy of the Black Panther Party." *Black Scholar* (November–December): 17, no. 6, 33–37.

Acoli, Sundiata. "A Brief History of the New Afrikan Prison Struggle." *Arm the Spirit*, November 30.

Ahmad, Muhammad. 1990a. "Malcolm X: Human Rights and Self-Determination." *Forward Motion* 9, no. 1 (March): 9–13.

———. 1990b. *Toward Black Liberation. Pt. 1*. Cleveland: Legacy Communications.

Ali, Tariq. 1969. *The New Revolutionaries*. New York: Morrow.

Alkalimat, Abdul. 1990a. "Black Marxism in the White Academy." In Abdul Alkalimat, ed., *Paradigms in Black Studies*, 207–25. Chicago: Twenty-First Century.

———. 1990b. "1990: Why Remember Malcolm X." *Forward Motion* 9, no. 1 (March): 3–8.

———. 1985. *Introduction to Afro-American Studies*. Chicago: Peoples College Press.

———, ed. 1991. *Perspectives on Black Liberation and Social Revolution*. Chicago: Twenty-First Century.

———. 1990. *Malcolm X for Beginners*. New York: Writers and Readers.

Alkalimat, Abdul, and Doug Gills. 1984. "Chicago: Black Power vs. Racism: Harold Washington Becomes Mayor." In Rod Bush, ed., *The New Black Vote*, 53–179. San Francisco: Synthesis Publication.

Alkalimat, Abdul, and Nelson Johnson. 1973. "Toward the Ideological Unity of the African Liberation Support Committee: A Response to Critics of the Statement of Principles Accepted at Frogmore, South Carolina, June-July 1973." Unpublished manuscript.

Allen, Ernest. 1996. "Religious Heterodoxy and Nationalist Tradition: The Continuing Evolution of the Nation of Islam." *Black Scholar* 26, nos. 3–4 (Fall–Winter): 2–34.

———. 1994a. "When Japan Was 'Champion of the Darker Races'" Sakota Takahashi and the Flowering of Black Messianic Nationalism." *Black Scholar* 24, no.1 (winter): 23–46.

———. 1994b. "Waiting for Tojo: The Pro-Japan Vigil of Black Missourians, 1992–1943." Forthcoming in *Gateway Heritage*.

———. 1991. "The New Negro: Explorations in Identity and Social Consciousness, 1910–1922." In Adele Heller and Lois Rudnick, *1915: The Cultural Moment*, 48–68. New Brunswick: Rutgers University Press.

———. 1985–86. "Afro-American Identity: Reflections on the Pre–Civil War Era." *Contributions in Black Studies*, no. 7:45–93.

———. 1979. "Dying from the Inside: The Decline of the League of Revolutionary Black Workers." In Dick Cluster, ed., *They Should Have Served That Cup of Coffee: Seven Radicals Remember the 60s*, 71–109. Boston: South End.

———. 1977. "The Cultural Methodology of Harold Cruse." *Journal of Ethnic Studies 5*, no. 2 (summer): 26–50.

Allen, Robert. 1976. "Racism and the Black Nation Thesis." *Socialist Revolution* 6, no. 1 (January-March).

———. 1974. *Reluctant Reformers: Racism and Social Reform Movements in the United States*. Garden City, NY: Anchor Books.

———. 1970. *Black Awakening in Capitalist America*. Garden City, NY: Anchor Books.

Alston, Jacquelyn. 1985. *Comparative Nationalism: Definitions, Interpretations and the Black American and British West African Experience to 1947*. Washington, DC: Historical Dimensions Press.

Amin, Samir. 1990a. *Delinking: Towards a Polycentric World*. London: Zed Press.

———. 1990b. *Maldevelopment: Anatomy of a Global Failure*. London: Zed Press.

———. 1988. "Accumulation on a World Scale: Thirty Years Later." *Rethinking Marxism* 1, no. 2 (Summer).

———. 1982. "Crisis, Nationalism, and Socialism." In Samir Amin et al., *Dynamics of Global Crisis*. 167–231. New York Monthly.

———. 1980a. *Class and Nation*. New York: Monthly Review.

———. 1980b. "Concerning Eurocommunism." *Contemporary Marxism*, no. 2 (Winter 1980): 27–39.

———. 1977. *Imperialism and Unequal Development*. New York: Monthly Review.

———. 1975. "Toward a Structural Crisis of World Capitalism." *Socialist Revolution* 5, no. 1 (April): 9–44.

———. 1974. *Unequal Development: An Essay on the Social Formations of Peripheral Capitalism*. New York: Monthly Review.

Amin, Samir, Giovanni Arrighi, Andre Gunder Frank,, and Immanuel Wallerstein. 1990. *Transforming the Revolution: Social Movements and the World-System*. New York: Monthly Review.

———. 1982. *The Dynamics of Global Crisis*. New York: Monthly Review.

Anderson, Elijah. 1994. "The Code of the Streets." *Atlantic Monthly*, May 80–94.

Anderson-Sherman, Arnold, and Doug McAdam. 1982. "American Black Insurgency and the World-Economy: A Political Process Model." In Edward Friedman, ed., *Ascent and Decline in the World-System*, 165–88. Beverly Hills: Sage.

Anthony, Earl. 1990. *Spitting in the Wind: The True Story behind the Violent Legacy of the Black Panther Party*. Malibu, CA: Roundtable Publishing.

———. 1970. *Picking Up the Gun: A Report on the Black Panthers*. New York: Dial Press.

Arrighi, Giovanni. 1990. "Marxist Century, American Century: The Making and Remaking of the World Labour Movement." *New Left Review*, no. 179 (January–February): 29–63.

———. 1978. "Towards a Theory of Capitalist Crisis." *New Left Review*, September-October, 3–24.

———. 1982. "A Crisis of Hegemony." In Samir Amin et. al., *Dynamics of Global Crisis*, 55–108. New York, Monthly Review.

Arrighi, Giovanni and Terence K. Hopkins. 1986. "Theoretical Space and Space for Theory in World-Historical Social Science." In Norbert Wiley, ed., *The Marx-Weber Debate*, 31–41. Beverly Hills: Sage.

Arrighi, Giovanni, Terence Hopkins, and Immanuel Wallerstein. 1991. "1989: The Continuation of 1968." Paper prepared for Eleventh International Colloquium on the World-Economy, "1989: The End of an Era?" Starnberg, June 28–30. Reprinted in *Review* 15, no. 2 (spring 1992): 221–42.

———. 1989. *Antisystemic Movements*. New York: Verso.

Arrighi, Giovanni, and Beverly Silver. 1985. "Labor and Long Waves." Paper prepared for the Second International Forum on the History of the Labor Movement and the Working Class, Paris, June 26–28.

———. 1984. "Labor Movements and Capital Migration." In Charles Bergquist, ed., *Labor in the Capitalist World-Economy*, 183–216. Beverly Hills: Sage.

Aya, Rod. 1979. "Theories of Revolution Reconsidered: Contrasting Models of Collective Violence." *Theory and Society* 8:1–38.

Bailey, Ron. 1973. "Economic Aspects of the Internal Colony." In Frank Bonilla and Robert Girling, eds., *Structures of Dependency*. Stanford: Institute for Political Studies.

Baker, Houston. 1993. "Scene . . . Not Heard." In Robert Gooding-Williams, ed., *Reading Rodney King, Reading Urban Uprising*, 38–48. New York: Routledge.

Baraka, Amiri. 1984. *The Autobiography of Leroi Jones*. New York: Freundlich Books.

Baron, Harold. 1978. "The Retreat from Black Nationalism: A Response to Robert L. Allen." *Socialist Review* 8, no. 1 (January–February).

———. 1975. "Racial Discrimination in Advanced Capitalism: A Theory of Nationalism and Divisions in the Labor Market." In Richard Edwards, Michael Reich, and David Gordon, eds., *Labor Market Segmentation*. Lexington, MA: D. C. Heath.

Baxter, Jack, and Jefri Aalmuhammed. 1994. *Brother Minister: The Assassination of Malcolm X*. Greenvale, NY: 3rd Millennium Entertainment Group.

Bennett, Lerone. 1964. *The Negro Mood*. New York: Ballantine.

Bergesen, Albert. 1983. "The Class Structure of the World-System." In William Thompson, ed., *Contending Approaches to World System Analysis*, 43–54. Beverly Hills: Sage.

———. 1980. "Cycles of Formal Colonial Rule." In Terence K. Hopkins and Immanuel Wallerstein, ed., *Processes of the World-System*, 119–26. Beverly Hills: Sage.

Bergquist, Charles. 1984. "Placing Labor at the Center: Introduction." In Charles Bergquist, ed., *Labor in the Capitalist World-Economy*, 7–19. Beverly Hills: Sage.

Bermanzohn, Paul, and Sally Bermazohn. 1980. *The True Story of the Greensboro Massacre*. New York: Cesar Cauce.

Bernstein, Dennis, and Julie Light. 1995. "The Life and Times of William Moses Kuntsler." *Z Magazine*, October.

Bernstein, Eduard. 1961. *Evolutionary Socialism: A Criticism and Affirmation*. New York: Schocken Books.

Beverly, Creigs, and Howard Stanback. 1986. "The Black Underclass: Theory and Reality." *Black Scholar*, September–October.

Black Radical Congress. 1997. "Principles of Unity," Chicago, IL, http://www.blackradicalcongress.com

Blair, Thomas L. 1977. *Retreat to the Ghetto: The End of a Dream?* New York: Hill and Wang.

Blake, J. Herman. 1973. "Black Nationalists." In Peter Rose, Stanley Rothman, and William Julius Wilson, eds., *Through Different Eyes: Black and White Perspectives on American Race Relations*, 72–87. New York: Oxford University Press.

Blauner, Bob. 1989. *Black Lives, White Lives: Three Decades of Race Relations in America*. Berkeley: University of California Press.

———. 1972. *Racial Oppression in America*. New York: Harper and Row.

Blauner, Bob, Harold Cruse, Stephen Steinberg et al. 1990. "Race and Class: A Discussion." *New Politics* 2, no. 4 (winter): 12–58.

Blaut, James. 1977. "Are Puerto Ricans a National Minority?" *Monthly Review* 29, no. 1 (May): 35–55.

Bloom, Jack. 1987. *Class, Race, and the Civil Rights Movement*. Bloomington: Indiana University Press.

Blum, Zahava, and Peter Rossi. 1968. "Social Class Research and Images of the Poor: A Bibliographic Review." In Daniel Patrick Moynihan, ed., *On Understanding Poverty: Perspectives from the Social Sciences*, 343–97. New York: Basic Books.

Blumer, Herbert. 1969. "Social Movements." In A. M. Lee, ed., *Principles of Sociology*. New York: Barnes and Noble.

Boggs, Carl. 1986. *Social Movements and Political Power: Emerging Forms of Radicalism in the West*. Philadelphia: Temple University Press.

———. 1972. "The Italian Left: A New Political Synthesis?" *Socialist Revolution* 2, no. 3 (May-June): 91–113.

Boggs, James. 1985. "What Now for Blacks?" *Monthly Review* 37, no.2 (June).

———. 1984. "Beyond Militancy." *Monthly Review* 26, no. 4 (September).

———. 1983. "From Rights to Power." Mimeo.

Boggs, James, and Grace Lee. 1974. "Marxism: Looking Backward and Forward." *Monthly Review* 26, no. 2 (June).

Bonacich, Edna. 1976. "Advanced Capitalism and Black/White Relations in the United States: A Split Labor Market Interpretation." *American Sociological Review* 41.

Bonilla, Frank. 1985. "Ethnic Orbits: The Circulation of Capitals and Peoples." *Contemporary Marxism*, no. 10.

Bonilla, Frank, and Ricardo Campos. 1982. "Imperialist Initiatives and the Puerto Rican Worker." *Contemporary Marxism*, no. 5 (summer): 1–18.

Bontemps, Arna, and Jack Conroy. 1966. *Anyplace but Here*. New York: Hill and Wang.

Boswell, Terry. 1989. "World Revolutions and Revolution in the World-System." In Terry Boswell, ed., *Revolution in the World-System*, 1–16. Westport, CT: Greenwood.

Bourdieu, Pierre. 1985. "Social Space and the Genesis of Groups." *Theory and Society* 14 (October): 723–44.

———. 1979. "The Disenchantment of the World." In *Algeria 1960*. New York: Cambridge University Press.

Boyd, Herb. 1995. *Black Panthers for Beginners*. New York: Writers and Readers.

Bracey, John. 1971. "Black Nationalism after Garvey." In Nathan Huggins, Martin Kilson, and Daniel Fox, eds., *Key Issues in the Afro-American Experience.* New York: Harcourt Brace Jovanovich.

Bracey, John, August Meier, and Elliott Rudwick, eds. 1971. *Conflict and Competition: Studies in the Recent Black Protest Movement.* Belmont, CA: Wadsworth.

———. 1970. *Black Nationalism in America,* Indianapolis: Bobbs-Merrill.

Branch, Taylor. 1988. *Parting the Waters: America in the King Years, 1954–63.* New York: Simon and Schuster.

Brandel, Fernand. 1972. "History and the Social Sciences: The Longue Durée." In Peter Burke, ed. *Economy and Society in Early Modern Europe,* 11–42. London: Routledge and Regan.

Braun, Denny. 1991. *The Rich Get Richer: The Rise of Income Inequality in the United States and the World.* Chicago: Nelson-Hall.

Braverman, Harry. 1974a. *Labor and Monopoly Capital: The Degradation of Work in the Twentieth Century.* New York: Monthly Review.

———. 1974b. "Marxism: Looking Backward and Forward." *Monthly Review* 26, no. 2 (June).

Breitman, George. 1968. *The Last Year of Malcolm X: The Evolution of a Revolutionary.* New York: Schocken Books.

Brisbane, Robert. 1974. *Black Activism: Racial Revolution in the United States, 1954–1970.* Valley Forge, PA: Judson Press.

———. 1970. *The Black Vanguard: Origins of the Negro Social Revolution, 1900–1960.* Valley Forge, PA: Judson Press.

Broderick, Francis L. 1969. "W. E. B. Du Bois: Entente with White Liberals, 1910–1920." In Melvin Drimmer, ed., *Black History: A Reappraisal.* Garden City, NY: Doubleday.

Brown, Elaine. 1992. *A Taste of Power: A Black Woman's Story.* New York: Pantheon.

Buhle, Paul. 1987. *Marxism in the United States: Remapping the History of the American Left.* New York: Verso.

Burawoy, Michael. 1974. "Race, Class, and Colonialism." *Social and Economic Studies* 23:521–51.

Burnham, Linda, Letisha Wadsworth, Gerald Horne, Utrice Leid, Ute Buesing, Andy Pollack, and Geoffrey Jacques. 1987. "Race, Class, and Howard Beach: The Debate in the City Sun." *Frontline Reprints,* March.

Burnham, Walter Dean. 1989. "A Comment on Harry Eckstein's 'Civic Inclusion and Its Discontents.'" *Daedalus* 113, no. 4 (fall): 147–60.

Bush, Rod. 1981. "Racism and the Rise of the Right." *Contemporary Marxism,* no. 4 (winter–spring).

———, ed. 1984. *The New Black Vote: Politics and Power in Four American Cities.* San Francisco: Synthesis.

Cabral, Amilcar. 1973a. "Connecting the Struggles: An Informal Talk with Black Americans." In *Return to the Source: Selected Speeches of Amilcar Cabral,* 75–92. New York: Monthly Review.

———. 1973b. "National Liberation and Culture." In *Return to the Source: Selected Speeches of Amilcar Cabral,* 39–56. New York: Monthly Review.

Campbell, Horace. 1987. *Rasta and Resistance: From Marcus Garvey to Walter Rodney.* Trenton: Africa World Press.

Campos, Ricardo, and Frank Bonilla. 1982. "Bootstraps and Enterprise Zones: The Underside of Late Capitalism in the United States and Puerto Rico." *Review 5,* no. 4 (spring): 556–90.

Cantor, Milton. 1978. *The Divided Left: American Radicalism, 1900–1975.* New York: Hill and Wang.

Carmichael, Stokely, and Charles Hamilton. 1967. *Black Power: The Politics of Liberation in America.* New York: Random House.

Carr, E. H. 1982. *Twilight of the Comintern, 1930–1935.* New York: Pantheon.

Carr, Leslie. 1981. "The Origin of the Communist Party's Theory of Black Self-Determination: Draper vs. Haywood." *Insurgent Sociologist* 10, no. 3 (winter): 35–50.

Carson, Claiborne. 1991. *Malcolm X: The FBI File.* New York: Carroll and Graf.

———. 1981. *In Struggle: SNCC and the Black Awakening of the 1960s.* Cambridge: Harvard University Press.

Carter, Alprentice (Bunchy). 1969. "The Genius of Huey Newton." *Black Panther,* March 3. Reprinted in Philip Foner, ed., *The Black Panthers Speak.* New York: Lippincott, 1970.

Carter, Greg. 1986. "In the Narrows of the 1960s U.S. Black Rioting." *Journal of Conflict Resolution* 30, no. 1 (March): 115–27.

Castells, Manuel. 1983. *The City and the Grassroots.* Berkeley: University of California Press.

Caulfield, Mina Davis. 1974a. "Culture and Imperialism: Proposing a New Dynamic." In Dell Hymes, ed., *Reinventing Anthropology.* New York: Random House.

———. 1974b. "Imperialism, the Family, and Cultures of Resistance." *Socialist Revolution* 4, no. 2 (October).

Caute, David. 1988. *The Year of the Barricades: A Journey through 1968.* New York: Harper and Row.

———. 1970. *Frantz Fanon.* New York: Viking.

Centers, Richard. 1949. *The Psychology of Social Classes.* Princeton: Princeton University Press.

Chaffe, William H. 1986. *The Unfinished Journey: America since World War II.* New York: Oxford University Press.

Childs, John Brown. 1981. "Concepts of Culture in Afro-American Political Thought, 1890–1920." *Social Text* 2, no. 1 (fall): 28–43.

Churchill, Ward, and James Vander Wall. 1990. *The COINTELPRO Papers: Documents from the FBI's Secret Wars against Dissent in America*. Boston: South End.

———. 1988. *Agents of Repression: The FBI's Secret Wars against the Black Panther Party and the American Indian Movement*. Boston: South End.

Clarke, John Henrik. 1992. "Black Pseudo-Scholars Are 'In' with White America, but They Deserve to Be 'Outed,' Says Historian." *Alkebulanian*, 3d Quarter, 4–8.

———. 1991. *Africans at the Crossroads: Notes for an African World Revolution*. Trenton: Africa World Press.

———. 1974. *Black Americans: Immigrants against Their Will*. Los Angeles: Center for African and African-American Studies Occasional Paper, April.

———. 1973–74. "Marcus Garvey: The Harlem Years." *Black Scholar* 5, no. 4:17–25.

———. 1973. "The Impact of the African on the New World: A Reappraisal." *Black Scholar* 4, no. 5 (February): 32–39.

———. 1961. "The New Afro-American Nationalism." *Freedomways* 1, no. 3 (fall): 285–95.

———, ed. 1990. *Malcolm X: The Man and His Times*. Trenton: Africa World Press.

Claudin, Fernando. 1975. *The Communist Movement: From Comintern to Cominform*. New York: Monthly Review.

Cleaver, Eldridge. 1970. "On the Ideology of the Black Panther Party." *Black Panther*, June 6. Reprinted in Philip Foner, ed., *The Black Panthers Speak*. New York: Lippincott.

Clegg, Claude Andrew. 1997. *An Original Man: The Life and Times of Elijah Muhammad*. New York: St. Martin's.

Cole, Johnetta. 1973. "The Black Bourgeoisie." In Peter Rose, Stanley Rothman, and William Julius Wilson, eds., *Through Different Eyes: Black and White Perspectives on American Race Relations*, 25–43. New York: Oxford University Press.

Collins, Sheila. 1986. *The Rainbow Challenge*. New York: Monthly Review.

Colon, Jesus. 1982. *A Puerto Rican in New York and Other Sketches*. New York: International Publishers.

Community Self-Defense Program. 1990. "From Self-Defense to Consolidating People's Power: History Goes Forward!!! Statement of the History and Political Line of the Community Self-Defense Program." Brooklyn: Spear and Shield Publications.

———. 1988. "Conversations in Fort Green; Black Liberation Movement at the Crossroads: Tactics and Strategy of Building a Mass Movement."

———. 1986. "Building Confidence among the Masses: Political Report to the Black Community and Black Liberation Movement." July.

Cone, James. 1991. *Martin and Malcolm and America: A Dream or a Nightmare.* Maryknoll, NY: Orbis Books.

———. 1980. "The Black Church and Marxism: What Do They Have to Say to Each Other?" Occasional Paper, Institute for Democratic Socialism, April.

Corrigan, Philip, Harvie Ramsay, and Derek Sayer. 1979. *For Mao: Essays in Historical Materialism.* London: MacMillan.

Cosgrave, Stuart. 1984. "The Zoot-Suit and Style Warfare." *History Workshop Journal* 18 (autumn): 77–91.

Cox, Oliver. 1987. *Race, Class, and the World System.* New York: Monthly Review.

———. 1950. "Leadership among Negroes in the United States." In Alvin Gouldner, *Studies in Leadership: Leadership and Democratic Action,* 228–71. New York: Harper and Row.

———. 1948. *Caste, Class, and Race: A Study in Social Dynamics.* New York: Monthly Review.

Cronon, E. David. 1959. *Black Moses: The Story of Marcus Garvey and the Universal Negro Improvement Association.* Madison: University of Wisconsin Press.

Cruse, Harold. 1987. *Plural but Equal: A Critical Study of Blacks and Minorities and America's Plural Society.* New York: Morrow.

———. 1974. "Black Politics: The Little Rock National Black Convention." *Black World* 23, no. 12 (October).

———. 1968. *Rebellion or Revolution?* New York: Morrow.

———. 1967. *The Crisis of the Negro Intellectual.* New York: Morrow.

Curtin, Philip. 1974. "The Black Experience of Colonialism and Imperialism." In Sidney Mintz, ed., *Slavery, Colonialism, and Racism,* 17–29. New York: Norton.

Dalfiume, Richard. 1969. "The 'Forgotten Years' of the Negro Revolution." In Bernard Sternsher, ed., *The Negro in Depression and War: Prelude to Revolution, 1930–1945,* 298–316. Chicago: Quadrangle Books.

Davis, Horace. 1978. *Toward a Marxist Theory of Nationalism.* New York: Monthly Review.

———. 1974. *Socialism and Nationalism.* New York: Monthly Review.

Davis, Mike. 1986. "The Political Economy of Late Imperial America." In *Prisoners of the American Dream,* 181–230. London: Verso.

Davis, Mike, Manning Marable, Fred Pfeil, and Michael Sprinkler. 1987. *Toward a Rainbow Socialism: Essays on Race, Ethnicity, Class, and Gender.* New York: Verso.

Davis, Terry. 1986. "The Forms of Collective Racist Violence." *Political Studies* 34:40–60.

DeCaro, Louis. 1996. *On the Side of My People: A Religious Life of Malcolm X.* New York: New York University Press.

Delgado, Gary. 1986. *Organizing the Movement: The Roots and Growth of ACORN*. Philadelphia: Temple University Press.

Denby, Charles. 1978. *Indignant Heart*. Boston: South End.

Diara, Agadem Lumumba. 1973. *Islam and Pan-Africanism*. Detroit: El-Hajj Malik El-Shabazz Press.

Dixon, Marlene. 1979. *In Defense of the Working Class*. San Francisco: Synthesis Publications,.

———. 1978. "Abstract: The Degradation of Waged Labor and Class Formation on an International Scale." *Synthesis* 2, no. 3 (spring).

Dixon, Marlene, Ed McCaughan, and Elizabeth Martinez. 1982. "Reindustrialization and the Transnational Labor Force in the United States Today." *Contemporary Marxism*, no. 5 (summer).

Dofny, Jacques. 1977. *Nationalism and the National Question*. Montreal: Black Rose Books.

Douglas, William. 1994. "Time to Heal: Black Caucus Leader Says Hurt Exists for Blacks and Jews." *New York Newsday*. A31, 3–22.

Drake, St. Clair. 1987. *Black Folk Here and There: An Essay in History and Anthropology*. Los Angeles: UCLA Press.

———. 1986–87. "Dr. W. E. B. Du Bois: A Life Lived Experimentally and Self-Documented." *Contributions in Black Studies*, no. 8:111–34.

———. 1982. "Diaspora Studies and Pan Africanism." In Joseph Harris, ed., *Global Dimensions of the African Diaspora*. Washington, DC: Howard University Press.

———. 1972. "The Black Experience in Black Historical Perspective." In Carlene Young, ed., *Black Experience: Analysis and Synthesis*. San Rafael, CA: Leswing Press.

———. 1971a. "Hide My Face? The Literary Renaissance." In Okon Edet Uya, ed., *Black Brotherhood: Afro-Americans and Africa*, 194–213. Lexington, MA: D. C. Heath.

———. 1971b. "Prospects for the Future." In Nathan Huggins, Martin Kilson, and Daniel Fox, eds., *Key Issues in the Afro-American Experience*, 280–305. New York: Harcourt Brace Jovanovich.

———. 1970. *The Redemption of Africa and Black Religion*. Atlanta: Third World Press.

———. 1969. "Urban Violence and American Social Movements." In Robert Connery, ed., *Urban Riots: Violence and Social Change*, 15–26. New York: Random House.

———. 1965. "The Social and Economic Status of the Negro in the United States." *Daedalus* 94, no. 4 (fall): 771–72.

Draper, Hal. 1977. *Karl Marx's Theory of Revolution. Vol. 1, State and Bureaucracy*. New York: Monthly Review.

Draper, Theodore. 1969. *The Rediscovery of Black Nationalism*. New York: Viking.

———. 1960. *American Communism and Soviet Russia*. New York: Viking.

———. 1957. *The Roots of American Communism*. New York: Viking.

Duberman, Martin. 1989. *Paul Robeson: A Biography*. New York: Ballantine.

Dubofsky, Melvin. 1988. *We Shall Be All: A History of the Industrial Workers of the World*. New York: Quadrangle.

———. 1985. *Industrialism and the American Worker, 1865–1920*. 2d Ed. Arlington Heights, IL: Harlan Davidson.

———. 1983. "Workers' Movement in North America." In Immanuel Wallerstein, ed., *Labor in the World Social Structure*, 22–43. Beverly Hills: Sage.

Du Bois, W. E. B. 1979. *Black Reconstruction in America*. New York: Atheneum.

———. 1975. *The Negro*. New York: Henry Holt.

———. 1973. "Marxism and the Negro Problem." In Theodore Vincent, ed., *Voices of a Black Nation: Political Journalism in the Harlem Renaissance*, 210–216. San Francisco: Ramparts Press.

———. 1970. *Dusk of Dawn: An Essay toward an Autobiography of a Race Concept*. New York: Schocken Books.

———. 1969. *The Autobiography of W. E. B. Du Bois*. New York: International Publishers.

———. 1961. *The Souls of Black Folk*. Greenwich, CT: Fawcett.

———. 1919. "I.W.W." *Crisis* 18 (June): 60.

Dyson, Michael Eric. 1995. *Making Malcolm: The Myth and Meaning of Malcolm X*. New York: Oxford University Press.

———. 1993. *Reflecting Black: African-American Cultural Criticism*. Minneapolis: University of Minnesota Press.

Eagles, Charles, ed. 1986. *The Civil Rights Movement in America*. Jackson: University Press of Mississippi.

Eckstein, Harry. 1989. "Civic Inclusion and Its Discontents." *Daedalus* 113, no. 4 (fall) 107–45.

Engels, Frederick. 1975a. *The Condition of the Working Class in England*. Peking: Foreign Language Press.

———. 1975b. *Socialism: Utopian and Scientific*. Peking: Foreign Language Press.

Epps, Archie. 1968. *The Speeches of Malcolm X at Harvard*. New York: Morrow.

Erikson, Erik, and Huey P. Newton. 1973. *In Search of Common Ground*. New York: Norton.

Essien-Udom, E. U. 1971. "Black Identity in the International Context." In Nathan Huggins, Martin Kilson, and Daniel Fox, eds., *Key Issues in the Afro-American Experience*. New York: Harcourt Brace Jovanovich.

———. 1964. *Black Nationalism: A Search for Identity in America.* New York: Dell.

———. 1962. "The Relation of Afro-Americans to African Nationalism." *Freedomways* 2 (fall): 395.

Essien-Udom, M. Ruby, and E. U. Essien-Udom. 1990. "Malcolm X: An International Man." In John Henrik Clarke, ed., *Malcolm X: The Man and His Times*, 235–67. Trenton: Africa World Press.

Evanzz, Karl. 1996. "Deadly Crossroads: Farrakhan's Rise and Malcom X's Fall." *National Times*, October.

———. 1992. *The Judas Factor: The Plot to Kill Malcolm X.* New York: Thunder's Mouth Press.

Fainstein, Norman. 1986–87. "The Underclass/Mismatch Hypothesis as an Explanation for Black Economic Deprivation." *Politics and Society* 15, no. 4.

Falk, Richard. 1987. "The Global Promise of Social Movements: Explorations at the Edge of Time." *Alternatives* 12, no. 2 (April): 173–96.

———. 1986. "Solving the Puzzles of Global Reform." *Alternatives* 11, no. 1 (January): 45–82.

Falk, Richard, and Samuel S. Kim. 1983. "World Order Studies and the World System." In William Thompson, ed., *Contending Approaches to World System Analysis*, 203–37. Beverly Hills: Sage.

Fanon, Frantz. 1967a. *Black Skin, White Masks.* New York: Grove.

———. 1967b. *A Dying Colonialism.* New York: Grove.

———. 1967c. *Toward the African Revolution: Political Essays.* New York: Grove.

———. 1966. *The Wretched of the Earth.* New York: Grove.

Farrakhan, Louis. 1994. "'They Suck the Life from You': An Interview with Minister Louis Farrakhan." By Sylvester Monroe. *Time*, February 28.

Farrell, Christopher, Michael Mandel, Michael Schroeder, Joseph Weber, Michele Galen, and Gary McWilliams. 1992. "The Economic Crisis of Urban America." *Business Week*, March 18, 38–43.

Fauset, Arthur Huff. 1971. *Black Gods of the Metropolis: Negro Religious Cults in the Urban North.* Philadelphia: University of Pennsylvania Press.

Feagin, Joe, and Harlan Hahn. 1973. *Ghetto Revolts: The Politics of Violence in American Cities.* New York: Macmillan.

Fields, Barbara Jeanne. 1990. "Slavery, Race and Ideology in the United States of America." *New Left Review* 181:95–118.

Fisher, Sethard. *From Margin to Mainstream: The Social Progress of Black Americans.* New York: Praeger.

Flacks, Richard. 1988. *Making History: The American Left and the American Mind.* New York: Columbia University Press.

Foner, Philip. 1978. "Cyril V. Briggs: From the African Blood Brotherhood to the Communist Party." Paper presented at the annual conference of the Association for the Study of Afro-American Life and History, Los Angeles, October 12–15.

———. 1977. *American Socialism and the Black American: From the Age of Jackson to World War II.* Westport, CT: Greenwood.

———. 1975. *A Documentary History of the Labor Movement in the United States.* New York: International Publishers.

———. 1974. *Organized Labor and Black Workers: 1619–1973.* New York: Praeger.

———, ed. 1970. *The Black Panthers Speak.* New York: Lippincott.

Foner, Philip, and James Allen, eds., 1987. *American Communism and Black Americans: A Documentary History, 1919–1929.* Philadelphia: Temple University Press.

Foner, Philip, and Ronald Lewis. 1989. *Black Workers.* Philadelphia: Temple University Press.

Forman, James. 1985. *The Making of Black Revolutionaries.* Washington, DC: Open Hand Publishing.

———. 1969. "Control, Conflict, and Change: The Underlying Concepts of the Black Manifesto." In Robert Lecky and H. Elliott Wright, eds., *Black Manifesto.* New York: Sheed and Ward.

Foster, William Z. 1970. *The Negro People in American History.* New York: International Publishers.

———. 1968. *History of the Communist Party of the United States.* New York: Greenwood.

———. 1947. *American Trade Unionism.* New York: International Publishers.

Frady, Marshall. 1996. *Jesse: The Life and Pilgrimage of Jesse Jackson.* New York: Random House.

Frady, Marshall, et al. 1996. "The Pilgrimage of Jesse Jackson." *Frontline,* April 30.

Franklin, Raymond S. 1991. *Shadows of Race and Class.* Minneapolis: University of Minnesota Press.

Franklin, V. P. 1992. *Black Self-Determination: A Cultural History of African-American Resistance.* Brooklyn: Lawrence Hill.

Frazier, E. Franklin. 1974. *The Negro Church in America.* New York: Schocken.

Friedly, Michael. 1992. *Malcolm X: The Assassination.* New York: Ballantine.

Frobel, Folker. 1982. "The Current Development of the World-Economy: Reproduction of Labor and Accumulation of Capital on a World Scale." *Review 5,* no. 4 (spring).

Frobel, Folker, Perry Anderson, Jurgen Heinrichs, and Otto Kreye. 1987. "Some Postulates of an Anti-Systemic Policy." *Dialectical Anthropology* 12, no. 1.

Frobel, Folker, Jurgen Heinrichs, and Otto Kreye. 1981 *The New International Division of Labor.* New York: Cambridge University Press.

Frobel, Folker, et. al. 1985. "Dead End: Western Economic Responses to the

Global Economic Crisis." In Herb Adoo, et al., *Development as Social Transformation*. Tokyo: UN University.

Gallen, David. 1992. *Malcolm X: As They Knew Him*. New York: Carroll and Graf.

Gamson, William. 1980. "Understanding the Careers of Challenging Groups: A Commentary on Goldstone." *American Journal of Sociology* 85, no. 5: 1043–60.

———. 1975. *The Strategy of Social Protest*. Homewood, IL: Dorsey Press.

———. 1968. *Power and Discontent*. Homewood, IL: Dorsey Press.

Garddell, Mattias. 1996. *In the Name of Elijah Muhammad: Louis Farrakhan and the Nation of Islam*. Durham: Duke University Press.

Garrow, David. 1988. *Bearing the Cross: Martin Luther King, Jr. and the Southern Christian Leadership Conference*. New York: Random House.

Garry, Charles. 1970. "The Old Rules Do Not Apply: A Survey of the Persecution of the Black Panther Party." In Phillip Foner, ed., *The Black Panthers Speak*. New York: Lippincott.

Gaughan, Joseph, and Louis Ferman. 1987. "Toward an Understanding of the Informal Economy." *Annals of the American Academy of Political and Social Science* 493 (September).

Gelfand, Donald, and Russell Lee, eds. 1973. *Ethnic Conflicts and Power: A Cross-National Perspective*. New York: John Wiley.

Gendzier, Irene. 1973. *Frantz Fanon: A Critical Study*. New York: Pantheon.

Genovese, Eugene. 1981. *From Rebellion to Revolution*. New York: Random House.

———. 1968. *In Red and Black: Essays in Southern and Afro-American History*. New York: Vintage.

Genovese, Eugene, and Elizabeth Fox Genovese. 1983. *Fruits of Merchant Capital*. New York: Oxford University Press.

Georgakas, Dan, and Marvin Surkin. 1975. *Detroit: I Do Mind Dying: A Study in Urban Revolution*. New York: St. Martin's.

George, Hermon. 1988. "Black America, the 'Underclass' and the Subordination Process." *Black Scholar* 19, no. 3 (May–June).

———. 1984. *American Race Relations Theory: A Review of Four Models*. New York: University Press of America.

———. 1980. "The Latest Scam in Ethnic Group Analysis." *Journal of Ethnic Studies* 7, no. 4 (winter): 93–98.

George, Nelson. 1992. *Buppies, B-Boys, Baps, and Bohos: Notes on Post-Soul Black Culture*. New York: HarperCollins.

Geschwender, James. 1977. *Class, Race, and Worker Insurgency*. New York: Cambridge University Press.

———, ed. 1971. *The Black Revolt: The Civil Rights Movement, Ghetto Uprisings, and Separatism*. Englewood Cliffs, NJ: Prentice Hall.

Giddens, Anthony. 1987. *Sociology: A Brief but Critical Introduction*. New York: Harcourt Brace Jovanovich.

———. 1977. *Studies in Social and Political Theory*. New York: Basic Books.

Giddens, Anthony, and Gavin Mackenzie, eds. 1982. *Social Class and the Division of Labor*. New York: Cambridge University Press.

Gilman, Stuart. 1981. "Black Rebellion in the 1960s: Between Non-Violence and Black Power." *Ethnicity* 8:452–75.

Gilmlore, Ruth Wilson. 1993. "Public Enemies and Private Intellectuals: Apartheid USA." *Race and Class* 35, no. 1 (July–September): 69–78.

Gilroy, Paul. 1993a. *The Black Atlantic: Modernity and Double Consciousness*. Cambridge: Harvard University Press.

———. 1993b. *Small Acts: Thoughts on the Politics of Black Culture*. London: Serpent's Tail Press.

———. 1981–82. "You Can't Fool the Youths . . . Race and Class Formation in the 1960's." *Race and Class* 23, nos. 2–3 (Autumn–Winter).

Gitlin, Todd. 1987. *The Sixties: Years of Hope, Days of Rage*. New York: Bantam.

Glantz, Oscar. 1958. "Class Consciousness and Political Solidarity." *American Sociological Review* 23:375–83.

Glascow, Douglas. 1980. *The Black Underclass: Poverty, Unemployment, and Entrapment of Ghetto Youth*. San Francisco: Jossey-Bass.

Glastris, Paul, and Jeanye Thornton. 1994. "A New Civil Rights Frontier." *U.S. News and World Report*, January 17.

Glazer, Nathan. 1971. "The Culture of Poverty: The View from New York City." In J. Alan Winter, ed., *The Poor: A Culture of Poverty or a Poverty of Culture*. Grand Rapids, MI: William B. Eerdsman.

———. 1961. *The Social Basis of American Communism*. New York: Harcourt Brace and World.

Glazer, Nathan, and Daniel Patrick Moynihan. 1963. *Beyond the Melting Pot: The Negroes, Puerto Ricans, Jews, Italians, and Irish of New York City*. Cambridge: MIT Press.

Goetz, Briefs. 1937. *The Proletariat*. New York: McGraw-Hill.

Goldman, Peter. 1979. *The Death and Life of Malcolm X*. 2d. ed. Urbana: University of Illinois Press.

Goldstone, Jack. 1980. "The Weakness of Organization: A New Look at Gamson's *The Strategy of Social Protest*." *American Journal of Sociology* 85, no. 5: 1017–42.

Goodwyn, Lawrence. 1976. *Democratic Promise: The Populist Movement in America*. New York: Oxford University Press.

Gordon, David, Richard Edwards, and Michael Reich. 1982. *Segmented Work, Divided Workers: The Historical Transformation of Labor in the United States*. New York: Cambridge University Press.

Gorz, Andre. 1990. "The New Agenda." *New Left Review* 184 (November–December): 37–46.

———. 1989a. *Critique of Economic Reason.* London: Verso.

———. 1989b. "A Land of Cockayne?" *New Statesmen and Society*, May 12.

———. 1985. *Paths to Paradise: On the Liberation from Work.* London: Pluto Press.

———. 1982. *Farewell to the Working Class: An Essay on Post-Industrial Socialism.* Boston: South End.

Gouldner, Alvin W. 1980. *The Two Marxisms: Contradiction and Anomalies in the Development of Theory.* New York: Seabury Press.

———. 1955. "Metaphysical Pathos and the Theory of Bureaucracy." *American Political Science Review* 49 (June): 496–507.

Grant, Joanne, ed. 1968. *Black Protest: History, Documents, Analyses, from 1619 to the Present.* Greenwich, CT: Fawcett.

Green, Charles, and Basil Wilson. 1989. *The Struggle for Black Empowerment in New York City: Beyond the Politics of Pigmentation.* New York: Praeger.

Green, Gil. 1971. *The New Radicalism: Anarchist or Marxist?* New York: International Publishers.

Greer, Edward, ed. 1971. *Black Liberation Politics: A Reader.* Boston: Allyn and Bacon.

Gregor, A. J. 1963. "Black Nationalism: A Preliminary Analysis of Negro Radicalism." *Science and Society* 27, no. 4:415–32.

Grigsby, Daryl Russell. 1987. *For the People: Black Socialists in the United States, Africa, and the Caribbean.* San Diego: Asante.

Grimke, Archibald. 1977. "What the NAACP Has Done for the Colored Soldier" [1918]. In Herbert Aptheker, ed., *A Documentary History of the Negro People in the United States, 1910–1932.* Vol. 3, 207–8. New York: International Publishers.

Gruder, Helmut. 1967. *International Communism in the Era of Lenin: A Documentary History.* Greenwich, CT: Fawcett.

Gurley, John. 1983. *Challengers to Communism.* San Francisco: W. H. Freeman.

Gutman, Herbert. 1976. *The Black Family in Slavery and Freedom: 1750–1925.* New York: Random House.

Hacker, Andrew. 1992. *Two Nations: Black and White, Separate, Hostile, and Unequal.* New York: Scribners.

Haines, Herbert. 1988. *Black Radicals and the Civil Rights Mainstream, 1954–70.* Knoxville: University of Tennessee Press.

———. 1984. "Black Radicalization and the Funding of Civil Rights: 1957–1970." *Social Problems* 32, no. 1 (October).

Hall, Raymond. 1978. *Black Separatism in the United States.* Hanover, NH: University Press of New England.

Hall, Stuart. 1993. "What Is This 'Black' in Black Popular Culture." *Social Justice* 20, nos. 1–2 (spring–summer).

Hampton, Fred. 1987a. "It's a Class Struggle, Godamnit." *Vita Wa Watu*, August, bk. 11, pp. 8–20.

———. 1987b. "Power Anywhere Where There's People." *Vita Wa Watu*, August, bk. 11, pp. 1–7.

———. 1987c. "We Have to Protect Our Leaders." *Vita Wa Watu*, August, bk. 11, pp. 21–23.

Hampton, Henry, and Steve Fayer. 1990. *Voices of Freedom: An Oral History of the Civil Rights Movement from the 1950s through the 1980s*. New York: Bantam.

Harding, Vincent. 1983. *There Is a River: The Black Struggle for Freedom in America*. New York: Random House.

———. 1982. *The Other American Revolution*. Los Angeles: Center for Afro-American Studies.

Harrington, Michael. 1989. *Socialism: Past and Future*. New York: Penguin.

———. 1986. *The Next Left: The History of a Future*. New York: Henry Holt.

———. 1984. *The New American Poverty*. New York: Penguin.

———. 1972. "The Other America Revisited." In Helen Ginsburg, ed., *Poverty, Economics, and Society*. Boston: Little, Brown.

———. 1967. "The Economics of Protest." In Arthur Ross and Herbert Hill, eds., *Employment, Race, and Poverty*, 234–57 New York: Harcourt Brace and World.

Harris, Janet, and Julius Hobson. 1969. *Black Pride: A People's Struggle*. New York: McGraw-Hill.

Harris, Robert L. 1985. *Teaching Afro-American History*. Washington, DC: American Historical Association.

Haupt, Georges. 1972. *Socialism and the Great War: The Collapse of the Second International*. London: Oxford University Press.

Haywood, Harry. 1978. *Black Bolshevik: Autobiography of an Afro-American Communist*. Chicago: Liberator Press.

———. 1976. *Negro Liberation*. Chicago: Liberator Press.

Headley, Bernard. 1991. "Race, Class and Powerlessness in the World Economy." *Black Scholar* 21, no. 3 (summer).

———. 1988. "War Ina 'Babylon': Dynamics of the Jamaican Informal Drug Economy." *Social Justice* 15, nos. 3–4 (fall–winter): 61–86.

Heath, G. Louis, ed. 1976. *Off the Pigs: The History and Literature of the Black Panther Party*. Metuchen, NJ: Scarecrow Press.

Heberle, Rudolf. 1951. *Social Movements: An Introduction to Political Sociology*. New York: Appleton-Century-Crofts.

Hechter, Michael. 1978. "Group Formation and the Cultural Division of Labor." *American Journal of Sociology* 84, no. 2:293–319.

Helmick, Jennifer, and Daniel Welch. 1990. "Black-Led Populism and the Defeat of the Democrats." *Forward Motion* 9, no. 1 (March): 46–54.

Henry, Stuart. 1988. "Can the Hidden Economy Be Revolutionary? Toward a Dialectical Analysis of the Relations between Informal and Formal Economies." *Social Justice* 15, nos. 3–4 (fall–winter): 29–60.

———. 1987. "The Political Economy of Informal Economies." *Annals of the American Academy of Political and Social Science*, no. 493 (September): 137–53.

Henwood, Doug. 1990a. "Compendium of Woe." *Left Business Observer*, September 14, 4–5.

———. 1990b. "Poor Counts." *Left Business Observer*, March 8, 8.

Herring, Cedric. 1991. "Class Based Reactions to Political Alienation." Unpublished manuscript.

Hertz, Susan Handley. 1981. *The Welfare Mothers Movement: A Decade of Change for Poor Women*. Washington, DC: University Press of America.

Higham, John. 1975. *Strangers in the Land: Patterns of American Nativism, 1860–1925*. New York: Atheneum.

Hill, Freddye. 1983. "An Analysis of the Communist Party's Theory on 'The Negro Question.'" Unpublished manuscript.

Hill, Herbert. 1987. "Race, Ethnicity and Organized Labor: The Opposition to Affirmative Action." *New Politics* 1, no. 2 (winter).

———. 1967. "The Racial Practices of Organized Labor: The Age of Gompers and After." In Arthur Ross and Herbert Hill, eds., *Employment, Race, and Poverty*, 365–402. New York: Harcourt, Brace and World.

Hill, Robert. 1987. *The Crusader*. Vols. 1–3. Los Angeles: UCLA Press.

Hilliard, David, and Lewis Cole. 1993. *This Side of Glory: The Autobiography of David Hilliard and the Story of the Black Panther Party*. Boston: Little, Brown.

History Task Force, Centro de Estudios Puertorriqueños. 1979. *Labor Migration under Capitalism: The Puerto Rican Experience*. New York: Monthly Review.

Hobsbawm, E. J. 1973. *Revolutionaries*. New York: New American Library.

———. 1962. *The Age of Revolution: 1789–1848*. New York: New American Library.

———. 1959. *Primitive Rebels: Studies in Archaic Forms of Social Movement in the Nineteenth and Twentieth Centuries*. New York: Norton.

Hobsbawm, Eric. 1984. *Workers: Worlds of Labor*. New York: Pantheon.

———. 1970. "Lenin and the 'Aristocracy of Labor.'" *Monthly Review* 21, no. 11 (April): 47–56.

Hofstadter, Richard. 1955. *Social Darwinism in American Thought*. Boston: Beacon.

Honey, Michael. 1984. "The Labor Movement and Racism in the South." In Marvin Berlowitz and Ronald Edari, eds., *Racism and the Denial of Human Rights: Beyond Ethnicity*. Minneapolis: MEP.

Hooker, James. 1967. *Black Revolutionary: George Padmore's Path from Communism to Pan-Africanism*. New York: Praeger.

hooks, bell. 1990. *Yearning: Race, Gender, and Cultural Politics*. Boston: South End.

———. 1988. *Ain't I a Woman: Black Women and Feminism*. Boston: South End.

Hopkins, Terence, and Immanuel Wallerstein. 1987. Capitalism and the Incorporation of New Zones into the Capitalist World-Economy." *Review* 10, nos. 5–6 (summer–fall): 761–79.

———. 1982. *World-Systems Analysis: Theory and Methodology*. Beverly Hills: Sage.

Horne, Gerald. 1995. *The Fire This Time: The Watts Uprising and the 1960s*. Charlottesville: University Press of Virginia.

———. 1994. *Black Liberation/Red Scare: Ben Davis and the Communist Party*. Newark, DE: University of Delaware Press.

———. 1988. *Communist Front? The Civil Rights Congress, 1946–1956*. Rutherford, NJ: Fairleigh Dickinson University Press.

———. 1987a. "The Horne-Pollack Debate Continues." *City Sun*, March 11–17.

———. 1987b. "Jackson Points to the Class-ic Issue." *City Sun*, February 4–10.

Hughes, Langston. 1968. "The Founding of the NAACP." In Joanne Grant, ed., *Black Protest: History, Documents, Analyses, from 1619 to the Present*, 210–14. Greenwich, CT: Fawcett.

Iglesias, Cesar Andreu, ed. 1984. *Memoirs of Bernardo Vega: A Contribution to the History of the Puerto Rican Community in New York*. New York: Monthly Review.

Jackson, George. 1972. *Blood in My Eye*. New York: Random House.

———. 1970. *Soledad Brother*. New York: Random House.

Jacobs, Jim. 1970. *Our Thing Is Drum!* Detroit: Black Star.

Jacques-Garvey, Amy, ed. 1968. *Philosophy and Opinions of Marcus Garvey*. Vols. 1–2. New York: Atheneum.

James, C. L. R. 1973. *Modern Politics*. Detroit: Bewick Editions.

———. 1969. *A History of Pan-African Revolt*. Washington, DC: Drum and Spear Press.

James, Joy. 1997. *Transcending the Talented Tenth: Black Leaders and American Intellectuals*. New York: Routledge.

Jennings, James, and Monte Rivera. 1984. *Puerto Rican Politics in Urban America*. Westport, CT: Greenwood.

Johnson, Timothy. 1986. "Marxism-Leninism and the Underclass." *Political Affairs*, September, 13–19.

Jonas, Susanne, and Marlene Dixon. 1979. "Proletarianization and Class Alliances in the Americas." *Synthesis* 3, no. 1 (fall).

Kaiser, Ernest. 1969. "Review of the Crisis of the Negro Intellectual." *Freedomways* 9, no. 1 (winter).

Kanet, Roger. 1973. "The Comintern and the Negro Question: Communist Policy in the United States and Africa: 1921–1941." *Survey*, autumn.

Karenga, M. Ron. 1978. *Essays on Struggle: Position and Analysis*. San Diego: Kawaida.

Karim, Benjamin. 1992. *Remembering Malcolm: The True Story of Malcolm X from inside the Muslim Mosque*. New York: Carroll and Graf.

Katsiaficas, George. 1987. *The Imagination of the New Left: A Global Analysis of 1968*. Boston: South End.

———. 1968. "The Meaning of May 1968." *Monthly Review* 30, no. 1 (May): 13–30.

Katz, Jon. 1992. "White Men Can't Rule: A Melting Pot Revolt." *Rolling Stone*, August 6.

Katznelson, Ira. 1981. *City Trenches: Urban Politics and the Patterning of Class in the United States*. Chicago: University of Chicago Press.

Kazin, Michael. 1988. "A People Not a Class: Rethinking the Political Language of the Modern U.S. Labor Movement." In Mike Davis and Michael Sprinkler, eds. *Reshaping the U.S. Left: Popular Struggles in the 1980s*, 257–86. New York: Verso.

Kelley, Robin D. G. 1994. *Race Rebels: Culture, Politics, and the Black Working Class*. New York: Free Press.

———. 1993. "The Black Poor and the Politics of Opposition in a New South City, 1929–1970." In Michael Katz, ed., *The Underclass Debate: Views from History*, 293–333. Princeton: Princeton University Press.

———. 1992a. "The Riddle of the Zoot: Malcolm Little and Black Cultural Politics during World War II." In Joe Wood, ed., *Malcolm X: In Our Own Image*, 155–82. New York: St. Martin's.

———. 1992b. "Straight from the Underground." *Nation*, June 8, 793–96.

———. 1990. *Hammer and Hoe: Alabama Communists during the Great Depression*. Chapel Hill: University of North Carolina Press.

———. 1988. "Comrades, Praise Gawd for Lenin and Them! Ideology and Culture among Black Communists in Alabama, 1930–35." *Science and Society* 52, no. 1:59–82.

Killian, Lewis. 1968. *The Impossible Revolution: Black Power and the American Dream*. New York: Random House.

Kilson, Martin. 1995. "On the Nationalism of Fools." *Boston Review* 20, no.4 (October/November).

———. 1988. "Truly Apocalyptic." *Nation* May 14.

King, Martin Luther, Jr. 1991. "Letter from Birmingham City Jail." In *A Testa-*

ment of Hope: The Essential Writings and Speeches of Martin Luther King, Jr. San Francisco: HarperCollins.

———. 1967. *Where Do We Go from Here: Chaos or Community.* Boston: Beacon.

———. 1963. *Why We Can't Wait.* New York: Penguin.

King, Mary. 1987. *Freedom Song: A Personal Story of the 1960s Civil Rights Movement.* New York: Morrow.

Kinloch, Graham C. 1981. *Ideology and Contemporary Sociological Theory.* Englewood Cliffs, NJ: Prentice Hall.

Klehr, Harvey. 1984. *The Heyday of American Communism: The Depression Decade.* New York: Basic Books.

———. 1978. *Communist Cadre: The Social Background of the American Communist Party Elite.* Stanford, CA: Hoover Institution Press.

Kohn, Hans. 1965. *Nationalism: Its Meaning and History.* Rev. Ed. New York: Van Nostrand.

Kondo, Baba Zak. 1993. *Conspiracys: Unraveling the Assassination of Malcolm X.* Washington, DC: Nubia Press.

Kuper, Leo. 1973. "Theories of Revolution and Race Relations." In Donald Gelfand and Russell Lee, eds., *Ethnic Conflicts and Power: A Cross-National Perspective,* 48–65. New York: John Wiley.

Kushnick, Louis V. 1981. "Racism and Class Consciousness in Modern Capitalism." In Benjamin Bowser and Raymond Hunt, eds., *Impacts of Racism on White Americans,* 191–216. Beverly Hills: Sage.

Ladner, Joyce. 1973. "The Urban Poor." In Peter Rose, Stanley Rothman, and William Julius Wilson, eds. *Through Different Eyes: Black and White Perspectives on American Race Relations,* 3–24. New York: Oxford University Press.

Laguerre, Michel. 1978. "Internal Dependency: The Structural Position of the Black Ghetto in American Society." *Journal of Ethnic Studies* 6, no. 4 (fall): 29–43.

Lasch, Christopher. 1969. *The Agony of the American Left.* New York: Random House.

Laue, James. 1964. "A Contemporary Revitalization Movement in American Race Relations: The 'Black Muslims.'" *Social Forces* 42 (March): 436–48.

LeBon, Gustave. 1960. *The Crowd: A Study of the Popular Mind.* New York: Viking.

Lee, Martha. 1996. *The Nation of Islam: An American Millenarian Movement.* Syracuse: Syracuse University Press.

Leggett, John. 1972. *Race, Class, and Political Consciousness.* Cambridge, MA: Schenkman.

———. 1963a. "The Uprooted and Working Class Consciousness." *American Journal of Sociology* 68 (May): 685–86.

―――. 1963b. "Working Class Consciousness, Race, and Political Choice." *American Journal of Sociology* 69 (September): 171–76.

Leid, Ultrice, and Ute Buesing. 1987. "Jesse Jackson's Tightrope Act." *City Sun*, January 21–27.

Lemelle, Anthony. 1995. *Black Male Deviance*. Westport, CT: Praeger.

Lenin, V. I. 1973. *Imperialism: The Highest Stage of Capitalism*. Peking: Foreign Language Press.

―――. 1972. *What Is to Be Done: Burning Questions of Our Movement*. New York: International Publishers.

―――. 1964a. "A Caricature of Marxism and Imperialist Economism." In *Lenin: Collected Works*. Vol. 23, 28–76. Moscow: Progress Publishers.

―――. 1964b. "Imperialism and the Split in Socialism." In *Lenin: Collected Works*. Vol. 23, 105–20. Moscow: Progress Publishers.

Lerner, Michael. 1992. *The Socialism of Fools: Anti-Semitism on the Left*. Oakland, CA: Tikkun Books.

Lewis, Michael. 1970. "The Negro Protest Movement in Urban America." In Joseph Gusfield, ed., *Protest, Reform, and Revolt*, 149–90. New York: John Wiley.

Lewis, Oscar. 1968. "A Culture of Poverty." In Daniel Patrick Moynihan, ed., *On Understanding Poverty: Perspectives from the Social Sciences*, 185–200. New York: Basic Books.

Lewis, Rupert. 1988. *Marcus Garvey: Anti-Colonial Champion*. Trenton: Africa World Press.

Liberatore, Paul. 1996. *The Road to Hell: The True Story of George Jackson, Stephen Bingham, and the San Quentin Massacre*. New York: Atlantic Monthly Press.

Liebow, Elliot. 1967. *Tally's Corner*. Boston: Little, Brown.

Lightfoot, Claude. 1968. *Ghetto Rebellion to Black Liberation*. New York: International Publishers.

Lincoln, C. Eric. 1973. *The Black Muslims in America*. Boston: Beacon.

Lipset, Seymour Martin. 1963. *Political Man: The Social Bases of Politics*. Garden City, NY: Anchor Books.

Lipsitz, George. 1990. *Time Passages: Collective Memory and American Popular Culture*. Minneapolis: University of Minnesota Press.

―――. 1988a. *A Life in the Struggle: Ivory Perry and the Culture of Opposition*. Philadelphia: Temple University Press.

―――. 1988b. "The Struggle for Hegemony." *Journal of American History* 75 (June): 146–50.

Lipsky, Michael. 1973. "Protest as Political Resource." In Donald Gelfand and Russell Lee, eds., *Ethnic Conflicts and Power: A Cross-National Perspective*, 266–84. New York: John Wiley.

Lomax, Louis. 1968. *To Kill a Black Man*. Los Angeles: Holloway House.

———. 1963. *When the Word Is Given: A Report on Elijah Muhammad, Malcolm X, and the Black Muslim World.* New York: Signet.

———. 1962. *The Negro Revolt.* New York: Signet.

Loury, Glenn C. 1995. "On the Nationalism of Fools." *Boston Review* 20, no. 4 (October/November).

Lubiano, Wahneema. 1997. "Black Nationalism and Black Common Sense: Policing Ourselves and Others." In Wahneema Lubiano, ed. *The House That Race Built: Black Americans, U.S. Terrain,* 232–52. New York: Pantheon.

Lynch, Hollis. 1971. "Pan-Negro Nationalism in the United States before 1862." In Okon Edet Uya, ed., *Black Brotherhood: Afro-Americans and Africa,* 241–56. Lexington, MA: D. C. Heath.

McAdam, Doug. 1988. *Freedom Summer.* New York: Oxford University Press.

———. 1983. "Tactical Innovation and the Pace of Insurgency." *American Sociological Review* 48 (December): 735–54.

———. 1982. *Political Process and the Development of Black Insurgency: 1930–1970.* Chicago: University of Chicago Press.

McCloud, Aminah Beverly. 1995. *African American Islam.* New York: Routledge.

McGuire, Randall, Joan Smith, and William Martin. 1986. "Patterns of Household Structures in the World-Economy." *Review* 10, no. 1 (summer).

McIntyre, Robert. 1991. *Inequality and the Federal Budget Deficit.* Washington, DC: Citizens for Tax Justice.

Madhubuti, Haki. 1994. *Claiming Earth: Race, Rage, Rape, Redemption.* Chicago: Third World Press.

———. 1978. *Enemies: The Clash of Races.* Chicago: Third World Press.

Magida, Arthur. 1996. *Prophet of Rage: A Life of Louis Farrakhan and His Nation.* New York: Basic Books.

Magri, Lucio. 1977. "Italy, Social Democracy, and Revolution in the West: An Interview with Lucio Magri." *Socialist Review* 7, no. 6 (November–December): 105–42.

———. 1970. "Problems of the Marxist Theory of the Revolutionary Party." *New Left Review,* 60 (March/April): 97–128.

Magubane, Bernard. 1987. *The Ties That Bind: African-American Consciousness of Africa.* Trenton: Africa World Press.

———. 1984. "The Political Economy of the Black World: Origins of the Present Crisis." In James Turner, ed., *The Next Decade: Theoretical and Research Issues in Africana Studies.* Ithaca, NY: Africana Studies and Research Center, Cornell University.

Malcolm X. 1989. *Malcolm X: The Last Speeches.* Ed. Bruce Perry. New York: Pathfinder.

———. 1971. *The End of White World Supremacy.* New York: Marlin House.

———. 1970. *By Any Means Necessary.* New York: Pathfinder.

————. 1966. *Malcolm X Speaks*. New York: Pathfinder.

————. 1965. *The Autobiography of Malcolm X*. New York: Grove.

Maldonado-Denis, Manuel. 1982. "Puerto Rican Immigration: Proposals for Its Study." *Contemporary Marxism*, no. 5 (Summer): 19–26.

————. 1973. "The Puerto Ricans: Protest or Submission." In Donald Gelfand and Russell Lee, eds., *Ethnic Conflicts and Power: A Cross-National Perspective*, 296–310. New York: John Wiley.

Manifesto, Il. 1971. "For Communism: Theses of the Il Manifesto Group." *Politics & Society* 1, no. 4 (August): 409–40.

Mann, Eric. 1974. *Comrade George*. New York: Harper and Row.

Mannheim, Karl. 1936. *Ideology and Utopia*. New York: Harcourt Brace and World.

Mao Tse-Tung. 1977. "On the Correct Handling of Contradictions among the People." In *Selected Works of Mao Tse-Tung*. Vol 5, 384–421. Peking: Foreign Language Press.

————. 1974a. "Talks with Yuan-hsin." In Stuart Schram, ed., *Chairman Mao Talks to the People: Talks and Letters: 1956–1971*, 242–52. New York: Pantheon.

————. 1974b. "Talk to Leaders of the Center." In Stuart Schram, ed., *Chairman Mao Talks to the People: Talks and Letters: 1956–1971*, 253–55. New York: Pantheon.

————. 1969. "Oppose Racial Discrimination by U.S. Imperialism." In Stuart Schram, ed., *The Political Thought of Mao Tse Tung*, 409–12. New York: Praeger.

————. 1967a. "The Chinese Revolution and the Chinese Communist Party." In *Selected Works of Mao Tse-Tung*. Vol. 2, 305–34. Peking: Foreign Language Press.

————. 1967b. "On Contradiction." In *Selected Works of Mao Tse-Tung*. Vol. 1, 311–47. Peking: Foreign Language Press.

————. 1967c. "On New Democracy." In *Selected Works of Mao Tse-Tung*. Vol. 2, 339–84. Peking: Foreign Language Press.

————. 1967d. "On Practice." In *Selected Works of Mao Tse-Tung*. Vol. 1, 295–310. Peking: Foreign Language Press.

————. 1967e. "The Question of Independence and Initiative within the United Front." In *Selected Works of Mao Tse-Tung*. Vol. 2, 213–18. Peking: Foreign Language Press.

————. 1967f. "Rectify the Party's Style of Work." In *Selected Works of Mao Tse-Tung*. Vol. 3, 35–52. Peking: Foreign Language Press.

————. 1967g. "Reform Our Study." In *Selected Works of Mao Tse-Tung*. Vol. 3, 17–26. Peking: Foreign Language Press.

————. 1967h. "Report on an Investigation of the Peasant Movement in

Hunan." In *Selected Works of Mao Tse-Tung*. Vol. 1, 23–59. Peking: Foreign Language Press.

———. 1967i. "The Role of the Chinese Communist Party in the National War." In *Selected Works of Mao Tse-Tung*. Vol. 2, 195–212. Peking: Foreign Language Press.

———. 1967j. "Some Questions Concerning Methods of Leadership." In *Selected Works of Mao Tse-Tung*. Vol. 3, 35–52. Peking: Foreign Language Press.

Marable, Manning. 1993. "Ben Chavis: New Leader for the NAACP." *Forward Motion* 12, no. 4 (September–October): 30–31.

———. 1990a. "Race, Class and Conflict: Intellectual Debates on Race Relations Research in the United States since 1960: A Social Science Bibliographical Essay." In Abdul Alkalimat, ed., *Paradigms in Black Studies*, 165–206. Chicago: Twenty-First Century.

———. 1990b. "Toward an American Socialism-from-Below." *Forward Motion* 9, no. 1 (March): 31–36.

———. 1986. *W. E. B. Du Bois: Black Radical Democrat*. Boston: Twayne.

———. 1985a. *Black American Politics: From the Washington Marches to Jesse Jackson*. New York: Verso.

———. 1985b. *Race, Reform and Rebellion: The Second Reconstruction in Black America, 1945–1982*. Jackson: University of Mississippi Press.

———. 1981a. "Beyond the Race-Class Dilemma: Toward a Black Politics." *Nation*, April 11.

———. 1981b. *Blackwater: Historical Studies in Race, Class Consciousness and Revolution*. Dayton, OH: Black Praxis Press.

———. 1980. *From the Grassroots: Essays towards Afro-American Liberation*. Boston: South End.

Marcuse, Herbert. 1972. *Counter-Revolution and Revolt*. Boston: Beacon Press.

———. 1969. *An Essay on Liberation*. Boston: Beacon.

Marek, Franz. 1969. *Philosophy of World Revolution*. New York: International Publishers.

Marsh, Clifton. 1996. *From Black Muslims to Muslims: The Resurrection, Transformation, and Change of the Lost-Found Nation of Islam in America, 1930–1995*. 2d ed. Latham, MD: Scarecrow Press.

Marshall, T. H. 1964. *Class, Citizenship, and Social Development*. Westport, CT: Greenwood.

Martin, Tony. 1983. *The Pan-African Connection: From Slavery to Garvey and Beyond*. Dover, MA: Majority Press.

———. 1976. *Race First: The Ideological and Organizational Struggles of Marcus Garvey and the Universal Negro Improvement Association*. Dover, MA: Majority Press.

Martinez, Elizabeth. 1989. "Histories of the 'Sixties': A Certain Absence of Color." *Social Justice* 16, no. 4 (winter): 175–85.

Marx, Karl. 1977. *Capital*, Vol. 1. New York: Random House.

———. 1970. *A Contribution to the Critique of Political Economy*. Moscow: Progress Publishers.

———. 1969. *The Eighteenth Brumaire of Louis Bonaparte*. New York: International Publishers.

Marx, Karl, and Frederick Engels. 1972. *The Manifesto of the Communist Party*. Peking: Foreign Language Press.

———. 1970. *The German Ideology*. New York: International Publishers.

Maxwell, Andrew. 1990. "The Myth of Underclass Culture." Unpublished manuscript.

Mazrui, Ali. 1987. "The World-Economy and the African/Afro-American Connection." In Adelaide Cromwell, ed., *Dynamics of the African Afro-American Connection: From Dependency to Self-Reliance*, 36–53. Washington, DC: Howard University Press.

Meier, August. 1971. *Negro Thought in America, 1880–1915*. Ann Arbor, MI: University of Michigan Press.

———. 1962. "Negro Class Structure and Ideology in the Age of Booker T. Washington." *Phylon* 23:258–66.

———, ed. 1970. *The Transformation of Activism*. New York: Aldine.

Meier, August, and Elliott Rudwick. 1976. *From Plantation to Ghetto*. 3ed. New York: Hill and Wang.

Meier, August, Elliott Rudwick, and Francis Broderick, eds. 1971. *Black Protest Thought in the Twentieth Century*. New York: Bobbs-Merrill.

Memmi, Albert. 1968. *Dominated Man: Notes toward a Portrait*. Boston: Beacon.

———. 1965. *The Colonizer and the Colonized*. Boston: Beacon.

Merton, Robert K. 1949. *Social Theory and Social Structure*. Glencoe, IL: Free Press.

Meyers, Barton. 1984. "Minority Group: An Ideological Formulation." *Social Problems* 32, no. 1 (October): 1–15.

Meyers, Michael. 1994. "Not N.A.A.C.P. of Old." *New York Times*, March 16, A20.

Mhone, Guy. 1975. "Structural Oppression and the Persistence of Black Poverty." *Journal of Afro-American Studies* 3, nos. 3–4 (summer–fall): 395–419.

Michels, Robert. 1962. *Political Parties*. New York: Free Press.

———. 1955. "The Origins of Anti-Capitalist Mass Spirit." In Contemporary Civilization Staff of Columbia University, ed., *Man in Contemporary Society*, 740–65. New York: Columbia University Press.

Miliband, Ralph. 1977. *Marxism and Politics*. New York: Oxford University Press.

Miller, John. 1992. "Silent Depression." *Dollars and Sense*, no. 175 (April): 6–9.

Miller, Walter B. 1958. Lower Class Culture as a Generating Milieu of Gang Delinquency." *Journal of Social Issues* 14, no. 3:5–19.

Milton, David. 1982. "*The Politics of U.S. Labor: From the Great Depression to the New Deal*. New York: Monthly Review.

Mintz, Sidney. 1974. *Caribbean Transformations*. New York: Columbia University Press.

———. 1953. "The Folk-Urban Continuum and the Rural Proletariat." *American Journal of Sociology* 59, no. 2:136–43.

Mintz, Sidney, and Richard Price. 1976. "An Anthropological Approach to the Afro-American Past: A Caribbean Perspective." *ISHI Occasional Paper in Social Change*. Philadelphia: Institute for the Study of Human Issues.

Mitchell, Roxanne, and Frank Weiss. 1981. *A House Divided: Labor and White Supremacy*. New York: United Labor Press.

Monteiro, Tony. 1988. "The Origins and Consequences of the Underclass Theory." *Political Affairs*, November, 18–25.

Montgomery, David. 1987. "Marxism and Utopianism in the USA." *New Left Review* 164 (July/August): 123–28.

Montgomery, David. 1983. Introduction to Immanuel Wallerstein, ed., *Labor in the World Social Structure* 9–16. Beverly Hills: Sage.

———. 1979. *Worker's Control in America*. New York: Cambridge University Press.

Moon, Henry Lee. 1972. *The Emerging Thought of W. E. B. DuBois: Essays and Editorials from the Crisis*. New York: Simon and Schuster.

Moore, Richard. 1971. "Africa Conscious Harlem." In Okon Edet Uya, ed., *Black Brotherhood: Afro-Americans and Africa*, 241–56. Lexington, MA: D. C. Heath.

Moore, Stanley. 1963. *Three Tactics: The Background in Marx*. New York: Monthly Review.

Morris, Aldon. 1984. *The Origins of the Civil Rights Movement: Black Communities Organizing for Change*. New York: Free Press.

Moses, Wilson Jeremiah. 1978. *The Golden Age of Black Nationalism: 1850–1925*. New York: Oxford University Press.

———, ed. 1996. *Classical Black Nationalism: From the American Revolution to Marcus Garvey*. New York: New York University Press.

Movimiento de Liberación Nacional. n.d. "Our Struggle from Within." Mimeo.

Moynihan, Daniel Patrick. 1968. "The Professors and the Poor." In Daniel Patrick Moynihan, ed., *On Understanding Poverty: Perspectives from the Social Sciences*, New York: Basic Books.

————. 1967. *The Negro Family: A Case for National Action*. In Lee Rainwater and W. L. Yancey, eds., *The Moynihan Report and the Politics of Controversy*. Cambridge: MIT Press.

————, ed. 1968. *On Understanding Poverty: Perspectives from the Social Sciences*. New York: Basic Books.

Murray, Charles. 1984. *Losing Ground: American Social Policy, 1950–1980*. New York: Basic Books.

Myrdal, Gunnar. 1944. *An American Dilemma*. Vol. 2, *The Negro Social Structure*. New York: McGraw-Hill.

Naison, Mark. 1983. *Communists in Harlem during the Depression*. New York: Grove.

————. 1978. "Communism and the Politics of Black Protest." *Marxist Perspectives* 1, no. 3 (fall): 20–50.

————. 1974. "Communism and Black Nationalism in the Great Depression: The Case of Harlem." *Journal of Ethnic Studies*, summer.

————. 1971. "Marxism and Black Radicalism in America: The Communist Party Experience." *Radical America*, May–June.

Nasar, Sylvia. 1992. "The 1980's: A Very Good Time for the Very Rich." *New York Times*, March 5, 1.

Navarro, Vicente. 1987a. "Race versus Class? More on the Rainbow and Class Politics." *Monthly Review* 39, no. 6 (November).

————. 1987b. "The Rainbow Coalition and the Challenge of Class." *Monthly Review* 39, no. 2 (June).

Network of Black Organizers. 1995. *Black Prison Movements, USA*. Trenton: Africa World Press.

Newfield, Jack. 1994a. "Widow Pins Malcolm X Murder on Farrakhan." *New York Post*, March 12, p. 2.

————. 1994b. "Farrakhan X-posed: Questions Raised over Role in Malcolm's Death." *New York Post*, March 1, pp. 5, 22.

Newton, Huey. 1996. *War against the Panthers: A Study of Repression in America*. New York: Harlem River Press.

————. 1973. *Revolutionary Suicide*. New York: Ballantine.

————. 1972. *To Die for the People*. New York: Random House.

Newton, Michael. 1980. *Bitter Grain: The Story of the Black Panther Party*. Los Angeles: Holloway House.

New York 21. 1971. *Look for Me in the Whirlwind: The Collective Autobiography of the New York 21*. New York: Random House.

Nicolaus, Martin. 1970. "The Theory of the Aristocracy of Labor." *Monthly Review* 21, no. 11 (April): 91–101.

Nkrumah, Kwame. 1970. *Class Struggle in Africa*. New York: International Publishers.

Nolan, William. 1951. *Communism versus the Negro*. Chicago: Henry Regnery.

O'Callaghan, Mary. 1980. "Introductory Notes." In UNESCO, *Sociological Theories: Race and Colonialism*. Paris: UNESCO.

O'Dell, J. H. 1967. "A Special Variety of Colonialism." *Freedomways* 7, no. 1 (winter): 7–15.

———. 1967. "Colonialism and the Negro American Experience." *Freedomways* 6, no. 4 (fall): 297–308.

Oliver, Melvin, and Thomas Shapiro. 1995. *Black Wealth/White Wealth: A New Perspective on Racial Inequality*. New York: Routledge.

Omni, Michael. 1980. "Book Review of *The Declining Significance of Race*." *Insurgent Sociologist* 10, no. 2 (fall): 118–22.

Omni, Michael, and Howard Winant. 1986. *Racial Formation in the United States: From the 1960s to the 1980s*. New York: Routledge and Kegan Paul.

Oppenheimer, Martin. 1969. *The Urban Guerrilla*. Chicago: Quadrangle Books.

O'Reilly, Kenneth. 1989. *Racial Matters: The FBI's Secret File on Black America, 1960–1972*. New York: Free Press.

Owen, Frank. 1994. "Gangsta Rap: The Real Story." *New York Newsday*, January 5.

Padmore, George. 1972. *Pan-Africanism or Communism*. Garden City, NY: Doubleday.

Pavlenko, A. 1983. *The World Revolutionary Process*. Moscow: Progress.

Pearson, Hugh. 1994. *The Shadow of the Panther: Huey Newton and the Price of Black Power*. Reading, MA: Addison-Wesley.

Perkins, William Eric. 1977. "Harold Cruse: On the Problem of Culture and Revolution." *Journal of Ethnic Studies* 5, no. 2 (summer): 3–25.

Perkins, W. E. and J. E. Higginson. 1971. "Black Students: Reformists or Revolutionaries?" In Rod Aya and Norman Miller, eds., *The New American Revolution*. New York: Free Press.

Perry, Bruce. 1991. *Malcolm: The Life of a Man Who Changed Black America*. Barrytown, NY: Station Hill Press.

———, ed. 1989. *Malcolm X: The Last Speeches*. New York: Pathfinder.

Pincus, Fred, and Howard Ehrlich. 1994. *Race and Ethnic Conflict: Contending Views on Prejudice, Discrimination and Ethnoviolence*. Boulder: Westview.

Pinkney, Alphonso. 1984. *The Myth of Black Progress*. Boston: Cambridge University Press.

———. 1976. *Red, Black, and Green: Black Nationalism in the United States*. Boston: Cambridge University Press.

Piore, Michael. 1979. *Birds of Passage: Migrant Labor and Industrial Societies*. New York: Cambridge University Press.

Piore, Michael, and Charles Sabel. 1984. *The Second Industrial Divide: Prospects for Prosperity*. New York: Basic Books.

Piven, Frances Fox. 1981. "Deviant Behavior and the Remaking of the World." *Social Problems* 28, no. 5:489–508.

Piven, Frances Fox, and Richard Cloward. 1992. "Normalizing Collective Protest." In Aldon Morris and Carol McClurg Mueller, eds. *Frontiers in Social Movement Theory*. New Haven: Yale University Press.

———. 1988. *Why Americans Don't Vote*. New York: Pantheon.

———. 1982. *The New Class War: Reagan's War on the Welfare State and Its Consequences*. New York: Pantheon.

———. 1979. *Poor People's Movements*. New York: Random House.

———. 1974. *The Politics of Turmoil: Essays on Poverty, Race, and the Urban Crisis*. New York: Pantheon.

———. 1971. *Regulating the Poor: The Functions of Public Welfare*. New York: Random House.

Plummer, Brenda Gayle. 1996. *Rising Wind: Black Americans and U.S. Foreign Policy*. Chapel Hill: University of North Carolina Press.

Pollack, Andy. 1987. "On the Economics of Racism." *City Sun*, February 18–24.

Pollack, Norman. 1962. *The Populist Response to Industrial America: Midwestern Populist Thought*. Cambridge: Harvard University Press.

Portes, Alejandro. 1972. "Rationality in the Slum: An Essay on Interpretive Sociology." *Comparative Studies in Society and History* 14:268–286.

———. 1971. "Political Primitivism, Differential Socialization, and Lower-Class Leftist Radicalism." *American Sociological Review* 36 (October): 820–35.

Przeworski, Adam. 1985. *Capitalism and Social Democracy*. New York: Cambridge University Press.

Puddington, Arch. 1994. "The NAACP Turns Left." *Commentary* 97, no. 1 (January): 35–39.

Quarles, Benjamin. 1970. *Black Abolitionists*. New York: Oxford University Press.

Randolph, A. Phillip. 1919. "Du Bois Fails as a Theorist." *Messenger*, December. Reprinted in August Meier, Elliott Rudwick, and Francis Broderick, eds., *Black Protest Thought in the Twentieth Century*. New York: Bobbs-Merrill.

Rawick, George. 1972. *From Sun-Down to Sun-Up: The Making of the Black Community*. Westport, CT: Greenwood.

Record, Wilson. 1971. *The Negro and the Communist Party*. New York: Atheneum.

Redkey, Edwin S. 1971. "The Flowering of Black Nationalism: Henry McNeal Turner and Marcus Garvey." In Nathan Huggins, Martin Kilson, and Daniel Fox, eds., *Key Issues in the Afro-American Experience*. Vol. 2, 107–24. New York: Harcourt Brace Jovanovich.

Reed, Adolph, Jr. 1996. "Ebony and Ivory Fascists." *Progressive* 60, no. 4 (April): 20–22.

———. 1994. "Behind the Farrakhan Show." *Progressive* 58, no. 4 (April): 16–17.

————. 1991a. "False Prophet I: The Rise of Louis Farrakhan." *Nation*. 252, no. 2 (January 21): 37, 51–56.

————. 1991b. "False Prophet II: All for One and None for All." *Nation*. 252, no. 3 (January 28): 86–92.

————. 1988a. "The Liberal Technocrat: A Review of William J. Wilson's *The Truly Disadvantaged.*" *Nation* 46, no. 5 (February 6): 167–70.

————. 1988b. "Reed Replies to Martin Kilson and William J. Wilson." *Nation*, May 14.

————. 1986. *The Jesse Jackson Phenomenon: The Crisis of Purpose in Afro-American Politics.* New Haven: Yale University Press.

————, ed. 1986. *Race, Politics, and Culture: Critical Essays on the Radicalism of the 1960's.* Westport, CT: Greenwood.

Research Working Group on World Labor of the Fernand Braudel Center. 1986. "Global Patterns of Labor Movements in Historical Perspective." *Review* 10, no. 1 (summer): 137–55.

Rex, John. 1986. "The Role of Class Analysis in the Study of Race Relations: A Weberian Perspective." In John Rex and David Mason, eds., *Theories of Race and Ethnic Relations*, 64–83. New York: Cambridge University Press.

————. 1982. "Racism and the Structure of Colonial Societies." In R. Ross, ed., *Racism and Colonialism.* Boston: Matinus Nijhoff.

————. 1970. *Race Relations in Sociological Theory.* New York: Routledge and Kegan Paul.

Rivers, Eugene. 1994/95. "Beyond the Nationalism of Fools: Toward An Agenda for Black Intellectuals." *Boston Review* 20, no. 3 (January/December).

Roach, Jack, and Janet Roach. 1978. "Mobilizing the Poor: Road to a Dead End." *Social Problems* 26:160–71.

Robinson, Cedric. 1997. *Black Movements in America.* New York: Routledge.

————. 1985. "The African Diaspora and the Italo-Ethiopian Crisis." *Race and Class* 27, no. 2 (autumn): 51–65.

————. 1983. *Black Marxism: The Making of the Black Radical Tradition.* London: Zed Press.

Robinson, Cyril. 1988. "Introduction: Exploring the Informal Economy." *Social Justice* 15, nos. 3–4 (fall–winter).

Rodney, Walter. 1969. *The Grounding with My Brothers.* London: Bogle-L'Ouverture.

Rodriguez, Clara E. 1989. *Puerto Ricans: Born in the U.S.A.* Boston: Unwin Hyman.

Rodriguez, Clara E., Virginia Sanchez Korrol, and Jose Oscar Alers, eds. 1980. *The Puerto Rican Struggle: Essays on Survival in the U.S.* New York: Puerto Rican Migration Research Consortium.

Roediger, David. 1989. "Notes on Working Class Racism." *New Politics* 2, no. 3 (summer): 61–66.

———. 1988. "'Labor in White Skin': Race and Working Class History." In Mike Davis and Michael Sprinkler, eds. *Reshaping the U.S. Left: Popular Struggles in the 1980s*, 287–308. New York: Verso.

Rollins, Judith. 1986. "Part of a Whole: The Interdependence of the Civil Rights Movement and Other Social Movements." *Phylon* 47, no. 1.

Rossanda, Rossana. 1971. "Mao's Marxism." *Socialist Register* 7:53–109.

Rossi, Peter, and Zahava Blum. 1968. "Class, Status, and Poverty." In Daniel Patrick Moynihan, ed., *On Understanding Poverty: Perspectives from the Social Sciences*, 36–63. New York: Basic Books.

Rubenstein, Richard. 1971. "Rebels in Eden: The Structure of Mass Political Violence in America." In Rod Aya and Norman Miller, eds., *The New American Revolution*, 97–142. New York: Free Press.

Rude, George. 1964. *The Crowd in History: A Study of Popular Disturbances in France and England, 1730–1848*. New York: John Wiley.

Rustin, Bayard. 1976. *Strategies for Freedom: The Changing Pattern of Black Protest*. New York: Columbia University Press.

———. 1965. "From Protest to Politics: The Future of the Civil Rights Movement." *Commentary* 39 (February).

Salaam, Kalamu Ya. 1974. "Tell No Lies, Claim No Easy Victories: African Liberation Day, an Assessment." *Black World* 23, no. 12 (October).

Saladin, Muhammed. 1987. "Toward a National Black Political Program for Black Workers." *International Correspondence,* no. 10 (winter).

Sales, William W., Jr. 1994. *From Civil Rights to Black Liberation: Malcolm X and the Organization of Afro-American Unity*. Boston: South End.

Samuels, Raphael. 1987. "Class Politics: The Lost World of British Communism, Part 3." *New Left Review*, no. 165 (September–October): 52–91.

Sanchez Korrol, Virginia A. 1983. *From Colonia to Community: The History of Puerto Ricans in New York City, 1917–1948*. Westport, CT: Greenwood.

San Juan, E., Jr. 1989. "Problems in the Marxist Project of Theorizing Race." *Rethinking Marxism* 2, no. 2 (summer): 58–80.

Sartre, Jean-Paul. 1962. "Materialism and Revolution." In *Literary and Philosophical Essays*. New York: Collier.

Sassen-Koob, Saskia. 1986. "New York City: Economic Restructuring and Immigration." *Development and Change* 17.

Savitch, H. V. 1978. "Black Cities/White Suburbs: Domestic Colonialism as an Interpretive Idea." *Annals of the American Academy of Political and Social Science*, no. 439 (September): 118–34.

Schwartz, Michael. 1976. *Radical Protest and Social Structure: The Southern Farmer's Alliance and Cotton Tenancy, 1880–1890*. New York: Academic Press.

Schweitzer, Arthur. 1944. "Ideological Groups." *American Sociological Review* 9, no. 2 (August): 415–26.

Scott, William R. 1993. *The Sons of Sheba's Race: African-Americans and the Italo-Ethiopian War, 1935–1941*. Bloomington: Indiana University Press.

Seale, Bobby. 1968. *Seize the Time: The Story of the Black Panther Party and Huey Newton*. New York: Random House.

Sellers, Charles, Henry May, and Neil McMillen. 1981. *A Synopsis of America History*. 5th ed. Boston: Houghton Mifflin.

Selsam, Howard, David Goldway, and Harry Martel, eds. 1970. *Dynamics of Social Change: A Reader in Marxist Social Science*. New York: International Publishers.

Selznick, Philip. 1952. *The Organizational Weapon: A Study of Bolshevik Strategy and Tactics*. New York: McGraw-Hill.

———. 1948. "The Foundations of a Theory of Organization." *American Sociological Review* 13, (February): 25–35.

Shakur, Assata. 1987. *Assata: An Autobiography*. Westport, CT: Lawrence Hill.

Shanna, Mwalimu, and Seldom Seen. 1986. "Notes on the Transition of the 'Black Liberation' Phrase, Concept, and Movement." *Vita Wa Watu*, January, bk. 8.

Shepperson, George. 1971. "Notes on Negro American Influences on the Emergence of African Nationalism." In Okon Edet Uya, ed., *Black Brotherhood: Afro-Americans and Africa*, 214–27. Lexington, MA: D. C. Heath.

———. 1962. "Pan-Africanism and 'pan-Africanism': Some Historical Notes." *Phylon* 23:353–54.

Shepperson, George, and St. Clair Drake. 1986–87. "The Fifth Pan-African Conference, 1945 and the All African People's Congress, 1958." *Contributions in Black Studies*, no. 8:35–66.

Shorter, Edward, and Charles Tilly. 1974. *Strikes in France, 1830–1968*. New York: Cambridge University Press.

Silver, Beverly. 1989. "Class Struggle and the Kondratief." Paper presented at the International Colloquium on "The Long Waves of the Economic Conjuncture: The Present Stage of the International Debate," Brussels, January 12–14.

Sitkoff, Harvard. 1981. *The Struggle for Black Equality, 1954–1980*. New York: Hill and Wang.

———. 1978. *A New Deal for Blacks: The Emergence of Civil Rights as a National Issue*. Vol. 1, *The Depression Decade*. New York: Oxford University Press.

———. 1971. "Racial Militancy and Interracial Violence in the Second World War." *Journal of American History* 58 (December): 661–81.

Sleeper, Jim. 1990. *The Closest of Strangers: Liberalism and the Politics of Race in New York City*. New York: Norton.

———. 1987. "Boodling, Bigotry, and Cosmopolitanism: The Transformation of a Civic Culture." *Dissent*, fall.

Smith, Joan. 1984. "Non-Wage Labor and Subsistence." In Joan Smith, Immanuel Wallerstein, and Peter Evans, eds., *Households and the World-Economy*, 64–89. Beverly Hills: Sage.

Smith, Michael Peter, and Joe Feagin, eds. 1995. *The Bubbling Cauldron: Race, Ethnicity, and the Urban Crisis*. Minneapolis: University of Minnesota Press.

Smith-Irvin, Jeannette. 1989. *Marcus Garvey's Footsoldiers of the Universal Negro Improvement Association*. Trenton: Africa World Press.

Sojourner Truth Organization. 1978. "Thesis on White Supremacy and the National Question." *Urgent Tasks*, no. 2.

Solomon, Mark. 1988. *Red and Black: Communism and Afro-Americans*. New York: Garland.

Soskin, William. 1967. "Riots, Ghettos, and the 'Negro Revolt.'" In Arthur Ross and Herbert Hill, eds., *Employment, Race, and Poverty*, 205–33. New York: Harcourt Brace and World.

Spear, Allan. 1971. "The Origins of the Urban Ghetto, 1870–1915." In Nathan Huggins, Martin Kilson, and Daniel Fox, eds., *Key Issues in the Afro-American Experience*. Vol. 2, 153–66. New York: Harcourt Brace Jovanovich.

Spero, Sterling, and Abram Harris. 1966. *The Black Worker: The Negro and the Labor Movement*. Port Washington, NY: Kennikat.

Stack, Carol. 1974. *All of Our Kin: Strategies for Survival in a Black Community*. New York: Harper and Row.

Stein, Judith. 1986. *The World of Marcus Garvey: Race and Class in Modern Society*. Baton Rouge: Louisiana State University Press.

Stein, Lorenz von. 1964. *The History of the Social Movement in France, 1789–1850*. Totowa, NJ: Bedminster.

Steinberg, Stephen. 1993. *Turning Back: The Retreat from Racial Justice in American Thought and Policy*. Boston: Beacon Press.

———. 1992. "Et Tu Brute: The Liberal Betrayal of the Black Liberation Movement." *Reconstruction* 2, no. 1:32–34.

———. 1989. "The Underclass: A Case of Color Blindness." *New Politics* 2, no. 3 (summer).

———. 1981. *The Ethnic Myth: Race, Ethnicity and Class in America*. Boston: Beacon.

Sternsher, Bernard, ed. 1969. *The Negro in Depression and War: Prelude to Revolution, 1930–1945*. Chicago: Quadrangle Books.

Stone, Chuck. 1970. *Black Political Power in America*. New York: Dell.

Streater, John Baxter. 1981. *The National Negro Congress, 1936–1947*. Ann Arbor, MI: University Microfilms International.

Street, David, and John Legget. 1961. "Economic Deprivation and Extremism: A Study of Unemployed Negroes." *American Journal of Sociology* 47 (July): 53–57.

Strickland, William. 1994. *Malcolm X: Make It Plain*. New York, Viking.

Stuckey, Sterling. 1987. *Slave Culture: Nationalist Theory and the Foundations of Black America*. New York: Oxford University Press.

———. 1975. "History of the Black Peoples of America." In *The World Encyclopedia of Black People*. Vol. 1, 221–40. St. Clair Shores, MI: Scholarly Press.

———. 1972. *The Ideological Origins of Black Nationalism*. Boston: Beacon.

Tani, E., and Kae Sera. 1986. *False Nationalism, False Internationalism: Class Contradictions in the Armed Struggle*. Chicago: Seeds Beneath the Snow.

Thomas, Bert, ed. 1982. *The Struggle for Liberation: From Du Bois to Nyerere*. Brooklyn: Theo. Graus.

Thompson, E. P.,1966. *The Making of the English Working Class*. New York: Random House.

Thompson, J. Phillip. 1994. "Do We Need a New Style of Black Leadership? *New York Newsday*, February 6.

Thompson, Vincent. 1969. *Africa and Unity: The Evolution of Pan-Africanism*. New York: Humanities Press.

Tilly, Charles. 1978. *From Mobilization to Revolution*. Reading, MA: Addison-Wesley.

Tilly, Charles, Louise Tilly, and Richard Tilly. 1975. *The Rebellious Century, 1830–1930*. Cambridge: Harvard University Press.

Times-Mirror. 1987. *The People, Press, and Politics*. Los Angeles: Times-Mirror.

Tomich, Dale. 1979. "The Dialectic of Colonialism and Culture: The Origins of the Negritude of Aime Cesaire." *Review* 2, no. 3 (winter): 351–88.

Touraine, Alain. 1985. "An Introduction to the Study of Social Movements." *Social Research* 52:749–91.

Traugott, Mark. 1985. *Armies of the Poor: Determinants of Working Class Participation in the Parisian Insurrection of June 1848*. Princeton: Princeton University Press.

T'Shaka, Oba. 1983. *The Political Legacy of Malcolm X*. Chicago: Third World Press.

Tucker, Robert. 1970. *The Marxian Revolutionary Idea*. London: George Allen and Unwin.

Tukufu, Darryl. 1990. "Jesse Jackson and the Rainbow Coalition: Working Class Movement or Reform Politics?" *Humanity and Society* 14, no. 2.

Turner, James. 1971. "Social Origins of Black Consciousness." In Rod Aya and Norman Miller, eds., *The New American Revolution*. New York: Free Press.

Turner, Lou, and John Alan. *Frantz Fanon, Soweto, and American Black Thought*. Detroit: News and Letters.

Turner, Richard Brent. 1997. *Islam in the African-American Experience*. Bloomington: Indiana University Press.

Tuttle, William. 1985. *Race Riot: Chicago in the Red Summer of 1919*. New York: Atheneum.

Tyner, Jarvis. 1987. *The Meaning of Howard Beach*. New York: Communist Party New York State.

Ucelli, Juliet, and Dennis O'Neil. 1990. "The Cost of Drugs: Toward a Progressive Agenda." *Forward Motion* 9, no. 2 (May): 2–9.

UNICEF. 1990 *The State of the World's Children, 1990*. New York: Oxford University Press.

United States House Committee on Internal Security. 1970. *The Black Panther Party, Its Origins and Development*. Washington, DC: U.S. Government Printing Office.

Valentine, Charles. 1968. *Culture and Poverty: Critique and Counter-Proposals*. Chicago: University of Chicago Press.

Van Deburg, William. 1997. *Modern Black Nationalism: From Marcus Garvey to Louis Farrakhan*. New York: New York University Press.

Vilar, Pierre. 1979. "On Nations and Nationalism." *Marxist Perspectives* 2, no. 1 (spring): 8–29.

Vincent, Theodore. 1973. *Voices of a Black Nation*. San Francisco: Ramparts Press.

———. 1971. *Black Power and the Garvey Movement*. San Francisco: Ramparts Press.

Vogel, Lise. 1983. *Marxism and the Oppression of Women: Toward a Unitary Theory*. New Brunswick: Rutgers University Press.

Wacquant, Loic. 1994. "'Dangerous Places': Violence and Isolation in Chicago's Black Belt and the Parisian Red Belt." In William Julius Wilson, ed., *Urban Poverty and Family Life in Chicago's Inner City*. New York: Oxford University Press.

———. 1990. "Making Class: The Middle Classes in Social Theory and Social Structure." In R. Fantasia, R. Levine, and S. G. McNall, eds., *Bringing Class Back In*. Boulder: Westview.

———. 1989a. "For a Socioanalysis of Intellectuals: On 'Homo Academicus'" (interview with Pierre Bordieu). *Berkeley Journal of Sociology* 34:1–30.

———. 1989b. "The Ghetto, the State, and the New Capitalist Economy." *Dissent* 36, no. 4 (fall).

———. 1989c. "The Puzzle of Race and Class in American Society and Social Science." *Benjamin E. Mays Monograph* 2, no. 1 (fall): 7–20.

———. 1989d. "Social Ontology, Epistemology, and Class: On Wright's and Burawoy's Politics of Knowledge." *Berkeley Journal of Sociology* 34:165–86.

———. 1985. "Heuristic Models in Marxian Theory." *Social Forces* 64, no. 1 (September): 17–46.

Wacquant, Loic J. D. and William Julius Wilson. 1989. "The Cost of Racial and Class Exclusion in the Inner City." *Annals of the American Academy of Political and Social Science* 501 (January): 8–25.

Wadsworth, Letisha, and Linda Burnham. 1987a. "Class Perspectives Must Explain, Not Obscure Racism in Howard Beach." *City Sun*, March 25–31.

———. 1987b. "Howard Beach and the Dump Koch Movement." *City Sun*, April 13.

Waller, Joseph. 1977. "The Political Aspects of Building a Mass Movement: The Tactical and Strategic Objectives for Black Liberation." For presentation at the Black Organizers Conference, University of Massachusetts at Amherst, April 15–17.

———. 1975. "Colonialism: The Major Problem Confronting Africans in the U.S." Mimeo.

Wallerstein, Immanuel. 1995. *After Liberalism*. New York: New Press.

———. 1991a. "Antisystemic Movements: History and Dilemmas." In Samir Amin et al., *Transforming the Revolution: Social Movements in the World System*. New York: Monthly Review.

———. 1991b. "The French Revolution as a World-Historical Event." In *Unthinking Social Science: The Limits of Nineteenth Century Paradigms*. Cambridge: Polity Press.

———. 1991c. "Introduction: The Lessons of the 1980s." In *Geopolitics and Geoculture: Essays on the Changing World-System*. New York: Cambridge University Press.

———. 1991d. "1968, Revolution in the World-System: Theses and Queries." In *Geopolitics and Geoculture: Essays on the Changing World-System*, 65–83. New York: Cambridge University Press.

———. 1991e. "Racism and Sexism vs. Universalism: The Ideological Tensions of Capitalism." In Etienne Balibar and Immanuel Wallerstein, eds., *Race, Nation, Class: Ambiguous Identities*. New York: Verso.

———. 1991f. "Who Excludes Whom? or the Collapse of Liberalism and the Dilemmas of Antisystemic Strategy." Paper prepared for Rencontre International du Forum de Delphis, Porus, (Greece), June 1–3.

———. 1990. "Culture as the Ideological Battleground of the Modern World-System." Paper presented at the International Symposium on "Cultural Change in the Period of Transformation in the Capitalist World-System: Some Reconsiderations," Hitotsubashi University, Tokyo, September 19–20.

———. 1989. "Marx, Marxism-Leninism, and Socialist Experiences in the Modern World-System." Paper for international conference on "Marxism and the New Global Society," Institute for Far Eastern Studies, Kyungnam University, Seoul, October 25–27.

———. 1988. "The Myrdal Legacy: Racism and Underdevelopment as Dilemmas." Lecture at University of Stockholm, Faculty of Social Sciences, November 10.

———. 1986a. "Marxisms as Utopias: Evolving Ideologies." *American Journal of Sociology* 91, no. 6 (May): 1295–1308.

———. 1986b. "Societal Development, or Development of the World-System?" *International Sociology* 1, no. 1 (March): 3–17.

———. 1985a. "The Centenary of Berlin: Simplifications, Soporifics, and Opportunities." Paper presented at African Studies Association, New Orleans, November 23–26.

———. 1985b. "The Construction of Peoplehood: Racism, Nationalism, and Ethnicity." Keynote address for conference on "Ethnic Labels, Signs of Class, the Construction and Implications of Collective Identity," October 11–12.

———. 1984a. "Economic Cycles and Socialist Policies." *Futures*, December.

———. 1984b. "Marx and History: Fruitful and Unfruitful Emphases." *Contemporary Marxism*, no. 9 (fall): 35–43.

———. 1984c. *The Politics of the World-Economy*. New York: Cambridge University Press.

———. 1983. *Historical Capitalism*. London: Verso.

———. 1980. "Imperialism and Development." In Albert Bergesen, ed., *Studies of the Modern World-System*, 13–23. New York: Academic Press.

———. 1979. *The Capitalist World-Economy*. Boston: Cambridge University Press.

———. 1974. *The Modern World-System I: Capitalist Agriculture and the Origins of the European World-Economy in the Sixteenth Century*. New York: Academic Press.

———. 1970. "Frantz Fanon: Reason and Violence." *The Berkeley Journal of Sociology* 15:222–31.

———. 1969a. *Africa: The Politics of Unity*. New York: Vintage.

———. 1969b. *University in Turmoil: The Politics of Change*. New York: Atheneum.

———. 1966. *Social Change: The Colonial Situation*. New York: John Wiley.

Wallerstein, Immanuel, and Terence K. Hopkins. 1997. *The Age of Transition: Trajectory of the World System, 1945–2025*. London: Zed Press.

Wallerstein, Immanuel, and Peter Phillips. 1991. "National and World Identities and the Interstate System." In Wallerstein, *Geopolitics and Geoculture: Essays on the Changing World-System*, 139–57. New York: Cambridge University Press.

Walton, John. 1984. *Reluctant Rebels: Comparative Studies of Revolution and Underdevelopment*. New York: Columbia University Press.

Walzer, Michael. 1979. "A Theory of Revolution." *Marxist Perspectives* 2, no. 1 (spring): 30–45.

Washington, Booker T. 1971. "The Atlanta Exposition Address—September 1895." In August Meier, Elliott Rudwick, and Francis Broderick, eds., *Black Protest Thought in the Twentieth Century*. New York: Bobbs-Merrill.

———. 1965. *Up from Slavery*. New York: Avon.

Waskow, Arthur. 1966. *From Race Riot to Sit-In: 1919 and the 1960s*. Garden City, NY: Anchor Books.

Weber, Max. 1978. *Economy and Society: An Outline of Interpretive Sociology.* Berkeley: University of California Press.

Weinglass, Leonard. 1997. *Race for Justice: Mumia Abu-Jamal's Fight against the Death Penalty.* Monroe, ME: Common Courage Press.

Weinstein, James. 1975. *Ambiguous Legacy: The Left in American Politics.* New York: New Viewpoints.

———. 1970. "The IWW and American Socialism." *Socialist Revolution* 1, no. 5 (September-October): 3–41.

———. 1967. *The Decline of Socialism in America, 1912–1925.* New York: Monthly Review.

Wenger, Morton. 1980. "State Responses to Afro-American Rebellion: Neo-Colonialism and the New Petit Bourgeoisie." *Insurgent Sociologist,* fall.

West, Cornel. 1994. *Race Matters.* New York: Random House.

———. 1992. "Malcolm X and Black Rage." In Joe Wood, ed., *Malcolm X: In Our Own Image,* 48–58. New York: St. Martin's Press.

———. 1991. "Nihilism in Black America: A Danger That Corrodes from Within." *Dissent,* spring, 221–26.

———. 1988. "The Crisis of Black Leadership." *Z Magazine* 1, no. 2.

———. 1987. "Demystifying the New Black Conservatism." *Praxis International* 7, no. 2 (July): 143–51.

———. 1982. *Prophesy Deliverance: An Afro-American Revolutionary Christianity.* Philadelphia: Westminster.

Wheaton, Elizabeth. 1987. *Code Name: Greenkil: The 1979 Greensboro Killings.* Athens: University of Georgia Press.

Whitney, R. M. 1924. *Reds in America.* New York: Beckwith.

Wilkins, Roger, et al. 1981. "Comments on Race and Class." *Nation,* April 11.

Willhelm, Sidney. 1986. "The Economic Demise of Black America: A Prelude to Genocide?" *Journal of Black Studies,* December.

Williams, Evelyn. 1993. *Inadmissible Evidence: The Story of the African American Trial Lawyer Who Defended the Black Liberation Army.* Brooklyn: Lawrence Hill Books.

Williams, Henry. 1973. *Black Response to the American Left: 1917–1929.* Princeton: Princeton University Press.

Williams, J. Allen, Nicholas Babchuk, and David R. Johnson. 1973. "Voluntary Associations and Minority Status: A Comparative Analysis of Anglo, Black, and Mexican Americans." *American Sociological Review* 38, no. 5 (October): 637–46.

Willie, Charles. 1979. *The Caste and Class Controversy.* New York: Grant Hall.

Willingham, Alex. 1986. "Ideology and Politics: Their Status in Afro-American Social Theory." In Adolph Reed, ed., *Race, Politics, and Culture: Critical Essays on the Radicalism of the 1960's,* 13–27. Westport, CT: Greenwood.

Willis, Daniel. 1976. "A Critical Analysis of the Mass Political Education of the Black Panther Party." Ph.D. diss., University of Massachusetts.

Wilson, Basil. 1982. "Marcus Garvey." In Bert Thomas, ed., *The Struggle for Liberation: From Du Bois to Nyerere*, 27–41. Brooklyn: Theo. Gaus.

Wilson, Basil, and Charles Green. 1988. "The Black Church and the Struggle for Community Empowerment in New York City." *Afro-Americans in New York Life and History* 12, no. 1 (January): 51–80.

Wilson, Edmund. 1972. *To the Finland Station: A Study in the Writing and Acting of History*. New York: Farrar, Straus and Giroux.

Wilson, William J. 1990. "Race Neutral Politics and the Democratic Coalition." *American Prospect* 1, no. 1 (spring): 74–81.

———. 1987. *The Truly Disadvantaged*. Chicago: University of Chicago Press.

———. 1978. *The Declining Significance of Race: Blacks and Changing American Institutions*. Chicago: University of Chicago Press.

———. 1973. *Power, Racism, and Privilege: Race Relations in Theoretical and Sociohistorical Perspectives*. New York: Free Press.

Winant, Howard. 1990. "Postmodern Racial Politics in the United States: Differences and Inequality." *Socialist Review* 20, no. 1 (January–March).

Withorn, Ann. 1984. *Serving the People: Social Services and Social Change*. New York: Columbia University Press.

———. 1978a. "Surviving as a Radical Service Worker: Lessons from the History of Movement-Provided Services." *Radical America* 12, no. 4:9–23.

———. 1978b. "To Serve the People: An Inquiry into the Success of Service Delivery as a Social Movement Strategy." Ph.D. diss., Brandeis University.

Wolpe, Harold. 1986. "Class Concepts, Class Struggle and Racism." In John Rex and David Mason, eds., *Theories of Race and Ethnic Relations*, 110–30. New York: Cambridge University Press.

———. 1975. "The Theory of Internal Colonialism." In Ivar Oxaal, Tony Barnett, and David Booth, eds., *Beyond the Sociology of Development*. London: Routledge and Paul.

Wood, Ellen Meiksins. 1986. *The Retreat from Class: A New "True" Socialism*. New York: Verso.

Woodis, Jack. 1972. *New Theories of Revolution: A Commentary on the Views of Frantz Fanon, Regis Debray, and Herbert Marcuse*. New York: International Publishers.

Woodward, C. Vann. 1974. *The Strange Career of Jim Crow*. New York: Oxford University Press.

Wright, M. Frank. 1974. "The National Question: A Marxist Critique." *Black Scholar* 5, no. 5 (February): 43–56.

Wright, Richard. 1995. *Twelve Million Black Voices*. New York: Thunder's Mouth Press.

Wynter, Sylvia. 1992. "No Humans Involved: An Open Letter to My Colleagues." *Voices of the African Diaspora* 8, no. 2:13–18.

Yeshitela, Omali. *The Road to Socialism Is Painted Black*. Oakland, CA: Burning Spear Press.

———. 1983. *Stolen Black Labor: The Political Economy of Domestic Colonialism*. Oakland, CA: Burning Spear Press.

———. 1982a. *A New Beginning: The Road to Black Freedom and Socialism*. Oakland, CA: Burning Spear Press.

———. 1982b. *Not One Step Backward! The Black Liberation Movement from 1971 to 1982*. Oakland, CA: Burning Spear Press.

———. 1981. *The Struggle for Bread, Peace, and Black Power*. Oakland, CA: Burning Spear Press.

Zald, Mayer, and Roberta Ash. 1987. "The Political Economy of Social Movement Sectors." In Mayer Zald and John McCarthy, eds., *Social Movements in an Organizational Society: Collected Essays*, 293–317. New Brunswick, NJ: Transaction Books.

———. 1973. "Social Movement Organizations: Growth, Decay, and Change." In Robert Evans, ed., *Social Movements: A Reader and Source Book*. New York: Rand McNally.

Zald, Mayer, and John McCarthy. 1987a. "Organizational Intellectuals and the Criticism of Society." In Mayer Zald and John McCarthy, eds., *Social Movements in an Organizational Society: Collected Essays*, 97–115. New Brunswick, NJ: Transaction Books.

———. 1987b. "Resource Mobilization and Social Movements: A Partial Theory." In Mayer Zald and John McCarthy, ed., *Social Movements in an Organizational Society: Collected Essays*, 15–42. New Brunswick, NJ: Transaction Books.

Zinn, Howard. 1980a. *A People's History of the United States*. New York: Harper and Row.

———. 1980b. *The Twentieth Century: A People's History*. New York: Harper and Row.

———. 1965. *SNCC: The New Abolitionists*. Boston: Beacon.

Index

About the Author

Rod Bush is Assistant Professor of Sociology and Anthropology at St. John's University, Jamaica, New York. Long an activist in the Black Power and radical movements of the 1968–88 period, Bush returned to SUNY Binghamton to obtain a Ph.D. in 1988. In 1984 he edited *The New Black Vote: Politics and Power in Four American Cities.*